A History of Modern Tourism

ERIC G. E. ZUELOW

macmillan education
palgrave

First published 2016 by
PALGRAVE

Palgrave in the UK is an imprint of Macmillan Publishers Limited, registered in England, company number 785998, of 4 Crinan Street, London, N1 9XW.

Palgrave Macmillan in the US is a division of St Martin's Press LLC, 175 Fifth Avenue, New York, NY 10010.

Palgrave is the global imprint of the above companies and is represented throughout the world.

Palgrave® and Macmillan® are registered trademarks in the United States, the United Kingdom, Europe and other countries.

ISBN 978-0-230-36965-8 ISBN 978-0-230-36966-5 (eBook)

DOI 10.1007/978-0-230-36966-5

This book is printed on paper suitable for recycling and made from fully managed and sustained forest sources. Logging, pulping and manufacturing processes are expected to conform to the environmental regulations of the country of origin.

A catalogue record for this book is available from the British Library.

A catalog record for this book is available from the Library of Congress.

In Loving Memory of my Grandparents

Slim and Alta
Gerald and Dagny

Table of Contents

Illustrations

Acknowledgements

The origins of this book date to the family vacations of my childhood. Each year, we loaded my parents' Volkswagen camper with equipment, packed up our flatulent dog Pippin (who only exhibited this distressing symptom on road trips), and headed down Route 101 to explore the Washington and Oregon coasts. For the next week or two, we visited fondly loved campgrounds, hiked on some of the world's most beautiful beaches, played on the sand dunes near Florence, Oregon, located petroglyphs carved by Native peoples and shipwrecks left behind by Europeans, and stopped at occasional roadside attractions such as the Sea Lion Caves (also near Florence) or the Enchanted Forest (near Salem, Oregon). I still savor the tasty one-pot meals that my mother whipped up on her Coleman stove, dream about the smell of the campground during the long summer evenings, recall the stories told around the campfire, and picture the incredible things that we found in tide pools along the way.

When I was twelve, careful saving allowed us to go to Britain for a five-week driving tour. It was eye opening. The experience of boarding my first airplane, a 747 called the "City of Westminster," was made that much better by the reality that my father earned his living by doing "flutter" analyses for Boeing on this very type of aircraft. By the end of that adventure I had fallen in love with Great Britain, with travel, and with history. These passions are still very much with me; a good thing as it is from them that I earn a living.

As I completed the last bits of my Ph.D. in 2004, I was fortunate to serve as George L. Mosse Distinguished Lecturer at the University of Wisconsin-Madison. Mosse, one of the greatest historians of the twentieth century, is a hero of mine. I was fortunate to meet him a year or two before his death, so I was especially excited to hold the title. It was almost equally thrilling that the class in question explored the history of modern tourism. I've now taught the course several times at two additional institutions, each different from the other and from the University of Wisconsin-Madison: West Liberty State College and the University of New England (UNE). Students always respond well, finding this subject exciting and engaging. More than any other class, I hear from them, sometimes years after graduation. "That class changed my world," they say. "I just cannot look at cities, parks, air travel, or anything else the same way." One student recently told me that "History of Modern Tourism" was among his favorite classes and he reminded me that the course led him to start a research group, to launch a weekly radio program, and even to get the chance to meet many of his favorite authors.

The thing is that tourism is an astonishing subject. While fascinating in and of itself, the topic is rendered more intriguing by its deep connections to virtually every aspect of the human experience. Tourism is linked to politics, economics, culture, aesthetics, medicine and health, the environment, technology, the history of ideas, nostalgia and memory, and much more besides. To study modern tourism is to examine the modern age—an important argument that runs throughout this book. Ultimately it was teaching that course, working with many talented students along the way, which inspired this project.

It is worth stressing right from the start that this book represents an overview of tourism history. The text does not cover everything and does not delve into the various scholarly debates about some of the subjects covered here. One of the most painful aspects of writing it was omitting stories that I love, subjects and debates that many of us who study the topic find fascinating. The maximum word count for this project was small, the subject massive. This said, hopefully the text will inspire curiosity and further enquiry. Interested readers will find a bibliography at the back that ought to assist with further exploration.

On that note, *A History of Modern Tourism* is a synthesis and it is based on the brilliant research of many, many fine historians, sociologists, economists, anthropologists, geographers, literary scholars, and others. Even a few years ago this book would not have been possible because the relevant literature simply was not developed enough. As it stands, the narrative remains Eurocentric with more written about Great Britain than virtually any place else. Some regions—Asia, for example—have received precious little historical treatment. Hopefully this book will play a role in encouraging further study of tourism, both on a global scale and more locally in areas where the phenomenon has yet to inspire considerable research.

I would like to thank all of the students who have taken my history of tourism course at University of Wisconsin-Madison, West Liberty State College, and the University of New England. Without their interest and the experience of working with them, writing this book would not have been possible. Two students, Jonathan Planer and Kelsey Heck, deserve special recognition for their help with this project. Jon aided me in building a bibliography of worthy secondary sources, as well as a list of newspapers (especially those relating to early rail travel). Kelsey's help at the end of the project was invaluable because she tracked down many of the images that are included here, as well as many others that we simply could not fit in. It was a pleasure working with both of them.

Anonymous reviewers offered tremendous feedback, both after reading an initial book proposal and later upon receiving the manuscript itself. Although I was not able to integrate all of their ideas, their suggestions were on my mind constantly throughout the writing and revision process. They have made this book considerably better than it might otherwise have been.

The UNE Library staff deserves special recognition for their help in acquiring the materials upon which this book is based. I am especially grateful to Brenda Austin, UNE's Interlibrary Loan Coordinator. Her efforts were tireless and extensive. Likewise, Laurie Mathes and Amanda Leen deserve special recognition for their assistance along the way. I literally could not have undertaken this project without their efforts.

Thank you to my UNE history colleagues, Paul Burlin and Rob Alegre, for their friendship and support. They make it fun to go to work and I always look forward to their company and conversation.

I would like to thank Jenna Steventon at Palgrave for believing in this project from the start, for her patience, and for helping to bring it to print. My project editor, Rachel Bridgewater, deserves special recognition for guiding me through the last stages of seeing manuscript to press. Likewise, Robert Diamond, Prudence Doherty, Sharon Eckert, Susan Gibbons, Paul Jarvis, Brian Kassel, Allison Myers, Joshua Larkin Rowley, Paul Smith, Sharon Thayer, and Susan Walker deserve recognition for their help with the images that are included here. A number of others, too numerous to list, also offered feedback and suggestions on this front as Kelsey and I tried to whittle down the illustrations to a manageable few. As with the text itself, limited space meant excluding photographs, drawings, and paintings that I truly wish could be seen here.

As often happens in scholarship, one project informs another. The editorial and advisory boards, as well as the contributors to the *Journal of Tourism History,* always inspire. They prompted me to think and rethink many of the points made in these pages. It is an honor to edit that journal and I am grateful to John K. Walton for giving me the opportunity to do so. He, along with Kevin J. James, also offered very helpful thoughts and ideas when I first started to think about writing this book.

As always, Katie Burns deserves special recognition. Not only does she brighten my days and offer constant encouragement, she is also an honest critic. Her copyediting and advice turned what might have been a rather staccato manuscript into a readable text. I am intensely grateful to her for the wonderful index at the end of this book as well as for her help preparing the manuscript for production.

My parents, Richard and Helen, cannot be thanked enough for taking me on all of those trips, for encouraging a passion for learning and exploring, and for instilling a sense of self-confidence that makes it possible to do what I do.

Finally, I want to dedicate this book to the memory of my grandparents: Dagny and Gerald Zuelow and Alta and Slim Lohmeyer. It seems especially fitting that the cover image was taken by Dagny and that my grandfather, Gerry, is the one wearing the hat on the far right.

Introduction: Modern tourism

According to license plates and roadway signage, the state of Maine, located in the extreme northeastern corner of the United States, is America's "Vacationland." During the summer, the various towns along the old coast road, Route 1, are packed with shorts-wearing, camera-toting, sandal-clad visitors racing excitedly from lobster shack to souvenir stand, beach arcade to sand towel. In Portland, the state's major population center, tourists flock to the Old Port. This district, mirrored in virtually every major New England coastal town as well as many others around the world, features cobbled streets, vintage-looking storefronts, copious bars and restaurants, and souvenir shops heavily stocked with t-shirts, refrigerator magnets, and a host of gifts that proudly celebrate the state's great claim to fame: lobsters and moose.

During the fall, the beaches are far less crowded, but visitors nevertheless return to the state to engage in "leaf peeping." In winter, things shut down along the ocean. Many shops and restaurants close, the streets are largely clear of outsiders. The locals return to old haunts avoided during the rest of the year. At this time, the short days of January, February, and March, inland areas boom. Ski areas come alive. Outsiders flood in. Shops open and the hotels are full for three or four months before the snow melts. When the days grow warmer and the leaves spring forth in an expression of rebirth and hope, the cycle starts again. Tourists begin to trickle and then flood back to the coastal towns. Shops remove their shutters. The "season" is on. There are other industries, of course—forestry, fishing, shipbuilding, agriculture, and some manufacturing—but it is tourism that defines the seasons as much as the temperature or hours of daylight.

Virtually the same story plays out in tourist areas around the globe. Tourism is the world's largest service sector industry. According to the United Nations World Tourism Organization the industry was worth about US$1.4 trillion worldwide in 2013. No small sum. It accounts for 6 percent of the world exports. Leisure travel contributes about 9 percent of gross domestic product worldwide and is responsible for one out of every eleven jobs globally. In 2013, there were 1087 million tourist arrivals worldwide and the industry was *growing* at 5 percent. Actually, the tourist industry has been growing more or less continually since World War II and the above totals represent an increase of more than 3000 percent over the same numbers in 1950.[1] If you want to make these figures more "real," try assembling a random group of people and ask them: "Have you ever taken a vacation?" Virtually every person in the room will raise his or her hand. If you change the question slightly and ask: "Have you taken or do you plan to take a vacation this year?" The response will probably not change.

What does this mean? Perhaps most importantly, it suggests that contemporary humans, at least in the developed world, spend a great deal of their time either traveling or thinking about traveling in pursuit of fun and escape. They remember past journeys and dream about future adventures. Given such intense focus the industry plays a role in helping to determine who we think we are. When we decide to go to one place rather than another, it says something about us. When we play host to outsiders, we must consider how we will present ourselves to them; we must determine exactly what we want to broadcast to the world. What makes us, as a culture, region, or group unique? How do we see ourselves and how should others see us? Because tourism plays such a noteworthy role both economically and culturally, it is exceptionally important politically. It is unimaginable to have a phenomenon that is as wide-reaching as tourism and not to have government clamoring to control it. In short, tourism plays a pivotal role in our world: socially, culturally, economically, and politically.

It was not always so. Before the eighteenth century, travel was carried out for a variety of reasons—searching for food, exploration and adventure, trade, religious ritual—but leisure was not *usually* a primary motivation. By contrast, modern tourism, the subject of this book, is about spending free time primarily in pursuit of enjoyment. The coming pages explore just exactly how it is that traveling for pleasure developed, became attractive to such a large proportion of the developed world, and came to encompass a remarkable range of activities.

Pre-modern travel

Mobility is not new.[2] The very earliest humans moved in pursuit of food. Most anthropologists believe that modern humans originated in Africa, somewhere around 100,000 years ago.[3] They did not stay put. Our distant ancestors quickly started to travel about in search of survival. As long as there was adequate food, there was little reason to move. But such a pleasant circumstance seldom lasted for long. Rising population, animal migration, and the seasonal nature of many food sources demanded that people be mobile. Early humans had to follow the herds and they needed to search for fresh fruits, grains, and vegetables.

Over time, these early hunter-gatherers covered considerable space. According to a growing body of archaeological evidence, it took only between ten and twenty thousand years for humans to inhabit every continent except Antarctica. It is clear that by 50,000 years ago, humans had reached Australia and Central Asia. They populated Europe by about 40,000 years ago. There is conflicting evidence about when humans reached the Americas. Until recently, anthropological orthodoxy held that so-called "Clovis" hunters arrived just after the last ice age, perhaps around 13,000 years ago. More recent findings, however, push that date back to as far as 50,000 years ago.[4]

Recent technological developments give scientists a previously unimaginable window into the distant past. It is possible to trace the paths taken by hunter-gatherers. Spear points, ancient fire pits, and both animal and human remains allow scientists to follow where early bands went, how long they stayed in a given location, and what they ate.[5] It is considerably harder to know or even to guess what they were thinking yet there are clues. From ancient burials, complete with standardized positioning of remains, grave goods, and even face painting, anthropologists infer that religion developed sometime between 130,000 and 35,000 years ago. This broad chronological range is supported by cave paintings that show dancing men and shamans presiding over what appear to be religious rituals.[6] By contrast, there is no evidence to suggest that early humans traveled for fun. Travel was undoubtedly arduous, taxing, and terrifying. When one left a shelter, one was subject to animal attack or to threats from rival bands of hunters. Any trip required a profoundly important purpose and food was the most justifiable motivation of all.

The Neolithic revolution, during which our ancestors decided to form settled communities, took place starting about 10,000 years ago. The first villages and then cities appeared separately but at roughly the same time in China's Yellow River Valley, between the Tigris and Euphrates Rivers in Mesopotamia (present day Iraq), along the Nile River in Egypt, and around the Indus River in what is now Pakistan. This might have occurred for a variety of reasons and scholars suggest various hypotheses. Perhaps it was the unexpected result of spilling a basket of grain. Maybe it was a geographic accident caused by the plentiful supply of edible grasses and large mammals that rendered continued migration unnecessary.[7] The first villages might even have been the result of an anxious drive to more reliably and regularly brew alcoholic drinks or bake bread.[8] Whatever it was, settled people were no less mobile than their unsettled forbearers. As people learned to grow more crops and to make more things, they soon started to engage with others beyond their city walls. The result was a new type of travel that ultimately defined a great deal of subsequent human history: trade.

Importing and exporting goods is as old as civilization itself, perhaps much older.[9] Historians John R. and William H. McNeill describe the result as a thickening "human web," claiming that the drive to create webs, "a set of connections that link people to one another," is a constant of human history.[10] Trade was integral to this process. When cultures met, they exchanged ideas. For example, grapes do not grow naturally in Egypt, yet, after making contact with Mesopotamian and Phoenician traders, the Egyptians learned to cultivate grapes and to make wine.[11]

Trade quickly emerged as a staple of human life and every subsequent civilization took part. Some early routes covered truly vast territory. The Phoenicians, for example, emerged from what is now Lebanon and northern Israel to develop a trading empire that spanned the Mediterranean, prompting "the majority of the maritime trade and naval activity" in that area by the seventh century BCE.[12] It was such a successful endeavor that others, perhaps most notably the Minoans and Mycenaeans of ancient Greece, were inspired to create their own trade-based cultures.[13]

Over time, routes grew more and more extensive, covering greater geographic space and involving more people and civilizations. The Roman Empire owed its success to trade and fostered routes that extended not only across Europe and North Africa, but also as far as India and China.[14] Later, the Vikings, a medieval group that started life in Sweden, Norway, and Denmark, developed a trading reach that extended from Scandinavia to the British Isles, Iceland, Greenland, and even to North America and Byzantium.[15] The available texts do not suggest that they traveled in search of a relaxing getaway. Trade was necessary for economic growth, for political power, and ultimately for survival. The people who engaged in it had little choice. They were forced to move.

In contrast to those mentioned above, what historian Eric J. Leed describes as "heroic" travelers left home by choice, often in pursuit of conquest and adventure. Yet here again, the motivation was not the same as that found among those who today wander the tourism cities of the world.[16] Gilgamesh is the hero of the oldest story that we have, the 5000-year old *Epic of Gilgamesh*. While not technically a travel narrative, the story does follow Gilgamesh and his friend Enkidu through many adventures. The pair's trips are a choice undertaken for the purpose of achieving specific goals: to kill a monster, to find eternal life, to better serve friends and subjects. It is never for fun or for seeing sights.[17] The top generals of the ancient world, men such as Alexander the Great of Macedon (356–323 BCE), who created a massive empire extending from Greece to northern India, or Temüchin, the future "universal leader" or "Genghis Khan" of Mongolia (1162–1227), who created the largest contiguous empire in human history, were probably very curious men. Yet their quest was a search for glory, revenge, wealth, and adventure. Such interests did not translate into sightseeing. Neither man apparently spent much time enjoying the scenery; such an activity was not part of the heroic traveler's vocabulary.[18] Nor was leisure a concern for the voyagers of the "age of exploration." The seamen who participated in Henry the Navigator's (1394–1460) effort to expand Portuguese influence and commerce wrote of the exotic things that they encountered, but their motives were decidedly unromantic.[19] Sixteenth, seventeenth, and even eighteenth-century European explorers moved around the globe in pursuit of undiscovered lands, sea routes, and potential regions to exploit for trade. Vast world empires and untold wealth for successful new colonialists resulted. Famous explorers such as Bartolomeu Dias (c.1451–1500), Pedro Alvares Cabral (1467–1520), Christopher Columbus (1451–1506), Walter Raleigh (c.1552–1618), and James Cook (1728–79), among others, sought wealth, both personal and national prestige, and adventure. Like Gilgamesh, their journeys were by choice. Yet they fit the rubric of pre-modern travel, little resembling modern tourists.[20]

Glimmers of the modern

If the majority of pre-modern travelers appear rather different from the souvenir shoppers, museum-goers, and rollercoaster riders of today, there are isolated places, a handful of individuals, a few selected historical moments, and some important practices that hint at what was to come.

According to historian Lionel Casson, there was nothing resembling tourism in Mesopotamia, however ancient Egypt inspired sightseers from as early as 1500 BCE. It appears that the massive temple and tomb complexes associated with both the Old (third millennium BCE) and the New (roughly 1550 BCE to 1077 BCE) Kingdoms were as amazing to inhabitants of the ancient world as they are to us today. Consequently, there is very old graffiti carved into even older walls.[21] Yet one must wonder how extensive such travel actually was. As Casson notes, there was little infrastructure in place to assist these "tourists." They found "no formal facilities for their food and lodging."[22] Surely if a suitable demand was present budding tradesmen would have anxiously offered services and souvenirs.

Herodotus (484–c.430 BCE), widely regarded as the first Western historian, may have been among the first tourists. His monumental *The History* is an account of the Persian Wars (499–449 BCE). The text reveals an author concerned with more than military exploits or heroic leadership (although there is plenty of both). Herodotus was deeply interested in context. He wanted to know what made the Persians Persian, the Egyptians Egyptian, and the Greeks Greek. Given this, Herodotus spends considerable space describing the habits and cultures of the different peoples impacted by the war. In many ways, *The History* is as much an example of travel writing as it is historical writing. It reflects a man who was attracted to travel for the sake of seeing the difference that existed around him. Herodotus evidently wanted to escape from what he knew in order to learn about what was beyond. Historians disagree about how much he actually traveled around the ancient world, whether he went to Egypt or the Black Sea, for example.[23] After all, simply writing about travel does not make one a traveler, let alone a tourist, just as writing about space flight does not make a person an astronaut. Nevertheless, if he traveled extensively, Herodotus likely did so largely out of curiosity. In this respect, he was not terribly far removed from many tourists.

It is possible that Herodotus was not alone in the Greek world, but the extent of Greek tourism is questionable. According to Lionel Casson, Herodotus suggests that "some" went to Egypt "to see the country itself." Evidently other travelers came to Athens to see the sites. Yet the number of such tourists must have been very small because "travel required leisure and money, and those who enjoyed such privileges in the fifth and fourth centuries BCE were but a wafer-thin crust of Greek society."[24]

The Roman world was different. While many Romans probably traveled as merchant traders or in the name of military service, others took a well-worn tourist track to Greece and Egypt, or summered on the coast. Historical sociologist Loykie Lomine leaves no doubt about how he views the evidence:

> ...contrary to common beliefs and assumptions, tourism existed long before the famous Grand Tour of Mediterranean Europe by English aristocrats. The sophisticated Augustan society offered everything that is commonly regarded as typically modern (not to say post-modern) in terms of tourism: museums, guide-books, seaside resorts with drunk and noisy holidaymakers at night, candle-lit dinner parties in fashionable restaurants, promiscuous hotels, unavoidable sightseeing places, spas, souvenir shops, postcards, over-talkative and boring guides, concert halls and much more besides.[25]

The Augustan period was Rome at its height. The empire attained its greatest reach and many of its people grew quite wealthy through trade and other employments. The empire extended from the Scottish border in the north, Africa in the south, Persia in the east. The network of roadways built by advancing Roman armies assured quick movement of troops, safe and efficient trade, and the possibility of leisure travel.

An established tourism route existed along which wealthier Romans made their way to Greece, on to Asia Minor, and finally to Egypt before returning to Rome. Along their journey, they visited many of the sites that attract tourists to this day: Delphi, Athens, Delos, Samothrace, Rhodes, Troy (and others associated with Homer [c. eighth century], the Greek poet who reportedly authored *The Iliad* and *The Odyssey*), as well as the Valley of the Kings and the Pyramids in Egypt.[26] More than just visiting impressive buildings or ruins, Roman tourists traveled for health, to see oracles, and to take in sporting events. There were restaurants and hotels, although the number of hotels was much smaller than would be true today because wealthier tourists could realistically expect to enjoy the hospitality of others along the way. It appears that Roman hotels might better be called brothels and that most available accommodations were humble at best. The Romans even had guidebooks, although these were so heavy that they were generally left at home in favor of utilizing locals who were only too happy to provide running commentaries about important sites.

It took as many as ten days to sail to Alexandria from Rome, quite some time to be away from gainful employments. Yet in this instance, the long travel times did not mean that only the rich pursued leisurely recreation. Rome was terribly hot and uncomfortable during the summer, so an assortment of tourism resorts sprung up closer to home in order to accommodate those anxious to escape from the city. Such spots offered a variety of places to stay and experiences to behold, not unlike modern seaside resorts.

Ultimately the evidence for Roman tourism is compelling, yet it does not make sense to tell the story of modern tourism beginning with Rome. First, even during the Roman period, tourism was not a cross-cultural phenomenon. Romans traveled within their own culture, never straying from the map of Roman influence.[27] This leisure travel was more limited than its modern equivalent. Second, as Lomine admits, the "Augustan age corresponded to the acme of Latin culture, while the 'decline of the empire was accompanied by the decline of tourism. The wealthy class was greatly reduced, roads deteriorated and the countryside became overrun by bandits, thieves and scoundrels, making travel unsafe.'"[28] When Roman tourism ended, it was done, leaving behind no legitimate offspring. It would take hundreds of years for anything like it to reappear.

Religious pilgrimage has a better paternity claim to modern tourism, though not a direct connection. Many of the world's major religions survived and flourished partly as a consequence of mobility. For example, following the death of Gautama Buddha, monks and traders spread the new ideas he founded widely, helped by the support of important state governments.[29] Islam, aided by a combination of weak emperors and angry populations across much of the Middle East, Central Asia, North Africa, and beyond, replaced many existing rulers and religions as a result of military exploit and trade.[30] Christianity (along with Buddhism and Islam) was a "missionary religion," a fact that allowed it to spread widely even if this was not the only factor responsible for its success in specific places.[31] Perhaps the importance of mobility for the spread of belief systems is responsible for the fact that religious pilgrimage "has been practiced for thousands of years and has been a feature of every major religion and very many minor cults across the world."[32]

Pilgrimage enters into the language of leisure travel as well as of faith and the idea of "making a pilgrimage" to Disneyland or to see some famous historic site or beauty spot is central to the motivation of many modern travelers. Tourists feel an obligation to visit specific sites. Going to London without seeing Westminster Abbey, the Tower of London, and Buckingham Palace is unthinkable. No respectable sightseer goes to Paris without visiting the Eiffel Tower and the Louvre. In this sense, tourism functions as "a form of secular ritual" or pilgrimage.[33] Yet on closer analysis, the motivations behind tourism and religious pilgrimage are different and one did not immediately beget the other.[34]

Religious pilgrimage, at least in the West, arguably reached its zenith during the high middle ages when Europeans left their homes in order to visit an astonishing network of holy sites such as Canterbury Cathedral in England, Santiago de Compostela in Spain, Rome, and, of course, the Holy Land itself. The practice expanded after about 1000 CE and grew still more popular during the twelfth and thirteenth centuries "when Christendom was swept by a wave of penitence." For pilgrims, travel was a sort of self-punishment, a way of repenting for sin and attaining forgiveness, and the destination had to be sacred.[35] There was a hierarchy of such sites. In England, the tomb of Thomas Becket (1118–70) at Canterbury was most important (and was featured in Chaucer's astonishing *Canterbury Tales*). On the Continent, Santiago and Rome were the top sites. Unsurprisingly, the Holy Land itself trumped everything, but was expensive and time consuming to get to so that only the wealthy were able to make the trek.[36]

For religious institutions, inclusion on a pilgrimage route was important for financial survival. Houses of worship went out of their way to accumulate sacred artifacts such as a piece of the true cross, the bone of a saint, or an item of clothing reportedly owned by a holy figure such as the Virgin Mary. The competition for relics was so fierce that serious questions arose regarding the authenticity of most items. There were so many pieces of the true cross in Europe, for example, that the implement used to bring about Christ's death would have been the size of a massive ocean liner. Likewise, John the Baptist's skull was such a popular item that no less than three churches claimed to have it. One possibly apocryphal story holds that a particularly observant pilgrim asked an attendant monk how it was possible to have seen the skull in two separate churches. The monk replied simply: "Maybe ... [the other skull] was the skull of John the Baptist when a young man, whereas this in our possession is his skull after he was fully advanced in years and wisdom."[37] Each site further accentuated profits by assuring that there were plenty of souvenirs for sale. Patches and broaches were especially common, usually made of "tin-lead alloy, or brass or clay." The surface was generally "stamped with either a portrait of the saint, a scene from the life or death, or a symbol associated with him."[38]

There is no question that the medieval pilgrimage generated its own economy. It is also true that pilgrims experienced an often very exciting array of attractions and experiences. Yet, the fact remains that the primary reason for travel was religion, not consumption or leisure.[39] Pilgrims were motivated to acquire indulgences and to assure themselves swift passage into heaven after death. Although modern travel promises to improve the traveler, the trip is not designed to inspire suffering. The goal is pleasure, prestige, and perhaps a certain amount of learning. It is about getting away from the everyday, not escaping into the eternal.

Modern tourism

Modern tourism, the topic of this book, is different from what came before. What is tourism? In essence, it is travel in pursuit of pleasure and an escape from everyday realities. Historian Rudy Koshar usefully describes it as "any practice arising from an individual's voluntary movement between relatively permanent 'settledness' and an extended moment of leisured displacement."[40] Such an activity, with few exceptions, is quite recent. At the same time, tourism is larger in scale and scope than what came before. It attracts almost everybody in the developed world beyond the very poor, encompasses a variety of experiences largely new to the current age, and focuses attention on sites/sights, using "lenses" that developed during roughly the past three hundred years. Above all, modern tourism is motivated by patterns of consumption, ideas about health, and notions of aesthetics that emerged after the middle of the eighteenth century.

This new type of leisure evolved from an elite (largely) English pastime that is especially associated with the seventeenth and eighteenth centuries and which is called the "Grand Tour." During the nineteenth century, when new railways made travel both faster and more affordable, a larger percentage of the population could realistically travel; the tourism industry was born. By the twentieth century, tourism represented a major focus of political attention. Regimes on both the left and right of the political spectrum tried to co-opt it for their own ends. After World War II, jet aircraft, higher standards of living, increased vacation time, and even better automobiles assured that still more people caught the travel bug and the industry exploded in size and scope. Today, in dramatic contrast to the past, the industry knows almost no borders and it concerns virtually everybody in one way or another.

Context, historians, and the "modern world"

Of course, the story of modern tourism is more complicated than the above summary suggests. For historians, context explains the evolution of the human story. In the simplest terms, people both respond to and make their environment. Human actions and reactions to a host of stimuli shaped everything that fills the pages of history books. Indeed, even the choice of things that historians write about, and the way that they write about them, is a product of historical context. Thus, the story of modern tourism is intimately connected to a host of intellectual, technological, economic, aesthetic, and political developments that will be outlined in the pages to come. At the same time, the very existence of this book is a product of a moment in which tourism is very widespread. If tourism were a minority concern, there might be little point in thinking about it.

This book argues that the tourism industry and experiences enjoyed by tourists were both shaped by and helped to create the modern world. Tourism grew from political, social, and cultural forces, emergent nationalism, new modes of consumption, intellectual change, and evolving technology—all of which, in turn, were themselves the products of various contexts and played important roles in the story outlined in the coming pages. Many of the earliest developments in the narrative are predominantly linked to England and Scotland, perhaps because industrialization was first a British story assuring that Britons enjoyed higher real incomes sooner than did others, but also that they experienced the trauma of urbanization (with its attendant pollution) against which ideas about the healthfulness of the natural environment took root. As it emerged, tourism impacted politics, expanded economies, altered culture, forwarded notions of good health and acceptable taste, inspired new technologies, created ideas about past and present, and more. Over time, tourism emerged as a central component of the "modern world" and of the controversial notion of "modernity."

Making this argument is not without risk; historians debate the very idea of a "modern world," of "modernization," and of something called "modernity" and the dispute is not without merit. The past is not inherently divided into discrete periods. Historians do this. Periodization helps us to make distinctions. At least in theory, breaking time into chunks defined by similarities and differences assists scholars in communicating with each other, with focusing their inquiries, and in defining their specializations. Historians *invented* "antiquity," the "middle ages," the "early modern period," and the "modern age." The challenge is that not all areas of the world followed the same trajectory, the same chronology. The schema just listed tends to represent a distinctly European evolutionary process.[41] Equally troubling, the words chosen to describe each period suggest a convenient linear progression from darkness into light. A "modern" person is clearly superior to someone who is "pre-modern." If Europe ushered in the modern age, then Europeans must be more advanced than non-Europeans. This is an unfair way to judge the past and the people who populate it. Our forbearers were not dumb, nor were they unsophisticated. One age is not inherently superior to another. One regional history does not outshine others. Chronological change does not represent a clear march toward anything but a time later than what falls before it on a timeline.

As the above discussion of pre-modern travel suggests, it is not always easy to confine specific behaviors or ideas to a single period. Herodotus may have looked upon travel in a similar way to that of a "modern tourist." Romans might have had a tourist trail. Medieval pilgrims likely found pleasure on their journeys. Yet we can also say without fear of contradiction that modern tourism *is* different. It encompasses more people, is largely based on different motives, and includes a range of experiences and desires that were anything but common in the past.

This fact raises one final point about the notion of the "modern world." However we describe the period from roughly the late-seventeenth century to the present, people *think* differently. For one thing, as historian C. A. Bayly notes, "an essential part of being modern is thinking you are modern."[42] But it is more than that. The modern world is organized in a manner that varies from other periods. Science and rational thought, while certainly important at other times, hold sway to an extent never known before. Consequently, ideas about health and wellness diverge significantly from what was true previously. Aesthetic sensibilities are unique. Consumption and consumerism play a far greater role in society. The individual matters more than in the past and, partly as a consequence, governments, even dictatorships and monarchies, are arranged much differently than they were in pre-modern times. Modernity is a "condition,"[43] not a value. We cannot escape that the world altered over the past three centuries. Likewise, those changes and this state of being are rooted in Europe: "The European origins of modernity cannot be denied."[44] The modern age is grounded in particular events—the Reformation, the Enlightenment, the Industrial Revolution—that were subsequently exported, often by violent force.

The story of tourism as we currently understand it is similarly rooted in Europe. It was born of the Grand Tour. It expanded as a result of changing aesthetics generated by the Enlightenment. It grew larger as a product of the Industrial Revolution and new technological innovations. It exploded in scope with the further expansion of wealth and with an ever-increasing sense that individuals are entitled to certain benefits and services. Military and economic dominance assured that Europeans could take their new pastime to every corner of the globe. When others encountered tourists, they both recognized the potential to generate wealth for themselves by capitalizing on tourists *and* wanted to become tourists themselves. Or, at least, this is the narrative that historians currently understand to be true. Future research may change the story.

Conclusion

People have always traveled and those journeys also sparked what anthropologist Stuart B. Schwartz describes as "readjustments and rethinking on each side" that forced those involved to reformulate ideas "of self and other in the face of unexpected actions and unimagined possibilities."[45] In this sense, modern tourism is little changed from what came before. If, however, one digs even a little bit deeper to explore what emerged over the past three hundred years, what exists today is profoundly removed from the past. This book explores that evolution and seeks to place it into historical context.

A History of Modern Tourism is structured chronologically. Chapter 1 examines the rise of the Grand Tour, finding roots in changing political needs and in the challenge of educating young aristocrats. During the sixteenth century, European states engaged in new forms of diplomacy and it was necessary to educate young men to meet new demands. At the same time it was necessary to reinforce the identity of a landed aristocracy relative to the rest of the population.

Chapter 2 explores changing ideas about aesthetics, the sublime and the beautiful. Europeans long viewed oceans and mountains with anxiety and concern, however the development of scientific thought, Dutch efforts to reclaim land from the sea and to prevent flooding, and the work of a new school of landscape painters all helped to spawn new notions of the Earth and unique ideas about how responses to that world impacted health and wellness.

Chapter 3 focuses on the evolution of steam power, looking specifically at the development of railways and trans-Atlantic steamers. This new technology made travel more affordable, at least on land, and considerably faster. It opened up new destinations to visit and created opportunities for those who would not previously have been able to afford even the shortest of holidays.

Chapter 4 looks at some of the new types of travel made possible by steam, describing the origin of package tours, the importance of spas to the development of water-based holidays as well as to connecting health with tourism, and it describes the rise of the seaside as a major vacation destination.

Chapter 5 covers the evolution of guidebooks and postcards, while also looking at the implications of tourism for landscapes, histories, and the built environment. Technology did not diminish as a major force behind the particular way in which tourism grew and changed.

New transportation technologies and the development of vast global empires made tourism a worldwide affair. Chapter 6 not only illustrates the globalization of tourism but also reflects the reality that leisure was increasingly useful as a means of showing difference. Tourists and tourism developers could use travel as a way of presenting a particular narrative of self to others during an age of both nationalism and global imperialism. It was a development that would have long-term implications for the politics of tourism around the world.

By the dawn of the twentieth century, tourism was a large industry. Chapter 7 looks at the rise of bicycles, automobiles and airplanes, showing how each exerted a major influence on the continued expansion of leisure travel. Chapter 8 shows how the three major types of political ideologies that vied for dominance during the twentieth century—communism, fascism, and democracy—endeavored to employ tourism as a path toward success.

Finally, Chapters 9 and 10 discuss developments after World War II, specifically a worldwide concern with tourism motivated by both political and economic considerations, as well as the rise of a truly mass tourism that involved people from all across the developed world and which made almost every corner of the globe a viable destination for escape. Together, the coming pages show how tourism moved from a geographically limited concern to become almost universal and how leisure travel changed from being the purview of a very few to being the obsession of nearly all. This is a book about how people grew to see themselves and their planet differently and about the contexts in which that change took place.

1
Beginnings: The Grand Tour

Edward Gibbon (1737–94), author of the epic six-volume *Decline and Fall of the Roman Empire,* started his education on a sour note. Hindered by ill health, he was a poor student and the future classicist did not immediately take to Latin or Greek. Worse, although he loved to read, the boy was largely unimpressed with his tutors. As a result, when Gibbon matriculated at Magdalen College, Oxford, in April 1752 he was unprepared for his studies. On arrival the future historian found this most wealthy, prestigious, and ancient of Oxford colleges sorely lacking. He huffed, "these venerable bodies are sufficiently old to partake of all the prejudices and infirmities of age. The schools of Oxford and Cambridge were founded in a dark age of false and barbarous science and they are still tainted with the vices of their origin."[1] Much as critics of large research universities today decry the use of teaching assistants, Gibbon was disgusted by the fact that professors seldom taught while the tutors were wholly inadequate. In the end, his fourteen months at Oxford "proved ... the most idle and unprofitable of my whole life."[2] It was all too much. A show of protest was called for; Gibbon converted to Catholicism, eschewing the established Church of England. Given a prohibition on Catholic attendance at Oxford, he was summarily tossed out of college.

Fortunately for Gibbon, eighteenth-century Britain offered its wealthy young men an alternative to university: Continental European travel. He was well suited. While at Oxford, Gibbon would dart off on excursions to various English cities to escape the miserable cloisters of Magdalen. What better than to go to Europe?

Of course, Gibbon's long-suffering father had little interest in setting his son on the European continent without guidance. The young Gibbon would have a tutor, the highly talented Daniel Pavilliard (1704–75), and he would remain in Lausanne, Switzerland learning French, German, Italian, Greek, and Classics. Equally important, the younger Gibbon came to detest the Catholic faith, renouncing his youthful conversion and, less desirably, eventually denouncing Christianity altogether.

As Gibbon matured under the guidance of his tutor and in an environment far removed from the warm yellow Cotswold limestone of Oxfordshire, he found himself taking to language and evermore attracted to the works of classical writers such as Marcus Tullius Cicero (106–43 BCE). He made contacts with contemporary scholars, was invited to formal gatherings, and started to become a man of letters. After nearly three years of extraordinary progress, Pavilliard obtained permission from Gibbon's father to take the young man on a tour of Switzerland. Now the lessons grew more cultural and political. Switzerland was a complicated state, divided into regions speaking diverse languages, exercising distinct political regimes, and even practicing different religious traditions. At every turn "we visited the churches, arsenals, libraries, and all the most eminent persons."[3] He was certainly seeing important institutions, but his tutor ensured that he gained a deeper understanding of Switzerland and of the Swiss people.

In 1758, Gibbon was called home to England. Over the following months, he half-heartedly looked for employment, wrote, and joined the national militia. Hungry for more adventure, five years after leaving the Continent the twenty-six-year-old scholar attained permission from his father to return to Europe, traveling throughout its various countries and kingdoms. Such a trip was not at all uncommon. He later wrote: "According to the law of custom, and perhaps of reason, foreign travel completes the education of an English gentleman." Gibbon was to embark on the "Grand Tour."

In Edward Gibbon's case, the journey lasted three months. He spent time in Paris, Switzerland, and finally Italy. The classical education that he had attained under the direction of Pavilliard paid off. He was accepted into the salons of Paris and, when he reached Italy, was captivated by the opportunity to visit the sites of so many ancient triumphs. "At the distance of twenty-five years," Gibbon wrote, "I can neither forget nor express the strong emotions which agitated my mind as I first approached and entered the eternal city [Rome]. After a sleepless night, I trod, with a lofty step, the ruins of the Forum; each memorable spot where Romulus stood, or Tully spoke, or Caesar fell, was at once present to my eye."[4] It was the stuff of dreams and boyhood fantasy. It was everything that the Grand Tour was supposed to be.

Parameters

By the end of the eighteenth century, major European cities such as Paris, Rome, or Venice might have had hundreds or even thousands of English men and women roaming their streets.[5] For many tourism historians, these travelers represent the first modern tourists.[6] They made the journey for many reasons but in doing so they played a significant role in fueling a growing passion for travel and adventure. Their trips, and their written accounts and acquired artwork, made others want to follow. Debate about the merits of travel was everywhere, driving the respectable classes to think about the potential adventures to be had by leaving home.[7]

The Grand Tour is generally associated with England's so-called landed elite and with the education of young nobles, so much so that one recent historian claims "the Grand Tour is not the Grand Tour unless it includes the following: first, a young British male patrician ...; second, a tutor who accompanies his charge throughout the journey; third, a fixed itinerary that makes Rome its principle destination; fourth, a lengthy period of absence, averaging two to three years."[8] While it is true that far more young Englishmen traveled around Europe than did members of other nationalities and that much of the debate that surrounded the trip centered on its pedagogical role, the reality is that this definition is too confining. Although Britons far outnumbered all others, many people of other nations went on the tour. Peter the Great (1672–1725), the Europeanizing Russian Tsar, famously made the trip and encouraged members of his court to go as well.[9] The German philosopher Johann Wolfgang von Goethe (1749–1832) took the trek.[10] These are but two famous examples. Many others traveled as well, from France, Russia, Germany, the Low Countries, and beyond.[11] Historian Chloe Chard ultimately expands the scope of her own definition of a Grand Tourist to say that he (or she) originated "somewhere in northern Europe" and aimed "to travel to the southern side of the Alps."[12] Likewise it was not simply young men who journeyed forth. English women such as the author Mary Wollstonecraft (1759–97), the widow Lady Mary Coke (1727–1811), and the fashionable socialite Lady Mary Wortley Montagu (1689–1762) all spent extensive time on the Continent where they escaped from unpleasant relationships, enjoyed freedom not possible at home, and attained the education usually limited to men.[13] Nor was age a barrier. Author Tobias Smollett made the trip later in life alongside his wife,[14] while at least some other older Britons ventured across the English Channel in pursuit of art to add to rapidly growing collections.[15] As the eighteenth century moved along, even some members of the middling sort, far removed from the blue-blooded aristocracy, braved the English Channel to embark on a European adventure.[16] Ultimately, any definition of the Grand Tour should take into consideration this diversity, focusing on the significant growth of European travel in the eighteenth century, on the various motivations behind those trips, and on the reality that more and more people, even removed from the male elite, found the idea of an extended stay on the Continent appealing. The Grand Tour was far from being mass travel, but it was a first tentative step in that direction.

Origins

While it may be satisfying and dramatic to focus on moments of upheaval, most of human history features slow evolution, not sudden revolution. Thus, eighteenth-century tourists did not spontaneously embark on trips around Europe. Although distinct from earlier travelers, they were the product of steady change that started in the Middle Ages and stretched forward into the seventeenth and eighteenth centuries. The Grand Tour is rooted in profound cultural, intellectual, political, social, and economic developments that emerged gradually across Europe during the late Medieval period. Indeed, while the Grand Tour is generally associated with the British, its origins are actually quite international in character.

The fifteenth century was a period of remarkable economic expansion in much of Europe. Part of the reason likely stemmed from the profound implications of mass mortality. Starting in 1347, a succession of plague epidemics washed over Europe, resulting in the death of between one-third and one-half of the population.[17] At least some survivors benefitted significantly by acquiring newly affordable land and by fostering marriages with wealthy heiresses that in turn made it possible for families to multiply wealth rapidly.[18] But the plague also had another implication. With a much smaller labor market, more efficient modes of production were developed—including stronger horses and efficient watermills that could produce food more cheaply, freeing investment in other areas. Some of the sail technology associated with the watermills transferred to ships, making them more efficient and facilitating trade. Land transport was similarly improved to accommodate better shipping. All of this depended upon investment and the banking sector grew to meet demand. Ultimately, more products were generated more efficiently, and were subsequently more widely traded.[19]

According to historian Fernand Braudel, trade routes between northern Europe, Belgium, Italian port cities, and the Asiatic world became routine, creating a "European world-economy."[20] The exchange of goods such as wool flourished and a significant number of merchants became affluent. These men sought ways to spend money. Many purchased items that would display prosperity and good taste: sculpture and paintings, for example. This made it possible for a growing list of painters, sculptors, architects, and authors to survive under the patronage of rich bankers, merchants, churchmen, nobles, and politicians. The Renaissance, or "rebirth," was the result—a period of extraordinary cultural production that initially looked to the classical world for inspiration. It was based, at least at first, in Italy. Between the late fourteenth and the early seventeenth centuries, Italian cities such as Florence emerged as beacons of good taste that both inspired artistic outpourings in other European cities while at the same time prompting northern Europeans to grow fascinated with Italian achievements.[21]

There were other significant results of greater opulence, at least two of which played a role in the development of tourism. First was expanding trade, combined with a desire among more people to explore the cities of Europe where original ideas and new artists might be found. Not only did merchants and traders venture around the metropolises of Europe, but a significant and growing number of travelers drawn from virtually every European country also set out to explore. These adventurers—and it was an adventure to brave the crime and pothole-ridden roads of the Continent—wrote about their experiences. A subsequent increase in demand for travel writing fueled further wanderlust.[22]

Second, Italy was anything but unified during the Renaissance. It was a veritable hodgepodge of city-states.[23] As wealth increased, Italian politics developed an increasingly "unstable equilibrium of power." Anxious to avoid chaos, Italian leaders responded by creating new modes of diplomacy. The resident ambassador was one of the most significant innovations. Within the short span of only thirty years (1420–50) such men assumed the role of "agents and ... symbols of a continuous system of diplomatic pressures." These Italians lived in situ in European cities and in Italian city-states, reporting back to their superiors and seeking to carry out diplomatic missions on behalf of their governments. The system worked, and by roughly 1500 such men were employed by other countries throughout Europe.[24]

By the end of the sixteenth century, English politics also became complicated. During her reign, Queen Elizabeth I (1533–1603) faced daunting tests. She was excommunicated in 1570 for pro-Protestant policies, weathered various internal challenges to her throne, confronted the Spanish Armada in 1588, and was relentlessly pursued by a host of other problems.[25] On one hand, this situation made journeying to Spain or Italy quite risky. Travel was inherently dangerous due to poor conditions and widespread thievery and it was made worse by the fact that upon return to England it created suspicion at court. To many officials, going abroad suggested undoubted tawdry dealings with foreign governments or, worse, treasonous activity.[26] On the other hand, the notoriously independent queen recognized the need for good information. Intelligence was critical as English policymaking was often "hamstrung by ignorance of enemy intentions."[27] In the past, at least some English monarchs traveled to the Continent to bolster diplomatic ties and to gather information for themselves. Although she reportedly loved to travel, Elizabeth was unable to make such a trip herself because she believed that venturing from England would result in "losing her monarchical power."[28] Consequently, Elizabeth relied on her councilors, on merchants and diplomats, on spies, and on other agents. It was an inadequate approach to intelligence as these figures often "told their paymasters what they wanted to hear." According to at least one historian, the employment of resident ambassadors might well have avoided early diplomatic hassles.[29] Evidently the queen agreed, for as time passed she grew anxious to develop a trained collection of diplomats. Unfortunately, British and European universities, once institutions of exceptional stature, went into steady decline during the late fifteenth and sixteenth centuries.[30] Oxford and Cambridge grew specialized—focusing on providing an exceptionally narrow education that was designed more to create an elite social class than to generate thoughtful leaders. Likewise, given their parochial nature, these schools failed to spawn a sense of curiosity about other cultures that might have inspired young men to become statesmen. They offered no instruction in languages other than Greek and Latin, making no pretense of celebrating a world broader than the English ruling class.[31] The only means of attaining the necessary servants was to send young men abroad so that they could learn about the languages, cultures, politics, personages, and military strengths of foreign lands. Toward this end the crown started to subsidize journeys, such as that made by Sir Philip Sidney (1554–86) in 1572–75.[32]

These trends combined so that by the early seventeenth century there was a sense among many that seeing Europe was beneficial to young men. The multi-talented Sir Francis Bacon (1561–1626) authored probably the most famous essay celebrating the value of travel. For the young, it was "part of education." Making "profitable" acquaintances, learning languages, observing foreign courts, touring churches and monasteries, visiting libraries, ruins, armories, and arsenals, or attending any of many other potential destinations, made such excursions valuable. The philosopher pointed out that it was vital to have a good tutor and to carefully record one's adventures in diaries and correspondence. Yet most of all, and anticipating later debates about the Grand Tour, Bacon informed the prospective tourist that travel should "appear rather in his discourse, than in his apparel or gesture; and in his discourse let him be rather advised in his answers, than forward to tell stories: and let it appear that he doth not change his country manners for those of foreign parts, but only prick in some flowers of that he hath learned abroad into the customs of his own country."[33]

Even as Bacon alluded to the fear that travel might make his young aristocratic countrymen somehow less *English*, he ignored the risks facing those journeying to the Continent. Europe was a dangerous place. According to popular historian Christopher Hibbert, early tourist Fynes Moryson

(1566–1630) braved many difficulties when he crossed the Channel in 1591. The young man departed from Leigh-on-Thames on May 1 only to narrowly escape pirates based at Dunkirk. Despite covering a relatively short distance, the Channel crossing took a monstrous ten days. Once in the Netherlands, Moryson faced no less risk and discomfort. The coastal roads in Holland were infested with a veritable swarm of highwaymen who robbed foreign travelers with impunity. Yet Moryson was ready for them. He dressed himself up as a "poor Bohemian" who was employed as a Leipzig merchant. The guise worked and the robbers stayed away. Unfortunately the scheme meant that Moryson was forced to pursue accommodations befitting his affected poverty. He had to sleep with the rabble in overcrowded and dirty inns. Rather than beds, they slept on benches. Once, when a maidservant spotted Moryson's silk stockings and recognized him for a disguised elite, the shrewd trekker got to sleep in a bed. It did not happen often. As further protection against thieves, the young man wore money-belts underneath his clothing. The tactic worked, though it meant that when he was caught in the rainstorms that are so frequent in northwestern Europe he could not change his clothes lest his numerous roommates spot his cash and try to rob him. Soggy nights followed.

Little changed when Moryson moved from the Netherlands into France and then on to Italy. When venturing from Rome to Naples, he hired sixty musketeers to protect him against bandits. It was money well spent because, although the tattered remains of drawn and quartered thieves were scattered along the roadway to dissuade others, there were criminals everywhere. In fact, despite all of his cleverness, Moryson was robbed while walking between the French cities of Metz and Châlons. Not only did the highwaymen steal his money, which would have been bad enough, but they also took his sword, his cloak, his shirt, and even his hat. No respectable man could be caught without his head covered, so Moryson was forced to acquire a greasy old French chapeau until he finally reached Paris and could attain something more desirable.

It could have been worse. Beyond thieves, tourists faced starving canines, horrendous roads, marauding soldiers, occasional wars, and the Inquisition that spread through large parts of Europe during the sixteenth century when desperate Catholics struggled to end the progress of Protestantism. English visitors were forced to proceed incognito lest they be captured, tortured, and executed for their religious beliefs. If all of this was not bad enough, at least one traveler reported seeing no less than thirty-four markers along the road between Danzig (Gdansk) and Hamburg denoting where a previous wayfarer had been murdered. In Brandenburg, murder was the least of it. Cannibalism was common. Disease was another threat. The writer John Evelyn (1620–1706) nearly died of smallpox in Geneva.[34]

Despite it all the Grand Tour was increasingly popular. Specific figures are difficult to come by and are anecdotal. We know, for example, that there were enough "English heretics" on their way to Venice in 1592 and 1595 for the Pope to complain. In 1612, there were reportedly more than 70 Englishmen in Venice—hardly a huge number but it indicates that there was enough of an increase in English travel to elicit notice. There were far more Britons in Europe in the first half of the eighteenth century than there were previously—somewhere between 12 and 30 in most European cities at a given moment. By the second half of the eighteenth century, the numbers climbed into the hundreds and perhaps thousands. There is even evidence that not all journeyers were from the most elite social class although we can be certain that they were anything but poor. Such tourists preferred less expensive, shorter trips. In short, by the eighteenth century we find a different scale of travel.[35]

The Grand Tour expands

The period between 1748 and 1789 was a relatively peaceful one in Europe and it was then that the Grand Tour reached its zenith.[36] Vast numbers of young Englishmen, and a few Englishwomen, ventured to Paris, Rome, Venice, Florence, and Naples. Some went to the Low Countries, Hanover, Berlin, Dresden, Vienna, Munich, Geneva, and Prague (the easternmost site visited by all but a very few tourists).[37]

Most sought education; the Grand Tour was a rite of passage from childhood to adulthood. It was truly a "customary" part of the schooling of landed aristocrats and the often unrealized goal of imbuing future leaders with knowledge of foreign languages, customs, politics, and culture remained intact. And yet the Grand Tour gradually reflected something altogether new, a hedonistic approach to consuming that was less evident during the previous century. The trip represented "a secularized ritual of commodification and consumption, whereby what was seen as a rite of passage itself is acquired in order to be put on show."[38] This new notion of display remains an important part of tourism today.

There was nothing affordable about traveling in Europe for months or years at a time, especially because tourists were advised to show their wealth at every turn. Guidebooks suggested that bleeding money was "the way to be respected" and being well thought of mattered.[39] In eighteenth-century Britain power derived from land. It had always been this way, of course, but after the Glorious Revolution, when Parliament essentially fired one king and hired another, the aristocracy stood atop the British political hierarchy as never before. Estates allowed them to inhabit a world of almost unimaginable opulence. They drew tremendous incomes from farming, rents, inheritance, and investment in trade. Status was linked to leisure and not needing to work, while at the same time spending a significant fortune on recreation was one way to display one's position in the class hierarchy.

During the eighteenth century, only about 3 percent of the population controlled Britain, both economically and politically.[40] Their power was based on vast holdings and palatial estates. From these rural seats, they controlled elections and largely defined legislative agendas. And yet, the aristocracy was increasingly worried about its status. The expansion of international trade and the initial growth of what would become the British Empire meant that a growing class of merchants grew rich, gradually catching up to the ancient and established families in monetary terms. Some of these had pretentions to join the gentry, crashing a party that was hundreds of years old. In addition, by the second half of the century the first rumblings of industrialization were underway and a new class of factory managers and owners began to desire the power of the property-owning classes. Yet even more than the arrival of what amounted to "new money," the traditional elite worried about its hold on power. Those who made money amid the expanding economic environment were the ones most directly impacted by government economic policies, yet they had virtually no say in politics. The landed elite controlled who ran for parliament and they defined how their tenants would vote. It was an irritating reality for those who felt unrepresented. By the 1760s, the first hints of radical politics emerged, gaining strength over the last half of the decade and continuing, haltingly, into the nineteenth century when a series of reform acts, beginning in 1832, gradually eroded landed control.[41]

During the eighteenth century the Grand Tour played an increasingly significant role in the expression of wealth. It was a question of taste. Members of the aristocracy could not be distinguished purely by their estates; they had to set themselves apart by the way that they displayed those acres, by the appearance of their houses, and by the way that they decorated their manors. Italy retained the cultural reputation gained during the Renaissance. It was truly "classic," an easily consumable expression of refinement. The Grand Tour offered a means of teaching young people to consume like landed gentlemen: A finishing school for the rich. In a world of manorial holdings, "political power depended on cultural display."[42]

Investing copious amounts on a Continental tour, to say nothing of related expenditures on art, architecture, landscaping, lavish clothing, and other expenses, was a way of hopefully staving off the inevitable. Travel certainly made it easy to spend. Trips were much longer than those taken by most twenty-first century vacationers and this necessitated arranging longer-term accommodations. Transportation was costly, much more so than it is at present, especially if the tourist was anxious to cover ground quickly. Many purchased their own carriages upon arriving in France, and then proceeded to complain bitterly at every turn about the outlays encountered along the way, especially in places such as Paris and Italy where post roads carried particularly high tolls. According to Grand Tour historian Jeremy Black, accidents represented an even greater expense and there was nothing rare about them. Altogether, it cost anywhere between £250 and £600 per year to go on the Grand Tour, but some spent far more. James Duff, the Second Earl of Fife (1729–1809), for example, managed to spend over £1700 during a stay of several weeks in Paris. Total expenditure varied wildly. Black notes that Lord (Frederick) North (1732–92) withdrew £70,000 from one banker alone during his 1753 tour. By contrast, a year later, Francis Hastings, the Tenth Earl of Huntingdon (1729–89), spent a rather more modest £5700. The British government, concerned about revenues lost to foreign governments, estimated that British travelers dispersed as much as £4 million per annum.[43]

Given the amounts and the reason for spending, it is hardly surprising that the idea of "packing light" was unheard of. Even in the seventeenth century, tourists were to take prayer books, swords and pistols, a watch, lice-proof bedclothes, waterproofs, hats, handkerchiefs, and more. By the eighteenth century, guidebooks added further items including special strongly made shirts, an iron fastener for securing hotel doors, tea caddies, penknives, seasonings, oatmeal, seasickness remedies, plenty of reading material, medicines, and so on. All of this added up. The Earl of Burlington (1694–1753) took no less than 878 pieces of luggage when he made his tour during the second half of the eighteenth century.[44]

Getting a taste for Europe

Historians debate when modern consumer society began. While many focus on the nineteenth century, especially after about 1850,[45] others note the beginnings of a change starting much earlier.[46] Either way, the extent to which the aristocracy pursued a lifestyle premised on exceptional levels of consumption is striking. Members of the elite spoke volumes when they hired a designer such as Lancelot "Capability" Brown (1716–83). The foremost landscape architect of his day, Brown created vast, carefully manicured estate grounds that resembled "open savannah" and projected "a sense of infinity."[47] Not only did the vistas suggest who was in control of nature, they gave a property a feeling of vast space. When elites constructed their houses, symmetry, order, and tasteful design told the world that the inhabitants were cultured, educated, and classy; because touring manor houses was almost as popular in the eighteenth century as it would later be in the twentieth and twenty-first centuries, these estates presented their impressive message to a wide audience.[48] It is no accident that the property class further projected their taste and control in the paintings they purchased or commissioned. Some made repeated trips to Italy to buy art, compiling huge collections in the process.[49] It was not uncommon for landed families to have themselves depicted with their estates or homes as a backdrop, with well-designed "natural" landscapes extending into the distance.[50] What people purchase speaks volumes.[51]

For sociologist Colin Campbell, the reason for all of this buying is not hard to see: Patterns of consumption underwent profound change, a veritable philosophical revolution that was closely tied to the growth of Romanticism in the second half of the eighteenth century. Fiction, art, and music all provided a flight into something that seemed better than the everyday. Escape made one feel good, offering a different perspective on the world. Buying art, then, was an exercise in self-improvement. The result was a new approach to consumption which Campbell calls "self-illusory hedonism." In essence, people spent a great deal of time imagining what they would like to have and feeling that they had improved themselves by acquiring things. This new pattern of behavior formed the foundation for the eventual "consumer revolution" and not long thereafter the first industrial revolution.[52] Although Campbell does not explicitly make the connection, these same developments were vital to the rise of modern tourism.

As noted above, the Grand Tour offered plentiful opportunity to spend and to pursue personal betterment through the development of taste. Grand Tourists also needed to bring something home that would display to everybody where they had been and what they had seen. A small industry developed to feed this need. Paintings depicted important sites such as the Pantheon and the Coliseum in Rome, the canals in Venice, the Parthenon in Athens, and Roman ruins wherever they might be. Equally important, the paintings nearly all feature tourists *looking* at the sites/sights in question. These figures visually consume the spectacle, while at the same time projecting the message to whomever looks on the canvas: The owner of this painting was here; he bought the experience. Paintings worked in much the same way as contemporary postcards emblazoned with the words "Wish You Were Here!" Such cards do not truly mean that the sender wishes that the recipient were literally underfoot, but rather announce that "I am seeing these places and you are not." They make a comment about the status accrued through travel. In some sense, the eighteenth-century paintings purchased by the box load by Grand Tourists are the first postcards, the first travel snapshots. These art works are physical reminders that travel was about consuming.[53]

Elites behaving badly

Although the purpose of the Grand Tour was supposed to be self-improvement, the reality was often rather different.

Edward Gibbon was an atypical tourist. He attained a solid education in Lausanne, then returned for his Grand Tour after some years had passed and following his stint in the national militia. Gibbon was more mature than the average tourist. He was 26 years old. Most made their trip between the ages of 18 and 25, the equivalent age of a twenty-first century undergraduate. These were students with virtually unlimited budgets and often little supervision. They frequently behaved accordingly.

Once in Europe, young elites did see the sites. They attended the papal fireworks at the Castel Sant'Angelo, toured Rome and Venice, spent time in Paris, hoped to see an eruption of Mount Vesuvius, and explored much of what was in between. They looked at art, visited gorgeous homes, admired monuments, and studied classical architecture. Some even learned a few words of French or Italian. As was true during the seventeenth century, there remained no fixed route. Major cities like Rome, Venice, Florence, and Naples were still popular. Travel was considerably safer than it had been, though periodic military and political conflict around Europe did define where tourists went to some degree.[54]

In theory, each sightseer employed a tutor who assured that all of these positive learning outcomes took place. The problem was that most instructors were untalented and inattentive, the very opposite of Gibbon's beloved Daniel Pavilliard. They were frequently failed writers, academics, or churchmen, essentially men who had fallen from favor at court and who had to earn a living in some other way. Given their decrepit status, most cared little about their young charges and often preferred to spend their time drinking and whoring. Unsurprisingly, their pupils often did much the same and chose their destinations accordingly.[55] Italy was long a leading center of sexual promiscuity.[56] Prostitutes were ubiquitous. Paris, meanwhile, was well known as one of the leading producers of condoms, dildos, and pornography.[57] Parisian wives had the reputation of being accommodating with their sexual favors, performing every imaginable act with travelers, especially when it was common for these young men to lavish

Figure 1.1 Young Grand Tourists were expected to travel with a tutor. Parents imagined that this individual would offer instruction in language, culture, history, and other important information. Very often this hope went unrealized. *"A Tour of Foreign Parts"* by Henry William Bunbury (artist) and James Bretherton (printmaker). Courtesy of The Lewis Walpole Library, Yale University.

gifts of as much as £1000 on them for services rendered.[58] Unsurprisingly, venereal disease was a real threat to tourists anxious to explore the more licentious side of Continental cities.[59]

Much like fraternity life today, drinking and gambling featured prominently on the itinerary. Both activities represented a significant component of eighteenth-century life both in Britain and elsewhere. Indeed, alcohol consumption in London during the eighteenth century was staggering by modern standards. In 1743, for example, the average ingestion of cheap spirits in London was 2.2 gallons per capita.[60] At one stage, there was one public house in Britain for every eighty-seven people.[61] Both statistics largely reflect the drinking habits of ordinary Britons, of course, but the amount of wine and spirits imbibed by the landed elite must have been impressively high as well. Yet the reality is that European cities offered extraordinary opportunity for debauchery outside of the ordinary strictures of an apparently sodden society, especially among unattended young men. Gambling losses were sometimes equally astonishing. Sir Carnaby Haggerston (c. 1700–56) wrote home constantly begging for more money to cover his expenses. Francis Anderton (dates unknown) lost nearly £200 (now equivalent to £17,000) in a single evening. John Thornton (dates unknown) was not far behind and lost £150 (now equivalent to £12,700).[62] Gambling was expensive, but drink was cheap. Many became "unhappily addicted to drinking to the highest degree."[63]

Not every traveler was male or ventured across the Channel in order to spend lavishly or to behave badly. Travel could offer an escape from oppression, especially for women. For example, Mary Wollstonecraft, author of *A Vindication of the Rights of Women* (1792), made the trip and her motivations are telling. Cultivating taste, learning languages, and seeing significant historic sites was part of it. But women like Wollstonecraft had another reason for traveling—to find scope for the imagination and to escape the male-dominated realities of eighteenth-century British culture.[64] Even women far less famous than Wollstonecraft found this sort of inspiration, focusing their attention more on "antiquities and works of art as well as cultural, social, and commercial developments" than on armies or politics.[65] Men were supposed to worry about earning money and running the country, women about managing the house. Thus, the 1747 book *The Art of Governing a Wife* advised that women were to "lay up and save; look to the house; talk to few; take of all within."[66] Georgian Britain was a gentleman's club and for independently minded women, it was stifling. Travel represented a reprieve.

While continental adventures offered escape they also raised very real concerns about the social order. What was to be made of women engaging in male pursuits? Besides, what possible benefit was there in female travel? They were not responsible for building landed estates or for purchasing the lavish décor of these places. No woman would serve in Parliament or make significant political decisions. At best, the experience of jaunting through European cities might improve a woman's chance on the marriage market by making her conversant in more languages and giving her something to chat about with suitors. Granted, the trip might almost make her *less* compelling to men. What man wanted a wife as interesting and erudite as himself? Given such prevalent attitudes, there is little surprising about the reality that women like Mary Wollstonecraft were rare. Adventurous women were the exception, not the rule.[67]

Most of the anxiety inspired by the Grand Tour was a result of the fact that parents, aware of the behaviors exhibited by many tourists, worried about their children. A fierce debate about the merits of continental travel resulted—perhaps the first significant and widespread discussion about the implications of going abroad. While many young people seemed to take touring foreign cities to be a license for sin, a few parents feared what their sons might get up to. Most anxiety did not center on sexual behavior or the risks of over-imbibing. Dr. Samuel Johnson (1709–84), though critical of sending unattended young men to Europe, summed up the majority view in a conversation with his traveling companion James Boswell (1740–95): "If a young man is wild, and must run after women and bad company, it is better this should be done abroad, as, on his return, he can break off such connections, and begin at home a new man, with a character to form, and acquaintances to make."[68] Evidently, travel *was* a license to move outside of social norms.

Instead, parents fretted about what their offspring might become. Edward Gibbon reports in his memoirs that his command of English declined while he was away. He came to love Switzerland and European culture more generally, getting evermore critical of English life as he spent more time away.[69] *This* was something to be concerned about. Bacon suggested that travelers should reflect their experience in discursive ability rather than in "apparel or gesture,"[70] yet an alarming number of tourists evidently returned to Britain as odd hybrids of English and European. Gibbon learned languages; most did not. Instead, they mastered a handful of words and filled in with strange accents and wild gestures. As one poem summarized:

> Returning he proclaims by many a grace,
> By shrugs and strange contortions of his face,
> How much a dunce, that has been sent to roam,
> Excels a dunce, that has been kept at home.

British adults were mortified. Historian Christopher Hibbert notes that the level of concern was so pronounced that an "Act Against Rambling" was proposed. If passed, the bill would have made it

> an offence to the debase purity of the English language "by a vile mixture of exotic words, idioms, and phrases," to make any unmeaning grimace, shrug or gesticulation, to use the world *canaille* more than three times in the same sentence, or wantonly to cast contempt on the roast beef of old England. Offenders against the Act were to be "flogged like schoolboys."[71]

Parents sent their children to Europe hoping that they would return as cultured members of the landed elite. What they often got in return were young people who eschewed the very emblems of English identity.

Conclusion: End of the Grand Tour

While the Grand Tour was customary in 1763, it was becoming a bygone memory by 1815. Part of the reason for this is immediately obvious: The French Revolution, followed closely by the Napoleonic Wars, swept across Europe starting in 1789 and extended until 1815. During the first conflict, many continued to travel around the Continent, but the second wave of hostilities was far more dangerous. By 1807, overland travel was risky and "sea routes had become impossible." When the fighting stopped, many visitors returned—even if only to see the damages of war—but this was no longer the old Grand Tour. Important ideas, especially about aesthetics and health, had changed, replacing the urban-centered and overwhelmingly aristocratic character of the eighteenth century trip.[72]

Of course, many of the trends inaugurated by the Grand Tour did not end. Elite tourism established a sense that travel generated prestige. There was something important to be gained by visiting the great European capitals. Foreign exploration and consumption made one a better person. It promised good mental health and a heightened intellect. This dream of self-improvement would ultimately connect closely to a desire for "self help" that permeated middle-class society during the Victorian age.

Likewise, the idea that good taste was partly to be found on the Continent also remained in place. As railways made it possible for ordinary Britons to view their own country, the sight of massive European-inspired manor houses and palaces was omnipresent. It was nice to see the British copies, but what about the real thing? Authenticity had its merits.

Perhaps most of all, the Grand Tour generated a body of literature describing travel adventures. These accounts did not disappear from the public consciousness. Yet the wave of new texts reflected the reality that something had changed. By the 1820s a new way of looking at the world, developing from at least the middle of the eighteenth century, had taken hold—a romantic vision of landscapes and history, a sense of excitement to be had in nature that European mountains and beaches offered in abundance. The old cities were still attractive, but more and more people wanted to escape the "beaten track" in order to locate "hidden secrets." They wanted to visit the mountains and to experience wild nature. They wished to enjoy "romantic travel."[73] What was soon known as the "sublime and beautiful" was very much on offer, if only you could leave home to find it. It was a goal that, increasingly, attracted tourists from all social classes and helps to explain the rise of a much more widespread wanderlust during the nineteenth century.

2

The sublime and beautiful

The romantic poet Samuel Taylor Coleridge (1772–1834) was prone to dependency. Like many others of his day, he was hooked on opium and in 1803 he cut short a trip around Scotland with fellow authors William (1770–1850) and Dorothy Wordsworth (1771–1855) partly because withdrawal symptoms became painfully pronounced. Laudanum, the most prevalent form of opium in the nineteenth century, was simply not available in the rural Highlands.[1] Yet this was not his only compulsion. The great romantic was strung out on something else, a fact clearly illustrated by an incident that took place during a hiking trip through England's Lake District in the first week of August 1802. "There is one sort of Gambling, to which I am much addicted," he wrote to love interest Sara Hutchinson. The poet continued: "It is this. When I find it convenient to descend from a mountain, I am too confident & indolent to look round about & wind about till I find a track or other symptom of safety; but I wander on, & where it is first possible to descend, there I go—relying upon fortune for how far down this possibility will continue."[2] As climbing historian Robert Macfarlane summarizes: "It was Russian Roulette, with the mountain-top the chamber of the gun and the ways off the mountain the bullets and the blanks."[3]

On August 6, Coleridge played his dangerous game on Sca Fell, the highest mountain in England. The climb upwards was uneventful, completed in pleasant conditions and without incident. Once on the summit, however, the poet looked for his way off as the first hints of a coming storm appeared on the horizon. The route choice was far from scientific: "the first place I came to, that was not direct Rock, I slipped down & went on for a while with tolerable ease." It did not continue. Soon, he found himself dropping down a seven-foot high patch of "smooth perpendicular Rock." There would be no going back, no way to climb upwards in search of a better path. Coleridge knew it. He recounted that the experience "put my whole Limbs in a Tremble." As well it might. There was nothing to do but continue ever downward. The storm grew closer and the author realized that his track would "in a very hard Rain ... [be the] channel of a most splendid Waterfall." Down he went. He slid this way. Then that. His clothes grew filthy and torn. Three smaller drops, each one increasing "the Palsy of my Limbs—I shook all over." All at once, he was stuck. The next drop fell to a ledge "[so] exceedingly narrow, that if I dropt down upon it I must of necessity have fallen backwards & of course killed myself." Consequently, he did what any normal person would do. Coleridge lay down and laughed "at myself for a Madman," while reclining "in a state of almost prophetic Trance & Delight."

Okay, so perhaps lying down to laugh is not an entirely *normal* response to such a situation, but eventually Coleridge got up and started looking around for another route. After a short search, he discovered a dead sheep near a heap of stones and concluded that if the sheep could climb up, then perhaps he could climb down. What was more, the pile of stones was not natural. Somebody had placed them there in an effort to get to the sheep. Further exploration revealed what climbers refer to as a "chimney," a place where slabs of rock form a channel into which a person can wedge him or herself in order to shimmy up or down a cliff face. Coleridge was saved, free to continue his descent, to find shelter from the storm, and to reflect on the excitement of his evidently quite perfect day.[4] Samuel Taylor Coleridge was addicted to the "sublime."

What is perhaps more striking is just how new this fixation was. Even sixty years earlier almost nobody would have climbed Sca Fell or any other mountain in pursuit of excitement. Before the mid-eighteenth century, people simply did not go into the mountains if they could help it. Little wonder. Greek mythology depicts Mount Olympus as the home of the gods, to ascend it was to engage in the "steep ascent of heaven." As one scholar comments, it "apparently did not occur to Greeks to climb mountains unless they wanted to get to the other side."[5] In the Old Testament, the Israelites, fresh from their advance across the Sinai, "camped before" Mount Sinai awaiting God's word. They were told: "Take heed to yourselves, *that ye* go *not* up into the mountain, or touch the border of it: whosoever toucheth the mount shall surely be put to death." Moses, of course, was instructed to climb up into the clouds where the Lord gave him the Ten Commandments.[6] Similar ideas evidently existed outside of Europe. Thus, for example, Inca tribesmen in Chile and Argentina sacrificed children to the gods high in the Andes, leaving the remains behind to be preserved by the cold conditions.[7]

Europeans spoke of "dismal mountains" and "frightful Alps." They "started with afright" at the very sight of spaces that diverged from the far more pleasing visage of ordered fields and controlled forms.[8] There were exceptions, of course. The Renaissance poet Francesco Petrarch (1304–74) evidently climbed Mont Ventoux, a barren, almost lunar-like peak in the center of France, in 1336 "solely from the desire to see [the mountain's] conspicuous height," but he was virtually alone: a strange exception to an almost universal rule. After the ascent, even Petrarch gave up climbing in order to pursue a more acceptable focus on self-reflection and faith. His reversal leads some scholars to refer to the climb as "nothing less than a halfway house between medieval and modern."[9] It would take more than four hundred years before very many others followed his lead above tree line.

Beaches were similarly taboo and for many of the same reasons. As social historian Alain Corbin explains: "With few exceptions, the classical period knew nothing of the attraction of seaside beaches, the emotion of a bather plunging into the waves, or the pleasures of a stay at the seaside. A veil of repulsive images prevented the seaside from exercising its appeal."[10] One need not look far to find the supporting evidence. Aspidochelone (a nasty sea turtle that lured sailors to their death), Leviathan (a Biblical sea creature that served as a gatekeeper to hell), Grendel (the great monster in the Anglo–Saxon epic *Beowulf*), Kraken (a giant squid-like being that destroyed ships), and a host of other sea monsters, to say nothing of the Great Flood that plays a role in everything from the *Epic of Gilgamesh* to the Bible, to Hindu and Greek mythologies, all demonstrate what people right through the Middle Ages thought of the ocean. It was a nasty place, a dangerous space. Boats were subject to rot and wood worms. Sailors were social outsiders and their weather-beaten faces only seemed to confirm that the ocean was unhealthy. The very fact that ocean travel often led to seasickness only confirmed just how deadly the sea could be. As God created man in his image, it followed that the land was divine. The beach was a transitional zone between heaven and hell. The people who lived at the shore were a component part "of the repulsive images" of the ocean. They occupied a boundary zone "where the Flood would mark its return and the chain of cataclysms be triggered."[11]

Despite these rather stark distinctions, at the same moment that Coleridge played Russian roulette with the mountains of northern England, sea bathing grew increasingly popular at lower elevations. Doctors suggested that "taking the waters" would cure a host of health problems from gout to impotence. The transformation of ideas about both mountains and seaside are closely connected, each a result of changing ideas about science and aesthetics, urbanization, and health. Put another way, both sites were re-imagined through a process of rationalizing nature, of making it something that could be made sense of intellectually, whether in scientific or aesthetic terms, and perhaps even controlled. Together, these changes represented not only a noticeably modern vision of the world, they also provided a new set of attractions that would serve as focal points for modern tourism.

Scientific rationalization

For students of the history of landscape, the scientific revolution and a transformation in thought about geologic time are pivotal. Throughout most of human history, time and the story of the earth's surface were defined in religious terms. So-called "primal religions" imagined the planet as atemporal, as existing outside of time.[12] Other faiths viewed it as a product of divine grace. The Abrahamic religions, for example, saw the globe as a product of God's intense effort over a very busy week. Geologic change was not a significant issue; the earth was as God made it. Consequently, it was possible to easily determine *precisely* how old the planet was. In 1650, James Ussher (1625–56), Archbishop of Armagh, did exactly that. Using clues found in the Old Testament, the venerable cleric insisted that the earth was created at 9 a.m. on Monday, October 26, 4004 BCE. This level of specificity was so admirable that many Christian texts continued to cite the date into the nineteenth century. Ussher assumed that the earth changed little after that mid-morning start. God was perfect, after all. He did not make mistakes. If the Lord wanted a mountain, he would construct one. If he wanted a valley, he would carve it. If he wanted a lake, river, or ocean, he would install the necessary divot and fill it with water.[13]

It was the Grand Tour that triggered the first major challenge to this worldview. In 1672, Thomas Burnet (c.1635–1715), a theologian and would-be Archbishop of Canterbury, was serving as tutor to a young tourist, the Earl of Wiltshire, a descendant of Thomas Boleyn, father of Henry VIII's ill-fated second wife, Anne. In August, the pair made their way over the Simplon Pass, a route utilized by many tourists anxious to visit Italy. By contrast with most other travelers, Burnet was captivated by the landscape. He embarked on a flight of creative fancy that started an intellectual revolution. The tutor wondered: Was it possible that the Biblical flood had left the land untouched? Even a rainstorm can bring mudslides and other damage. How much water would it take to cover the high mountains? Eight oceans, he thought. Could that many oceans fall in forty days and forty nights? Surely not. One ocean seemed a more likely estimate. Even if eight oceans had fallen, what happened to them afterward? Where did they go?

In an effort to reconcile Christian doctrine with his own observations, Thomas Burnet proposed an alternative solution, his "mundane egg" model. It held that God created a perfect spherical earth, free of topography or drama. When the flood came, only one ocean was required to cover everything. Inside the sphere, however, was a very different story. The globe was comprised of layers of concentric strata that fit together like a matryoshka doll. The bands were filled with tumult: lava and magma, all begging to escape if only the crust would rupture. And crack it did. The flood opened fractures, prompting sections of the earth's surface to fall away. All at once, there was topography, a globe with hills and valleys, a single ocean lapping at newly made continental shores. Burnet published

Figure 2.1 Thomas Burnet first published the English translation of his *Sacred Theory of the Earth* in 1684 (the original Latin version appeared in 1681). It started a process whereby the earth attained a history, previous ideas about a planet perfect and unchanged since inception were abandoned, and Europeans grew evermore curious about the physical world around them. Image courtesy of Rare Books Collections, University of Sydney Library.

his hypothesis in *Telluris Theoria Sacra, or Sacred Theory of the Earth* (1681). The book created a stir. Churchmen were mortified. Burnet's candidacy for high office in the Church of England was canceled.[14] But it was not for nothing. The argument changed everything, spawning an entirely new scientific field of study. His book was a "constant" reference point throughout the eighteenth century and it even "foreshadowed the great changes in the field of aesthetics which were eventually to lead people to sample [the] hideous beauty" of mountains and beaches.[15]

Over the next two hundred years, rationally minded scientists built upon Burnet's contribution. One book after another, the natural history of the earth took shape. First, Georges-Louis Leclerc, Comte de Buffon (1707–88), a flashy Frenchman, published a substantial multivolume essay entitled *Histoire Naturelle* (1749–88). The series laid out a story that divided global history into seven epochs spanning 75,000 years. *Histoire Naturelle* sparked considerable debate, leading to still more publications.[16] In the last years of the eighteenth century, James Hutton (1726–97) published a series of papers and books that outlined how natural processes such as the cycle of freeze and thaw, the rushing of rivers and the crashing of seas, the explosion of volcanoes and the shaking of earthquakes all played their part in altering the globe.[17] During the 1830s, Charles Lyell (1797–1875) built on Hutton's work by publishing a highly readable three-volume text entitled *The Principles of Geology: An Attempt to Explain the Former Changes of the Earth's Surface by Reference to Causes Now in Operation* (1830–33). It clearly made the case for an evolutionary history of geology.

It was this notion that the earth evolved with time that proved profound. Lyell's book was widely read and it captured the imagination of one of the greatest scientists of the nineteenth century: Charles Darwin (1809–82). The idea of earthly change must have been foremost in the mind of the future author of *Origin of Species* (1859) when he reached Chile in 1835. Disembarking from the HMS Beagle, the father of evolutionary theory famously climbed into the mountains. Once at altitude, he discovered fossilized seashells. The implications were huge. If the earth could evolve, leaving sea creatures thousands of feet above sea level, then surely the same was true of the sea creatures themselves. They too could evolve.

Darwin's experience was not confined to erudite scholarly texts. He recounted it in a very popular travel narrative widely known as *The Voyage of the Beagle* (1839). It was a hit. The trip represented the height of adventure and the discoveries that Darwin made along the way were enticing. Victorians realized that they too could engage in exploration. Climbing mountains in the Scottish Highlands might yield fossils. Walking along sea cliffs or gazing at rugged mountains laid bare the layers of rock that function like a timeline of geo-history.[18]

Taking control

Looking for fossils or walking amid the layers of geological history was ultimately about rationalizing nature. Visitors could make sense of the world around them through observation. If knowledge is power, knowing something about the planet represented a way of exercising that power to understand the vast and incomprehensible realities of time and space. Yet intellectual exploration was far from the only way to render the world less frightening. In the case of the oceans, engineering promised another avenue toward control. Here again, the Grand Tour played a pivotal role in changing European ideas about nature.

The Netherlands represented a popular destination for Europe's elite tourists. Holland was an economic powerhouse during the early modern period. Yet this fact represented a paradox. Tulips do not usually grow empires, yet Holland was a superpower, "a richer country than England,"[19] without many obvious natural resources. Clearly there was something present among the windmills worth learning from. Yet the Netherlands offered another more intriguing lure: much of the country is *below* sea level. Generations of Dutchmen reclaimed land from the sea and they implemented programs to mitigate the omnipresent risk of flooding. They "tamed the fury of the oceans."[20]

Initially, the Dutch controlled the waters through complex networks of drainage channels. By the thirteenth century these proved inadequate because drained lands have a tendency toward subsidence, making them more prone to flooding. Eventually, the drainage scheme created "what can only be described as an environmental crisis. A *waterwolf* stalked the land." The Dutch responded by "fashioning a complex system of dikes, dams, sluices, and drainage canals designed to perpetuate drainage while protecting against inundation."[21] By the fourteenth century, complex water boards (*waterschappen*) managed the process, the bureaucratic structure evolving over time to match changing demands and to meet evolving challenges.[22]

When large numbers of rich tourists arrived they encountered an astonishing example of the conquest of human ingenuity over nature. As early as the seventeenth century, the Duke of Rohan declared that "Holland is a marvel"; the landscape, he said, was astonishing. While the Dutch had not so much "disturbed the Creator's work," they had "completed it."[23] Visiting the Netherlands, then, allowed tourists to witness a "harmony between God and man" and to witness the "sight of a nation struggling with the sea," evidently winning.[24] For most people, the ocean was terrifying, yet for the Dutch it was something to be tamed. Humans need not live in terror of the godless deep because they could pacify it. Holland was a symbol of what man could accomplish using rational thought and engineering knowhow.

At least theoretically, the Grand Tour promised to enrich those who went by improving taste, teaching languages, and introducing new cultures and traditions. Changing ideas about science and man's ability to master nature suggested that travel might do more. It could familiarize people with their world, with their place in history, and even motivate them to take control of their environment. In other words, the Grand Tour played a role in inspiring and spreading rational thought. Tourists increasingly believed that travel would make them better people by acquainting them with astonishing feats of engineering and with an understanding of the earth and mankind's place on it.

Altered lenses: a revolution in aesthetics

The concept of the "sublime" was not new to the eighteenth century; literary-minded thinkers had utilized it as early as the Greek and Roman periods in relationship to the divine and to nature,[25] but it was only after the 1750s that it took a vice-like hold on the European imagination. Edmund Burke (1729–97), one of the most important thinkers and British politicians of the second half of the eighteenth century, was the reason. Burke was born in Dublin, son of a Protestant barrister and a Catholic mother. After studying at Trinity College, Dublin, the future leading Whig headed to London to pursue a legal career. He soon established a reputation as an essayist and later emerged as a founder of modern conservative political thought; his most widely known essay, *Reflections on the Revolution in France* (1790), argues strongly against rapid revolutionary change. Burke was of his time, a product of the Enlightenment and a believer in rational thinking, without completely eschewing religion. The young man engaged in debates about philosophy and science, evidently feeling that careful analysis and observation could open the secrets of the universe. He published his first essay in 1756, *A Vindication of Natural Society*, and then embarked on the paper that would change aesthetics: *Philosophical Enquiry into the Origin of Our Ideas of the Sublime and Beautiful* (1757).[26]

Burke's essay set out to compare the human response to different "objects," whether natural or artistic, the "beautiful" versus the sublime. He saw profound contrast:

> For sublime objects are vast in their dimensions, beautiful ones comparatively small: beauty should be smooth and polished; the great, rugged and negligent; beauty should shun the right line, yet deviate from it insensibly; the great in many cases loves the right line, and when it

> deviates it often makes a strong deviation: beauty should not be obscure; the great ought to be dark and gloomy: beauty should be light and delicate; the great ought to be solid, and even massive. They are indeed ideas of a very different nature, one being founded on pain, the other on pleasure. ...[27]

Beautiful things are regular, proportionate, and predictable. Imagine a green field populated by Holstein cows chewing happily. By contrast the sublime represents the opposite. It is unpredictable and chaotic. These contrasts had different implications. One would cause pleasure, the other temporary pain born of a fear of death. One relaxed the body; the other tightened it up. Taken together, the two responses could cause "delight," the result achieved by "the removal of pain or danger."[28] While beautiful things soothe the mind, sublime ones prompt a combination of pleasure and terror. The heartbeat increases. Body hair stands erect. A shiver runs down the spine. Although initially horrifying, "at certain distances, and with certain modifications, they may be, and they are, delightful..."[29] Being afraid is exhilarating, like rock climbing or driving fast on a curvy road. Although seemingly contradictory, the possibility of destruction results in a kind of natural high. Harmless terror is fun.

Burke was not interested purely in enjoyment, however. He suggested that raised heart rate, sweaty palms, and general exhilaration are healthy. Burke's eighteenth-century contemporaries found this plausible. It was long accepted that men should spend time in the military and that the experience of war was a positive thing. The sublime was little different from the battlefield, though if done properly it was almost certainly safer.

The application of the idea of the "sublime and beautiful" to landscape had profound implications, providing "a new impulse for eighteenth-century tourism."[30] Writing his memoirs at the end of the eighteenth century, Edward Gibbon recalled that when he finally took his Grand Tour, "the fashion of climbing the mountains and reviewing the glaciers, had not yet been introduced by foreign travelers, who seek the sublime beauties of nature."[31] The situation changed quickly. Burke's ideas flooded across Europe as prominent thinkers adopted them. Those who could afford to integrated the sublime into their daily routines. Intellectuals and tourists sought out mountains and beaches. For example, when traveling through Scotland, Dr. Samuel Johnson (1709–84) made a point of seeing the Bullers of Buchan, a rock bridge on the rugged coastline north of Aberdeen. On arrival, he remarked that no man could see the formation "with indifference, who has either sense of danger or delight in rarity."[32] James Boswell (1740–95), Johnson's traveling companion and biographer, was even more vivid in his description, remarking that the site represented "a monstrous cauldron."[33] Still, Johnson was not to be dissuaded by the prospect of venturing onto the Bullers and peering down into the thrashing torrent of waves below. It is a marker of the impact of Burke's essay that Johnson could not leave the site without remarking: "[T]errour without danger is only one of the sports of fancy, a voluntary agitation of the mind that is permitted no longer than it pleases."[34] It was just the sort of voluntary agitation that Europeans were now anxious to find, or even to create.

England's aristocrats were in a particularly strong position to reproduce the sublime and beautiful on their lands. Thus, Sir Richard Hill (1732–1808), a Shropshire landowner, dug out a two-mile-long lake, focused attention on a "300-foot-high white sandstone outcrop," and constructed an elaborate grotto along with caves, complete with a resident hermit whose short-lived presence was supposed to enhance the sublime qualities of the manufactured landscape. Samuel Johnson visited the estate in order to scale the hill and he described the experience using language not very different from that used to speak of the far more authentic Bullers of Buchan.[35] Among the wealthy, Hill was not alone. The gardens at the Swedish estate of Forsmark offered much the same. Irregular landscapes, wild spaces and dark corners. The park was "a wilderness, not sweet and beautiful, but strong and beautiful." It even included the requisite hermit, though in this case the landowner added a model "dressed up in a deep purple cloak" and with "a gentle but serious expression" rather than a paid actor. Unfortunately, while Hill's hermit evidently only lasted for three weeks before demanding payment and quitting to seek less taxing employment, the Forsmark hermit was wax. Rats quickly devoured it.[36]

By the early nineteenth century, this pursuit of pleasure gave way to a new movement in art, literature, and music called Romanticism. The Romantic movement celebrated emotions and experience, providing an alternative to the cold rationalization of the Enlightenment ideas from which it grew. Leading Romanticists such as Sir Walter Scott (1771–1832) and William Wordsworth, as well as the sublime-addicted Samuel Taylor Coleridge, were literary rock stars with huge followings. The natural environment was very often a central, even *the* central, component of their writing. In music, great composers such as Ludwig van Beethoven (1770–1827) attempted to capture the environment orchestrally. His sixth symphony, the "Pastoral," evokes nature in music. In a similar vein, Felix Mendelssohn (1809–47) traveled to Scotland where he composed his "Scottish Symphony" and "Hebrides Overtures"—both of which reflect the sublime character of the Scottish Highlands and Islands. In the world of painting, Caspar David Friedrich (1774–1840) captured the romantic zeitgeist with his "The Wanderer Above the Sea of Fog." The archetypal image shows a man gazing from a mountain summit, leg planted strongly on a rock outcrop. Wisps of cloud shroud trees, rocks, and hills beyond. By standing at the edge, he experiences the sublime. Striking the pose that he has, he shows that he has taken it all in, conquering both the land and embracing emotion.[37]

Tourism and the sublime

Travel offered an opportunity to pursue the sublime. The nascent sport of mountaineering, for example, afforded one such experience. While the Dutch conquered nature by beating back the ocean, climbers could attempt a similar feat on a smaller scale by surmounting peaks. A few Europeans on their Grand Tours began climbing higher up mountainsides to look at glaciers as early as the 1740s.[38] Mont Blanc, Western Europe's highest mountain, was first climbed in 1786.[39] By the second decade of the nineteenth century, Europeans developed what climbing historian Robert Macfarlane calls an "adoration for the summit."[40] Interest only expanded, especially after a middle-aged journalist named Albert Smith (1816–60) reached the top of Mont Blanc alongside three Oxford students and sixteen guides on August 12, 1851. Smith used the experience as the basis for a popular one-man show at the Egyptian Hall, Piccadilly. It was a multimedia extravaganza. According to historian Peter H. Hansen, "Smith festooned the stage with '[c]hamois skins, Indian corn, alpenstocks, vintage baskets, knapsacks, and other appropriate matters.' At the intermission, Saint Bernard dogs lumbered through the room with chocolates in barrels under their necks." The public response was astonishing. Two hundred thousand people attended the show, which earned over £17,000 in gross receipts. *The Times* declared it to be one of the "sights of London" and the Prince of Wales was among the audience. The production ran for six years and thousands of performances.[41]

"Mont Blanc mania," as the *Times of London* described it,[42] inspired greater and greater interest in the Alps. It made climbing "genteel." The pursuit of the sublime was available to everybody, prompting the formation of the world's first climbing club in London in 1857. It was comprised of respectable men, lawyers, businessmen and teachers, civil servants, churchmen, and others. Similar clubs formed throughout Europe during the 1860s and the 1870s, appearing further afield thereafter.[43]

Painted landscapes

Of course, there were other ways to become captivated by landscape and to be inspired to explore the natural world. Even before Burke's essay, Dutch landscape painters pointed the way for tourists to view scenery, especially coastal scenery, differently. Initially, these painters produced art that was in keeping with European conventions: roads, trees, fields, buildings, and people. Yet gradually, some painters began moving in another direction. Jan Van Goyen (1596–1656), for example, was intrigued by man's relationship to the sea. His paintings show workers busily employed on a sandy beach. These laborers did not yield to the ocean; they did not shy away from the beach. The sea itself was a font of fertility, a "daily miracle of the multiplication of herrings" in the Bible. This artist's work was not concerned with sea monsters or with the "eroticism of bathing," it illustrated man's symbiotic connection to nature. According to the historian Alain Corbin, Van Goyen soon became so intrigued by the beach that he hired ships to take him along the shore so that he could depict it from new angles. The artist even went so far as to paint himself seated on the beach, relishing the scene.[44]

By the middle of the seventeenth century, more and more artists followed Van Goyen's lead and Dutch painters attained a reputation for showing fishermen, beaches, and seascapes. Between 1635 and 1665, Dutch artists reached their zenith of popularity, so liked that painters elsewhere in Europe, including England, started to produce similar scenes. For artists, the sea now represented the perpetual cycle of life, more closely related to God than Satan.[45]

Aesthetic tastes obviously vary with time. As Dutch painters produced more and more seascapes, all quickly snapped up by wealthy travelers, those same tourists learned to look at the landscape around them in much the same way that the painters did. It was the early modern equivalent of a vacation photograph, almost all of which, regardless of who the photographer is, look alike. We take snapshots that appear almost identical to postcards. We learn to frame things based on the images that we have seen elsewhere. Put simply, seventeenth and eighteenth-century tourists learned how to look at scenery based on the art that they collected. Very often they wanted to experience the places depicted for themselves.

Rise of the urban and the pursuit of health

At the moment that landscapes were rationalized and made aesthetically pleasing, and while wealthy tourists flooded across Europe in growing numbers, something that was both profound and shocking took place in

Britain: industrialization and urbanization. Growth happened quickly, a dizzying, even horrifying, experience for those who went through it. In 1695, there were just over five million people living in England and Wales. By 1801 that number increased to nearly nine million. The population reached a staggering 14.9 million people in 1841.[46] Almost overnight, whole new cities sprang up as people flooded into growing urban centers. Manchester, for example, appeared where once there was but a tiny village creating what historian Asa Briggs calls the "shock city" of the nineteenth century in Britain.[47] In 1750, London was the only town in England with a population of 50,000. At the turn of the century there were eight such cities. By 1851 the number was twenty-nine.[48] In 1800, only about 19.2 percent of the population in the United Kingdom lived in cities with 5000 or more inhabitants. In 1850 the percentage was 39.6 percent. By 1900 it was 67.4 percent.[49] The same level of change took place on the Continent as well, in places such as Germany's Ruhr valley, where tiny towns became massive industrial cities in as little as fifteen years.[50]

There was no blueprint for this kind of growth. Nothing like it had happened before. Consequently, living conditions were often dreadful and contemporary observers, men such as Friedrich Engels (1820–95) and Karl Marx (1818–83), looked on in horror. Workers lived in overcrowded rooms. As there was no urban planning, slums were labyrinthine and the lack of running water assured the presence of trash and sewerage everywhere. Homes and factories alike ran on coal, so the air was thick with smoke and dust, sometimes turning day into night.[51]

Although not the only idea about disease prevalent in early modern Europe, there was a long-lived belief that "bad air," called "miasma," was harmful to one's health. Laboring under a long legacy of ideas of the Greek medical theorist Galen of Pergamon (130-200 CE), European doctors believed that "[b]ad air was dangerous because it could disrupt the balance of bodily humors." One did not become sick as a result of germs, but because they inhaled "corrupt vapors."[52] There was no shortage of such odors. Putrid smells marked urban life in Europe, and it was little wonder.[53] In London, as in many other urban centers, public sewers and running water were unknown until the second half of the nineteenth century, so waste was simply dumped into the streets or left to stand in stagnant cesspools. Wastewater drained into streams and rivers, the same places where people disposed of their trash, which were also the predominant source of drinking water.[54] As a consequence, cholera struck London (and other European and American port cities) during the nineteenth century, killing thousands in successive outbreaks of the disease.[55] Thick clouds of coal smoke joined the stench of human detritus.

It did not take a scientific mind to recognize that urban living was unhealthy, even if the precise cause of illness was misunderstood. Getting out of town was the obvious answer. Both mountains and beaches offered logical destinations (for more on spas and the seaside, see Chapter 4). Not only could one improve him or herself by looking for clues to natural history in a cliff face, by consuming the sublime beauty of a seaside landscape (see Chapter 5 for discussion of the picturesque), or by feeling a rush of fear when peering over a precipice, the most sublime places were also prone to constant winds and health giving breezes. Travel was good for you.

Conclusion

It is vital to recognize the interconnectedness of the Grand Tour, the growing primacy of new patterns of consumption, the altered aesthetic sensibility ushered in by Burke's notion of the "sublime and beautiful," the role of Dutch engineering, the expanded popularity of a new style of painting, and the spread of Enlightenment thought about everything from geo-history to health. The context created by these factors in combination generated the ideological framework that girds modern tourism. They created a sense that travel was good for the mind as well as the body and shaped notions of what tourists ought to see on their travels. The transformation of mountains and beaches from satanic horrors into desirable spaces not only ushered in a host of new pastimes from mountain climbing to the construction of sandcastles, it also created new ways of framing the world.

Although many of the essential ingredients for modern tourism were in place, there was something missing. To this point, the overwhelming majority of tourists were wealthy. For the notion of tourism to gain a wider footing, travel needed to become cheaper, faster, and more comfortable. What is more, a greater number of people needed to learn how to travel—whether through organized trips or by reading guidebooks. Steam-driven transportation promised to set in train a series of changes that made exactly these things possible, launching new modes of tourism and making leisure-centered mobility global in scope.

3

The age of steam

Prior to the proliferation of the iron horse, travel was a misery. Roads, both in Europe and elsewhere, were terrible. Going to the North of England assured routes that were little more than "trackways for ponies" along which no cart could move. Even in Oxfordshire during the mid-eighteenth century, a distance of less than sixty miles from the capital, roads "were in a condition formidable to the bones of all who travelled on wheels." Even if the surface was smooth, crime was a problem, stagecoach travel was dangerous and it was slow. It was not unheard of for horses to run away with their drivers after being startled. Bandits raised the threat of theft or worse—as poor Fynes Moryson discovered on his Grand Tour, and as many others realized when they confronted highwaymen such as the infamous Dick Turpin (1705–39) closer to home. A trip from Edinburgh to London took anywhere from four days on horseback to ten or more via stagecoach. Unless you had a substantial amount of time to spare and money to spend, this was no way to get around.[1]

According to the 1555 Highways Act, British roads were under the charge of churchwardens and constables. Parishes were always strapped for cash, so little was done to promote transport. Following the Restoration, Parliament passed a new Turnpike Act that privatized some roads, putting them under the charge of operators whose profits depended on passable routes. It helped, but only on some roads and in a few places. Technological improvements also made things easier with time. For example, engineers Thomas Telford (1757–1834), John Loudon McAdam (1756–1836) and "Blind Jack" Metcalf (1717–1810) turned their attention to roadways during the last years of the 1700s. They developed blacktop, learned to create better foundations to avoid subsidence, and started building roads with a convex shape so that water would drain off. Smoother surfaces that resisted flooding were the result. As with the turnpikes, there simply were not enough miles of improved road to ease transport of raw materials, industrial machinery, and travelers in more than a few places.[2]

Things were worse on the water. Sail was an ancient technology by the nineteenth century, and it had changed comparatively little, though ships did evolve. Sail shapes and rigging got more efficient. Hull designs passed through the water more easily. The craft grew slightly larger with time. It hardly mattered. Ships bobbed around on the ocean like so much flotsam and jetsam. With a good crew, tall ships were unlikely to sink or break apart, even in the roughest storms, but this was small consolation for seasick passengers for whom death probably seemed preferable to going forward.[3]

Sailing vessels offered two classes of accommodation: cabin and steerage. Most, anxious to emigrate, traveled in steerage. Conditions were poor, even awful. One historian describes lodgings as "not much of a cut above those on the recently outlawed slave ships." They were dirty, overcrowded, and uncomfortable. Passengers seldom cleaned up after themselves, even failing to "be decent with respect to the common wants of nature." Steerage passengers had to supply and prepare their own food—a problem if the ship's progress was slow due to poor winds, assuring insufficient supplies and hungry days.[4] The inadequate food, cramped accommodations, and poverty were a lethal combination. Disease was common. Most extreme during the Irish Potato Famine (1845–51), steerage passengers died in large numbers. Many who boarded "coffin ships" were already sick with "famine fever" and they soon spread their illness to others. Perhaps 50,000 people died either on board or shortly after arriving in North America.[5] Descriptions are horrifying: "Water covered the beds, cooking vessels, etc. of the dead. Ghastly appearance of boats full of sick going ashore never to return. Several died between ship and shore. Wives separated from husbands, children from parents."[6] The coffin ships represent an extreme example—even for ships from Ireland during the late 1840s—but the general unpleasantness of steerage conditions should not be underestimated.

Things were better in first class, although far from luxurious. Cabins were located at the back of the ship (stern). There was no running water, so hygiene was lacking.[7] Accommodations were cramped, especially when packed full of the passengers' belongings.[8] On the positive side, journeyers with cabins were supplied with food, but it came at a cost. In an age before refrigeration, sustenance was either dried and salted, or was carried live.[9] Chickens, cows, pigs, and sheep added an assortment of sounds and smells that were probably anything but pleasant.

Travel was also boring. People on ships amused themselves by playing various games, practicing musical instruments, shooting, and holding parties and dances. Even so, a windless ocean could leave any sailing vessel stranded for days or even weeks and months. Fighting was frequent. Even the pigs would quarrel "like so many schoolboys, abusing the little ones and biting their ears off." Sometimes, overcome by tedium, respectable men or members of the crew would make their way below decks to turn virgin Irish girls into "outcasts"—a practice so common that the American Congress passed legislation in an effort to eliminate "transatlantic dalliance."[10]

The age of steam promised a revolution. Steamships and trains could follow a fixed and predictable schedule, bringing speed and relative comfort. Much larger in size, an improved economy of scale meant reduced costs. The Grand Tour was limited to the very wealthy. Steam presented the opportunity for many others to engage in leisure travel. Not for the last time, technology was to fundamentally alter the story of tourism.

Arrival of the iron horse

Trains were not new to the nineteenth century. A mid-fourteenth-century stained-glass window in the Minster of Freiburg im Breisgau, Germany depicts "something resembling a railway."[11] Horse-drawn trains were in use across Britain by at least the sixteenth century in order to haul ore out of mines. During the late seventeenth century, Louis XIV had a small train on the grounds of his estate at Versailles outside of Paris. The problem was that none of these trains had a viable power source that would allow for adequate speed, make long up-hill travel possible, or facilitate hauling huge payloads.

A few engineers had endeavored to use steam to move trains since Nicolas-Joseph Cugnot (1725–1804) played with the idea in Paris in 1769. Unfortunately, his experimental machine promptly rolled into a wall and flipped over, causing authorities to ban further tryouts in the interest of public safety.[12] A Cornish engineer named Richard Trevithick (1771–1833) took the next step by designing a steam carriage that was supposed to roll along existing roadways. His first attempt worked, but it lacked a suitable steering mechanism. When Trevithick demonstrated it to a group of local gentry, the train launched into a ditch, burst into flames, and exploded. He was back two years later with an improved model, and then introduced yet another still better version in 1803. At five miles per hour, however, these early engines were not going to supplant horses. Consequently, many believed that the future lay in horse-drawn trains and this view was still very much in play as late as 1822.[13]

Even when faster trains came on line early in the 1820s, fostering the first commercial railway—the Stockton and Darlington started operations in 1825 to much fanfare if not to immediate economic success—engines were underpowered and unreliable. This was not the only anxiety. Steam trains were loud and, even at less than twenty miles per hour, comparatively fast. People worried that cattle "would be so terrified by horseless carriages hurtling past them that their udders would dry up."[14] When trains finally broke the thirty-miles-per-hour barrier, skeptics warned that such speeds might prove fatal. One critic, Thomas Creevey MP (1768–1838), lamented "it is impossible to divest yourself of the notion of instant death to all upon the least accident happening."[15] Others feared that the sound of two trains passing in a tunnel would lead to insanity.[16]

Perhaps there was reason to be scared. For one thing, railways might upend existing investments and force businesses or even whole communities into obsolescence. Many had sunk fortunes into canal construction during the closing decades of the eighteenth century. If successful, railways might undermine this business and cause investors to lose huge sums. Similarly, townspeople situated along canal routes rightly feared that trains would divert business away from their shops.[17] Others doubted the equipment itself.

Whatever the anxiety level, there was significant demand for a new transportation technology that would carry both hard goods and passengers. The Liverpool and Manchester Railway, the first railway company to make much of its profit from passenger travel, was the result. Launching the venture was anything but easy. The idea for the company was proposed to Parliament in 1824, *before* a suitable engine existed to make such an undertaking viable. Despite this minor problem, the route was needed. With the onset of industrialization Manchester grew from a tiny village to become a massive textile center, a "shock city" of the nineteenth century.[18] Cotton does not grow in Britain, so raw materials were shipped to the closest major port, Liverpool. Unfortunately, transportation from Liverpool to Manchester was inefficient. It took longer to get the critical white fibers from the port to the factory than it did to ship it across the Atlantic. The delay was costly. Seeing a need, a Liverpool corn merchant proposed a bill to Parliament authorizing construction of a railway to fix the problem. The trader went bust before the legislation passed, leaving an already well-known railway engineer named George Stephenson (1781–1848) to push the plan and to battle the skeptics. After two years of fierce debate, Parliament approved the scheme and construction began.[19]

While bridges were built, tunnels dug, and track laid, Stephenson got to work on a better steam engine. Whereas previous boilers featured a small number of large tubes in which steam pressure built up, he increased the number of smaller pipes in order to generate considerably more pressure and therefore more power. In addition, Stephenson also introduced "blastpipe exhaust," a design that essentially injected excess steam into the chimney, thus causing the fire to burn hotter and therefore more efficiently.[20]

At the same time a significant prize was promised to the creator of a steam engine that could match criteria to be tested at a rigorous competition, the Rainhill Trials, held in October 1829. Engines had to travel quickly, tow considerable loads, cover extended distances, and make their way up inclines. Stephenson's entry, the *Rocket,* represented the culmination of its designer's long-term experimentation and experience. By contrast, his competition was largely unfamiliar with the new technology. Whereas the *Rocket* went through its exercises with aplomb, easily meeting and exceeding each test, the other engines often overshot stopping areas as a result of inexpert operation or suffered from broken parts due to slipshod engineering and maintenance. When it was all finished, Stephenson was the easy winner.[21]

The Liverpool and Manchester Railway unveiled its new service on September 15, 1830 after years of controversy. There was much to rejoice about and spirits soared. Celebrities were everywhere. Arthur Wellesley, the First Duke of Wellington (1769–1852), who was then Prime Minister, and Sir Robert Peel (1788–1850), the Duke's successor, were there. Prince Paul Anton Esterházy (1786–1866), a Hungarian noble, was on hand. Naturally, important local members of Parliament, such as Mr. William Huskisson MP (1770–1830), a former cabinet minister and the minister for Liverpool, attended. The plan was for several trains stocked with wealthy VIPs to follow the line from Liverpool to Manchester. The vehicles would stop along the way to take on coal and water, as well as to allow throngs of spectators to marvel at the astonishing new machines. Once in Manchester, a massive dinner allowed the celebrities to rub elbows and to toast a great success.

All did not go according to plan and the initial effort to inaugurate a profitable railway service soon generated the first railway tragedy. When the trains stopped at Park Side to take on water a number of passengers failed to heed instructions and disembarked to wander the tracks. Suddenly *The Rocket* arrived causing the assembled pedestrians to leap out of the way, most successfully climbing back aboard the *Northumbria*. Huskisson was not so lucky. While at King George IV's funeral the previous June the MP developed an illness that resulted in partial paralysis on one side of his body. Consequently, he was in no way capable of fast movement.[22] The *Observer* newspaper recounted the awful results in vivid detail. As the train arrived,

> He hesitated, staggered a little, as if not knowing what to do, then attempted to run forward, found it impossible to get off the road ... and attempted again to get into the car. As he took hold of the door to do this, he must have thrown his gravity too much upon it, for

> on its suddenly turning on its hinges, on being seized by him, the rotation threw him off his balance, and before he could recover he was thrown down directly in the path of the *Rocket*. ... He contrived to move himself a little out of its path before it came in contact with him, otherwise it must have gone directly over his head and breast. As it was, the wheel went over his left thigh, squeezing it almost to a jelly, broke the leg and thigh in two places, laid the muscles bare from the ankle nearly to the hip, and tore out a large piece of flesh as it left him.[23]

Thinking quickly, George Stephenson had the fallen minister loaded onto his train for a mad dash to Manchester at an astonishing thirty-five miles per hour. Despite constant attention from a doctor who witnessed the

Figure 3.1 Steam travel inspired fear and anxiety from the beginning; the death of William Huskisson MP at the opening of the Liverpool and Manchester Railway certainly did not help. Critics worried about the health effects of speed, noise, and vibrations for both man and beast. Even in the 1860s, nearly three decades after the first trains carried passengers, concern remained, any disaster whether on land or sea assuring its perpetuation. In 1865, *Harper's Magazine* captured the anxiety often associated with steam-driven transportation. The publication lamented: "The graphic but by no means extravagant illustration ... scarcely needs any word of comment or explanation. ... Every day the record of mortality is continued from the day before, being only diversified in the manner of its occurrence." "Horrors of Steam Travel," *Harper's Weekly*, September 23, 1865. Image courtesy of the Brooklyn Historic Railway Association.

accident, it was all to no avail. Huskisson died what early Victorians would have imagined a perfect death: he asked for the last rites, consoled his distraught wife, and even had a last drink of wine and water—all despite violent spasms and untold levels of wrenching pain.[24]

The death captured headlines and still continues to dominate accounts of the launch of the Liverpool and Manchester Railway, perhaps because it so clearly reflected the horror attendant to rapid change. Even so, it did little to stop expansion of British and, indeed, global railways. In the United Kingdom profit sparked the laying of more track. Consequently, there were three great railway booms—1824–5, 1836–7, and 1845–7—each resulting in significant investment and construction.[25] Growth was "steady" rather than "spectacular." By 1843 there was somewhere between 1829 and 2050 miles of track in Britain. Sixteen years later the number was up to 9800 miles and climbing.[26]

Other countries followed suit. While Prussia had only 115 miles of track in 1840, by 1847 citizens were rolling along on 1506. The mileage simply climbed thereafter, hitting 22,744 miles on the eve of World War I.[27] In the New World, the United States was an early adopter of the new technology. Beginning in 1830 various developers along the Eastern Seaboard constructed tracks. Within a decade there was a "thin, broken network stretching along the Atlantic coast from Portsmouth, New Hampshire, to the Carolinas" and including rail lines in every one of the twenty-six states except Arkansas, Missouri, Tennessee, and Vermont. By 1850 there were railway tracks extending westward to Ohio and Michigan.[28]

The American urge toward expansion did not stop. There were calls for more track and to build a transcontinental railway. Delayed by the Civil War, serious efforts to construct the line moved ahead after the conflict. It was not only about economic growth; investors also imagined that the railroad would shift the country's attention from the destruction of war to the "possibilities of the west." It would allow people to travel, learning about their country from sea to shining sea.[29] The iron horse would also make it possible to exploit the land and its resources. After a herculean effort, the transcontinental railway was completed in 1869.[30] Further lines and more rails followed thereafter, augmenting the American railway network from 3000 miles in 1865 to 12,000 in 1870; from 32,000 miles in 1880 to 127,000 in 1920.[31]

Construction was not limited to industrial powerhouses and it became increasingly obvious that the reasons for building railways extended beyond immediate financial gain: "'*Railpolitik*' became a corollary to *realpolitik* calculations." As one observer commented at the dawn of the twentieth century, "the path to Empire is along the railway track."[32] Countries such as the United Kingdom and Russia recognized this long before the fin de siècle.

In Russia, Tsar Nicholas I (1796–1855) viewed railway building as an essential part, not only of creating a transportation network in his country, but of bringing Russia into the modern age. Imperial status required keeping up with the "advanced" technologies available elsewhere. Consequently, on January 13, 1842, Tsar Nicholas informed his closest advisors that Russia required a line between St. Petersburg and Moscow. At 400 miles in length, the route was to be the longest in the world to that point. During the 1850s, the government added a line from St. Petersburg to Warsaw, then one from Moscow to Odessa. In the 1860s, despite a disastrous experience during the Crimean War, additional lines from Moscow to Nizhny Novgorod and from Moscow to Theodosia in the Crimea were completed.[33] Although the network was far from adequate, it was an impressive leap forward for a country that did not emancipate its serfs until 1861—something that most of Europe had done hundreds of years before.

Britain also embarked on major projects across its massive global empire. In India, the Raj "was famous for its railways."[34] The imperialists imagined they could unite the famously divided subcontinent by laying track. Thus, even before a violent and bloody anti-colonial uprising in 1857, referred to as "the Mutiny" by Britons, trains started crisscrossing the country. After 1857 Britain's efforts sped up, linking isolated areas to major urban centers.[35] One way or another, railways spread across Latin America, Africa, Canada, and even China where Western pressure finally assured significant construction at the turn of the century.[36]

Experiencing railways

In the beginning, travel by rail was anything but comfortable. Carriages were connected using chains; they slammed violently into one another when accelerating or decelerating. Conditions could be decidedly unpleasant. Third class (and sometimes even second-class) accommodation could be cold, wet, and when cars were located near the engine, even fiery. Third-class passengers occasionally froze to death in cold weather and in one case a railway company even carried a hypothermic customer outside the station, leaving him to die on the sidewalk lest the firm get a reputation for killing clients.

This was not the least of the indignities suffered by those in third class. Initially, there was no food service on trains. (The first dining car was only introduced in 1868.) This meant that hungry passengers had to disembark to buy food from a selection of entrepreneurs who sold sandwiches, snacks, and ale on station platforms. Getting off the train could be risky, as there were often just moments during which to make a purchase. Eventually, several railway companies opened cafeterias in their stations where first and second-class travelers could race to buy notoriously bad food. Third-class passengers were forced to leave the station in search of sustenance.[37]

Although conditions remained spartan in places such as India and even New Zealand, railways in Britain, Europe, and the United States made dramatic improvements in terms of speed and comfort. There was something of a trickle-down effect. The first comparatively pleasant carriages were limited to people such as Queen Victoria (1819–1901), whose fear of railways was overcome with the addition of more wheels (and thus a smoother ride) and greater luxury. The giant leap forward, however, took place in the United States. American travelers faced much longer trips than did most Europeans. In the earliest days of railway transport carriages certainly did not live up to the challenge of distance traveling. The first American sleeper car, which debuted long before any such cars appeared in Europe, was thirty-four feet long and eight feet wide. Equipped with three-tiered bunk beds and lacking adequate suspension, the ride quality was brutal.[38] Being shaken and beaten, unable to sleep or to eat conveniently was no recipe for economic success. When George Mortimer Pullman (1831–97), a man who earned a powerful reputation by successfully moving large hotels with the customers still inside, introduced bigger, heavier carriages that were not only comparatively lavish but also featured more wheels and springs to cushion the journey, he found rapid success. His cars were expensive, as much as five times the cost of an ordinary railway car (extravagant models built for wealthy buyers, such as the banker and financier J.P. Morgan [1837–1913], might cost far more), but patrons were willing to pay. Pullman offered a range of models, from sleeping to dining cars. By the 1870s, carriages were even equipped with toilets featuring technology more advanced than a hole in the floor or a chamber pot under the seat. Pullman did not stop there. In order to assure adequate service aboard the cars that he built, the Pullman Company employed its own porters—10,500 of them by the 1920s, working on some 9800 railway cars. Pullman cars, as well as luxury carriages built by other builders such as Webster Wagner (1817–82) and George Nagelmackers (1845–1905), soon found service in Britain, Latin America, and beyond.

Velocities climbed as well. While the first trains only traveled at twenty or thirty miles per hour, there were routes that averaged forty to fifty or more by the 1850s and speeds rose thereafter in the face of growing competition. In most places, railway travel was comfortable and swift by the dawn of the twentieth century, a viable option for most travelers.[39]

Train stations also went through a process of evolution. They stood as "living temples to the worship of King Steam," cathedrals for the modern age and the single most significant architectural contribution of the nineteenth century.[40] Stations embodied national distinctiveness, sometimes standing as symbols of empire as at St. Pancras in London,[41] other times reflecting the diversity of a country as in the United States.[42] In Latin America, railway stations reflected the informal imperialism still present despite decolonization as well as a growing search for new and unique national characteristics.[43] Meanwhile, Asian stations illustrated the importance of European power.[44] To an extent, then, travelers venturing outside of Europe could see difference even as they boarded or disembarked from the train. At the same time, reminders of the Grand Tour were everywhere in the sculpture, paintings, and stained glass. Old tropes, such as the tutor, were everywhere. The railway age significantly increased the number of women traveling. Railway station art celebrated this by casting male escorts as tutors, assuring that tourism retained its eighteenth-century association with education and self-improvement.[45]

Trains and mass mobility

While it is an exaggeration to say that trains immediately "marked the end of the *ancien régime* in transport," they did alter the landscape dramatically and not everybody welcomed the change. Whereas once most people stayed put, now movement was to be a fact of life and many believed the implications would be profound. The headmaster of Rugby, one of the best known of England's elite boarding schools, remarked that trains would ultimately bring an end to the aristocracy, "feudality had gone forever."[46] The Vice-Chancellor of Cambridge University was equally concerned, demanding that the railway station be located at least one mile from the city center. Ideally, such a spatial arrangement would prevent a full-on attack by working-class day-trippers.[47] Some European countries sought to slow the pace of railway development for the same reason. What exactly would happen if people started moving around? At least at first and for some, the answer was too frightening to imagine.

This anxiety may explain why some railway companies actively worked to limit access to passenger travel. The Liverpool and Manchester Railway initially demanded that tickets be purchased a day or more in advance. Prospective passengers also needed to supply information about age, place of birth, and occupation. The restrictions did not last, but it speaks volumes that the company felt them necessary in the first place. Some European governments were even more prohibitive such that passengers were "checked and supervised at all stages to a degree that astonished the British traveller."[48]

Control extended beyond determining who could travel or how they did so. The railways also wanted to rule time. Trains needed to depart and arrive according to established schedules. Timetables published by railway companies started to appear within a few years of the Liverpool and Manchester Railway unveiling, growing longer and more detailed as years passed.[49] At first, the major problem with these listings was the unreliability of the trains, but there was yet another significant challenge. There was no common way of determining time across Britain, let alone across Europe or the world. Consequently, one timetable offered the following information: "London time is about four minutes earlier than Reading time, seven and a half minutes before Cirencester and fourteen minutes before Bridgwater."[50] For perspective, it is worth noting that Reading is only about 45 miles from London, while Bridgwater is less than 160 miles distant. Obviously this could not stand. Gradually, Britain adopted "Railway Time," more commonly known as "Greenwich Mean Time" (GMT), a "testimony to the efficacy of the railways and their inflexible tables in imposing a single national standard of time-keeping." GMT was formally implemented across Great Britain in 1880.[51]

Despite challenges, it took little time for leisure, once the purview of the very rich, to draw from other social groups. Third-class tickets were affordable. As labor legislation slowly limited hours spent in factory drudgery, workers engaged in Sunday excursions, gradually got out of town on Saturdays, and eventually took advantage of longer blocks of time to escape for annual seaside holidays. The middle classes found greater opportunities for leisure as companies such as Thomas Cook & Son created package tours to more exotic and far-flung destinations using trains for transport. The top of society, of course, also took advantage of railroads—the richest even buying their own railcars lest they suffer alongside the "great unwashed."

On water

The earliest experiments with steam-powered watercraft long-predated a similar application on land. French engineers reportedly played with the idea starting in 1615. James Watt (1736–1819) constructed an efficient steam engine in the 1760s. Claude de Jouffroy d'Abbans (1751–1832) built a boat that ran for fifteen minutes against a river current in 1783.[52] William Symington (1763–1831) invented an even better steamboat in 1787 and he quickly followed this up with a paddleboat just two years later. Hundreds of spectators lined the Forth and Clyde canal to see him test the new technology, which blazed smoothly along at five miles per hour. In 1802 a tug called the

Charlotte Dundas successfully pulled two seventy-ton barges along the canal, but the company that operated the waterway feared that if the boat were to race back and forth too quickly it might damage the passage. It was scrapped. Across the pond in New York, a similar craft suffered the same fate.[53]

The world's first regular passenger service finally debuted on the River Clyde near Glasgow, Scotland in August 1812.[54] Similar services launched in various places in Britain, the United States, and beyond in short order. The routes were popular, as data from Margate, in East Kent, England shows. There were reportedly 17,000 visitors to Margate in 1812–13, conveyed there from London aboard sailing ships. The advent of steam, first serving the resort in 1815, dramatically increased these numbers. Traffic rose to 44,000 by 1820–21, then again to an average of 85,000 by the 1830s. Numbers on the Clyde saw similar rises, as did other areas where steamships plied waterways.[55] On the Mississippi River in the United States, where the first steamboat launched in 1811, the new technology soon dominated. By 1821, steamers visited New Orleans 1200 times per year.[56]

The earliest steamships were well suited to lakes, rivers, and immediate coastlines: anywhere that fuel was accessible. They were not efficient enough to venture further away from shore, so efforts to cross the Atlantic demanded hybrid craft that mixed steam and sail. They looked much like tall ships, with two or three masts and essentially the same hull design used for sail-only craft. Hybrids diverged from their long-serving sail-only relatives by adding a steam engine and side-mounted paddle wheels. When the wind blew, the engine was turned off to conserve fuel. If the breeze slowed, steam power kept the boat moving through the water. Efficiency did come at a cost. The engine took up considerable space. Narrow hulls meant cramped accommodations and smaller payloads.

Nevertheless, the technology worked. In 1819, the *Savannah* made claim to becoming the first steamship to cross the Atlantic. The problem was that the boat did it almost entirely by sail, only running its engine in sight of anybody upon whom an impression might be made. Others soon made similar crossings, but none of these captured imaginations or inspired serious thinking about steam as a viable technology for oceanic crossings.[57] Even the *Royal William*, which paddle-wheeled from Nova Scotia to London in 1833, made hardly a splash in the minds of the masses.[58]

Things changed in 1838 when two ships, the *Sirius* and the *Great Western*, competed to see who could travel back and forth faster. The result was a kind of "steamship fever" that captured headlines. It was not long before Samuel Cunard (1787–1865), along with his business partner, a Glasgow shipbuilder named Robert Napier (1791–1876), launched a regularly scheduled steam-driven trans-Atlantic mail service.[59] The line also carried passengers, but in rather less than spectacular accommodations.

Seeing an opening whereby fancier digs might attract clients, American Edward K. Collins (1802–78) launched his own steamship line featuring far nicer rooms and more space. His craft were soon dubbed "palaces of the ocean" and he even attained a US government contract to compete with Cunard carrying mail in order to supplement the passenger business. The problem was that all of the lavish accommodations cost money. Collins could not compete, even with government subsidies to support his business. It did not even matter that one of his boats, the *Pacific*, became the first to cross the Atlantic in less than ten days on April 19, 1852. The Collins Line was out of business by 1858.

In some ways, the failure hardly mattered: competition beget greater comfort. The bad old days of austere rooms and painfully long crossings ended.[60] Still, luxury and speed did come at a price. It was imperative to develop improved technologies that allowed for more passengers—especially in steerage, where people were numerous and required few amenities—to offset costs. Larger ships, metal hulls, more efficient and reliable engines, as well as more and more routes that not only spanned the Atlantic, but increasingly the globe, helped.[61]

The last three decades of the nineteenth century brought more change. Paddle wheels gave way to screw propellers, allowing for taller and wider ships. Compound steam engines assured far greater power than was possible with older technologies.[62] Turbines went further, sequencing "compression and decompression of steam cylinders" to eventually turn a succession of ever-larger turbine rings, extracting the maximum amount of energy from the steam. The result was a massive boost in wattage without a significant increase in fuel consumption.[63] Together, the technologies allowed for the creation of ever-larger ships. Comfort and speed could both be improved exponentially as a consequence. The days of being soaked by waves were left behind; Atlantic crossings dropped from eighteen days to only about eight.

It took a few years for engineers to fully recognize the design potential engendered by the new technology, but when they did, the results were dramatic. Ships got larger and larger. While once boats were barely 200 feet long, the new palaces were as much as 1000 feet in length. Whereas sailing ships weighed little more than 2000 tons, the new craft exceeded 30,000 tons. Ships got wider and taller as well, shifting from little more than 25 feet across to as much as 119 feet, and going from just two decks to seven. Speed far from suffered. The fastest steamship in history, the *United States*, the final winner of an informal trans-Atlantic race called the Blue Riband, crossed the Atlantic in just 3 days, 10 hours, and 40 minutes in 1952.[64]

With technology getting better, emigrants seeking to escape from Europe, and a growing class of elite travelers willing to spend handsomely to go abroad for pleasure, there was plenty of competition to create steamship companies. Virtually every major power had at least one firm vying for business. Belgium, Germany, France, Great Britain, the United States, Spain, and others all entered the fray.

Crossing in luxury

Accommodations shifted from grim to grand. The greatest ships of the steam age, the *Queen Mary*, the *Lusitania*, and the *Normandie* were floating grand hotels, moving palaces for the über-wealthy. They were designed to carry passengers in a style in line with the newly created luxury hotels that started serving major cities during the mid-1850s and 1860s.[65] Steamship lines offered first-class clients the best of everything. Furnishings were ornate: elaborately carved wood, grand staircases, glorious lighting fixtures

Figure 3.2 The *R.M.S. Lusitania* is most famous for being sunk by a German U-boat off the coast of Ireland in 1915, however it is also notable as an example of the massive steamships that carried both wealthy and steerage passengers across the Atlantic Ocean during the late nineteenth and first half of the twentieth centuries. These craft featured extravagant accommodations befitting the rich and famous. Even so, shipping companies made most of their money by carrying legions of emigrants in more spartan accommodations below deck. Photograph by George Grantham Bain. Courtesy of the George Grantham Bain Collection, Library of Congress.

(electric lights were used on board steamships before they were introduced on city streets). While earlier craft offered no running water, the floating hotels had marble bathtubs.[66] Every type of entertainment was on offer. There were gymnasiums, swimming pools, games, photography dark rooms, libraries, and numerous bars. Kitchen staff worked hard to present a wealth of selection. At any given time, there were at least twenty different cooked meals available. Lunches included choices of soups and salads, multiple hot and cold dishes, and plenty of vegetable options. Dinners featured ten to twelve courses and chefs prided themselves on being able to prepare anything that a wealthy passenger might desire.[67]

Traveling with this kind of luxury was as much about showing off to others as it was about getting to a destination. The type of over-the-top consumption pattern that helped define the Grand Tour was everywhere. Daily life reflected this, marked out in time by regular changes of costume. Travelers wore evening dress to dinner on all but the first and last nights. Both men and women put on tweeds for lunch. Ladies donned elaborate dresses for tea. Those who managed to impress earned an invitation to the captain's table—the supreme honor and a source of social bragging rights.[68]

Of course, not everybody sailed first class and even during the second half of the nineteenth century steerage passengers, increasingly called "third class," far outnumbered their wealthier fellow travelers on the upper decks and generated most of the profits.[69] As in the past, they were accommodated in open berths, divided into single women, single men, and married couples. At the start of the voyage, each third-class passenger was given a tin cup, silverware, and a small metal plate. They were responsible for keeping these implements clean and for bringing them along to meals, served at long tables. The food was far from that offered in first class, but it was edible. Similarly, entertainment was also lacking. There were no deck chairs—or even any place to sit for that matter—and the only activities were those developed by the passengers themselves.[70]

Whether enjoying glorious conditions on the upper decks or crossing the sea in steerage, the floating palaces were popular with just about everybody. The larger ships bobbed around in the water far less than their smaller predecessors. Seasickness did happen, but less often than in the past. Regardless of class, boarding a steamship was exciting and the prospect of what would be found on the opposite shore was exhilarating. The ship represented a sort of "world between worlds," a third place that existed between one's point of origin and one's terminus. Most boarded the ship because they were looking forward to reaching a destination and to experiencing new sights, sounds, languages, and experiences, yet the ship itself also represented an important "site of imagination."

In terms of tourism, the ease of passage created for wealthy passengers (third-class tickets were almost always one-way) created an appeal for far-off places that simply could not exist previously. Americans, for example, could do more than dream about a European sojourn. The destination represented an escape, a kind of dream world that would allow one to get a better sense of self. As one traveler put it, going to Europe "will be a very good thing for the present, or as long as I'm in this irresolute mood. If I understand it, Europe is the place for American irresolution." Travel might help one discover a vocation or decide on a future. As in the eighteenth century, voyagers might use the journey to meet important people. For some, "Serendipitous encounters during their travels became an essential part of voyagers' personal, professional, and intellectual development." Travel was still about self-improvement.[71]

The great floating palaces created a market for trans-Atlantic tourism. During the 1920s, two additional classes of travel were added: "tourist" and "cabin" class, opening long-distance ocean voyages to younger and less affluent tourists. These categories offered much less expensive accommodation than was found in first class with more services, better rooms, and more entertainments than could be found in steerage.[72] Even at just under four days, steamships were too slow to appeal to those drawn from anything beyond the upper and middle strata of society. Tourist-class tickets were useful, but they did not create more time. Working people still had to choose making an income over pleasure.

Conclusion

And yet, steam created opportunities for new types of leisure travel. Railways made it possible for a growing number of promoters to develop what came to be known as excursions, short day and overnight trips aimed at the working classes. The seaside soon proved especially popular. Middle-class tourists engaged in longer journeys. A growing number of Americans could realistically dream of going to Europe and Europeans could visit the United States—or virtually anyplace else that the great nineteenth-century "age of imperialism" made available. Package tour companies turned these plans into reality by creating well-organized, all-in group tours, utilizing both railways and steamships, that would take the anxious globetrotter virtually anywhere he—and increasingly she—wanted to go. Tourism was going global and there were more and more guidebooks aimed at telling people where to go, what to do, and how to do it. Steam opened the way for widespread tourism.

4

Packaging new trips

The steam age and industrialization did not create the idea that tourism is healthy or introduce workers single-handedly to the notion of leisure, but it certainly helped to expand opportunities. Most people had long enjoyed the occasional day off from their labors. Religious holidays, seasonal festivals, and saints' days were an established part of the annual calendar. By the first decade of the nineteenth century, there were forty-four bank holidays in England. Although that number declined to only four by 1839, some factories introduced their own holidays. Sunday was long a day of rest and Parliament eventually added half-days on Saturdays, then whole weekends.[1] From the 1840s, labor legislation and rising real wages brought very real improvement to the lives of many, if not most, workers. The rise of railways provided a backdrop for these developments.[2] British tourism promoters and seaside resort developers conspired to help workers, as well as their middle-class countrymen, fill leisure time with trips and adventures. The nineteenth century was a period of significant tourism growth, marked by continued emphasis on health, as well as increasing coordination.

Organizing package tours

Excursions, short one or two-day package trips aimed primarily at working-class holidaymakers, appeared soon after the founding of railways and were, at least through much of the nineteenth century, unique to Britain.[3] Working-class groups such as Mechanics' Institutes and Friendly Societies arranged the first ones. These journeys usually involved destinations that would provide some measure of "self-improvement." Very often organizers hoped to forward a temperance agenda. According to tourism historian Susan Barton, most excursions included "brass bands, jollity and feasting." Even if the participants had little interest in taking the no-drink pledge, the prospect of riding a train, going someplace new, and experiencing the festive atmosphere associated with a planned trip was enticing. A single venture drew hundreds of individuals. At least one early Mechanics' Institute program attracted 2400 people, far outnumbering actual members of the body. Small wonder as the price represented a truly affordable expense for nearly everybody with an income—only two shillings for third class.[4]

Members of the middle class appreciated the temperate, "rational recreation" offered by early excursions as a means of rectifying what they perceived as the "growing 'problem' of the leisure of the masses." By leading loud, godless, heavy-drinking workers from their traditional pastimes and "riotous gatherings" and into the countryside with its pure air, they hoped to eliminate "tumultuous, disorderly, and intemperate scenes . . . in which wives and children cannot and ought not to participate." Travel could offer a "civilizing" influence.[5]

By the later nineteenth century, at least some companies believed that offering holidays to their employees would yield more productive workers. While smaller businesses often sponsored events, the large trips arranged by corporations such as the Bass Brewery stand out the most. Some such excursions drew as many as 10,000 hired hands and their guests, demanding numerous trains. Organization for such events was taxing, and employers made certain to tell their subordinates how to behave. It was not uncommon to read that you would be "LEFT BEHIND," as one set of instructions put it, if you arrived for the journey in a manner not in keeping with expressed codes of conduct.[6]

The growth of working-class outings stirred anxiety as well. In an assembly of thousands of people, one ill-mannered person might lead others astray. It did not help that some members of the laboring classes arranged group ventures for the sake of spectating at disreputable events such as prizefights, horse races, and even executions. In 1848, for example, the hanging of a multiple murderer at the Liverpool Gaol attracted some 100,000 spectators, thousands of whom arrived via an excursion train. The Bodmin and Wadebridge Railway had promoted a similar outing in 1836. With so many people on hand, it was very easy for riots to break out, as happened during a trip to the Epsom racecourse near London in 1838. Public order and crowd control could pose a serious problem.[7]

Whatever the challenges and debates, leisure travel and especially working-class tourism soon constituted a significant portion of the railways' profits. Between 1836 and 1840, railways carried some 1.25 million passengers and a significant portion of these journeyed for pleasure. While it is difficult to tell precise numbers because the companies did not record the reasons for travel, one need only acknowledge that individual "monster excursions" might consist of thousands of customers transported in hundreds of carriages with up to nine locomotives pulling them.[8] There was very real money to be made developing short leisure holidays for laborers and, ultimately, longer trips for the middle and upper classes.

Thomas Cook and the continued rise of package tours

The obvious potential for profit led a number of individuals to form businesses devoted to prearranged travel. Although they often note some of these early developers—Henry Gaze (1825–94) and John Frame (dates unknown), for example—historians thus far have only shown significant interest in Thomas Cook (1808–92) and his son John Mason Cook (1834–99). Many writers even incorrectly claim that he invented excursions and package holidays.[9] Although it is disappointing that Gaze and others have yet to find their historian, the story of Thomas Cook offers an important window into the early development of organized tourism both inside Great Britain and beyond.

According to Piers Brendon, the principal scholarly historian of the Thomas Cook & Son travel agency, Cook was very much a product of his background. The early package travel promoter's maternal grandfather was a co-pastor of the Melbourne flock of the New Connexion of General Baptists. Like other evangelical groups during the Methodist revival period of the late eighteenth and early nineteenth centuries, the sect believed in an ongoing process of conversion and advocated moral improvement at every turn. The General Baptists criticized the Methodists, usually seen as very strict, as painfully lax. As a young man, Cook internalized this severe outlook.

Initially Thomas Cook trained to be a printer and a cabinetmaker but his real passion lay in preaching and advocating the virtues of temperance.[10] The 1830s were one of several periods in British history when teetotalers gained a wide following. More moderate reform advocates designed the 1830 Beer Act to dissuade people from visiting gin shops in favor of drinking beer, widely believed to be a more temperate beverage. The act eased restrictions on attaining a permit to sell beer. In 1831, authorities issued 31,937 of the new licenses. The legislation, however, did not please strident opponents of alcohol. "Everybody is drunk," as one dissatisfied person described matters. "Those who are not singing are sprawling."[11] Cook agreed that more needed to be done to halt this terrifying turn of events.

At first, the future tourism promoter devoted himself to preaching the evils of drink. Then one day in early 1840, Cook had an idea likely inspired by working-class-led trips.[12] He would capitalize on the astonishing popularity of the new railways to promote his cause. Cook set out to hire a train, sell tickets to hundreds of passengers, and take them to a temperance rally. It would be, he believed, at once exciting and morally uplifting for those who went. The outing, held on July 5, 1841, attracted 570 passengers. They each paid a shilling to travel round trip from Leicester to Loughborough, where they listened to anti-drink speakers and temperance bands. Not only did the journey sell out almost instantly, thousands lined the track to *watch* the train go by.[13]

Encouraged by the success, Cook led more temperance trips and soon found that he enjoyed the organizational challenge. In the summer of 1845, he decided to pursue a more middle-class clientele by piecing together an outing of greater complexity. This time, he took travelers to Liverpool with side trips to Caernarfon Castle and Mount Snowdon in Wales. The basic fare was fourteen shillings for first class and ten shillings for second. As workers could not be expected to leave their jobs for long enough to take part, Cook offered no third-class seats. Once again, the tour sold out almost immediately, a few tickets later turning up again on the black market. Cook was onto something.[14]

Figure 4.1 Although the earliest trains inspired fear, there was also a great deal of excitement. Many Victorians raced to the rail lines to witness the new machines first hand. A number of largely working-class groups almost immediately organized inexpensive "excursion" trips to historic sites, scenic destinations, boxing matches, executions, and other attractions. Thomas Cook famously made his first foray into arranging such adventures when he promoted a trek between Leicester and Loughborough so that temperance advocates could attend a rally. Photo courtesy of Thomas Cook Archives, Peterborough, UK.

The following year, he organized his first trip to Scotland. In theory, it was an excellent idea. The rough landscape represented the very epicenter of the sublime. Since the late eighteenth and early nineteenth centuries, the wild hills and rugged scenery drew extensive interest from Romantics such as Sir Walter Scott, William and Dorothy Wordsworth, and the composer Felix Mendelssohn. More than that, it had Scottish people, and the English had long believed them to be particularly exotic types who were stronger than oxen and possessed of a positively strange culture.[15] In contrast to their neighbors to the south, they practiced rigid Sabbatarianism, often spoke in Gaelic, and wore curious tartan clothing. Scots represented an "other" within the British Isles that could be efficiently seen by those from England with time and money enough to venture north of the border.[16] Equally important, Queen Victoria and her beloved consort, Prince Albert (1819–61), visited Scotland in 1842 and absolutely loved it. The press coverage of the visit, as well as the couple's subsequent purchase of a home near Balmoral in Deeside, inspired others, especially sportsmen, to consider their own trips.[17]

The challenges posed by arranging such an adventure were profound and the undertaking nearly ended Cook's business before it truly got started. Scotland was comparatively undeveloped relative to England. There were no trains running from England into Scotland, fewer rail lines in Scotland itself, and those that did exist failed to connect with one another. Cook's trip would need to make use of a combination of trains, carriages, and steamships—an organizational nightmare. Once in Scotland, accommodations were in shorter supply than in much of England. Scottish weather is also often unreliable. It sometimes snows in July.

Problems started almost immediately. There were no toilets on the train and the tourists were only given a very short stop in Manchester to use the facilities. It was not sufficient. In Preston, Cook planned to provide tea. It never materialized. In Fleetwood, food was served, but there was not enough of it to go round. Once on board the steamship that was to take the group from England to Scotland, passengers discovered inadequate cabin facilities. Many very proper, middle-class Victorians found themselves sleeping on deck chairs. While not good, the lack of indoor accommodations became disastrous when the boat sailed into a storm. Now many guests were both "completely drenched" and "very ill." Weather, amenities, and services improved once the group reached Glasgow though. A brass band played. Guns were fired in celebration. Temperance orations filled the air. Yet few of the passengers had taken the no-drink pledge, and the speeches did not sit well with them. In fact, after the difficult passage on the Irish Sea, nearly all of them were anxious to locate some liquid courage as quickly as possible. (Cook eventually abandoned the teetotal aspect of his trips.) Nevertheless, the journey westward to Stirling, on to Ayrshire, and along Loch Lomond was without fault. Unfortunately, the damage was done. Word of mouth was anything but positive. Cook's first "Tartan Tour" left his nascent company in bankruptcy.

Cook was down, but he was not out. In 1847, he led two other groups around Scotland and by 1848 was directing an aggressive schedule of jaunts north of the border. Having ironed out the kinks, the Scottish circuit formed the backbone of his business.[18]

Even as Cook's longer tours began to attract a middle-class clientele, the working-class excursion trade was never far from his mind. The Great Exhibition of 1851, therefore, proved to be very important to Cook. Originally conceived in 1849 at least partly by Queen Victoria's beloved husband Prince Albert, the objective of the event was simple enough: celebrate Britain's industrial and colonial might. The massive "Crystal Palace," built expressly for the occasion in London's Hyde Park, set the scene. There, attendees examined displays on "Machinery and Mechanical Inventions," "Decorative Manufactures," "Raw Materials of Manufactures, British Colonial and Foreign," and "Sculpture Connected with Architecture and Plastic Art Generally."[19] As the presentations disproportionately showcased products made by members of England's working class, it made sense to encourage their attendance. Railway companies were pressured to offer discounted travel to the elaborate public show.[20] Yet the tickets remained out of reach for some workers and local subscription clubs formed so that interested people could pay a little bit at a time toward their trip to London.[21] Excursion organizers such as Thomas Cook also sold tickets, arranged lodgings, and otherwise made it possible for heretofore unheard of numbers of travelers to visit the biggest city in the world. Ultimately, six million people, about one fifth of the population, made the trip.[22] Thomas Cook transported 165,000 of them to London.[23] The Great Exhibition of 1851 was a huge success for all concerned and unmarred by any public order problems. Respectable contemporaries were impressed and the excursion movement gained greater acceptability as a result.[24]

As for Cook, his business continued to grow and drew new clientele. In 1860, he took 50,000 tourists to Scotland.[25] His customers, however, were no longer predominantly men or couples. For the first time, large numbers of women started to travel unaccompanied. Cook had little time for the idea that "unprotected females" should avoid adventure and he instead described his female patrons as "heroines who required no protection, beyond what the arrangements and companionships of the tour afforded." Cook himself was their "travelling chaperon." Given the amount of effort that Cook put in to the argument that women were equally right to travel, it is perhaps unsurprising that "more ladies than gentlemen went on

Cook's tours. Thomas Cook thus made a significant contribution to female emancipation. He assisted the angel to move away from the hearth, though she was very far from moving into a state of equality with the 'lords of humankind.'"[26]

By 1862, Cook's company was flourishing. Excursions continued to increase in popularity and other forms of tourism expanded as well. But there was a problem, at least for Cook's Scottish dealings. He made it look too easy. As a result, the Scottish railway companies stopped cooperating with Cook and decided to organize their own tours. Overnight, the cornerstone of Cook's fortunes vanished. The change might have been a major blow had the Great Exhibition not bolstered his excursion business as well as his other trips aimed at respectable tourists. Instead of destroying Thomas Cook, the demise of the "Tartan Tours" had a rather different outcome. Thomas Cook and his son John Mason, who joined the concern in 1851 to help with the Great Exhibition, simply took tourists abroad. British people had larger real incomes than virtually anybody else in the world and could therefore afford to take longer, more involved trips.[27] Thomas Cook & Son became the leading British travel company and, due to the firm's efforts, more people around the world came into contact with tourists who exemplified what until then were largely British modes of leisure.

Water and leisure: The spa

Almost from the start, tourism was said to make one better. It provided cultural capital, had either an enlivening or a relaxing impact on the mind through viewing landscapes or ruins, and offered to teach travelers good taste. Another aspect of the story assured that one might also be made physically healthy by travel and this thread ultimately helped generate connections between water and leisure that would impact the shape of tourism.

Most world religions assign water an important place. Reference to it is found in the opening and closing passages of the Christian Bible. Water is identified with the "underlying principle and foundation of the universe" in Vedic Hinduism. It is also vital to both Jewish and Islamic belief, as well as central to Taoism.[28] For many faiths, water represents the source of life and so it is hardly surprising that, as historian Ian Bradley explains, it "has a long association with both physical and psychological healing which goes back to the earliest civilizations and cultures."[29]

In Europe, the Romans developed an elaborate network of bathing practices; these largely disappeared with the demise of Roman power in

Western Europe.[30] Interest in mineral springs renewed gradually during the later Middle Ages and the notion that visiting a spring had healthy benefits was well established, at least on the European continent, by the seventeenth century.[31]

In Britain, however, water cures generated apprehension among Protestants who associated them with Roman Catholic practices. Yet even in Britain, there were those keen to visit healing waters and at least some made regular treks across the English Channel to visit Spa in the Spanish Netherlands—a Catholic country actively pursuing an inquisition against those deemed heretical. Such trips worried English authorities and intelligence agents warned that a "fifth column" of Papists was forming that might try to precipitate an invasion of England. To avoid the risk, and goaded by doctors anxious to make a name for themselves, authorities allowed for the promotion of English spas.[32] The change sparked the creation of various publications that advocated taking mineral baths, hot and cold bathing, drinking mineral water, and a host of other cures. The number of Britons making their way to the baths, whether located in France, Germany, the Netherlands, or even England and Scotland, increased significantly as elites grew convinced of the healing benefits of water.[33]

At first, spas were overwhelmingly about health. Doctors prescribed that most visitors take mineral water baths and drink the water. It was not necessarily a pleasant script. As one visitor to Vichy at the end of the eighteenth century described: "I took the waters this morning my dear friend, and oh were they bad! One goes at six in the morning to the fountain and finds that everyone is already there. One drinks, then walks around the fountain, then takes a longer promenade, and then drinks more of the disagreeable water. This is what one does until midday." Another patient noted that after a dozen glasses he could think of no greater desire than to "purge myself."[34]

Although at least some spas offered assistance to help sick members of the poor attain treatment, the overwhelming majority of early spa goers were members of the elite and they were attracted at least partly because it was fashionable.[35] In England, royal endorsements assured that other members of the aristocracy were anxious to fill themselves with foul liquid.[36] Yet the wealthy clientele was not simply a result of fashion. As with other types of travel, only the wealthy were able to shoulder the expense. Many spas in France, for example, were quite isolated and required long treks over terrible roads. Once there, it took considerable time—often about three weeks—to attain the desired cure. Those unfortunate enough to need a job to survive did not enjoy the luxury of that much time away from dutiful labor, or the ability to employ transportation for the long, arduous journey.[37]

Over time, spas grew eager to attract more and higher-class visitors. Places such as Baden-Baden (Germany), Bath (England), and Spa had huge reputations, but many newer sites were less known. By the early part of the nineteenth century the most acceptable marketing scheme consisted of regularly published "lists of visitors."[38] They included details on the number of persons attending a given facility, but the tallies also advertised when people of merit were in attendance. Others were naturally anxious to go where the stars went. More and more "middle class" visitors consequently turned up at spa towns.

Efforts to attract more customers went beyond creating public catalogs of the well heeled. Added attractions not only drew people to the spa but also showcased the social opportunities to be had in the setting of the surrounding town. Taking the waters entailed associating with the upper crust while passing through beautiful buildings, visiting massive drinking halls, and strolling through landscaped gardens.[39] In short, spas became resorts.

When transportation costs dropped due to the advent of railways, visiting spas grew more affordable. In France, at least, even the lower echelons of the bourgeoisie found water cures within their reach.[40] This was far from working-class leisure, but it paved the way for a new type of holiday that built on the aesthetic changes described in Chapter 2 and which caught the popular imagination: the seaside.

Water and leisure: The seaside

Workers had a local tradition of sea bathing in Lancashire dating at least to the middle of the eighteenth century, but it is safe to say that the rising popularity of the practice among the upper classes, partly inspired by their experience in spas, played a greater role in popularizing the waves.[41] The notion that saltwater bathing might toughen the body, promoting good health, took hold following the appearance of John Floyer's (1649–1734) *Psychrolousia or, the History of Cold Bathing* in 1715. The process grew more prescribed as time passed and additional commentators chimed in. According to virtually everybody, taking a dip in the cold ocean calmed the nerves and could cure all manner of ills ranging from "phrenzy" to nymphomania. The trick, according to a book published by Dr. Richard Russell (1687–1759) in 1750, was to do it properly, generally under the guidance of a trained "dipper" whose job it was to dunk the bather into the water repeatedly and for set lengths of time. It was necessary to rest before swimming ("dipping" is actually a better term as few bathers knew how to swim until the notion of propelling oneself through the water gained popularity in the 1860s and 1870s)[42] and bathing was best done just before sunset. Typical patients learned to throw themselves "energetically into the sea." After shivering twice, it was important to leave the water, to dry off, and to sleep in a comfortable bed in order to rest up. For most, thirty or forty treatments would do the trick. There were variations, of course. Impotent men, for example, were advised to rush urgently into the waves and to supplement this regime by eating plenty of fresh fish in order to become "essentially procreative."[43]

Sea bathing gained popularity quickly among the upper tiers of the social hierarchy, both in the British Isles and beyond. It did not hurt the rise of this regime that it was enthusiastically prescribed to royal clients. George III of Britain (1738–1820), for example, famously started to suffer from a genetic illness called porphyria during the 1780s. The disease is tremendously rare among the general population but is not uncommon among European royal families. It features alarming symptoms that range from bouts of madness—George III was convinced that the trees growing in Windsor Great Park were foreign ambassadors and he reportedly carried on diplomatic talks with some of them—to bluish urine.[44] His doctors tried various cures but were particularly anxious that the king stay in Weymouth to undergo an extensive course of therapy that entailed dips in the waters along the Dorset coastline. The townspeople were so excited to have him in their midst that they provided a band to accompany his daily treatments. Later, the king's eldest son, the future George IV (1762–1830), took to sea bathing at Brighton in an effort to remedy a painful case of gout along with other health concerns.[45] If sea bathing was good enough for the royals, it was good enough for their noble relations. Soon, the British aristocracy was swimming away all that ailed them.

From out of the factory and into the surf

It did not take long before the increasing numbers profiting from industrial growth started to "demand their place at the seaside" and members of rural society quickly joined them.[46] By the end of the eighteenth century, "plain and unrefined" London tradesmen had already adopted the upper-class penchant for the beach.[47] Blackpool, later one of the most popular working-class resorts in Britain, attracted its share of middle-class visitors by the turn of the century.[48]

It took longer for a considerable segment of lower-class excursionists to fully adopt the beach, primarily because they needed to have the financial resources for the journey. Consequently, working-class leisure culture did not really start to change until the middle of the nineteenth century. Some members of the labor aristocracy, as of the mid-1840s, began to take longer trips lasting for multiple days.[49] By the 1870s, the explosion of excursion travel after the Great Exhibition, continuing economic prosperity, shorter working hours and longer weekends, and the Bank Holiday Act of 1870—which generated more holiday opportunities for workers—all created the prospect for seaside trips.[50]

According to historian John K. Walton, precise numbers for growth are difficult to come by and exist for only a few places. Nevertheless, he cites a handful of Lancashire examples that reflect the expansion of demand. In July of 1854, 1400 people booked travel from Darwen to vacation at the seaside. This figure rose to nearly 7000 by the mid-1860s and to almost 10,000 by 1872. In 1889, 13,000 made the trip. At the same time, seaside visits apparently grew longer. In 1854, only 500 purchased a four-day ticket, and as many as 2328 did so in 1866. By the 1880s, "many working-class Lancastrians were already staying away for a full week." Yet the most significant change came slightly later. In 1905, 15,000 of 30,000 seaside visitors stayed for seven days or more.[51]

Clear distinctions in leisure cultures quickly emerged that can be loosely defined by social class. To begin with, there were differences in the way that bathers approached the water. For the respectable, getting in and out of the sea without attracting the attention of voyeurs was important. The solution was the "bathing machine," a wheeled box either pulled by horses or drawn in and out of the surf using ropes and pulleys. The first such appliance was spotted in Scarborough in 1735, its originator unknown. Benjamin Beale (dates unknown), often credited with inventing the contraption, debuted his own version at Margate with the name "bathing machine" in 1753. It featured an additional umbrella that could be extended or retracted when the bather entered the water in order to provide further protection from prying eyes. Over the years, bathing machines spread to virtually all of Britain's seaside resorts and were adopted by continental bathers as well. The Belgians hold the distinction of creating the only truly luxurious version complete with ornate details, beautiful paintwork, and extensive engravings.

For all their popularity, however, bathing machines were not pleasant. Most did not have windows and were very dark inside. The ride down the beach and into the water could be bumpy. Changing into swimming attire while bobbing along the sand proved quite a challenge. The smell of rotting wood mixed with brine made this already awkward experience even more disagreeable. The constant contact with water, after all, rendered many bathing machines quite "dank." Yet for those anxious to preserve their social standing and decorum these were small prices to pay.

Workers, however, rejected the contraptions altogether. For them, the concern was money, not social standing. Companies anxious to make a profit controlled access to the machines.[52] Even with the benefit of cheap excursion fares, workers had little left over to pay for the opportunity to ride into the water in a claustrophobic, malodorous, wooden shed on wheels. They had spent their money to visit the ocean and that was all they wanted to do.

This was not the only point of class difference. Middle-class aspirations during much of the Victorian era can be aptly summarized in the title of Samuel Smiles' (1812–1904) best selling *Self Help*. The goal was self-improvement and it extended to the shoreline. Beaches offered an opportunity to explore the natural environment, to collect scientific samples, and to study the landscape. For those interested in the arts, the seaside featured beautiful light and stunning rocks worthy of paint and canvas.[53]

By and large, such things were less interesting to the working classes. They were accustomed to a more group-oriented culture.[54] Workers wanted entertainment. Consequently, as time passed, a host of facilities evolved to meet demand. Along the seaside arose amusement parks and piers, fish and chip shops and public houses, freak shows and distorting mirrors. Donkey rides were tremendously popular and remained so into the twentieth century.[55] Working-class visitors were also visibly different. In comparison to those studying the tide pools, they were less well-dressed and prone to "boisterous fun."[56]

As for the very wealthy, the ones who largely launched the seaside habit, they wanted little to do with either the middle or the working classes. Consequently, the upper crust often crossed the channel to visit a growing number of continental destinations. Provence, attractive to visitors since the Grand Tour, drew many. The French and Italian Rivieras gained devotees. Many opted for famous European spas and others pursued their leisure time in search of mountain scenery in Switzerland or beyond.[57]

Within this context, the seaside resort evolved into a unique environment, even if one often resembled another because of the particular architecture, buildings, and types of amusements. At first, sites of interest to middle-class visitors, such as bathing machines, libraries, and theatres, dotted the landscape.[58] Piers were an early addition, the first built at Ryde on the Isle of Wight in 1814. Initially, these structures provided a place for boats to dock and trade to occur, but the influx of working-class tourists turned them into moneymaking enterprises. There were admission fees and entertainments, opportunities to promenade and places for refreshment. By the 1880s and 1890s, piers offered whole pleasure pavilions, a lure in and of themselves.[59] They were not confined to Britain and quickly became draws at many American resorts (which often resembled their

British antecedents) such as Atlantic City, New Jersey; New York's Coney Island; Santa Cruz, California; and Old Orchard Beach in Maine to cite but four. Even Chicago, located on Lake Michigan, built its equivalent, Navy Pier, during the first years of the twentieth century. As a greater variety of visitors arrived, attractions grew more diverse: pleasure gardens, aquariums, wax museums, lawn bowling greens, music halls, and more.[60]

The convergence of dissimilar leisure cultures assured a certain amount of class conflict. The middle classes balked whenever vacations were not "rational" or "self-improving." They complained little when offered "educationally stimulating" facilities, but cried foul as thousands of working-class tourists descended to pursue fun. "Rich and poor, respectable and ungodly, staid and rowdy, quiet and noisy," according to John K. Walton, "not only rubbed shoulders in the centres of what were still, in most cases and for most of this period, small towns or mere villages; they also had to compete for access to, and use of, recreational space."[61] The evolution of many resorts reflected such divisions. In Southend-on-Sea, a popular destination for London-based holidaymakers starting in the 1790s among elites and expanding to include growing numbers of working-class excursionists in the 1850s, the spatial makeup of the town mirrored rival traditions: wealthy at one end, poor East Enders at the other. As soon as workers discovered the town and started to arrive in significant numbers, their social betters "retreated to the western cliff top built up by the New South End scheme, leaving the lower seafront to the incomers." The result was a long-term struggle between the town council, dominated by "upper middle class" members who endeavored to highlight their town's propriety in brochures and other marketing materials, and the less respectable holidaymakers who entertained no such concerns. They debated land use, architectural styles, and the type of activities available along the "Golden Mile."[62] It was not simply the built environment that reflected the discord. Whole stretches of beach were often off-limits to "the sedate and serious-minded, anxious to keep their children away from the moral and even physical dangers of these seashore fairgrounds."[63]

While England spawned the seaside holiday, the country did not long retain a monopoly. At Biarritz, local Basque villagers had an established tradition of visiting the beach during the warmer months to splash about in the cooling salt water, but it was elite patronage that made the site a popular resort, especially for the wealthy. Napoleon visited twice in 1808 to enjoy the water, inspiring the French upper crust from Bordeaux and Lyons to mimic well-off Britons by renting accommodations there. This influx was soon followed by a stream of "Castilian dukes, English lords, and French counts" anxious to relax at the beach.[64] Dieppe, France followed a similar trajectory, soon attracting aristocratic Parisians who set up their summer residences near the shore.[65] In the German states, Holland, and Belgium, merchants played a greater role in forming bathing establishments, but the rich quickly moved in to situate themselves by the sea.[66]

Just as many English resorts constructed promenades along their beachfronts to allow holidaymakers to both see and be seen, so too did continental sites such as Dieppe. There were differences, as well. Designers drew on more indigenous European models, tipping their hats to efforts in Naples, Venice, and Palermo to create walkways that were distinctively European. It took little time for Palermitans to "seek fresh air and coolness" while parading along the marina in their carriages; "the promenade [turned] into a stage and a focal point of gallantry. No husband, it was said, would dream of forbidding his wife to walk at night in the shade of the marina."[67]

As had been true in Britain, workers soon sought their share of the seaside and class conflict was not far behind, albeit with regional variations. German laborers and their social betters, for example, wrestled with vastly divergent ideas about sex. Workers were too promiscuous to be seemly, felt the respectable classes. Consequently, the sexes were separated into different bathing spaces and strict regulations were passed concerning nudity. By contrast, Basques were perfectly fine showing a little skin and officials introduced no such segregation.[68]

By the end of the nineteenth century, similar stories unfolded in the United States where elites socialized with their own kind in places such as Newport, Rhode Island; Bar Harbor, Maine; and Marblehead, Massachusetts. The riffraff flooded onto the fifty-four seaside cities offering oceanfront recreation in the one hundred miles between New Jersey and Delaware. Like their English counterparts, many working-class American beachgoers believed in "abandoning limits."[69] Those better off were far more reserved.

Swimming and sunbathing

As seaside resorts evolved, so too did the behaviors tourists exhibited. At first, seaside visitors went largely for health reasons. They thrashed about in the waves, shivered, and hoped that their various ailments would float away on the tide. By the 1860s and 1870s, it became fashionable actually to propel oneself through the water. Brighton's swimming club held its first races in 1861. Competitions quickly cropped up in other places. In 1875, Captain Matthew Webb (1848–83) successfully swam across the English Channel, the first person ever to do so. Others soon sought lessons, which officials at seaside resorts promptly provided. They also, during the 1870s, began to offer exhibitions of "fancy swimming" by Professor Harry Parker (1849–1932) and his son Harry Junior (dates unknown). Diving displays and other performances followed, inspiring members of the public to try out leaping great distances into the water for themselves.

There were other new pastimes. During his 1778 voyage to the Hawaiian Islands, Captain James Cook (1728–79) and his crew encountered native peoples who rode the waves aboard curious looking planks. By 1867, some English swimmers made their own surfboards and began demonstrating them in the waves off various resorts. While surfing did not really take off until after World War I, it is significant that more and more people engaged with the water in increasingly varied ways.

Different forms of movement demanded newfangled forms of dress. Although many men swam naked during the eighteenth century, by the middle of the nineteenth century Victorians decked themselves out in "little more than a shapeless sack gathered at the neck and sleeves." The costume certainly did not encourage mobility. Swimming, diving, and surfing required that outfits evolved to provide greater range of motion. Correspondingly, by the end of the century the notion that pale white skin was preferable to color died out. Tanning grew fashionable, and melanin is not produced beneath thick layers of cloth. Beachwear changed to offer up more of the body to ultraviolet rays. So with the onset of a new century came a gradual evolution away from the Victorian bodysuit towards the revealing outfits favored by twentieth-century beachgoers.[70]

Conclusion

Differences about how and where to travel were not completely defined by social class or gender, of course. As companies such as Thomas Cook & Son added destinations to the list of available excursions and tours, as transportation options increased the list of viable places to visit, and as the variety of experiences on offer at seaside resorts or spas grew, personal choice undoubtedly played a significant role in decision-making. But selections were not made in a vacuum. There is nothing natural about tourism; people learn how to do it.

There was no shortage of groups of individuals anxious to tell others how to travel. Excursion organizers hoped to teach moral lessons or to dissuade people from drink. Doctors prescribed often very specific regimes to engage at beaches and spas. The middle classes hoped to teach workers how to behave, usually without success. Elites managed to lead by example, only to race off anxiously to new and often more isolated locations in the hope of escaping from a monster of their own making.

All of this happened through what could be called technologies of control: tourist guidebooks, travel and health-related literature and fiction writing, and even images produced for sale helped to define touristic behavior and understanding. Many saw this as important work and were anxious either to produce such technologies or to consume them. While not a new invention, the growth of tourism after the end of the Napoleonic Wars in 1815 assured that there was also an expansion in the variety and type of guides on offer, especially from publishing houses such as those operated by Karl Baedeker and John Murray among others. All of this, in turn, had further implications for how people saw their world, what they wanted to save of the past, how they thought about their present, and how they imagined the future.

5
Guidebooks and the importance of seeing the sights

Great literature does more than present a good story or interesting characters; it plunges the reader into life. It reveals truth about a time, a place, and a people. We should therefore take notice when the protagonist of E.M. Forster's (1879–1970) novel *A Room with a View* (1908), Lucy Honeychurch, tears up outside Basilica di Santa Croce in Florence, Italy. She is without her Baedeker: "How could she find her way home? How could she find her way about in Santa Croce?" Entering the famous Franciscan church, she is without moorings. Where are the famous frescoes by Giotto? Which tomb was "most praised by Mr. Ruskin?" Earlier, in preparation for her day out and before her far more adventurous friend Miss Lavish made off with the Baedeker in an effort to force Lucy to "simply drift," the young tourist had poured over her guidebook carefully memorizing important dates in Florentine history.[1] Such was the obligation of a respectable sightseer.

This episode reveals at least two important pieces of information. First, by the dawn of the twentieth century when Forster wrote the novel, guidebooks were a vital piece of the tourist's packing list, an essential item to be carried everywhere. These books not only provided directions home, they told readers what to value. They promised to tell visitors "what ought to be seen."[2] Second, and closely related, we learn that many travelers were utterly dependent on being given this information. They could not leave home without it. As another character advises Lucy upon learning of her loss, "If you've no Baedeker, you'd better join us" lest she miss out on something important or become otherwise adrift.[3]

Tourism was supposed to make people better: more cultured, educated, relaxed, and healthy. Self-improvement and/or a genuinely rewarding holiday called for an efficacious approach; it demanded a kind of tutor, someone or, as was the case in the nineteenth and twentieth centuries, some*thing* able to provide the right kind of direction and instruction.

Paintings or other images that celebrated particular locations or views, literature, travel narratives, and books written explicitly to tell tourists what to see, where to stay, and how to behave, helped mediate the travel experience. They played (and play) an important role in shaping what one author calls the "tourist gaze,"[4] teaching anxious sightseers how to be tourists and how to improve themselves through seeing vital places. While guidebooks in particular offered instructions about where to eat or sleep, arguably their more important task was to instruct leisure-seekers what to see and how to see it. The manuals directed people where to stand and how to look. Such tips defined tourist landscapes, generated narratives about culture and society, and fueled interpretation of the past.

Guidebooks

Guidebooks in whatever form were not a new addition to the story of travel in the nineteenth century. Pausanias (c.110–c.180 CE), a Romanized-Greek, authored the first "Itinerary-based" guide in 150 CE. He designed it to help Romans to see and enjoy "the temples and other religious sites of Ancient Greece." Later, medieval pilgrims utilized travel guides to follow their pilgrimage routes correctly, finding all of the available holy sites along the way in order to maximize their experience and their acquisition of indulgences. It hardly mattered that the information contained in these books was often "inaccurate, even completely fictional" as long as the pilgrim made it to the church on time. Early Grand Tourists also had their manual: a massive six-volume series weighing five kilos and more useful for home reading than as a companion for travel. More concise handbooks were subsequently printed for those unfortunate enough not to have a tutor in tow.[5]

While there were earlier examples, a profound uptick in the number and variety of guidebooks happened in the nineteenth century. It started before the railways. In Scotland, for example, an 1807 manual entitled *New Picture of Scotland* offered a variety of tours "which plotted the most manageable and interesting means by which to see those sights most peculiar to an area." Steamship operators followed this up in the 1820s with books focused on directing passengers to make the tour of Scotland's Western Isles aboard company steamers.[6]

Yet the real explosion in tourism guidebooks came with the rise of railways. Both authors and publishers hoped to meet the demands (or, perhaps to create them) of a growing middle class that swelled dramatically on the back of industrial expansion.[7] Like the elites of the eighteenth century, the bourgeoisie was anxious to travel. For them, self-improvement was essential.

They worshipped the idea of "self-help." Respectability, a vital component of middle-class identity, was partly borne of possessing culture.[8] Largely based on railway routes, the new breed of tourist handbook provided "five distinctive and fundamental elements: a preface, an introduction, one or more specialist commentaries on the (high) culture of the country, maps (both of the railway network and the geographical areas covered as well as town plans and panoramas), and a comprehensive, mainly geographical, index as a basis for elaborate cross-referencing." Sized for convenience, the books were available in multiple languages because tourists were increasingly drawn from European states other than Britain.[9] In short, Baedeker and the other guidebooks replaced the eighteenth-century tutor and provided the middle-class Victorian with a clear track along which to see everything essential, developing a keen sense of the culture and landscapes of the expanding world around them.

John Murray II (1778–1843) issued among the first in this new wave of guides directed at middle-class tourists in 1836, and Karl Baedeker (1801–59) followed suit shortly thereafter.[10] Numerous others, including package tour organizers such as Thomas Cook and Henry Gaze, joined the frenzy in relatively short order.[11] Even the railway companies, at first reluctant to venture too deeply into promoting tourism themselves, offered a few booklets.[12] Gradually, as the century moved on and as tastes evolved and new forms of tourism arose, a greater and greater diversity of publications appeared. There were guides to mountain climbing,[13] to literary shrines,[14] and to an ever-increasing number of non-European countries.[15] What is more, although the largest market for guidebooks was the middle class, more and more manuals were printed that were aimed at the respectable working class. Such texts focused on particular cities or regions rather than whole countries, allowing time and cashstrapped travelers to see the essentials in short order.[16]

As the Lucy Honeychurch example attests, guidebooks also opened the door for respectable women to travel. Baedekers and the like acted as "a great leveler of knowledge and culture" and, thus, gave women who lacked the same type of education afforded to men the ability to travel in pursuit of adventure and knowledge. Just as Honeychurch memorized the important dates in Florentine history, so could other women master the particulars of great artists, local cultures, historical developments, and literary masterpieces. Consequently women enjoyed much "greater freedom of maneuver" than ever before.[17]

Yet there was a down side. Historian Rudy Koshar begins his history of German travel guidebooks with an anecdote from Bayard Taylor (1825–78), a nineteenth-century American travel writer. Sailing down the Rhine, Taylor was in awe of the scenery, but he was equally taken by the sight of English tourists: "With Murray's Handbook open in their hands, they sat and read about the very towns and towers they were passing, scarcely lifting their eyes to the real scenes, except now and then to observe that it was 'very nice.'"[18] The scene hints at a characteristic of modern tourism: more people of all stripes travel to see the sights, and yet, many of them never escape from a tried and true "beaten track"[19] or even look up from the printed page to *see* what is around them. Because these manuals told nineteenth-century tourists "what ought to be seen," many opted to follow itineraries, failing to "simply drift" as Miss Lavish encouraged Lucy to do. Baedeker and Murray guides represented the "holy scriptures" of tourism and questioning the divinely ordained was not done.[20] The tourists' task was to stand where they were told in order to view a site in a particular way, to visit only specified sites/sights, and to understand the cultures they were gazing upon through pre-defined lenses—to consume what was around them in a particular manner. In some ways, a guidebook was as much a catalogue of products as a holy book for a converted faithful.[21]

There are at least two implications of this. First, because travel guides were written for specific markets, they tended to reflect the biases of their particular audiences while at the same time reinforcing their prejudices. They helped to shape national identities, as well as to define both self and other (an important role, as will become clear in subsequent chapters).[22] Murray's embodied the insularity of Victorian and early Edwardian Britain. Baedeker was undeniably "Germanic."[23] There were sometimes horrible downsides to these viewpoints, including their reflection of European racial and imperialist attitudes. Comments, so closely and uncritically poured over by tourists, could be insulting or worse to the focus of their gaze. One Baedeker manual offered advice on "Intercourse with Orientals," on the one hand advising visitors to be respectful, while on the other declaring Muslims to be "like mere children."[24] Colonial outlooks and superiority were on virtually every page, all the more obvious as the country-specific books expanded to include more and more locations. Locals were children, the Europeans were sophisticated, and imperial holdings, such as India for example, were improved at every turn under paternalist European guidance.[25]

The second implication is that nineteenth-century tourism, at least for the middle classes, focused on a handful of prescribed sites and ways of seeing. Tourist manuals invited readers to look at landscapes, at specified buildings or ruins, and to see places through the eyes of famous writers, even going so far as endeavoring to step into the lives of these individuals. As a result, nineteenth-century tourism was often about the commodification of specific panoramas, built environments, and literary reference points as mediated through texts.

Landscape, history, and the built environment

Eighteenth-century notions of the sublime, beautiful, and romantic did not disappear in the nineteenth century; landscapes and ruins continued to top the list of "must visit" locations. Guidebook writers were anxious to instruct tourists on *how* to see such places. The trick was to capture a view from a specific angle and, perhaps, to sketch it for posterity. Adam and Charles Black, one of the most important publishing houses in nineteenth-century Scotland, for example, directed visitors to one of Scotland's most famous lakes: Loch Lomond. The descriptions in their guidebook present historic narratives, suggestions about sites to visit, and depictions of what might be seen from particular spots. Readers learn that

> Inchcailloch (the Island of Women), [is] so-called from its having been the site of a nunnery. The last named contains the old parish church of Buchanan and the burial-ground of the lairds of MacGregor, and other families claiming descent from the old Scottish King Alpine.

If the historic credentials were not enough, the text pointed out each beautiful hill and advised visitors to climb one in particular from which they could see "the finest views of the loch." Those who were particularly fit were encouraged to climb Ben Lomond itself, for

> It is difficult to describe the scene from the top. Grand and lovely to a high degree, we see on one side the Grampian mountains indefinitely swelling westward, mound after mound; on the west the Argyleshire hills; and on the south and east the great Scottish Lowland district, with its minor mountain ranges.[26]

Such accounts were not limited to Black's, or to Scotland. Karl Baedeker's English-language *Handbook for Travellers on the Rhine, from Switzerland to Holland* (1861) points out similar attractions. The publisher told tourists to the Black Forest to ascend the Blauen, a 3589-foot peak that ranks among the five highest in the region. It is close to the Rhine and offers views of "[f]our different mountain chains" that are "visible to the naked eye." The book also listed other hills, instructions given for transportation to and from, and the promise of beautiful views.[27]

With virtually every handbook reinforcing a similar list of destinations it is little wonder that a particular touristic optics took root.[28] While some disagreed with that aesthetic—favoring more "productive" landscapes such as industrial cities or mines, for example—there was little room for dissention. Defacing the sublime and beautiful was unacceptable. In 1786, for example, William Gilpin (1724–1804), an artist and author associated with helping to create the idea of the picturesque which predominated during the nineteenth century, utilized a footnote in his discussion of England's Lake District to chastise a local landowner for doing "almost everything, that one would wish had been left undone." Landscapes that did not match what "purists of the Picturesque" liked were condemned with "enough violence to provoke some visitors into reasserting the old-fashioned claims of utility and convenience against the new craze for judging gentlemen's estates by the painter's eye alone."[29]

The notion that preserving landscapes and structures was desirable predated such claims, but it certainly picked up steam following the spread of tourism. Pope Pius II (1405–64) passed the first preservationist edict in the fifteenth century and the German philosopher Johann Wolfgang von Goethe pushed the notion of saving historic structures in the 1770s. The French author of *The Hunchback of Notre Dame* (1831), Victor Hugo (1802–85), advocated much the same, claiming "long histories make great peoples." Physical markers of the past stood as evidence of this timelessness.[30] As more tourists followed their travel manuals to ancient piles of stone, preservationist ideas attained still wider circulation. Tourism and preservation had a symbiotic relationship, one fueling the other.[31]

Thus, by the end of the nineteenth century a new breed of preservationist made saving the natural and built environment a priority. In England, the drive to protect attractive places and spaces fueled the foundation of the National Trust, an organization that neatly embodies a view of Englishness coterminous with manor houses, historic sites, and pastoral landscapes. Octavia Hill (1838–1912) first suggested the idea of forming a body tasked with saving English sites in 1884 and she soon had the support of like-minded individuals such as Robert Hunter (1844–1913), Hardwicke Rawnsley (1851–1920), and Hugh Lupus Grosvenor (1825–99).[32] Within a year, they named the nascent organization the National Trust. One year later it acquired its first property. The group participated in the restoration of St. Mary-le-Bow Church in Cheapside, London in 1898. A year later, the National Trust attained its first nature preserve. In 1900, it received a castle.[33] A similar impulse informed the creation of America's national parks, and the idea of creating similar bodies to the Trust eventually spread to other parts of the world, including Ireland (1948),[34] Western Australia (1959),[35] and the United States (1949).[36]

As the list of properties acquired by the National Trust suggests, ruins were every bit as important as landscapes. Gilpin, the poet William Wordsworth, and several artists all made Tintern Abbey famous, for example, because it fulfilled the "picturesque ideal of nature ... so precisely and demandingly imagined by writers on aesthetics." This was a site upon which one could gaze, taken by flights of creative fancy. So many leisure-seekers were anxious to enjoy the experience that beggars clustered around the abbey starting in the last decades of the 1700s.[37] Yet during the nineteenth century tourists also moved beyond simply admiring ruins. Europeans grew interested in the historic value of certain structures. This is reflected in guidebooks' expanded efforts to carefully describe architectural features and historic associations.[38]

As will be discussed in the next chapter, the nineteenth century was an age of nationalism. Born amid both the French and industrial revolutions, this new ideology helped to integrate disparate populations into an increasingly urbanized environment.[39] History played an important part in this effort because it provided national communities with a common yet distinctive sense of the past; national histories could "sustain and develop national identities and allegiance to the nation-state."[40] The provenance of historic sites played into these new narratives. Domestic tourists could come to see their patrimony, foreign ones to view national difference. Travel handbooks led the way and helped to drive further the rise of historic preservation.

Literary tourism

Nineteenth-century writers also promoted a new type of tourism that was not unrelated to landscapes, buildings, and ruins: literary tourism. The notion of meeting with famous authors was not new. James Boswell spent a significant part of his Grand Tour seeking out Enlightenment philosophers such as Jean-Jacques Rousseau (1712–78) and Voltaire (1694–1778).[41] Yet the type of bookish sightseeing that emerged at the dawn of the nineteenth century was different. The authors in question were usually dead, sometimes long so. The new breed of tourist hoped to experience the environment associated with a given writer, to know what it was like to breathe the same air, to walk the same roads and trails, even to stand inside the same buildings. Experiencing written work in a way that expanded upon merely reading a beloved poem, novel, or play motivated literary travelers. You could "visit a dizzying array of places where your chosen author was born, grew up, courted, lived or died, you may visit where your favorite books were written, or places where they are set, and buy the postcard too."[42]

Stratford-upon-Avon, a small town in the English Midlands, inaugurated the trend and attracted the first text-focused tourists. The birthplace of William Shakespeare (1564–1616) features many of the buildings associated with arguably the greatest English playwright. Lovers of *Hamlet* and

Macbeth could see where the Stratford man was born, where he courted his wife, and where he was buried. Fans first arrived for a two-hundredth anniversary celebration in 1769 and they never stopped coming.[43] The central attraction was (and is) a "three-story timber framed building from the sixteenth century." It may or may not be the actual birthplace, but this detail seems largely irrelevant to the legions anxious to experience "England's Poet" in the most tactile way possible. A private trust purchased the building as a national memorial in 1847 and within five years it already attracted 2000+ visitors annually. In 1874, interested parties launched a Shakespeare Memorial Trust to establish a theatre. Other buildings, such as Anne Hathaway's cottage and Mary Arden's House, subsequently joined the pantheon of must-see locations. Town planners either razed or simply ignored buildings that were not built in the sixteenth century—even much older medieval structures. Tourists wanted to experience what they imagined to be William Shakespeare's Stratford-upon-Avon, seeing what *he* saw, breathing the air that *he* breathed, and doing so in a prescribed manner.[44] Visitors could engage in a secular pilgrimage, moving from station to station in a nearly liturgical manner outlined by the likes of Karl Baedeker, who used very methodical, directed language to guide readers around the town. People were to start at the birthplace, noting that the timber framework was largely "unaltered" from Shakespeare's day. From there, visitors walked up High Street, past an Elizabethan building undoubtedly known to the Bard, en route to see a statue and portraits of the playwright at the town hall. Next, they ventured up Chapel Street to "the New Place, the site of the house in which Shakespeare resided on his return to Stratford in later life, and where he died on April 23, 1616." On and on the tourist traipsed: to a mulberry tree, to see the burial site, to enjoy "pleasant" views of the Avon River, and to take in "jarring statues" added almost contemporary to publication of the guidebook.[45]

Stratford-upon-Avon might be the first literary tourist destination, but it is not the last or even the most popular. According to the 1887 Baedeker handbook, 13,000 to 14,000 wandered Stratford each year, "while over 30,000 annually visit the birthplace of [Robert] Burns, near Ayr"[46]—the second major literary tourist site to develop in Britain. Burns, the Scottish national poet, was born on January 25, 1759 in Alloway, Ayrshire. It is, and remains, a small agricultural community in the Scottish Lowlands. He lived in a variety of other locations before dying in Dumfries in July 1796.[47] Burns's poems are rich with local color, depicting engaging characters and scenic beauty in a manner that captured the late eighteenth and nineteenth-century imagination like few others. For this reason, Ayrshire and its environs attracted rapidly growing throngs within only a few years of the poet's death. Tourists wanted to see the churchyard where Tam o' Shanter, one of the more famous literary dipsomaniacs, encountered a gaggle of partying witches. Visitors dreamed of then crossing the bridge over which the hapless drunk escaped from those magical emissaries of Satan. As at Stratford, seeing the writer's birthplace was a priority as well. Three years after Burns died, poet Richard Gall (1776–1801) wrote "Verses written on visiting the house in which the celebrated Robert Burns was Born, and the Surrounding Scenery, in Autumn 1799," describing the sensations experienced while seeing "Whare infant Genius wont to smile."[48] *Scots Magazine* carried an engraving of the cottage in 1805. In 1818, visitors found carefully placed portraits of the poet at sites associated with him. By 1838 the landowner provided "a regular visitors' 'album'" at the birthplace and some 350 evidently made the pilgrimage to the house in September alone. Guidebooks and carefully delineated Burns tourist routes followed,[49] often including snippets of poetry where appropriate. Oliver and Boyd's *Scottish Tourist* (1852) is a case in point, offering Burns tourists not only bits of verse, but careful mention of farmsteads occupied by Burns, the rent that he paid in various places, sites mentioned in the poems, and the precise locations where he authored particular works.[50]

Not all were satisfied. The great English poet, John Keats (1795–1821), for example, traveled to Scotland in 1818 in an effort to follow his literary hero. He made his way to the birthplace, "ready for a marvelous experience" but was horrified by what he found. The homestead was now a public house and "the landlord, one of Burns's old drinking buddies, annoyed and depressed Keats with his stories about the dead poet." Keats had wanted to write a brilliant poem under Burns's roof, instead what he penned was a disappointment and he blamed the drunken proprietor.[51] Nathaniel Hawthorne (1804–64), the great American writer, was evidently even more distressed. He visited in 1857 and, forgetting that Burns was born into a poor farming family, bitterly complained that the cottage was "inconceivably small, considering how large a space it fills in our imagination before we see it." Just as terrible, it smelled.[52]

Enthusiasts added more sites to the literary tourist trail. Pilgrims could see William Wordsworth's Lake District,[53] visit Walter Scott's Abbotsford estate,[54] look for the Brontës' Yorkshire,[55] or slum in Dickens' London.[56] This branch of tourism did not end with the water's edge. Thus, in the United States, Harriet Beecher Stowe (1811–96) attracted tourists[57] and Rider Haggard (1856–1925) drew visitors to South Africa where they sought the sites depicted in *King Solomon's Mines* (1885).[58]

Like landscapes or historic places, literary sites virtually demanded that tourists step into a world of sublime and beautiful imaginings. Such locations could be a useful resource for developers, such as railway companies anxious to draw visitors. Henry Wadsworth Longfellow's (1807–82) poem

"Evangeline: A Tale of Acadie," written in 1847, is a case in point. It tells the story of a young woman's lost love, set against a rustic Nova Scotia backdrop. While the story is compelling, the evocative accounts of scenery are equally notable. Longfellow describes a "forest primeval" that is "bearded with moss, and in garments green." There is a "thatch-roofed village" filled with Acadian farmers. As is true of much good literature, when one reads the poem it is difficult not to *feel* the place. The Annapolis Railway Company, later renamed the Dominion Atlantic Railway Company, recognized the potential touristic appeal of the saga and consequently branded Nova Scotia the "Land of Evangeline" beginning in the early 1880s. They named their trains according to the poem, included images of a lovely young woman in their marketing materials, and whisked visitors along the "Land of Evangeline Route." Together, the company sent a message that "the setting for the poem and the land owned by the railway were one and the same." As Keats discovered when he visited the Robert Burns birthplace, the reality of the imagination did not match up with physical truth. There was "little in the area able to live up to Longfellow's imagination."[59] Bits and pieces were present, but the totality was certainly not there. It did not matter. Reality can be created and the imagination can fill in tremendous gaps.

Wish you were here

Tourism is also mediated visually. Although postcards are a nineteenth-century invention,[60] the notion of collecting inexpensive artwork has deeper and more multinational roots. Popular prints have attracted the public from at least the eighteenth century. Printmakers such as William Hogarth (1697–1764) succeeded financially and by so doing created an astonishing visual record of the time in which they worked. For example, just after the end of a period of dizzying gin consumption in London, sometimes called "gin mania," Hogarth released two prints that drew an impressive response: *Beer Street* and *Gin Lane*. The prints captured the horror that shot through respectable society at the thought of working-class people, especially women, getting spifflicated on spirits. Gin Lane shows a woman dropping her baby from a staircase amid all manner of destitution. The only businesses excelling on Gin Lane are the coffin maker and the pawnbroker. By contrast, Beer Street features happy industrious people going about their daily lives. Today these illustrations are essential sources for historians.[61] During the seventeenth century they represented affordable art, not unlike postcards.

Dr. Heinrich von Stephen (1831–97), a German postmaster, first proposed the postcard as a means of correspondence in 1865. The idea was immediately shot down. The Austrians revived it three years later. Within only one month, 1.5 million picture-less cards were sold. Cheaper than sending a letter, the cards represented an affordable way to keep in touch with friends and loved ones. By October 1870, every European country offered postcards. The United States followed in 1873.

Postcard historians debate when pictures were first added to the cards. The Swiss included mountain scenery as early as 1872. The Germans might have predated this with images of their newly unified state. Either way, advertising was quick to appear on cards, as were overtly nationalist images. Postcards had the power to sell, whether a consumer product or a national identity. During the 1880s, for example, Germans used them as a means of publicizing important national monuments such as the *Hermannsdenkmal* statue near Grotenburg—a massive structure featuring a giant representation of "Herman the German," a national military hero who defeated the Romans at the Battle of Teutoburg Forest in 9 CE. The French took things further by issuing an Eiffel Tower postcard at the Paris Exposition of 1889. Rather than simply release the cards, fair officials made it possible to buy, write on, and mail them from the observation deck of the tower itself—perhaps the first opportunity to say: "You'll never believe where I'm writing to you from" and really mean it. Other sites such as Mount Snowdon in Wales followed with a similar service complete with a postmark that verified the author's location at the time of composing.

Initially, governments limited the utility of postcards by refusing to allow their use beyond national borders. Popularity increased dramatically following an international agreement regarding acceptable sizes as well as the use and dimension of images. The resulting standard from very early on was 5.5 × 3.5 inches, though British officials refused to accept this until 1894 when they finally gave up on demands for 4.5 × 3.5-inch measurements.[62] For a number of years writers were not allowed to pen their messages on the same side of the card as the address. This meant that images could only take up part of the front of the card. The British proposed including a line down the back that divided the sender's greetings from the recipient's location. This innovation made it possible for images to occupy the entire front side. Other countries were slow to agree, only consenting to the idea over a period of time between 1905 and 1907, assuring that British cards had limited reach abroad.[63]

After various governments finally settled upon common standards, postcards quickly caught on. People began collecting them and keeping carefully maintained scrapbooks of their finds. Cards ranged from photographs to paintings, to national symbols, to beauty spots, to political messages.[64]

There were bawdy cards issued at seaside resorts that featured questionable humor.[65] In one card, which ran afoul of censors, a man is depicted on the beach with an attractive young woman leaning on his shoulder. He tells her: "I must send a postcard to the missus, but I haven't got anything exciting to tell her!" The wife, meanwhile, sprints into the upper left of the card with an angry look on her face and a nasty looking club in her hand.[66]

As the cards gained popularity, they became what ethnologist Orvar Löfgren describes as "a powerful medium for organizing and presenting ideas about vacation preferences, tastes, and attractions." They reinforced how people saw landscape or other scenery and therefore contributed to what Löfgren calls a "marked conservatism of scenic viewing." People tended to look at the world from the vantage point of the postcard, reproducing the same views and perspectives: "[O]nce scenery has been institutionalized through various media it becomes in a way frozen and taken out of time."[67] The desirable scene was the postcard scene, or the guidebook perspective. It was not that postcards remained stagnant, never changing or evolving, or that new perspectives never again emerged after the first photographer printed an image on a card for widespread distribution, rather that particular tropes developed and became enshrined. These images were markers of the tourist experience to be recreated in drawings and then tourist snapshots following the development of easily transported cameras.

Conclusion

Even as guidebooks, postcards, and other technologies tell tourists what ought to be seen and how to see it, consumers have a voice too. Photographers and guidebook writers must react to their audience every bit as much as the reader or viewer responds to the guide. For instructions to be effective, somebody needs to study them. John Hinde Studios, an Ireland-based postcard production business that started operations in the 1950s, presents an excellent example. Although color postcards existed previously, new photography and printing advancements during the 1930s and 1940s created the possibility for much wider use of color photographs as well as of considerably more vivid tones. John Hinde (1916–97) believed that the new technology offered an opportunity, thinking that consumers wanted color—and lots of it—in their postcards. He developed a new style: "By introducing bright foreground colours in his cards… He stuck primary colours prominently in the foreground to accentuate to viewers that, yes, they were looking at a COLOUR photograph… He was shrewd enough to realise that an audience used to seeing black and white pictures didn't just want to see a bit of colour tinting, it wanted to see a COLOUR PHOTOGRAPH."[68] Hinde did not simply wish to *believe* that this is what consumers wanted, he needed to *know*. As a result, John Hinde spent the night in Shannon Airport with a notebook listening to what customers had to say.[69] Armed with this information, the photographer began issuing postcards featuring deep blue skies, hyper-green grass, and splotches of bright red, whether in clothing or blossoms. He carefully staged his compositions, even going so far as to place flowers into scenes in order to introduce the right reds and purples.[70]

For John Hinde and his photographers, it was critical to meet consumer demand, whatever it took. One story can stand for others. The plan was to capture an Aran Island fisherman working on his nets while a group of men launch a boat in the background—a classic image that played on ideas of nostalgia for an idyllic past and on romantic notions of the hardy Irish fisherman. Every tourist knows that such men wear authentic Aran

Fishermen on the Aran Islands, Co. Galway, Ireland.
Photo: D. Noble, John Hinde Studios.

Figure 5.1 John Hinde provided postcard buyers with images that showcased color, but that also captured scenes in a way that the consumer expected. A careful study of this picture shows men carrying a boat to water's edge in their Sunday suits and a fisherman in a sweater several sizes too small, but it also captures an appealing view of life in the Aran Islands of Ireland that proved tremendously popular with tourists. Image courtesy of John Hinde Archive. Copyright and trademark, John Hinde Archive.

sweaters—much like those carried in many an Irish souvenir shop today. The problem was that the actual fishermen were apparently unaware of the dress code. There was only one sweater on the island. It was tiny and full of holes. The photographer still needed his shot, however, so he posed the fisherman in such a way that the holes did not show and he positioned the sleeves so that it was not immediately obvious that they were several inches too short. That was not the only challenge though. The fishermen launching their boat in the background arrived at the shoot immediately after leaving church. With no chance to change, they marched boldly into the water in their Sunday best, certainly not a usual practice among fishermen. From a sales standpoint, the effort was a success and the resultant postcard proved immensely popular with consumers who beat a path to the shops to buy copies.[71]

Ultimately, tourism is as much about ideas as it is specific places and spaces. Guidebook publishers, authors, photographers, and artists have long mediated the meanings attributed to various sites as well as the ways in which those spots should be experienced. This reality forms a vital element of modern tourism and it assures that leisure travel is well placed to forward ideas about collective identity, common cultural characteristics, and distinctions relative to other groups. It generates and builds upon a sense of difference. Little wonder that tourism plays a role in the creation and perpetuation of national identities, as will become obvious in subsequent chapters.

But guidebooks also present a paradox, raising the old distinction between tourists and travelers that emerged during the Grand Tour when some members of the landed aristocracy fiercely questioned the merits of sending teenage boys to France or Italy where they might get into all sorts of trouble without ever learning more than a word or two of the local vernacular or acquiring even a shred of information about the culture. Being respectable during the nineteenth century required using a guidebook, just as a successful Grand Tour was contingent on the employment of a qualified and motivated tutor. Yet after tourism started to attract more and more people drawn from across the class spectrum, guidebooks had the effect of creating what historian James Buzard called a "beaten track." Everybody followed essentially the same routes, saw the same things, and became just like everybody else.[72] This is a significant problem for groups anxious to distinguish themselves from others, as is apparent when members of the aristocracy, the middle, and the working class all refused to occupy the same beach. Where one spent their free time and how they spent it mattered.

The challenge is that social prestige through travel comes partly from seeing something different, from branching out and going one's own way.

It demands that people demonstrate individualism. Lucy Honeychurch begins *A Room with a View* as a tourist, wedded to her Baedeker. By the end of the novel she returns to Italy with her new husband and without her guidebook. The novel is about her development, about her acceptance of being an individual and her willingness to step outside of strict social conventions. The loss of her Baedeker can therefore be read as an indication of her growth as a human being; it is a statement of a sense of personal uniqueness and it defines her as stepping off the beaten track.

Many tourists probably imagine themselves to be travelers rather than tourists, even as they delve deeply into the pages of their Baedekers. They are distinct, different from the rest, breaking free of the maddening crowd. Consuming one holiday destination or another, engaging in one form of tourism or another, is a mode of self-expression—every bit as much as buying one type of car over another makes a statement. Image producers such as John Hinde Studios and guidebook publishers following in the footsteps of John Murray must recognize this, even as they inform their users how to see the world. The interplay of perceived self-expression combined with the ability of tourism to present powerful messages about self and other made leisure travel a potentially potent political tool—a major theme as tourism continued to evolve.

6

Tourism in an age of empires and nationalism

The nineteenth century was an "age of empire,"[1] a period when European countries, led by Great Britain, assumed control of territory around the world. Related news coverage, travel accounts, adventure stories, and exotic art circulated widely.[2] Perhaps as a result, people in both Europe and the United States grew more interested in the world around them. Some pursued colonial service. Others avidly followed accounts of far-off adventure in the pages of books or newspapers, such as Henry Morton Stanley's description of his search for Dr. David Livingstone.[3] Still others either set out alone, or joined an organized tour, to see the world.

It was also a century of nationalism. At first, this meant building a sense of liberal community beyond social class, a notion that people were part of something larger than themselves and that their efforts at work represented more than a paycheck. Modern industrial society demanded "a certain kind of egalitarianism" because "[m]en can tolerate terrible inequalities, if they are stable and hallowed by custom."[4] At the same time, members of a nation are equal because "regardless of the actual inequality and exploitation that may prevail in each, the nation is always conceived as a deep, horizontal comradeship."[5] During the second half of the century the message changed. Nationalism became more exclusive. It was about who was in and who was out, about difference.[6] Racial science, a new development during the second half of the century,[7] offered one explanation of otherness as well as the possibility for hierarchy: white races above others, but even they were divided into strata with Anglo-Saxons superior to Celts, for example.[8] For imperialists, it was surprisingly easy to merge race, nation, and empire and to use the notion of white European superiority to justify everything from the governance of far-off places to the murder of whole populations as happened under British rule in Tasmania.[9]

Travel afforded one way in which group members and the *other* were distinguished from each other and this "interaction of the self with the outside world" allowed "the European psyche" to "refine" itself, "seeking knowledge and power, but also self-understanding ... through this deliberately sought encounter with the world."[10] While small numbers of both men and women had long traveled widely beyond the confines of Europe,[11] the advent of steam power between roughly 1850 and World War I made tourism on a global scale possible for far more people. Package tour companies such as that of Henry Gaze and his far more famous rival Thomas Cook & Son made it feasible for even members of the middle class to make long trips. Yet travel "abroad" could take place closer to home. Beginning in 1851, regular "world's fairs" were held in various European cities, showcasing what countries could be proud of, both nearby and abroad. These events represented a chance to explore multiple countries without actually boarding a ship or crossing an ocean.

Tourism thus spread beyond Europe. Non-European governments could capitalize by forming alliances with tour operators. There was money in promoting leisure travel and it was useful as a means of pointing to differences between communities. As noted in the previous chapter, guidebook writers were not above depicting foreign groups as "children" and therefore as inferiors. As discussed below, it was possible to utilize tourist attractions as a means of advancing positive national stereotypes and of forming imagined communities. The nascent United States, for example, could forward a particular variety of tourist sites in order to show that America was different from other places and that it had much to offer and a good deal about which to be proud. Tourism had a class politics, a fact seen clearly at the seaside, and there was also a national and an international politics: a growing economic, cultural, and social significance.

World's fairs: The world in one place

The British Empire was well established by 1850. While excitement was not universal, there were those who were intensely pleased with British imperial efforts and none more so than the Prince Consort, Queen Victoria's husband Prince Albert. Members of a committee anxious to hold a national exhibition—Henry Cole (1808–82), John Scott Russell (1808–82), Thomas Cubitt (1788–1855), and Francis Fuller (1807–87)—met with Albert in late June of 1849 to suggest holding a "Great Exhibition" in 1851. They wanted a chance to celebrate Britain while promoting "exhibition, competition, encouragement." The Prince Consort enthusiastically endorsed the plan and set to work helping to make the event a reality.[12] He believed that an exhibition would "lessen international hostility by demonstrating the similarity of men's interests everywhere." Of course, it would also promote British objectives both inside the country and without, showcasing its remarkable worldwide accomplishments.[13]

The 1851 Great Exhibition took place in a majestic "Crystal Palace," situated in Hyde Park, London and it proved to be a resounding success. As noted previously, Thomas Cook and other package tour operators transported large numbers of trippers to London to experience the display. Nearly 60,000 foreigners traveled to the capital to take part; as many as 100,000 people per day visited during the summer months.[14] The success proved infectious. Other countries soon promoted their own events. New York hosted a fair in 1853. Paris did so in 1855, 1867, 1878, 1889, and 1900. Vienna put on an exposition in 1873, Philadelphia in 1876, Sydney in 1879 and Melbourne in 1880. Boston hosted a similar event in 1883 and Chicago offered up an epic fair in 1893.[15] Attendance at these spectacles was high. The Paris Exposition Universelle et Internationale in 1900 set the ultimate record; more than 50 million people.[16] Between 1851 and 1937, 200 million people traveled to world's fairs in Europe alone.[17] These were the first "global gatherings of mass numbers of people" and they arguably stand as "the most important international mass events of the modern era."[18]

For attendees, world's fairs promised something remarkable: a chance to experience myriad places while physically visiting just one. As one fair-goer enthused:

> The Grande Avenue formed the border between France and England, and with a single leap we could get from England to Mexico or into a log cabin of the North American hinterland. "I promised to meet with a friend in Morocco, could you be so kind as to show me the way?" "Gladly. You start here from North America via Italy, pass between Tunisia and Egypt, leave Syria on your right, at the Temple of Edfou turn in the direction of China, … and turn, when you see the tower of Romania on your right, into the street, which leads straight on Morocco lies before you. In half an hour, you can be back in Russia." I have to admit that such a route seems fantastic enough, though crossed the globe in even stranger leaps later on, irrespective of language, conventions, and customs of the peoples, whom I wanted to visit in their own house, or whose territory I had to cross.[19]

One could "visit 'the world' with a journey to just one place, just one city." Countries competed with one another to showcase distinctiveness. National "villages" were built, reflecting the unique styles and architecture of each country. Attendees could see "authentic" Indian wigwams from the United

States, experience "Oriental" street scenes,[20] and even watch beautiful Irish peasant girls serve milk from real Irish cows.[21] Indigenous peoples from Africa, Asia, or South America "welded the otherwise separated European onlookers together, united in a specific view of the non-white 'other' as strange, inferior, and backward."[22] Food from around the world was available, including spicy dishes that were as yet exotic to European palates.[23] One could see curious dances and masks from far-flung places, drink exotic teas, and explore interesting architecture. Foreign languages were there to hear and even new ones debuted—Esperanto made its first appearance on the world stage at the 1900 Paris exhibition.[24] Even the people touring these fairs amounted to part of the exhibit. Although elites all dressed very much the same by 1900, "it was still expected that the bourgeoisie of each nation would dress distinctively. Peasants flocked to Paris in 1900 and wore their ... national costumes."[25]

New display technologies constituted a perennial element of each successive fair as members of participant countries endeavored to present a desirable image of themselves to the international community. Whenever one strategy proved successful, it was adopted by others and reintroduced at a later event.[26] Presentations that worked well also found their way into the day-to-day marketing of a place: "changes ... trickled down on activities on the national, regional, or local level."[27] In other words, the process of competing for recognition at the fairs helped to define the presentation of national spaces, places, and people: feeding the process of inventing modern European nations and their external "other."

The progression was not always straightforward and competition could be as marked within a particular national community as it was between nation-states. So it was that two separate women developed Irish villages for the Chicago fair in 1893. Presentations overlapped somewhat, but varied significantly in other respects. One promised a traditional Donegal village. The other pretended to encompass all that was Irish. They offered "different approaches to home industries and rural poverty in Ireland," diverging thanks to the conflicting social views of their creators, Alice Hart (1848–1931), a merchant's daughter, and Lady Aberdeen (1847–1939), an aristocrat with an obsession with her Scottish ancestry and title.[28] Between them, the villages demonstrate the challenge of developing a singular national product when there was sometimes minimal consensus about the invented traditions that comprise any given modern nation.[29]

All of this had important implications. As historian Cristina Della Coletta points out, "World's Fairs became catalysts of popular taste and promoters of mass culture. They gathered all social classes around bourgeois values and drew the lower social strata into modern market economies and consumption systems." The fairs themselves were painstakingly constructed, of course. They offered "carefully managed aesthetic and pedagogical messages," tied together through an elaborate process of mapping. They were "utopias of readability" and fair-goers were "empowered ... to play the part of universal interpreters when scouting, reconnoitering, and mapping these ordered compendia of the world."

The expositions were tremendously persuasive. Visitors were "convinced that they were watching a veritable compendium of the world, concentrated in a few square miles." Fairs made the world "knowable."[30] It was as if the visitor had actually seen distant lands, internalized the notion that doing so was desirable, and gained a sense of accomplishment at having successfully "read it" all at the same time. Most would never take travel further. They could not afford to. But the fairs nevertheless supported the idea that touring abroad is desirable as well as stressing notions of self and other in the face of a world growing evermore globalized due to steam-based propulsion.

Colonialism, package tours, and the start of global tourism

The relationship between empire and travel was not new. For example, the stability provided by the Ottoman Empire—which emerged in the fourteenth century and lasted until just after World War I—facilitated mobility.[31] Citizens moved about in pursuit of trade, family visits, and religious pilgrimage. Elites may even have traveled for leisure.[32] Yet nineteenth century imperialism was different. It took place on a grander scale, extending over much of the globe. Likewise it developed at a time when tourism was growing in Europe and America, the standard of living was rising, and transportation was more widely available and efficient. There was a window of opportunity and some people sought to benefit. Muhammad Ali of Egypt (1769–1849) is a case in point. Between the end of the Napoleonic Wars in 1815 and 1848 he endeavored to provide transportation and infrastructure in order to attract visitors to his country.[33] At the same time imperial powers such as Great Britain sometimes used tourism to promote crown authority, to create the infrastructure needed to maintain political and military might, and even to generate positive relationships within their sphere of influence. Leisure travel could help form tighter bonds with Egypt that might be useful. Such synergy meant that tourism "was inseparable from the west's conquest of the Middle East"[34] and probably of other territories as well.

It is somewhat surprising that, despite separate and growing literatures on tourism and empire, historians have yet to systematically explore connections between the two.[35] What does exist is largely focused on particular areas such as Canada, Jamaica, and Egypt, on the activities of Thomas Cook & Son, and on the evolution of leisure travel in the United States, a former British colony whose tourism advocates used the industry to create a unique identity relative to the Old Country. Historian Eric T. Jennings traces the relationship between French imperialism, travel, and health.[36] There are also a small number of publications addressing "hill stations" created by colonial elites in India during the Raj, sites that offered healthy sanctuary from lowland heat as well as more comfortable locations from which officials could govern.[37] The picture that emerges is limited, but it does offer a sense of how tourism spread and of the shape that it took in differing contexts. Colonies, and even former colonies, offered a range of sites/sights for various tastes. Such variety meant that people could define themselves by the places they visited and by the people they saw there, while the destinations could emphasize unique qualities in an effort to establish separate identities.

Where the wild things are: Canada

Eighteenth and nineteenth-century elites believed hunting to be the height of masculine respectability. Doing it properly demanded following established rituals and practices, all carefully taught and learned in Britain's exclusive public boarding schools such as Eton, Harrow, and Rugby.[38] Aristocrats jealously guarded the rights and traditions associated with hunting. In Great Britain, the Black Act threatened death to those caught shooting or trapping illegally on private lands.[39] In India, preventing natives from engaging in this white man's pursuit led to legislation, anxious efforts to define the Indian people as effeminate and therefore unworthy of carrying a weapon, and considerable spilled ink communicating the problem to anybody who could read.[40]

During the nineteenth century, the British Empire provided sportsmen with a remarkable opportunity to seek out larger game, to venture into terrifying remote areas, and to demonstrate self-control and restraint under potentially scary circumstances. Big-game hunters could reaffirm "the superiority and rightness of British character, conduct, and ideals." Writing about the experience "reassured imperial readers at home that white hunters remained civilized in the face of primitive cultures and the savage frontier."[41] At the same time, the larger the trophy and the more one received, the greater the hunter's "masculine prowess,"[42] and, one assumes, status as a powerful figure in British society.

India, Africa, and Canada all offered superb opportunities for the pursuit of big game. Prince Rupert's Land, the area surrounding the Hudson's Bay, was among the most important places in North America in this regard.

While Scotland was closer to home and afforded hunters the chance to chase red deer,[43] the mighty moose provided far greater rewards and could be pursued amid a still more expansive sublime landscape. At first the number of visitors to the region was small and confined exclusively to the very elite, but by the 1880s the Canadian Pacific Railway launched an aggressive advertising campaign designed to celebrate the picturesque excitement of hunting in Canada's untamed places.[44]

At the same time, Canada handed visitors a confrontation with a primitive exotic, whether people or wild animals. The backwoods of the country represented a temporary escape from the "civilized world." Meeting native people further emphasized this distance, offering an authentic encounter with a rapidly disappearing past.[45] One sightseer described "the strange sensation one has, thus thrown for a time beyond the bounds of civilized humanity."[46] Tourists were able to disembark from their steamship and to cast their eyes over the native Ojibwe population, seeing "native life first hand, always superficially and at times intrusively." While members of First Nations did sell various handicrafts and could attain some money by providing goods and services, their more important role for tourists was to offer an "other" which reinforced the experience of escape for European tourists. Natives provided whites the appearance of authentic difference and so helped to assure them of their self-identified civility.

Exchange moved in at least two directions: tourists were attracted to wildness and nascent Canadian identity was connected to the natural world and demanding conditions. Canada was closely aligned with Britain through much of the nineteenth century—despite gaining dominion status in 1867, it followed Westminster's lead in international politics until just before World War II[47]—but that did not negate a sense of difference. The challenge was to arrive at "signs and symbols with which to assert national identity." For Canadians, this meant devising a contrast with the "picturesque English landscape" and "the raw beauty of the Precambrian Shield could readily constitute such a vehicle of national meaning and feeling in Canada."[48] Creating deeply felt national identities does not happen overnight. It takes time, requiring an exchange of ideas about what it means to be inside or outside of a group.[49] The arrival of tourists anxious to confront wilderness certainly played a part in that process.

Tourism in the tropics: Jamaica

While Canada represented a sublime, exotic, and adventurous tourist destination during the nineteenth century, Jamaica and other tropical locations were something else altogether. For most Europeans, the island had long represented little more than a place to make money through sugar production. Then, when the bottom fell out of the sugar industry and many planters returned to Europe, former slaves who were subjected to some of the most shameful treatment ever meted out by one man to another turned to violence in an effort to acquire their own land in 1831. For Britain, the island now represented a political and military nightmare.[50]

Above all, however, Jamaica and its island neighbors represented a "graveyard for white folks," a place where one was far more likely to catch malaria, yellow fever, any of a number of strains of distemper, dropsy, dysentery, leprosy, cholera, typhoid, or yaws than to enjoy a relaxing holiday. Such illnesses were virtually inescapable. British troops stationed there died at an alarming rate of 121.3 per thousand between 1817 and 1836.[51] African slaves had a better chance of survival because they acquired resistance to diseases such as malaria before being ripped from their homes. Once in the New World, and assuming that they continued to be bitten repeatedly by infected mosquitos, they maintained it. White slave owners were less fortunate. They tended to die before attaining immunity.[52] Even after the sugar industry collapsed, for Europeans, Jamaica was a place to be avoided, not a place to fantasize about or visit.

Although it was widely believed that little could be done to fix the problem, evolving understanding of the causes of disease during the second half of the nineteenth century gradually reduced the risk of sickness and death. For example, when scientists realized that polluted water may result in an illness such as cholera, typhoid, or dysentery, efforts were made to improve the water supply, moving away from the use of wells that were "saturated with decayed excreta" to filtered water piped into towns from a sanitary reservoir. Officials also tried to expand sewerage, to develop accommodations, to move settlements away from mosquito-infested swamps, and to increase hygienic precautions throughout the population.[53]

The reduction of disease created an important condition of possibility for tourism, but there were other challenges that entrepreneurs and the British colonial administration had to overcome: a shortage of accommodation and the long-term negative perception of Jamaica among potential leisure travelers. Despite these issues, there were those who believed that tourism represented a way to make money. American banana traders led the way. Fruit companies already operated steamships to and from the island, calling at important ports such as Boston, New York, Philadelphia, and Baltimore. It was easy enough to offer round-trip passage to Jamaica, assuming, of course, that hotels existed to host the visitors after arriving on the island. Consequently, the growers set about constructing a 150-room facility called Hotel Titchfield.[54]

The colonial government was equally aware of the need for housing. Hotel Titchfield aside, most available lodging was truly subpar: unpleasant with unsanitary rooms, located mostly in taverns, both bug-infested and moth-eaten. To right this wrong, the government passed legislation, the Jamaica Hotels Law of 1890, in the hope of inspiring the erection of more suitable lodging. A number of hotel companies quickly formed and building construction soon followed. Service frequently remained poor and profits did not match expectations, at least prior to World War I, but the changes paved the way for future development.[55]

The secret to filling beds was to transform attitudes about tropical destinations, to create a sense of these places as something other than a health risk. Potential sightseers needed to believe in the desirability of where they were going—certain that an adventure would be forthcoming without proving fatal. Publicity took two forms. On one hand, Jamaican authorities held an international exhibition in 1891 in order to encourage investment and to inspire visitors.[56] On the other, the Merchant's Exchange met in February 1904 to push the creation of a tourism bureau that would look after guests while also producing various guidebooks and advertising. It took time and the Jamaica Tourist Association did not formally launch until September 1910.[57]

There are no tourism statistics for Jamaica prior to 1906. In that year, 7000 people visited the island. In the years thereafter, growth was rather unspectacular. There were 4023 tourists in 1911–12, 11,318 the next year, and just 3000 the one after. The country was rumored to be too expensive for all but those with money and it had a reputation for exploiting people.[58] Nevertheless, before the Great War colonial administrators and private companies took important steps toward making the island safer to see, creating infrastructure, and changing perceptions about what a stay at a tropical, sunny destination might provide. In the years after World War I, numbers increased dramatically: more than 11,000 in 1926, over 26,000 in 1930, and in excess of 65,000 in 1937.[59] Attitudes had clearly altered.

Packaging the world: Australia, Egypt, and beyond

While developers in Canada and Jamaica gradually attracted more and more visitors, perhaps the largest single factor driving the globalization of tourism was the effort of package tour companies. These organizations, often with the support and encouragement of local administrators, worked tirelessly to magnify the infrastructure, promotional materials, and travel packages necessary to draw large numbers of sightseers to places such as Egypt, Palestine, and Australia. The long-term implications of their efforts could be dramatic. Thus, for example, at least one historian argues that Thomas Cook is almost entirely responsible for the development of tourism in Australia starting in the early 1870s.[60]

Package operators did not create the Egyptian tourism industry out of nothing. Ancient Egypt interested outsiders almost from the first. "[T]he pharaohs' monumental buildings" fascinated the first Greek historian, Herodotus. As noted in the introduction, Roman travelers were anxious to visit Egypt and were absolutely astonished by what they saw there. Both British and French elites were captivated by Egypt during the eighteenth and early nineteenth centuries. Thus, when Napoleon Bonaparte (1769–1821) invaded the country in 1798 he took Egyptologists with him and endeavored to collect as many artifacts as he could.[61] Victorians were so obsessed that even a cursory meander through many nineteenth-century British or American manor houses will yield Egyptian artifacts or even mummies, while a short walk through rural cemeteries such as Highgate in London or Mount Auburn in Cambridge, Massachusetts reveals numerous grave monuments featuring pyramids, sphinxes, and the like.

After the Napoleonic Wars and as a result of the waning power of the Ottoman Empire, Great Britain gradually gained influence in Egypt. Nominal command was held by Egyptians such as Muhammad Ali, who ruled from 1805 until 1848. During the first half of the century, Britain grudgingly supported the Ottomans, only to assume greater and greater direct control after construction began on the Suez Canal in 1855 (completed in 1869). British authorities insisted that the country was self-governing—a claim maintained even after the crown purchased a dominant share of the Suez Canal in 1875, forcing the Colonial Office in London to secure its investment by asserting evermore power in both Egypt and neighboring Sudan.[62]

With fiscal challenges to solve, Ali recognized the economic possibilities of tourism and he did his best to open the country to tourists immediately after Napoleon's collapse in 1815. By 1819, Egypt represented a comparatively peaceful and inviting destination.[63] Outsiders were impressed. Alexander Crawford (1812–80), for example, commented "Whatever one's opinion of the Pasha's domestic policy, travellers owe him much, for throughout his dominions (in Egypt and Syria, at least) they may travel in the Frank dress with perfect safety."[64] Ali left behind a country in which "tourism was a feature of life ... with all its component parts, transportation, lodging, established sights, accepted routes, supporting travel literature, guidebooks, and locals engaging in trinket sales and sightseeing services. Consequently, more and more Europeans made the trip; as many as 20,000 tourists traveled to Egypt each year by 1850."[65]

This environment was very attractive to package tour companies and especially to Thomas Cook & Son. Cook and his son, John Mason,[66] initially surveyed the Middle East, Turkey, Syria/Palestine, and Egypt in

Figure 6.1 During the second half of the nineteenth century, the Thomas Cook & Son travel agency developed an extensive tourism network in Egypt and attracted large numbers of female, as well as male, clients anxious to see ancient sites. Photo courtesy of Thomas Cook Archives, Peterborough, UK.

1868 and he led his first tour a year later in the spring of 1869. There were challenges: finding suitable translators, currency issues, and various obstructions arising from a few government officials. On this last point, Cook soon noted the importance of fostering close relations with people in power. He did not waste time and quickly developed a friendship with the Viceroy and other key officers in Egypt and Palestine. Cook was especially keen to nurture ties to colonial officers for

> [w]ithout the protection of the world's leading power, without favours and patronage of a fiscally-strapped Egyptian government that was increasingly dependent on the European powers for its survival, and without the profits and prestige derived from the extension of British imperial rule, Cook & Son could not have realized its goal of implanting a tourist structure on the banks of the Nile.

Henceforth, the company's Egyptian and Middle Eastern tours ran smoothly. In fact, when one of Cook's tents was robbed in Jerusalem, local administrators leapt into action with such gusto that nearly all of the stolen items were quickly recovered.[67]

Cook faced physical trials as well, especially at first. Tourism in Egypt was easily accomplished because most sites were accessible from the Nile River. The company needed only to utilize steamships, whether owned by Thomas Cook & Son or leased from others, to transport visitors in comfort. Expanding into the Holy Land was more challenging. Groups had to stay in tents and spend days in the saddle to get from one place to another. All provisions had to be carried in the same way and numerous attendants were required. Every trip represented a significant organizational feat, yet that is precisely what Thomas Cook promised his clients—a well-organized, all-in trip to once very hard-to-reach places.[68] The results were impressive. Despite recent political strife, 11,000 tourists went to Cairo in 1889–90 and 1300 of these sailed down the Nile. Numbers increased annually. By the winter of 1893, 1000 explored the city in one week alone. By the turn of the century, the firm developed a relay network of resorts, accommodations, and facilities along the Nile, extending from Cairo to Khartoum. It consisted of five tourist "stations" connected by steamships. Travelers could move comfortably from one to the next, enjoying "a range of conveniences" at each stop. In Cairo, the concern provided an assortment of lodgings from pensions to grand hotels, assured easy access to churches, offered telegraph and postal services, maintained European physicians to address any health concerns, conducted city tours, and more. Travelers could easily get whatever they needed.[69]

The company's clients could go just about anywhere. In 1872–3, Cook embarked on perhaps his biggest challenge—an around-the-world tour. It visited Australia, Europe, India, South Asia, and the United States. The audacious trek was repeated. When Thomas Cook died in 1892, over twenty groups, perhaps 1000 people, had duplicated the route using Thomas Cook & Son to lead them.[70] For at least some of the countries visited, the arrival of the company's trips spelled the start of modern tourism. Leisure travelers might want some adventure, but it needed to be easily managed. There must be regular timetables and accommodation. Easy access to transportation was a necessity. Guidebooks were required. Sites/sights had to be readily available to capture attention and to incite interest. That first round-the-world journey in 1872–3 inspired developers in Australia to produce just these things, fueling a budding industry as a result while at the same time benefiting Australian citizens.[71]

As the process of creating tourism took hold in more places around the world, made possible by empire and by the growing ease of travel, the industry contributed significantly to the formation of difference. It allowed promoters to concoct something new, to market a sense of what made one country distinct from another, to re-establish perceptions of places such as Jamaica, and to help a country such as Canada form a unique identity.[72]

Developing American tourism

In the United States, as in Europe, tourism took shape during the nineteenth century. Partly as a result of the demands of recently acquired independence, partially due to the horrific divisions engendered by civil war in the 1860s, the new pastime played a significant role in shaping a sense of American national identity.

The privileged among Americans were no strangers to travel; they had gone back and forth to Europe almost from the first settlements in the New World.[73] Doing so reflected good taste and connected the country's small elite to cultural traditions still valued by the upper crust on both sides of the Atlantic. These trips were not easy, but they were expected. As steamships got faster and more comfortable, doing one's own "Grand Tour" grew less difficult. At the same time, independence generated a desire to distinguish the United States from Europe and an impulse to create a distinctly "American" tourism.[74] About what did the new country have to be proud? Europeans enjoyed a long history traced to antiquity and beyond. They could boast romantic castles and other ruins. The United States had none of this. There was no long history—at least not one that text-obsessed whites appreciated—and no ancient sites or architectural wonders.

When tourism-minded American patriots looked around themselves, they sought sites/sights that were distinctive and impressive. According to historian John F. Sears, these men and women were different. They were steeped in religious traditions. Early America boasted more religious sects than anywhere else on earth. Nearly everybody understood themselves according to their relationship to God and to God's earth. Viewed from this perspective, the United States was virtually a Garden of Eden. God's handiwork was everywhere. It existed in massive waterfalls and mammoth cliffs. The Christian God was visible in vast forests and lakes, deserts and caves. Europe had natural beauty, but the sublime and beautiful available in the United States was on a grander scale. America might not have castles on the Mississippi or an ancient coliseum in Cincinnati, but neither could Europeans point to the equivalent of Niagara Falls or Mammoth Cave. These were America's "temples." Because such great natural wonders were unique to the New World, American tourists (and tourism developers) took great satisfaction in them—a pride that eventually grew to become a central component of the American national myth and of American national identity.[75]

As in Europe, poor transportation initially held back American tourism development. Few roads existed and travel came with numerous risks associated. Of course, new modes of transportation did eventually come to the aid of would-be tourists. The first steamboat service on the Hudson

River was inaugurated in 1807.[76] Railways appeared around the Northeast during the 1830s.[77] Easier mobility rendered tourism more appealing and made possible the development of the country's first great tourist destinations.

From as early as the 1810s, Niagara Falls, first discovered by Europeans in the seventeenth century, dominated itineraries.[78] Contemporaries believed the massive cataract to be "one of God's greatest creations"; a notion "that attained official recognition in 1861 when Pope Pius IX (1792–1878) established a pilgrim shrine" there. Some referred to the site as a "cathedral" and one enthusiast wrote: "I feel as if I had entered a living temple of the Eternal." Thomas Moore (1779–1852), an Irish poet, went so far as to imagine that the cascading water might convert even the most steadfast atheist.[79]

Most American religious sects believed in the significance of a conversion experience; as Moore suggested, Niagara was supposed to provide one. Visitors were meant to feel not only closer to God but also a deep, satisfied feeling akin to divine ecstasy. The problem was that many who saw the site failed to experience such a thing. They looked on and exclaimed how beautiful and impressive the tumbling water was, but no great conversion followed. This prompted people to stay longer in the hope that they would "see the light" if only God were given time to work on them.[80] Hotels sprang up, souvenir sellers proliferated, guides promised tours of the site that were designed to provide a celestial encounter. Virtually all of the literature concerning the great cascade certainly celebrated such a purpose. The novelist Nathaniel Hawthorne, for example, noted "The beholder must stand beside [Niagara] in the simplicity of heart, suffering the mighty scene to work its own impression."[81] It was a similar attitude to that held by religious pilgrims during the Middle Ages and the liturgy, with its pacing and gazing, was not all that different either.

Niagara Falls even had its own hermit—a man who arrived in pursuit of his conversion experience and found it impossible to leave. Visitors were fascinated and handbooks told the saga in detail:

> He was a young man then, tall and well-formed, but emaciated and haggard; of an easy and gentlemanly deportment, but sufficiently eccentric in his appearance to arrest the gaze of the stranger.
>
> Clad in a long, flowing robe of brown, and carrying under his arm a roll of blankets, a book, portfolio, and flute, he proceeded directly to a small, retired inn, where he engaged a room for a week, stipulating, however, that the room was to be, for the time, exclusively *his*, and that only a *part* of his food was to be prepared by the family. Soon after, he visited the village library, entered his name, and drew books. About the same time, also, he purchased a violin. At the expiration of a week he

> returned to the library, where, falling into conversation, he spoke with much enthusiasm on the subject of the Falls, and expressed his intention of remaining here some time longer.
>
> Shortly afterward he asked permission of the proprietor of these islands to erect a cabin on Moss Island, that he might live here in greater seclusion than the village afforded him. Failing in this request he took up his abode in part of a small log-house, which then stood near the head of Goat Island. Here for nearly two years he continued to live, with no companions but his dog, his books, and music—blameless but almost unknown. On this island, at hours when it was unfrequented by others, he delighted to roam, heedless, if not oblivious to danger. At that time a stick of timber about eight inches square extended from Terrapin Bridge eight feet beyond the precipice. On this he has been seen at almost all hours of the night, pacing to and fro beneath the moonlight, without the slightest apparent tremor of nerve or hesitancy of step. Sometimes he might be seen sitting carelessly on the extreme end of the timber—sometimes hanging beneath it by his hands and feet. Although exquisitely sensitive in his social habits, he seems to have been without an apprehension in the presence of danger. After residing on Goat Island two winters, he crossed Bath Island Bridge, and built him a rude cabin of boards at Point View, near the American Fall. Although brought into the immediate neighborhood of the villagers, he held but little intercourse with them; sometimes, indeed, refusing to break his silence by oral communication with anyone. At times, however, he was extremely affable to all, easily drawn into conversation, and supporting it with a regard to conventionalism, and a grace and accuracy of expression that threw a charm over the most trivial subject of remark.[82]

The hermit's name was Francis Abbot (1800–31) and he provided the same symbolic meaning to the falls that Richard Hill hoped to inspire by employing a hermit to inhabit the grotto at his estate in Shropshire. The discovery of the curious man's body among the rocks below the falls augmented this sense. Nobody knows whether it was suicide or an accident, but that was irrelevant. Abbot's death reinforced the power of the place.[83]

Accidents enhanced the mythology of Niagara. As with the hermit, guidebook writers were anxious to repeat the stories. In one tale, a 22-year old named Charles Addington (1827–49) and Antoinette DeForest (1841–9), his 8-year old charge, enjoyed a picnic by the waterside. All at once, DeForest fell into the river and Addington leapt in after her. Together the two tumbled to their deaths. In another horrifying episode, a group of people wandered atop a frozen bridge that formed every winter above the falls. When the ice cracked, three people were stranded upon the resulting floe. At least one reportedly dropped to his knees to pray just as his iceberg crested the edge and tumbled into the abyss.[84] Tragedy reinforced notions of the sublime and visitors could not get enough.

It could not stay divine forever. Showmen started to do stunts for the benefit of tourists as early as 1829. Tightrope walkers made their way across the chasm and thrill-seekers went over the brink in barrels. Souvenir stands and entertainment pavilions were not far behind.[85] As more people came to Niagara, hotels overlooking the water soon dominated the scene. Engineers discovered that it was possible to generate electricity by harnessing the power of the rushing torrent. Industrial structures sprung up, blighting the view.

It was not long before Niagara's meaning started to change, emerging as a symbol of what could go wrong, of the negative side of tourism. In 1879, Frederick Law Olmsted (1822–1903), perhaps the greatest American landscape architect of the nineteenth century, was hired to fix the problem. He planted trees and erected small hills to frame specific views. The landscape had to be preserved. It was a realization that would have a profound impact on the subsequent development of American tourism.[86]

While there were other natural sites—Mammoth Cave and the White Mountains, for example, America also offered other "divine," if at first curious, things to see: lunatic asylums, prisons, and hospitals for the blind and deaf. People living during the nineteenth century were fascinated by technology. As a consequence, new treatments for social outsiders were viewed as little different from trains or steamships. These sites stood in contrast to what was found elsewhere. The approach that Americans developed to address insanity, crime, and physical challenges was dissimilar from that of Europeans. It seemed more humane, more in line with Christian teaching; at least that is how Americans and a growing tide of European visitors saw things.[87]

As in Europe tourism gradually democratized in the United States, increasingly accessible to people from across the social spectrum. On Martha's Vineyard, participants in an annual Methodist revival meeting held at the edge of the town of Oak Bluffs gradually extended their time on the island to include more than just sermons and religious study. They arrived early and stayed after the religious events to enjoy the scenery and beaches. With time, developers added amusements such as a popular carousel to entice the vacationing Methodists. The Vineyard, once a whaling and farming community, emerged as an evermore popular holiday destination.[88]

The development of parks offered another path to working-class leisure. As in Britain, growing American cities were both densely populated and

Figure 6.2 Niagara Falls was one of the first major American and Canadian tourist destinations. Initially, visitors hoped to confront the sublime and anticipated a divine experience. Developers later added other attractions, hotels were constructed, and the site became a popular destination for honeymooning couples. Photo courtesy of Richard G. Zuelow.

polluted, prompting concerns about health. One solution, based largely on the example of the Père Lachaise cemetery in Paris, was to move crowded graveyards perhaps three or four miles from urban centers. These new cemeteries were meticulously landscaped to look peaceful and rural. Many had lakes, carefully planned labyrinthine pathways, and otherwise park-like grounds. That is just what these "garden cemeteries" were: the first parks. In the United States, developers constructed cemeteries at Mount Auburn

(1831) in Cambridge, Massachusetts, Laurel Hill (1836) in Philadelphia, Pennsylvania, and at Greenwood (1837) in Brooklyn, New York among other places.

These new burial grounds were unbelievably popular. In 1860 alone, 140,000 people visited Laurel Hill and between 400,000 and 500,000 wandered the paths at Greenwood. The demise of cemeteries as parks certainly did not result from a lack of people anxious to spend a quiet afternoon in the presence of the dead. Instead, success bred a change of habits. Many started to question whether it was proper to enjoy leisure in a graveyard, wondering if it was disrespectful.

The solution was to create dedicated urban leisure areas: parks. Central Park in New York City is one of the most famous. It was designed by Frederick Law Olmsted to be a natural space—similar to the cemeteries but without the corpses. Visitors were supposed to forget about the close proximity of the city and time was meant to lose all importance. Parks were intended to be democratic spaces. Everybody from the very poor to the very rich could find relaxation and pleasure in their class-free borders.[89]

The creation of early parks had long-term implications. They inspired a sense that natural spaces were important and that people should have access to nature. Many Americans started to believe that they had a responsibility to make such spots available. The result was the creation of the first national parks.

White settlers "discovered" Yosemite, which is located about 150 miles from San Francisco, California, in 1833 when a military unit chased a group of Native Americans into the mountains. The valley was soon forgotten: only to be "rediscovered" in 1851.[90] Astonished by the massive granite cliffs, impressive rock forms, and high waterfalls, a man named J.M. Hutchings (1820–1902) wrote about the area. He poured out his heart, celebrating the "marvelous grandeur of the Yo Semite."[91] While Niagara was impressive, Yosemite featured taller waterfalls and some of the most amazing mountain scenery in the world. Hutchings was not alone in his admiration. The first hotel and hiking trail appeared in 1855. Thomas A. Ayres (1828–1913) started sketching the cliffs that same year. The first photographer reached the Yosemite Valley in 1859.[92] The notion of creating a "national park"—an as yet undefined concept—followed shortly thereafter.[93]

Even as the American Civil War raged (1861–5), Congress recognized the tourism potential of the Yosemite Valley. It was unique and a clear example of what set America apart. It might even play some role in knitting the country back together after the fighting stopped. The national park idea gained further public attention when a steamship service to San Francisco began and as Americans learned of a planned transcontinental railway. Uneasiness with the impact that development had on Niagara shaped interest in the plan, too.

Yosemite was officially declared America's first national park on June 30, 1864. Almost immediately, a whole new collection of paintings, sketches, and photographs circulated. The first tourist guidebook to the park was published in 1868. The few who could afford to visit Yosemite believed they were going to the Garden of Eden—a place more beautiful than Niagara had ever been.[94]

For railway companies, the creation of Yosemite National Park was economically promising, but it was not enough to assure profits. If people were to be drawn to the West, there had to be a whole series of uniquely American attractions to see. Railway owners saw their lines of track as the embodiment of "Manifest Destiny" and they wanted to show Americans that despite the unfortunate civil war, the country was intimately connected. The task, as far as the rail companies were concerned, was to create more national symbols—a network of them—that would unite Americans both through the pride the sites inspired and by the desire to see those sites.[95] As a consequence, railway companies soon lobbied for the creation of further national parks.

Yellowstone followed Yosemite. By the early 1870s, the West was the subject of considerable fascination in the populous East. It was the stuff of dime store novels. The task for railway companies was to exploit the romantic excitement that an imagined "West" held for huge numbers of people, both in America and beyond.[96] Yellowstone was perfect. It featured a stunning variety of landscapes that included rugged mountain scenery, endless forests, a great diversity of wildlife, as well as other-worldly geysers, bubbling mud pits, and hot springs. From the perspective of the nineteenth century Yellowstone's strangest sites were not temples. They were freak-shows. If Yosemite represented the Garden of Eden, Yellowstone was Hell, access made easy by the close proximity to the new transcontinental railway.

As with Yosemite, the effort to establish the park involved sending pictures to Congress. Proponents argued that creation of a second national park represented the height of patriotism. It would allow for the protection of important scenery and would make it possible for Americans to experience their patrimony in a very corporeal way. It worked. Congress officially designated the park on March 1, 1872.[97]

More followed: Mount Rainier (1899), Glacier (1910), Grand Canyon (1919), among others, all showcasing a new slogan: "Go to Europe if you must, but see America first." Tourism would generate money. It would encourage people to go west. It would help the country heal after the Civil War by showing that everything really was connected. It would make the United States something special, unique, and valuable.[98]

Figure 6.3 When the American Congress established Yellowstone National Park in 1872, its geysers and other volcanic features—none more famous than "Old Faithful"—represented "hell" to the "heaven" visible at Yosemite National Park. Photo courtesy of Richard G. Zuelow.

Conclusion

The global empires constructed by European states during the nineteenth century gradually collapsed in the twentieth. Like so many other legacies of the era, however, the wider geographic scope of leisure travel as well as the ties between tourism and identity persisted. By the fin de siècle, the trend was toward democratizing tourism, making it something that everybody could engage in. Expanding leisure opportunities, and the attendant identity politics, had political implications for governments anxious to establish their popular following and to sell often heavily nationalist messages.

Yet before boosters could create truly mass tourism another stage of technological development occurred: the invention of bicycles, automobiles, and airplanes. Steam had made it possible for workers to take excursions and for tourism to expand into distant places associated with European empires. Bicycles and automobiles made it considerably cheaper and more flexible to leave home. Car owners, whose ranks swelled with the advent of inexpensive vehicles, could go almost anywhere that they wanted, whenever they desired. No schedule required. Aircraft opened up the possibility of even longer-haul trips done more efficiently than could be accomplished on board a ship. Tourism attained greater popularity in the nineteenth century, drawing in more and more people, but it would become a truly mass phenomenon in the twentieth.

7

Bicycles, automobiles, and aircraft

By the end of the nineteenth century tourism was global in scope and popular among a growing number of social actors. New inventions played a significant part in this process by reducing costs and increasing the number of people who could take part in travel. At the dawn of the twentieth century, three new technologies contributed to the development of mass tourism: bicycles, automobiles, and airplanes. Each new vehicle followed a similar trajectory. It was first the purview of elites. Then, new production techniques and novel inventions helped to increase accessibility while also spawning more uses—car camping, for example. Finally, each mode of conveyance caught the popular zeitgeist, became a regular part of daily life, and an accelerant for mass tourism.

The bicycle

The notion of mechanical, human-powered transportation was not new to the nineteenth century. Jacques Ozanam (1640–1718), a French mathematician, suggested the concept as early as 1696. The problem was arriving at a usable design. At first, the best idea available was to suspend a padded board between two wheels. It was called a "draisine" (after inventor Karl von Drais [1785–1851]), or a "velocipede" (Latin for "fast foot"). Riders sat on the board and ran, the wheels significantly improving speed, especially downhill, and making forward motion easier. The device spawned a public response, but it was not the efficient human-powered transportation imagined by Ozanam.[1]

During the 1860s an assortment of rear-drive "bicycles" came to market. These new machines were more efficient than the draisine, but they were also complicated and costly. When the great "breakthrough," the first true bicycle, saw daylight in Paris in 1867, it "completely changed the character of the vehicle." The two-wheeled wonder spun along "as though it were alive, and with a smooth grace alike exhilarating and beautiful to behold."[2] For wealthy and respectable European men, it was a must-have toy.

Unfortunately, production remained slow. The bikes were hard to come by and they were painfully expensive. Up to the 1890s, bicycles cost roughly 500 francs, an amount equivalent to three months of a teacher's salary at the time.[3] During the last decade of the century, however, a slew of largely European inventors improved the design. Ball bearings, new frame shapes, rubber tires, and other additions assured that bicycles were more comfortable and efficient. A revolution in assembly-line type manufacturing brought prices down by the early 1890s.[4] Now ordinary people could afford to buy. By 1909, a used bicycle could be purchased for just 50 francs in Paris. Costs fell at a similar rate in the United States.[5]

There were at least two significant results. On one hand, bicycle racing exploded in popularity on both sides of the Atlantic and the creation of new races fed the public's desire to watch the "giants of the road"[6] as well as to go riding themselves. In the United States, track cycling attracted a massive following and the velodrome at Madison Square Garden in New York City drew huge numbers of spectators, as did similar tracks in most American cities. It is no exaggeration to say that bicycle racing, not baseball or American football, was the national sport at the end of the century.[7] Although there were other professional sports, "It was the bicycle racers who pulled in the big bucks."[8] Road cycling, and especially multi-day "stage races," introduced legions of fans to places they might otherwise never know, but now could imagine visiting. The French, for example, learned about the varied geography of their country following the advent of the Tour de France in 1903.[9]

The second implication was that inexpensive bicycles allowed people from nearly all walks of life to travel beyond a narrow geographic range. The machines made it viable for workers to live further afield from their places of employment. Just as important, they allowed everybody from the top of the social pyramid to the bottom to venture into the countryside, to ride to adjacent towns, and to participate in cycling clubs that organized regular group outings as well as more extended excursions to significant sites/sights. The resulting "cycle craze," which struck fear into the hearts of some elites—just as railways had before—also inspired ideas of improvement. If workers could be taught to behave in a particular way, to ride their bikes in the respectable pose of a horseman, to enjoy the benefits of healthy outdoor exercise, and to learn more about the national patrimony, the political and social implications of cycling might be very positive indeed.[10] Far more than was true during the railway age, the ability to move from place to place was individualized: "Personal mobility, independent of railway timetables and stations, had previously been restricted to the minority who could afford a horse and carriage. Even carriages, however, had limitations in terms of flexibility and distance which the bicycle could easily overcome."[11] What was more, the implications were not limited to men. By the mid-1890s, women, especially from the bourgeoisie, took to the road by the thousands.[12] Bicycles promised a degree of liberty and autonomy that was entirely unavailable previously,[13] even under the auspices of a Cook's Tour.

For Americans, the cycle craze was comparably short-lived, while many in Europe continue their love affair with the bicycle today. The machines opened up the notion that leisure travel to almost anyplace could be available to virtually anybody. That idea never disappeared.

The automotive revolution

Similar to bicycles, cars promised freedom and independence. As anthropologist Orvar Löfgren summarizes: "The steam engine had collectivized travel, now the car offered a new individualism and a freedom to go (almost) wherever you fancied."[14] It helped shape the self-image of those involved, transitioning them (at least in their own minds) "from character to personality; from inner-direction to other-direction; from utilitarian to expressive individualism; from sovereign to social selfhood." It "offered opportunities for the traditional crafting of character through expedition and hardship, even though such crafting took place within the culture of leisure." Motoring "promised not only transportation, but transformation."[15] Railways had time schedules. They had fixed routes, going only to a handful of places, severely limiting flexibility. Automobiles helped to generate new forms of leisure, prompted the creation of parks, sparked a transformation of overnight accommodation, allowed more people to travel to more places, and led to entirely new ways of seeing the landscape and of imagining identity.

The idea for motorized overland travel dates at least to the eighteenth century. A Swiss engineer named Nicholas-Joseph Cugnot earned a subsidy from the French government to build steam-powered trucks between 1765 and 1770, ideally to carry heavy canons. Horses proved more efficient. As noted in Chapter 3, Richard Trevithick built a steam engine that was set loose on the roads of Cornwall between 1801 and 1803. It ended up in a ditch, with potential investors less than impressed. Oliver Evans (1755–1819) attempted to build a steam-powered vehicle in the United States around the same time. This too failed. Steam was simply not a suitable power source.[16]

Various inventors on both sides of the Atlantic developed the internal combustion engine over a period of time; it occurred to a number of people that this new creation might well be used to power an overland vehicle. They built miscellaneous machines, but it was only between 1885 and 1895 that a flurry of "automotive activity" resulted in engineers Karl Benz (1844–1929) and Émile Constant Levassor (1843–97) building a car with "commercial feasibility." These one-cylinder tricycles appeared at the Paris Exhibition and soon found their way into limited production. Only the very wealthy could afford one, but for the exalted few the car represented a magnificent new plaything.[17]

Motoring was not a hobby without challenges. Road builders constructed routes for horses and buggies so surfaces were not necessarily well suited to speedy vehicles. Many worried about the implications of mixing horseless carriages with those using equine engines. The concern was real enough, and the railway lobby strong enough, that British lawmakers passed the Locomotives Act in 1865 limiting the speed of "road locomotives" to 2 miles per hour in towns and 4 miles per hour on the open road. The law did not stop there. It demanded that any motor-driven horseless carriage employ an attendant to walk sixty yards ahead carrying a red lantern to warn of the approaching machine. In the United States, railway magnates assured that roadways remained remedial in order to dissuade the use of stagecoaches.[18]

Such prohibitions did not last. Automotive enthusiasts formed clubs almost as quickly as they bought cars. In 1895, Harry Lawson (1852–1925), an early devotee, formed the Motor Car Club. Within a year he helped assure passage of the Locomotives on Highways Act, legislation that opened British roads to motorcars. Parliament raised the speed limit to 12 miles per hour. By 1903 it climbed again, this time to 20 miles per hour. Encouraged, enthusiasts formed other automotive organizations. The Self-Propelled Traffic Association, for example, published a journal called *Autocar* and promoted events that enjoyed royal patronage.[19] In the same year that Lawson formed his group, French enthusiasts started the Automobile Club of France, largely with the goal of promoting long distance races such as Paris-Bordeaux-Paris.[20] American automotive activists launched a New York-based group in 1899 and the American Automobile Association formed in 1902. Australia followed suit; an automobile club started activities in 1903. There was even a transnational motoring group in Europe, the Fédération Internationale de l'Automobile, from 1904. Others followed in short order. There were two clubs in Argentina (1904, 1907); a club was founded in Cape Town, South Africa in 1901; twenty-eight petrol-minded drivers started the Natal Automobile Club in 1908. The Automobile Club of Rhodesia launched in 1923.[21] The Danish Touring Club started activities in 1909.[22] The list goes on.

At first many of these clubs focused on the promotion of distance races—something in which the press quickly developed an interest. The *Chicago*

Times-Herald newspaper sponsored the first automobile race in America in 1895.[23] It covered fifty-five miles in freezing temperatures and "through deep snow, and along ruts that would have tried horses to their utmost."[24] The cars broke down so often and the weather was so bad that it took several attempts before the race was completed.[25]

For drivers such challenges provided a chance to test their vehicles and themselves. Early cars were anything but reliable and the roadways assured frequent breakdowns. Any budding motorist had also to be a mechanic and possibly even a blacksmith. Driving a car was the very definition of adventure. The appeal was significant and many contemporaries felt that it was actually good for those involved, more akin to taking exercise on the back of a horse than inside a railway carriage. As one scholar notes, "There was a horselike willfulness and unreliability to early automotive technology, which broke many a starter-cranking wrist and oversteered many automobiles into ditches." It made people better, stronger, and tougher.[26]

Historian Rudy Koshar describes this earliest phase of automotive history as a "pioneering mode." It was an age when "drivers often literally had to create their own roads, or rather paths, through landscapes that in some cases have never been traversed by an automobile."[27] Newspapers anxiously reported on each new feat for an evidently fascinated public. In 1900, for example, three Frenchmen captured headlines when they arrived in New York anxious to be the first to drive an automobile to the Klondike.[28] In August 1903, a Boston couple managed to reach the Arctic Circle using their car.[29] It hardly required something quite so grand to make the paper; another pair captured headlines in 1903 by driving their car through the Adirondack Mountains.[30] All of this was impressive, but there was an even bigger prize available. Just as the pioneers captured the American imagination by conquering the frontier, now car owners sought a similar prize: to cross the American continent in a horseless carriage. John D. Davis (dates unknown) and his wife, Louise Hitchcock Davis (dates unknown), made the first attempt in 1899. They started in New York, hoping to reach San Francisco. Constant mechanical problems ended the trip in Chicago. In terms of popular impact, it hardly mattered. An automotive company sponsored the trip, the Good Roads Association generated maps to help out, and publications such as *Scientific American* publicized it. The magazine reported that "[T]here is no more delightful way of seeing the country than to view it from the comfortably cushioned seats of an automobile vehicle."[31] It was mostly "small boys" who materialized to see the couple off—suggesting, perhaps, that the motor age would create a new kind of hero.[32]

Dr. Horatio Nelson Jackson (1872–1955) was the first to successfully make the trip from coast to coast. In 1903, driving a Winton automobile nicknamed "Vermont" and accompanied by a mechanic (and former bicycle racer) named Sewall K. Crocker (1881–1913) and a goggle-wearing bulldog named Bud, the Vermont-based physician set out from San Francisco. Just over sixty-three days later the trio arrived in New York, beating two other cars in the process. It was no easy journey. They negotiated dry streambeds through the mountains, the brakes becoming so overheated that they had to be cooled off in pools of mountain water. They wore out tires, continuing by wrapping the threadbare rubber in rawhide and rope in order to keep moving forward. As there were no gas stations in the United States until one was built in St. Louis in 1905, Jackson purchased fuel at convenience stores, sometimes facing inflated prices at the hands of unscrupulous storeowners.

Figures 7.1 and 7.2 Horatio Nelson Jackson, his mechanic, Sewall K. Crocker, and Bud the bulldog were the first to drive successfully across the United States. While their experience earned particular historical recognition, they were but three among many others anxious to engage in automotive endurance tests. Early motoring demanded driving skill, mechanical acumen, navigational ability, and more than a little bravery. Around the world, automotive associations evolved to help by printing maps, lobbying for roadway construction, promoting events, and more. Photos courtesy of University of Vermont Special Collections.

(*continued*)

Figures 7.1 and 7.2 (continued)

All too often it was necessary to wait for parts, and at other times blacksmiths fabricated them. It was one of the wettest years on record and the three adventurers were frequently forced to extract their car from the mud, sometimes employing local horses. In short, it was a very difficult trip, but they made it to New York City.[33]

Although transcontinental racing ran well beyond the means of most, there was no shortage of Americans anxious to take to the roads. By 1910, there were 458,500 motor vehicles registered in the United States.[34] Although initially dominated by males, women joined the motoring masses as well. At first ladies were encouraged to drive electric cars because they were slower and deemed more reliable, but the advent of the electric starter ended this division. Besides, women wanted to enjoy the same freedom, adventure, and character-building benefits sought by men. The automobile market grew accordingly.[35] As this happened, the car helped to alter the female role in family life, at least in the United States, because it "helped loosen family ties, reduce parental authority over children, introduce women to new opportunities for recreation, romance, and work outside the home; and, in general, expand social contacts between the sexes."[36]

British manufacturers could not match American production numbers, but that hardly diminished the desire to own an automobile. By 1906, there were 23,000 cars speeding through the hedgerows and across the moors. In 1925 there were nearly two million registered vehicles clogging the roadways.[37] Notable variations existed and not every country embraced the motorcar immediately. Germans, for example, were more hesitant to welcome car culture, but the trend shifted toward what Koshar calls a more "democratic" period of automotive history—a period when more and more people, men and women, elites and their social inferiors, started driving.[38]

New manufacturing techniques, expanding product lines, and the availability of low cost vehicles made automobile ownership more widely available. It is interesting to note that the earliest objections to cars, which often held them to be the "opulent" toys of wealthy socialites, largely dissipated as prices fell.[39] Many scholars credit Henry Ford (1863–1947) for this development. He organized the Ford Motor Company in 1903, concluding that automobiles would soon "supersede the horse."[40] He was right. The company launched the Model T in 1908; it initially cost $850 and Ford advertised the new vehicle by saying: "No car under $2000 offers more, and no car over $2000 offers more except the trimmings." Ford, alongside a team of engineers, was committed to reducing the already comparatively low price. The goal was to produce as many of the cars as possible, eventually developing an assembly-line system that saw the company turning out vehicles at a previously unimaginable pace. In 1910, Ford built 32,053. In 1916 the number was 734,811 and climbing. The price dropped accordingly. By 1916, the Model T runabout sold for just $345. A larger touring version dented pocketbooks by only $360.[41] By the time that the last Model T rolled out of the company's Dearborn, Michigan factory on May 27, 1927 the trusty little car cost only $290. It was one of the more than 15 million Model T Fords issued.[42]

The manufacture of much more reliable and affordable vehicles was not limited to the United States, although Americans certainly built more cars than anybody else during the first few decades of the automotive age. In 1911, Ford opened a factory in Trafford Park, an area of greater Manchester, England, where parts shipped from Michigan were assembled for the British, imperial, and European markets. By 1913 the company produced more than twice the number of vehicles made by its closest British competitor, Wolseley. British entrepreneurs were in no way dissuaded from entering the fray. The Morris Motor Company opened in 1913 and set about building the Morris Oxford—widely known as the "Bullnose Morris"—a car that cost roughly the same as the Model T. Production far from matched Ford, but that did not hinder the new company. By the 1920s, Morris was the largest car company in Britain and it continued to produce automobiles that sold handsomely. Its most successful vehicle, the Morris Minor, launched in 1931.[43] Like the Model T, the Morris Minor eventually became part of countless holiday memories.[44]

More motorists meant more political clout. The demand for better, more expansive roadways quickly grew in both Europe and the United States. In the States, for example, enthusiasts built upon the "See America First" idea to promote the notion that motoring and nationalism went hand in hand. Advocates claimed that good roads would improve commerce by allowing manufacturers and merchants, agriculturalists and others, to get around swiftly and easily. In 1916, President Woodrow Wilson (1856–1924) of the United States gave his "good roads" speech in which he argued that roadways would assure economic development, erode provincialism, and otherwise serve the national interest.[45] But roads would do more. They would educate the people. Historian Marguerite Shaffer cites one enthusiastic supporter: "Mothers must aid in creating good roads sentiment, so that their children will as future citizens be educated to the axiomatic truth that good roads are the milestone that backs the advancement of civilization." More, roads would unite the nation, teaching people about their land, making them better Americans.[46]

Simply calling for better roads did not necessarily lead to immediate action. Writing in 1907, activist William Pierrepont White (1867–1938) summed up part of the problem:

> Everyone is interested in the improvement of the highways, but the residents of the towns want to put the expense on the county, and the residents of the county want to put the expense on the state, and the residents of the state want to put the expense on the nation; but the nation uses its surplus for the improvement of rivers and harbors, and so everyone commences all over again, trying to find someone who will stand the expense of road improvement.[47]

Some problems seem nearly timeless. Certainly the American government was loath to spend money and contented itself with studying the issue. This left private organizations, highway associations, and state governments to do most of the heavy-lifting, at least until a Federal Highway Act was passed in 1916, offering "$75 million in federal aid for state highway construction to be distributed over the ensuing five years." World War I delayed the funding, but more money and additional highway acts followed the war. A network of national highways developed as a result.[48]

The push for roadways was not without controversy, especially when building a road might jeopardize protected scenic beauty. Many wanted to see rivers of tarmac flowing into America's most revered landscapes, but this was a contentious idea. Would automobiles harm the scenery? Might they be dangerous? How would they interact with non-motorized traffic? Mount Rainier National Park in Washington State was the first to admit cars, doing so in 1908. Other places were more circumspect. Those facilities associated with railways, Glacier National Park, for example, feared that the automobile would reduce visits into "mere day-trips" while stealing profits. Zipping along, sightseers would not encounter much of the scenery, enjoying little of the pedagogical value of getting back to the land. It would "cheapen the park experience." Authorities at Yosemite National Park were famously opposed to cars, but even they had to admit by 1912 that automobile clubs enjoyed too much clout. Certainly car enthusiasts clamored for roadway construction deep into the heart of America's most sacred places. These groups buried the Secretary of the Interior's office with demands that politicians understood. Roads would boost car sales and fuel the construction of more roadways, building the economy. It hardly needed to be said that drivers represented a powerful and growing voting bloc.[49] Roads soon penetrated into the interiors of every American national park, carefully designed to frame the views seen by motorists. Their construction aimed to showcase the parks, not just to bring people in. The visitor experience was, thus, mediated through the windscreen.[50]

Controversy was not only about who would pay or about the scenic impact. Others were anxious to assure that their town or state would benefit. Arguably the most famous and perhaps important American highway is a case in point, the transcontinental Lincoln Highway. In 1911, Indiana businessman Carl Graham Fisher (1874–1939) proposed the idea of building an improved road across the United States.[51] Recognizing the challenge of financing such a project, Fisher imagined finding donors who would foot the bill. Pledges and words of support soon rolled in. Among other contributions, the president of Packard Motor Company—a stanch patriot and fan of the sixteenth president—suggested calling the road the "Lincoln Highway," a much nicer name that the previous working title of the "Coast-to-Coast Rock Highway."

While Fisher proposed the idea and offered a way to fund it, he proved less interested in the mundane day-to-day planning and unwilling to proffer a clear route other than to say that it should move from New York to San Francisco. Herein was a problem. Political leaders in Missouri, Kansas, and Colorado were all anxious to see the Lincoln Highway cross their states. The governors of Kansas and Colorado went so far as to promise their constituents that the road was coming. As with the arrival of railways, these men knew that having a major highway meant jobs, money, and development. Fisher was happy to have the conflict, believing that it would keep his proposal in the news, assure public interest, and inspire donations. When the route was eventually publicized, Colorado was not on it. The governor was furious. Other similarly slighted states also grew angry. As a result a series of longer bypasses and scenic highways were added. Fisher's straight road across the country now had a host of bumps and protrusions.[52]

More thoroughfares were built after World War I. During the conflict, railways became hopelessly bogged down with the needs of the war effort. Roadways offered a way to fix the bottleneck. Similarly, farmers made clear that successful commerce required accessible routes along which to ship their products. Roads were the answer. Starting in 1923, the Bureau for Public Roads advocated for and ultimately built a network of arterial highways spanning thousands of miles. By the middle of the decade there were "numerous interstate highways" of uneven quality. Standardization—coded signs, route numbers, and improved road surfaces—came later.[53]

Parkways represented another type of roadway and enjoyed a brief period of popularity between the 1920s and the 1930s. This American invention built on the idea of the European boulevard, integrating landscape and tarmac while excluding the growing number of businesses and attractions that usually proliferated wherever there were large numbers of cars. These routes were faster and safer than conventional roads and it took little time for other countries to emulate them.[54]

As time passed, and similar to the debate over extending roads into America's national parks, there was a reaction to the worldwide expansion of blacktop and concrete. In Scotland, critics worried about danger to people and animals, about dust and mud, about the implications for townsfolk and country-dwellers, and about the effect that heavy automobiles would have on roadways. Who would pay for the damage?[55] Such concerns existed in the United States as well, but there was a different anxiety also. Some asked as early as the 1910s, 1920s, and 1930s: if roads went everywhere, representing the relentless march of progress, how would one get away from it all? How could one escape from civilization—one of the objectives that formed the basis of tourism almost from the start of the previous century?

The resulting backlash produced the Wilderness Society, an organization formed in the 1930s. The group argued that "wilderness was a sanctuary in the modern world for nature untrammeled by humanity, if it was to remain one of the places on earth where the primitive conditions of the frontier could be experienced at first hand, then the intrusions of automobiles and highways must be resisted at all costs." Cars, and the tourists they carried, might destroy the last few wild places.[56] Truly mass tourism was yet to fully materialize, but the combination of technology, numbers, and nature still merged to raise questions about what is sustainable. Once started, the debate did not disappear.

Automobiles and the mounting number of people owning and driving them had immediate and growing implications. While some drove for business, most of these early motorists were on the road primarily for fun.[57] The myriad automobile clubs and associations around the world reflected this recreational bent with more and more attention to the publication of guides, maps, and travel magazines. The National Roads and Motorists Association (NRMA) in New South Wales, for example, spent many of its resources on "touring." The group's periodical reflected the leisure focus, identifying different types of tourist and offering articles tailored to the interests of adventurists, families, fishermen, "eight-hour" holidaymakers, and others.[58] The Touring Club of Denmark published a magazine, *Motor,* that celebrated the idea of driving for pleasure, offering suggestions and ideas for where to visit, and eschewing the notion of competition. In a famous early incident, Frederik Bagge (1861–1928), vice-president of the club, was touring the Rhine Valley with friends. When one driver suggested a race, Bagge replied: "Gentlemen, we do not make this tour to drive. We drive to do the tour." Members of the club thrilled at the suggestion and repeated the story often. "[L]eisure, freedom, and adventure" were much the preferable activity, something that car owners everywhere should seek.[59]

Just as with the first nineteenth-century guidebooks, manuals focused on motor touring told tourists what ought to be seen. They listed accommodations, suggested routes, and advised on the best sites/sights. Some told tourists how to pack and how to engage in "the family vacation." People are not born to be tourists. They must learn. Guidebooks (and automotive travel writing) played the role of instructor.[60] Thus, a 1921 book by Elon Jessup (1885–1958), a particularly enthusiastic proponent of car touring, told prospective car campers "about vehicle preparation, camping equipment, food, clothing, and temperament." He then declared "motor camping the most democratic sport in America."[61] Such excitement was not limited to the States. In Australia, guidebooks encouraged travelers to move beyond the scenic beauty of the countryside and to use their cars in order to explore historic sites.[62] In Scotland, they pointed out must-see sites/sights and played up an almost mystical relationship between roadway, driver, and holiday.[63]

In France, guides did something else; they told motorists where and what to eat. The Michelin rubber company largely manufactured the idea that France is notable for its cuisine. The organization started life during the nineteenth century making bicycle tires, but by the fin de siècle its main business was the automobile. Two brothers managed the corporation. Edouard Michelin (1859–1940) knew advertising and his brother André (1853–1931) brought engineering know-how as well as a fascination with marketing. Together they turned the concern into a global empire.

André devised the *Michelin Guide* in 1900 as a way of reminding car tourists about Michelin tires. The guidebook, a small red volume that fit easily into a breast pocket, was designed to give drivers a quick and easy reference to the best hotels and roadways along their route, while at the same time closely associating Michelin with driving in the consumers' mind. The idea represented a significant gamble because in 1900 automobiles were extremely expensive—a rich man's hobby. Nevertheless, André pulled together the little guide and distributed it for free. Readers were asked to confirm his assessments and he promised to continually up-grade the book as time went along, assuring that it was always current.

Michelin used stars to rate the hotels and inns that he listed. This was not original to the company—Baedeker had been doing the same for some time—but it was useful and it matched easily with a collection of other symbols that he already utilized. For example, a symbol denoted all the various fuels available at gas stations, whether there was a flush toilet, if bath/shower was available, and whether or not there was a darkroom for developing film. As the books expanded, André began including city maps. The manuals were distinguished from others because they focused explicitly on the driving experience rather than on sites of historic interest.

The guidebooks soon became required equipment for all motorists. Despite their popularity, Michelin used every avenue available to publicize them further. He purchased newspaper advertisements, created posters, and even reported a case in which a young married couple had been unable to consummate their marriage because they lacked the text needed to point them toward a suitable hotel.

Gradually, Michelin offered books covering more and more states. In 1915 the company published a guidebook to Germany as though it were possible to simply enter the country during World War I. Why did he do this? It was a patriotic gesture. André wanted to assure that when his countrymen broke through enemy lines they would know exactly where to go and how to get there. On a related point, when the Allies stormed the beaches at Normandy in 1944, soldiers carried the little red books, Allied commanders having been assured that they were the best available to help navigate a newly liberated France.

In 1925 Michelin began using the star system to rank restaurants. The very best received three stars. The authors never explained how they arrived at a ranking, but people quickly began to trust the score. It was not long before the whole world knew that if you had a Michelin guide you could eat your way around France. Chefs recognized that receiving a star or two was a ticket to fame and fortune. Small towns that housed a ranked restaurant were suddenly on the map. Tourists would come. The new fascination with anyplace that had a good spot to eat meant that everybody in the new tourist centers from the baker to the candlestick maker had something to gain. Restaurants all across France worked tirelessly to assure they would get stars. They remodeled, worked year round to produce the best food, developed their presentation, and generally went all out to create the most impressive experience available anywhere. As a result, France became globally associated with great cooking.[64]

There were other very physical changes engendered by cars as well. Accommodations changed. Prior to the automobile, hotels existed along stagecoach and railway routes, they sprang up adjacent to established tourist attractions, or they provided destinations where wealthy patrons could enjoy an extended and luxurious holiday amid a community of their peers.[65] Just as the automobile allowed travelers to move more or less spontaneously, so, too, it freed hoteliers, and the proprietors of the newly invented motel, to build in more places. Drivers could point themselves in any direction and be reasonably assured that affordable accommodations were available.[66]

Many women were thrilled to try their hand at motor touring. A 1925 magazine concluded that the expanding range of labor-saving camping equipment was directly linked to the number of housewives at campsites. Closely related, family holidays became a popular pastime on both sides of the Atlantic. In Britain, working-class campers made their way to caravan parks where they could set up amid communities of like-minded holiday-makers.[67] In the United States, army surplus tents, boots, and packs became required equipment. There were also companies anxious to create new items that quickly became essential. For example, the Colman Lantern Company began marketing gas camp stoves. By 1937, trailer construction became the fastest growing industry in America and there were already 100,000 of them on the road. It is a measure of just how deeply (and quickly) car touring entered the American psyche that even the Great Depression only inspired a short-lived dip in car-based travel.[68]

With all of these people anxious to go camping, a problem emerged: they had no place to go. While the national parks offered obvious destinations, many lacked easy access or the time required to visit far-away sites. Without other options, many simply pulled off to the side of roadways, pitched their tents, and proceeded to relax. Such camps were not aesthetically pleasing, but there were also concerns about healthfulness and sanitation. Campers would scavenge the landscape for firewood, tamp down the soil and trample vegetation, pollute the water, and leave behind human waste. Some guidebooks even instructed readers in how to cut down trees and bushes in order to construct beds or shelters. Litter proliferated. It was as if a biblical plague of motorized locusts was descending. Authorities had to act. The state parks movement was one result. Commissioners initiated campgrounds in National Forests. Private facilities opened.[69] When President Franklin D. Roosevelt launched the New Deal in an effort to put Americans to work during the Great Depression, state parks and campgrounds represented one of the important construction projects undertaken.[70]

A dilemma emerged in Norway, fueled by car camping expositions that attracted tens of thousands of people as well as by encouragement from motoring groups whose members urged their countrymen to try out the new pursuit. At first, with few organized campsites, Norwegians engaged in "wild camping," simply stopping by the roadside and pitching tents. Farmers were not amused by the "descent of noisy, undisciplined and drunken hordes spreading litter all over valuable farmland." Rather than a new deal, the solution came from drivers' associations that launched campsite construction programs.[71]

Of course, as parents well know, arriving at a destination is probably less than half the battle. Help was soon at hand. Guides instructed parents to take regular breaks from driving, visiting sites along the roadside.[72] In the years just before and after World War II, major tourist routes, especially in the United States, sprouted a new type of site designed especially for the driver anxious for a short break from a vehicle-imposed imprisonment with loved ones. Roadside attractions did not need to meet a very high standard "for they were not required to sustain long-term entertainment." These were places at which motorists stopped only for a break, a chance to divide up the drive for their children.[73] Dinosaur parks, wigwam villages, giant statues of mythical figures such as Paul Bunyan and his famous blue ox Babe, and seal caves entertained the frazzled driver.[74] Even the architecture could draw visitors. There was nothing quite like a BBQ restaurant that looked like a pig or an ice cream shop that resembled a cone of strawberry-flavored goodness.[75]

At the end of the day, cars opened up tourism to more people and from more walks of life. This new type of transport freed men, women, and children to hit the road. It encouraged developers to invent whole new things to see and places to go. It created novel ways to spend a holiday and prompted the creation of facilities to help. The advent of automobiles, then, was nothing short of a revolution. The same can be said of aircraft.

Birth of air travel

It was cold in Kitty Hawk, North Carolina on December 17, 1903, but that did not stop Orville (1871–1948) and Wilbur Wright (1867–1912), two bicycle shop owners from Dayton, Ohio who had started experimenting with gliders in 1900, from flying the first powered aircraft. A grainy one minute thirty second film captures the event. A horse-drawn trap, anachronistic beside the manmade bird, drags the plane into place. The twin props turn over and start. Then, a weight drops from an enormous tripod thrusting the plane forward. The primitive bi-plane is airborne, soaring.[76] The famous first flight lasted just twelve seconds and covered only 120 feet, but it was a foundation. Three flights followed later in the day, one covering 852 feet and lasting nearly a minute.[77] A modest distance to be sure, but the implications were enormous.

Initial progress was surprisingly slow after that day and technology changed little in the next eleven years, despite the development of new aircraft by the Wright Brothers and various European competitors.[78] This is not to say that there were no signs of things to come. Louis Bleriot (1872–1936), one of the first men to fly across the English Channel, tested a plane designed to carry passengers in 1911. He called it the "Aero Bus." Within weeks, he debuted the "Aero Taxi," also a passenger plane, displaying it to crowds at the 1911 International Aeronautical Exhibition in Paris.[79] The first regular passenger air route, the St. Petersburg-Tampa Airboat Line, commenced flying on January 1, 1914. It offered curious travelers a twenty-two-mile, twenty-minute flight for the healthy rate of $5 (heavier passengers were obliged to pay more). Within only a few months the company went bankrupt.[80] Yet, when World War I started in August 1914, planes remained little more advanced than they had been in 1903. Handling was poor, flight distances unimpressive.[81]

The war changed everything. The opposing sides found themselves living in trenches that they burrowed into the mud of northern France. Battles followed a soon familiar pattern. Unimaginable artillery barrages, designed to remove enemy machine gun nests, lasted for up to a week. Then, commanders ordered their men "over the top" and the soldiers were left to run across a barren "no man's land" in an effort to take enemy positions at bayonet point. It was an inefficient strategy. Neither side ever gained more than a few hundred feet of territory and the death tolls were unlike anything previously imagined. At the Battle of Verdun there were 300,000 French and German dead as well as 750,000 wounded. At the Battle of the Somme, British forces lost some 420,000, the French 200,000, and the Germans anywhere from 450,000 to 650,000.[82] Author Gertrude Stein (1874–1946) famously referred to the result as the creation of a "lost generation."[83]

Terrible as it was, the realities of combat had astonishing technological implications. As soldiers and their officers lay hunkered down in the cold mud, trying desperately to stave off a fungal disease called "trench foot" and avoid being eaten alive by rats,[84] military strategists looked for any advantage that might break the stalemate. Aviation seemed a promising option and officials poured money into the search for better aircraft with which to prosecute the world's first air war.[85]

When the first military aircraft took to the skies, they were adept at one thing: flying in a straight line. They were not powerful enough to carry bombs and none were designed to field a machine gun. Incapable of the type of aerial acrobatics necessary to engage with an enemy, planes only conducted short reconnaissance flights over enemy trenches to gather information that would increase the accuracy of artillery. Pilots avoided contact with enemy aircraft.[86] Had this remained the only use for military planes, few design changes would have been necessary. Of course, that is not what happened. French pilot Roland Garros (1888–1918), for example, carried a marksman with him in his aircraft and took part in dogfights with German pilots almost from the first moment he reached enemy airspace. After confronting a German plane armed with machine guns, Garros started the process of arming French aircraft in a similar manner: Anything to improve his ability to engage. As a result, and building on the experiments of an earlier engineer, Garros developed a propeller that was protected against the bullets fired by his own machine gun. By March 1915 his new innovation made him virtually unstoppable, until, of course, the Germans developed a gear that would modulate their machine guns, halting fire whenever the propeller passed in front.[87] At the same time, aircraft designers built planes that could turn, dive, and climb in such a way as to allow pilots to use more and more effective maneuvers when encountering the enemy.[88] It took very little time for aircraft engineering and design to make quantum leaps forward and a new class of fighter "ace" emerged.

The public was enthralled. Against the hellish backdrop of the trenches, the pilot emerged as "an airborne knight armed with a machine gun who jousted in the sky." Men such as Germany's Manfred von Richthofen (the "Red Baron"; 1892–1918), Britain's Edward Mannock (1887–1918), and America's Edward Rickenbacker (1890–1973) were soon household names. While the reality was quite different, the public imagined these men as the embodiment of chivalry, never anxious to shoot down a wounded competitor, always ready to do the right thing. Journalists did their best to sell this narrative, promoting particular aces almost as sports-writers celebrate specific athletes. Artists depicted pilots fighting a good fight and, when the end came, dying heroic deaths with angels carrying them skyward to heaven aboard winged horses. Posters and postcards followed, elevating pilots to exalted status.[89]

There were two results. First, aircraft after World War I were worlds ahead of those which came before. It was night and day. Postwar planes showed real utility, whereas before the war they were little more than novelty. Second, flying now enjoyed a level of romance, especially in Europe, that was attractive to the masses. Even when flight was not romanticized, it still captured peoples' attention. Writer Virginia Woolf (1882–1941), for example, used aircraft to symbolize a sort of modern alienation. In *Mrs. Dalloway* (1925), Woolf describes a skywriting plane as it scrawls an advertisement across the London sky. Her language is telling. For Woolf, the plane is not graceful or beautiful, heroic or majestic. Instead, it "*bored* ominously into the ears of the crowd." She repeats the use of the verb "bore" a page later as if to suggest that this technology, even more than the automobile which first captures the primary character's attention and is then ignored when the plane appears, will pierce society.[90] Whether positive or negative, the reality is the same: aircraft could not be disregarded.

Whereas some worried about this brave new world, the majority wanted a taste of flight. Although it was illegal in Britain to engage in commercial aviation until April 1919, some retired Royal Air Force (RAF) pilots pursued careers taking members of the public on short trips as soon as the ban was lifted. In June and July of that year, aerialists took Blackpool holidaymakers on short flights for money. At least 10,000 people went up for rides in just two months. The jaunts, and the fact that so many undertook them, soon made many Britons feel comfortable with flying and it did not take long before entrepreneurs made longer flights available. Even in the days immediately after the legal restrictions were lifted, an air route between Manchester and Liverpool was opened for businessmen and wealthy pleasure-seekers.[91]

From the moment the ban on air travel outside of Britain ended during the late summer of 1919, the Aircraft Travel and Transport Company (AT & T) opened a passenger service between London and Paris, making 147 flights during the first ten weeks of operation. Its remarkable record was certainly helped by a railway strike during the autumn months.[92] It was not, however, impressive enough. At £21 for a round-trip ticket and few seats available on the earliest planes—retired and slightly modified World War I bombers—mail carrying was the primary source of income alongside state subsidies. The problem for AT & T was that the British government was reluctant to offer large enough subsidies to meet costs. In contrast to European governments such as those of Belgium, Holland, Denmark, Sweden, and Russia which all poured money into national airlines that appeared within weeks of AT & T, the British government proved little interested in offering an adequate subvention for the start-up.

While the British Parliament debated how deeply to support civil aviation, European governments justified their support for the industry along a number of lines that often had little to do with passenger travel or mail transport per se. Airplanes were symbols as much as modes of conveyance. For a state such as Germany, angry about the harsh sanctions imposed upon it by the Treaty of Versailles that ended World War I, starting a commercial airline symbolized a semblance of sovereignty. For the new Communist government in Russia, it demonstrated an embrace of modernity. For imperial powers such as Belgium, Holland, Italy, Spain, and Portugal, it promised easier access to colonial holdings. Consequently, these states quickly offered money to their new airlines.[93] By 1921, the British recognized their error and launched into a concerted debate about how best to pursue aviation development, eventually providing greater subsidies and even pushing for the amalgamation of a number of small airline businesses into a single company called Imperial Airlines in 1924.[94]

As enticing as many governments found aircraft, and as fascinated as many in the public were with the technology, the cost and discomfort of early travel created a challenge when trying to attract paying customers.[95] One passenger aboard a very early Aircraft Travel and Transport Company flight across the English Channel describes a plane furnished with four armchairs. Much like today, customs took too long and the man's flight left the ground thirty-five minutes late. Once in the air, he found the experience exhilarating, but painfully loud. The plane did not feel "steady" in the air, although "nobody was actually sick." In order to communicate with the passengers, the pilot scribbled on notepaper and handed it back into the cabin. The flight from Hounslow (London) to Le Bourget (Paris) took two hours and twenty minutes. On the return trip, the plane encountered a storm and the flight lasted three hours as a consequence. Despite the gale, the pioneering airline customer found it impossible "to feel uneasiness—such a sense of security is given by these reliable machines and fine pilots."

Some passengers were a little too confident in the new airplanes. They demanded to fly in all weather and at night. Forecasts were sketchy at best and pilots always had to rely on their own judgment, but the over-eager passengers created another challenge. On one hand, if the pilots could successfully carry passengers through near hurricanes, they would make more money and gain healthy reputations that would lead to even greater financial returns. On the other hand, if they crashed, their careers and possibly their lives were done. It was often a difficult choice that the airline itself had to balance with the growth of the insurance industry. The inherent hazards of flying soon led to the creation of an agency concerned entirely with aviation, the British Aviation Insurance Group.[96]

Given the hazards associated with air travel, to say nothing of the expense, the wider public, especially in the United States, was reluctant to abandon earlier technologies such as steam trains. Women played an important role in changing the narrative in the States. The public was fascinated with "intrepid birdmen," which pilot fans imagined to be "a breed apart," a kind of "modern superman." Aviation magazines urged that people see things differently, noting that "No special 'air sense' or divine gift is required," but the masses were skeptical. Female pilots altered the story. Manila Davis (1898–1973), a particularly outspoken pilot, informed her countrymen "if I can fly and land a plane successfully, weighing as I do but 105 pounds, almost anyone ought to be able to." Many female pilots sold planes, raced, and completed flights aimed to promote aircraft and other products. They could seldom attain work flying passenger planes because "the public simply doesn't have confidence in women fliers," but their existence did not go unnoticed. They played up their femininity, many were married, and they "made every 'sacrifice' to insure that people thought of flying 'in the best light.'" It paid off. Women "made flying acceptable to the masses primarily by acting as lady-fliers." [97] They domesticated the air. If women could do it, then surely it must be safe for everybody else.

Demand grew and there was a rapid push by the various world airlines to increase available routes. Colonial powers were anxious to assure easy access to distant colonies. By the mid-1930s itineraries were created from Belgium to the Congo, from Germany to Russia, and even from the Netherlands to Djakarta in Indonesia.[98] It was not so much about making money as it was about symbolism and the exercise of power. Control demanded unrestricted entry and rapid communication—both more easily provided by air.

The early long-distance routes were tenable because they negotiated only comparatively short passages over water, meaning that the major challenge was diplomatic—countries had to allow access to their airspace—rather than technological. These trips did involve a great deal of up and down, however. A passenger flying from London to India in 1927 enjoyed stops in "Dijon, Marseille, Pisa, Naples, Homs, Benghazi, Sollum, Aboukir, Bushire, Lingeh, Jask, Pasni, Karachi and Jodhpur," before finally arriving in Delhi. The flying time was sixty-five hours.[99]

Even in the United States, getting from one side of the continent to the other via the air was no easy task. The States came to commercial aviation very late—there were no American companies until 1926—but, after that date, it quickly committed itself to getting people across the country. Transcontinental Air Transport (TAT) inaugurated its service in 1929. It took passengers forty-eight hours to reach San Francisco from New York and the trip was anything but a straight shot. Planes could not fly at night, so the aircraft landed in order to unload passengers onto a special train that carried them through the darkness until it was bright enough to fly again. Because planes could not go great distances or fly in adverse conditions, there were airfields every ten to twenty miles where planes could refuel or wait-out storms. Naturally, things did get faster. Just one year after their first flight, the trans-US time was cut to thirty-six hours and these periods dropped as night flying became safer.

Although the airlines certainly made an effort to provide comfort, long journeys must have been especially taxing. TAT trips, for example, featured wicker chairs that slid around the cabin, a dearth of insulation insuring that it was usually quite cold, enough vibration that passengers had difficulty keeping their glasses on, and noise so loud that intrepid travelers were forced to stuff their ears with wool or go deaf.[100] European airlines were no better. During the 1920s pilots were instructed to fly routes such that railways were never visible to passengers lest paying customers realize that they might actually travel both faster and in more comfort on a train.[101]

If regular chances to land were unavailable, such as when flying the North Atlantic between Europe and the United States, long-haul trips were more difficult. There were at least two promising technologies. The first, flying boats, represented a real option, but they were not without challenges. In particular, one had to refuel. Pan-American airlines looked into landing on various islands, or perhaps setting down in the arctic. Neither was viable. Imperial Airways explored the possibility of airborne refueling. Again, the technology did not work out. Similarly, efforts carried out during the 1930s to develop a truly long-haul flying boat capable of negotiating the distance failed to take shape until the eve of World War II.[102]

During the interwar years, the most promising technology for trans-Atlantic flights was not an airplane at all but, rather, the German Zeppelin. These aircraft were large hydrogen-filled balloons with luxurious cabins strung below. Flying by Zeppelin was comfortable. The cabins were relatively large and passengers could move around to take advantage of dining rooms, viewpoints, a small library, and even a specially designed smoking room. The promenade decks were the most significant attraction. As an American passenger recalled some years later:

> Outboard of the public rooms, and separated from them by a low railing, were fifty-foot promenades connected by a cross-passage between the two sides of the A deck. This afforded a walking distance of nearly 200 feet for transatlantic passengers used to the daily constitutional around a steamer deck. Outboard of the promenades were six large Plexi-glass windows, slanting outwards at 45°, often left open as there was no draught in or outwards even at an air speed of eighty knots. Here the passengers stood or sat for hours on low cushioned seats, enthralled by the sight of foaming waves, tossing ships, forests, towns, rivers and cities, going by only a few hundred feet below. Curtains drawn at night between the promenade and public rooms enabled the travelers to enjoy the sight of moonlight on the waves, the brilliance of the stars, without the glare and reflection of artificial lighting.

Perhaps best of all, these great flying machines made the crossing in just forty-three hours.[103] At the time, it seemed probable that trans-Atlantic flight would remain the exclusive domain of the Zeppelin.

The Hindenburg disaster ended the dream. On May 6, 1937, the largest and most luxurious of the Zeppelins burst into flames while landing in Lakehurst, New Jersey, killing thirty-six people. The fireball, depicted in newsreel footage and in a remarkable commentary by newscaster Herbert Morrison (1905–89), quickly broke the popular love affair with Zeppelins. Some other form of trans-Atlantic transport would be needed.[104]

When World War II erupted in September 1939, trans-Atlantic leisure and business travel all but ceased. Yet as with World War I, World War II introduced technological and social changes that ultimately made mass leisure travel possible. In particular, the need to carry out long-distance bombing runs generated pressurized cockpits. Planes could now travel higher and faster while requiring less fuel. German engineers developed the jet engine, a technology that would eventually make it possible to fly hundreds of miles an hour faster than in propeller-driven aircraft. The widespread use of planes to carry troops during the war created a generation of men familiar with air travel and spartan accommodations. Luring customers with promises of luxury became less necessary, assuring that airlines could adopt seating plans that packed passengers into their planes in closely spaced rows.[105]

Conclusion

Bicycles, planes, trains, and automobiles (as well as steamships) assured that tourism was increasingly a mass concern. It catered to people from across the class spectrum, offering freedom and escape, fun and good health. After the Great War, the Western world represented a new political landscape. Three different ideologies vied with one another for dominance and they looked for ways with which to gain the favor of the masses. Tourism promised to be a useful tool, a new chapter in the politicization of leisure.

8

Tourism during the interwar years

The nineteenth century was remarkable, filled with technological and cultural innovation, a rising standard of living, and widespread, though far from universal, optimism about the future. World War I (1914–18) changed much of this, especially for Europeans. It was a very different conflict from those of prior centuries. The Great War went on and on, seemingly without end. Casualty rates were dizzying, a sharp contrast with what had taken place in the past. Technology was supposed to make life better, yet on the battlefield it seemed only to result in mass death and vicious dismemberment. Young men, once the picture of health, were reduced to shadows.

When many historians look back at this time, they see a world thrown into a sudden and profound transformation. The war spelled the beginning of the end of empire, started the process of turning the United States into the premier global economic powerhouse, and ushered in the vote for women in several countries. It challenged the hegemony of nineteenth-century class hierarchies, largely because so many members of the elite died in Flanders. The bloody clash altered the way that people commemorate their dead, and started to change the character of administration in many countries, introducing a sense that the state should adopt a more paternal role. Governments ought to care for the people and assure that they have homes to live in, healthcare to keep them well, and money to spell them during times of crisis. Sometimes the war created change, at times it sped up existing trends, but it stands as a shocking zero hour, a starting point for what philosopher Isaiah Berlin (1909–97) called "the most terrible century in Western history" and what Nobel Laureate author William Golding (1911–93) described as "the most violent century" ever.[1]

After the Great War the world *did* look different. Far more than in the past, governments recognized the necessity of appealing to a mass audience. The days of hereditary rule were over. According to historian Mark Mazower, the result was a three-way conflict over how best to govern, over how to appeal to the masses. Democracy, fascism, and communism all promised "their own utopia as an End to History—whether in the form of universal communism, global democracy or a Thousand Year Reich."[2] Each depended on universal support, on a willing public that believed in the efficacy of the state and its ideology.

That is where tourism entered the frame. Its development over the previous two hundred years assured that it now stood variously as a synecdoche for rest, relaxation, health, adventure, identity, and affluence. During the war, the industry's fortunes varied from place to place. Blackpool, on England's northwest coast, offered an escape for servicemen and others from the wartime grind, while being safely removed from the front lines. Scarborough, bombed at the start of the war, was less fortunate.[3] Although a few areas in Scotland continued to attract tourists, the interruption of shipping lines as well as food rationing generally led to a serious drop in visitor numbers. Leisure travel to the Continent, meanwhile, all but dried up.[4] Across the pond, in the United States, the inaccessibility of European tourism destinations had profound implications, especially for the national parks which emerged as America's "preeminent tourist attractions," largely because "touring the parks was presented as a ritual of citizenship" at a time when patriotism was already at a premium.[5]

Whatever the varied implications of war, by 1918, both bicycles and automobiles made it possible for people to travel far from their homes. There existed a sense that mobility brought cultural capital and social prestige. Many believed that getting away from day-to-day tedium was healthy, even vital to a long and happy life. Not everybody bought into these ideas, of course, but governments of all stripes imagined that leisure travel offered a way forward, a tool for mastering the masses. As a consequence, states used it to accomplish one or more of at least four different goals. First, many hoped to use holidays to improve the health of the population. Closely related, leisure travel granted an opportunity to teach citizens about the nation, its landscapes and culture, and the racial and/or political superiority of the state and its people. Third, tourism offered a showcase for modernity. Highways, cars, great cruise ships, fancy resorts, and more could stand as symbols of a regime's modern outlook. Finally, the budding new industry offered a source for economic growth,[6] whether for underdeveloped regions or for countries anxious to move beyond poverty.

Fascist tourism

The origins and characteristics of fascism are among the most hotly contested issues in modern history, largely because the various fascist movements often appear to be quite different from one another. Each reflected the unique demands of its country of origin. What worked in Italy did not necessarily function in Brazil; Germany was different from Japan or Spain. As a consequence, at least one historian suggests that it is better to define fascism in terms of what broad similarities do exist rather than according to a fixed checklist. These movements were intensely nationalistic, adopted "corporatist" economic models, were anti-liberal and anti-communist, made great use of theatricality, believed in the value of violence, and so forth.[7] Paradoxically, fascist states were often virulently anti-modern at the same time that they utilized hyper-modern technologies and ideas, what historian Jeffrey Herf calls "reactionary modernism."[8]

Tourism represented a useful tool for such governments because it allowed the state to focus attention on what made the nation great, generate comparisons with other countries deemed inferior, and promote the healthfulness of its people.[9] At the same time, providing holidays to citizens made it possible for the state to show that it was *doing* something for its inhabitants, to create a contrast with the dysfunctional governments that preceded the rise of the new ideology.

Italy instituted the first fascist government. Benito "Il Duce" Mussolini (1883–1945), the child of devoted socialists, started the movement. Although he spent his youth reading Marxist theory, an encounter with the work of German philosopher Friedrich Nietzsche (1844–1900) sent him in a different direction. The future dictator imagined marrying socialism with Nietzschean ideas of the "superman," a strong leader around whom the state would revolve. Postwar Italy was an ideal place for such an experiment. The government was unstable and no parliamentary party could achieve a strong majority, necessitating frequent elections. Economic problems, large strikes, internal division, and other issues all seemed intractable. After carefully organized political theater, orchestrated street violence, and clever politicking, Mussolini assumed power, gradually implementing his new "fascist" politics.[10]

Il Duce's new ideology involved integrating government tightly into people's lives economically, culturally, and socially. Leisure was one means toward this end. European workers are traditionally associated with the political left. Mussolini's regime represented a significant departure from this alignment and laborers were not always enthusiastic. Tourism and leisure provided an opportunity to win their support by showing that the party could provide tangible benefits. Fascism could be fun. *Opera Nazionale Dopolavoro* (OND), the Italian leisure organization usually referred to simply as *Dopolavoro* ("After Work"), was designed to teach Italians how to use their spare time. Left alone, they might waste free moments and engage in activities that were not beneficial to the state. Such behavior would reflect badly on Italy. Careful instruction could fix the problem.

The Dopolavoro idea did not originate with the Fascists themselves. It was the brainchild of Mario Giani (dates unknown), a former manager of the Westinghouse Corporation's subsidiary in Vado Ligure. The idea was simple. A carefully designed leisure group might offer a sort of social engineering scheme designed to inspire "'healthy' and 'praiseworthy pastimes' ... selected according to 'criteria of practicality, efficiency, and enlightened modernity.'"[11] At the same time, it would be good business, improving relations between workers and management. The new organization would offer suitable activities, strive to attain control over existing clubs, and encourage good behavior.

The plan was not an overnight success. Founded in 1923 using private funds, only 13,000 people had joined by mid-1924. Still, the group did not go unnoticed. The notion of organizing leisure caught the attention of the National Confederation of Fascist Syndicates which was anxious to replace existing working-class groups with their own labor associations. The challenge was to develop programs that might draw the interest of skeptical workers. Following a brief political crisis in June 1924, the "social question" became a leading priority for the government, prompting Mussolini and his supporters to nationalize Giani's organization. Within months, the OND provided the new dictatorship with a means of closely coordinating "national policy with locally sponsored initiatives."[12]

Dopolavoro pursued an agenda of "promoting the healthy and profitable occupation of workers' leisure hours by means of institutions for developing their physical, intellectual, and moral capacities."[13] The new group devoured extant clubs and the Fascists used preexisting infrastructure to make the transfer of power easier. By 1937, the body sponsored "some 50,000 foot marches, day outings, and tours." Bunting, contests, speeches, group singing, and fanfares all helped to raise trips planned by the Dopolavoro from the commonplace to the exciting.

Inexpensive activities were the most popular. Cycle tours, for example, were particularly well liked (one of the largest preexisting groups that the OND took over was the Italian Touring Club, a major cycling group originally founded in 1892). Such outings were easy on the pocket, "the one pastime almost every *dopolavorista* could afford." Beginning in August 1931, Dopolavoro expanded its offerings to encourage affordable excursions by rail. The OND provided workers with discounted tickets so that they could embark on short group holidays. Not only did the price reductions promise to help workers travel, they were also designed to bolster the state railways.

And yet the OND was not an unbridled success. Mussolini and his leadership had little interest in "low culture" and took over Dopolavoro more out of expediency than true belief. They were loath to provide adequate funding in order to really explore the potential of tourism as a political tool.

Without money, the OND was in no position to offer large-scale cruises or truly affordable long-stay holidays. Even with its low-cost offerings, ordinary workers often could not afford the tickets that were available.[14]

In Germany, the Nazis created a much better financed and more expansive equivalent to the Dopolavoro. The National Socialist Democratic Party (NSDAP) assumed control of Germany in 1933. When the Nazis came to power, they did so on the shoulders of a broad coalition drawn from across the social spectrum. Even so, Adolf Hitler (1889–1945) and his leadership felt that their hold on the working class was weak. Most laborers supported the largest party in Germany, the Socialist Democratic Party (SDP), the Communist Party (KDP), or an assortment of smaller left-leaning groups.[15] This was threatening to the National Socialists so they quickly crushed their political opponents. Within only six months, "the largest and best-organised workers' movement in the world" was eliminated.[16] Something had to fill the void so the Nazis quickly built their own working-class organizations: the German Labor Force and *Kraft durch Freude* (KdF), or "Strength through Joy," which was based on the Italian leisure group.[17]

More than just a replacement for Weimar-era bodies, the KdF promised to improve the health of the population by offering outings and raising living standards. It proposed to teach the people to be better Germans while distinguishing the Nazi regime from either hated communist or market-driven governments.[18] It would showcase the state's modernity even while emphasizing older landscapes and traditions. And the KdF would fuel economic growth, especially in underdeveloped areas such as rural Bavaria, while simultaneously breaking down the barriers between social classes within the "Fatherland."

KdF director Robert Ley (1890–1945) traveled to Italy as early as 1932 to observe how Italians handled "free time." He was impressed with the OND but did not believe that it went far enough. The workplace had to be addressed as much as leisure did. It was necessary to draw together far more elements than the Italians attempted. He envisioned sporting events, hiking trips, excursions, resorts, cruises, and other extended holidays. There would even be an easily affordable automobile: the KdF Wagon, widely known as the Volkswagen Beetle.[19]

All of this cost money and Ley drew funds from a variety of sources. First, he redirected cash from the now defunct leftists groups abolished by the Nazis in 1933. Next, he demanded that businesses pay dues to the KdF. Finally, he raised money by charging for performances and organized trips. Although some workers were selected to travel free of charge, most had to pay for their KdF holidays—though the organization did manage to keep prices far lower than were offered by commercial concerns.[20]

Most workers suffered very low wages. The average salary was a scant 25DM per week. This meant that many could not afford to participate in organized trips despite the low cost.[21] An even larger barrier was cultural. Laborers grew accustomed to saving their money for the purchase of food, furniture, rent, and other tangible items during the long period of economic crisis that followed World War I. Convincing them that they should spend their resources on recreation was not always easy.[22] Yet efforts were not a total wash. In 1938–9 alone, 27,610 companies provided funding so that 463,800 employees could go on KdF vacations.[23]

Once in operation, the organization set about trying to meet its economic and ideological goals. Although most Germans who took part in Strength through Joy trips were from urban areas, the KdF used tourism as a means to aid disadvantaged communities. Many parts of rural Bavaria, for example, were quite poor, so planners used their holiday packages as an opportunity to promote economic development; they utilized local residences and small hotels to house tourists. This approach not only kept costs down, potentially increasing the number of lower to middle-income travelers, it also pumped resources into local communities rather than into the pockets of commercial leisure providers.[24]

Germany is often associated with "blood and soil" nationalism. That is, being German is defined both by having the right blood and by having a link to the national landscape.[25] Hiking trips made this connection to the land immediately tangible. Outings to characteristically German areas such as the Black Forest and Bavaria allowed citizens to see their culture on display in the form of traditional architecture or costumes. Still other expeditions visited major cities such as the international port of Hamburg. Here, the KdF emphasized the country's growing industry. Tourists were able to see the nation's greatness blossoming before their eyes.[26] There were also excursions that ran much further afield, allowing officials to draw a distinction between the prominence of Germany and the inferiority of other states. There were still more closely related lessons. Only Aryans could participate; Jews and others deemed inferior were excluded. Officials showed racial elites how much the Nazis were doing for *them* while camouflaging the horrible implications of Nazi policy for the rest of the population. Leisure operated as a wedge between racial groups.[27]

That travelers got the message was not left to chance. Kraft durch Freude provided careful instruction through testimonials in its magazine. Readers were treated to stories that reflected the organization's goals. One article told of the impact that a KdF trip had on a thirty-two-year-old worker. As far as the Nazis were concerned, the man was irresponsible because he had never bothered to wed or even to consider marrying. While on a Strength through Joy trip, however, he met a young woman from Berlin. They hit it off, but only as the tour was coming to an end. After returning to their respective homes, they stopped corresponding until she sent him a scrapbook of images from their time together. He was overcome and rushed to Berlin where he found her and immediately proposed. Through the KdF he had become a responsible German. He had learned to be a man. Other testimonials stressed the poverty of other countries and the glories of Germany.[28]

Cartoons also underlined German superiority. One depicted a spear-carrying, human bone-lugging African chieftain named "Wahatupa" who was naked save for a loincloth. The chief informed his tribesmen: "No one eats a KdF vacationer on my watch. We too have to show that we're cultured." While the cartoon reflected German respectability, it also served as a subtle way of teaching KdF holidaymakers how they should act. Obey orders and show the world that you are well behaved.[29]

Strength through Joy offered its first package tours only three months after its founding. Initially, the group leased cruise ships, but in 1938–9 it bought two of its own. Destinations varied from the Isle of Wight in the English Channel (which Hitler promised to give to the KdF for development as a holiday resort after he conquered Britain), Genoa, Naples, Lisbon, and even Cairo, Istanbul, and Jerusalem. There was nothing innocent about these choices. Poverty was often on display, creating a stark contrast with the Fatherland's rising affluence. Visitors were meant to conclude that Germany was superior and Hitler's desire to attain greater "living space" for his people was justified. The trips also reflected Hitler's foreign policy objectives. One of the most popular cruise endpoints was Madeira—long a destination for wealthy English holidaymakers. By taking the German working class to this elite outpost, the Nazis demonstrated that they had no time for the class system and even less respect for what was previously "British" territory.[30]

The KdF reached an impressive number of Germans. In 1934, participants in KdF cultural activities totaled 9,111,663. By 1938 this number increased to 54,568,467.[31] Still more were exposed to Strength through Joy advertising and propaganda. The organization's tourism activities "enabled nearly forty-three million Germans to participate in its day outings, weekend excursions, and longer domestic and overseas vacation trips."[32] In other words, the group's message of respectability, classless society, racial and national superiority, and economic development reached a broad audience.

Communist tourism

Communism represents the opposite end of the political spectrum from fascism, yet tourism presented similar opportunities to the Bolsheviks who assumed control of Russia after the October Revolution of 1917.

The Soviet Union was a revolutionary state, based on the formation of a classless society.[33] For some Soviet intellectuals, tourism offered a path toward this new utopia. Although communists typically associated leisure travel with capitalism, wasted time, and diminished productivity, it nevertheless promised the chance to create a sense of fundamental difference. The Soviet Union could invent a *new* type of tourism, while at the same time improving the health of Russians, both mentally and physically.

Tourism was not new to Russia. Before the Bolshevik Revolution, members of the bourgeoisie, like their Western counterparts, visited spas and the seaside. They enjoyed beautiful views. Most of them wanted to explore Western Europe although there were also opportunities for adventure in the "Motherland" itself. [34] For the revolutionaries who overthrew the old Tsarist political system, such activities were a lesson in sloth and were the very embodiment of class hierarchy. The problem for Vladimir Lenin (1870–1924) and his followers was that this brand of tourism failed to symbolize classless society. It was anything but egalitarian.

Soviet tourism had to be different. As historian Diane P. Koenker summarizes:

> The Soviet project rested its appeal and legitimacy on the theory that under socialism, the contradictions of bourgeois life would disappear. Instead of a society in which one person's pleasure was bought at the expense of another's toil and in which toil, pleasure, and learning remained separate and mutually exclusive activities, socialism would allow every individual to share in every social activity. This was a totalist ambition: under Soviet socialism, everyone would work, everyone would engage in productive self-improvement, and everyday life would acquire a new meaning because it would combine work, self-improvement, and pleasure in one.

Soviet ideologues dreamed of creating a unique "proletarian tourism" that would be collective yet also self-improving.[35]

There were two difficulties. First, there existed a variety of competing ideas about how to craft this new style of leisure. Second, the men who promised to create proletarian tourism were hopelessly informed by the consumer-centered ideas detailed throughout this book.[36] Still, new ways of running and/or thinking about tourism emerged. One focused narrowly on health, another promised more types of leisure, but did so on a commercial basis, and a third offered variety while endeavoring to remain tied to more collectivist models of organization.

In the first instance, and drawing on modern "science," medical professionals determined the "best form of rest: whether a six-week recuperation in a tuberculosis sanatorium, a month-long stay at a 'climate' rest home, or a long-distance backpacking trip for the physically healthy but emotionally drained urban worker." Armed with a certificate, patients were ready to go on holiday[37]—often on their own, regardless of marital status, because there was no guarantee that everybody in a family would receive the same diagnosis. Some officials felt that time apart might even be good for couples.[38] For propagandists, such a vacation provided opportunity to draw distinctions between Soviet Russia and the rest of the world. Promotional films celebrated the "combination of medicine, luxury, contemporaneity, and fun." Everything was up-to-date. All was modern.[39] Like most things in the Soviet Union, much of this was exaggeration.

It was not the sort of holiday that appealed to everybody. Some wanted to see new sites and to visit new places rather than spending time in a single location, especially if that spot was essentially a hospital. For officials, there was nothing wrong with this, as long as it had a useful purpose. Soviet tourism had to be distinguished from capitalistic modes of leisure by an emphasis on "purpose and rigor." It would "invite broad masses of workers, peasants, students, and intellectuals to become purposeful tourism activists, to develop tourist skills, and to choose the rigors of the road for their annual vacations from work." The challenge was to create a network of facilities to service these travelers.[40]

Sovetskii turist, or *Sovtur* was devised to meet this demand. Sovtur saw tourism as an educational opportunity and sought to "use the rest and leisure of toilers to broaden their production horizons."[41] The new body functioned as a travel agency, organizing package tours on a commercial basis while also striving to construct recreational facilities around Russia, assuring infrastructure in often previously undeveloped areas.

Proletarian tourism put Russians in touch with their country. Like the KdF's trips to places in rural Germany, this brand of travel "led to a heightened sense of patriotism." It allowed people from different backgrounds to meet, while teaching travelers skills that might also have "critical military significance" such as map reading and navigation. "Fostering the love of one's country," as historian Diane P. Koenker further explains, "would encourage the tourist to defend it if the need arose."[42] Sometimes these tourists also engaged in what twenty-first century tourism scholars call "voluntourism." They traveled to faraway places and then helped the locals by repairing equipment, engaging in childcare, and transporting reading materials.[43]

Yet Sovtur walked a dangerous ideological tightrope. By developing package tours it resembled the bourgeois leisure that existed in capitalist states. For devoted Soviets, the commercial aspect of the program was too much to stomach.[44] Consequently, another organization, the Society of

Proletarian Tourism, formed in 1928 to create something more in keeping with leftist ideas. Toward this end, the body attempted to form "tourist cells" or "sections" by developing a support base within Soviet factories. By 1932, after four years of effort, the group had 800,000 members and claimed to serve as many as three million tourists—an involvement of between 33 and 60 percent of all "toilers."[45]

Democratic tourism

Democratic states were as interested in tourism and leisure as fascist and communist ones, although they approached it rather differently. According to historian Gary Cross, "The vacation was not merely mass escapism as Europe prepared for war; rather, the paid holiday was a deeply felt social need which, after the war, became one of the most valued entitlements in Europe."[46] Some of the reasons for this matched those in "totalitarian" countries. As in fascist states, officials often saw leisure as "a vehicle for a 'politics of consent.'" It created loyalty by showing workers that the state cared and helped to create a sense of shared purpose.[47] Remunerated time off also "created 'a democratic civilization' with a tendency 'toward social equality.'" The philosopher Bertrand Russell (1872–1970) argued the point well, noting "that instead of a leisure class, which 'produced a few Darwins and many fox hunters,' ... 'ordinary men and women, having the opportunity of a happy life, will become more kindly and less inclined to view others with suspicion.'"[48] Tourism would make better citizens by allowing them to "discover the beauties" of their country—promoting patriotism and a sense of national identity in the process.[49]

Many believed that paid leave for leisure would generate stronger families and healthier citizens. The vacation was a gift that a man could give his family. A shared respite allowed couples and their children to live together under one roof uninterrupted by work time, to relax together, to play on the beach as a unit. Harried husbands and wives, often seeing one another only after a long day of toil, too tired to see straight, could rediscover their mutual affection. It was possible to use the occasion to visit aging relatives elsewhere, thus strengthening the extended family.[50] Time off from work was also good for the individual. A "change of environment" was deemed absolutely necessary for good health.[51] Echoing an idea that was by now well established, the "vacation was necessary for self-development."

There was little dissent concerning these views and even some employers admitted "vacations are necessary in the modern world." They hoped that paid rest would increase worker discipline and could "implant in the minds of the employees that they are actually part of the business." By scheduling the annual leave during seasonal periods of low demand for production, it was possible to attain these benefits without costing the company revenue.[52]

Governments recognized that the holidays with pay idea was a transnational movement. Between 1919 and 1925 "legislation extended paid vacations to various workers in six Eastern and Central European countries."[53] By 1935, fourteen different states, including Brazil, Chile, Peru, Mexico, and Cuba, as well as many more in Europe, legislated that workers should enjoy paid time off from work.[54] French and British leaders were certainly aware of the trend. In 1934, 1936, 1937, and 1938 Germany hosted major international hotels and tourism conferences—making the KdF "the showpiece" of the 1936 World Congress for Leisure Time and Recreation.[55] At least some were convinced. Irish officials, busily building their own tourism industry, looked to the Third Reich for ideas and sent officials to Germany to observe the Strength through Joy program in action.[56] French representatives, meanwhile, saw an opportunity to draw a contrast; tourism should bring "joy," "spontaneity," and "unity," they said. It was about a "breaking-down of the walls" separating social groups. By contrast, the KdF was squarely about "national self-promotion or voluntary obedience." Whereas German leisure fueled negative contrasts between people, French holidays promised to make societies "less prone ... to make war" because time off "promotes peace for it magnifies life and makes one love life."[57]

Against this backdrop, on June 20, 1936, a Socialist-leaning government in France led by Léon Blum (1872–1950) passed legislation mandating a fifteen-day paid vacation for workers every year.[58] The British were more circumspect, relying on employers to offer compensated holidays on their own. The approach worked relatively well. 1.5 million wage earners, unburdened by concern about lost salary, enjoyed relaxing time off in 1935 and the number jumped to 7.75 million by March 1938—roughly 40 percent of the workforce.[59]

In contrast to fascist and communist states, democratic ones tended to depend on private efforts and on the free market, a faith in capitalism that could be read as a political lesson in itself. In France, a variety of groups—working-class organizations, the Catholic Church, and employers—stepped in to "provide low-cost vacation opportunities distinct from the existing tourism and vacation industry."[60] Before 1936, French leisure was squarely aimed at elites, often revolving around luxury hotels. Such facilities, as depicted in the 1932 Oscar-winning American film *Grand Hotel*, catered to every need. Legions of bellhops were on hand to collect bags, deliver food, do laundry, and arrange travel. Fancy hotel bars and restaurants offered not only food and drink, but also dancing and entertainment. French laborers knew nothing of such experiences. Tourism boosters had their work cut out for them, needing to teach workers how to enjoy time away from their toils.[61] Just as Germans had to be instructed to spend money on leisure rather than squirreling it away, so French workers had to learn how to use their free time. Pro-tourism class-based groups thus generated programs that made cheap excursion tickets available. They created guided tours of Paris for those from the countryside. They built inexpensive accommodations (especially for young people) and they constructed sports facilities.[62]

The British government was not anxious to throw itself into the tourism business either, taking only small steps to facilitate private initiative. Thus, the state passed legislation in 1921 permitting resorts to use "profits from municipal enterprises up to the equivalent of the penny rate" to advertise the health and pleasure industry.[63] Along similar lines, the Department of Overseas Trade "supported," but did not take part in or finance, a movement launched by a group of hoteliers in 1926 advocating that outsiders "Come to Britain." Such initiatives were anything but aggressive and the numbers do not lie. The French government gave £25,000 to its tourist agency and was widely criticized for being miserly. The Italians gave theirs £250,000. Germany spent £60,000 on publicity alone. By contrast, the "Come to Britain" scheme managed to raise a mere £1,945. It failed. Despite this, state-sponsorship increased little with time. During the 1930s and against the backdrop of development efforts on the continent, the Board of Trade offered a small, one-time payment of £5,000 to support the creation of a group called the Travel Association (TA). The TA lasted through the 1930s and beyond, but the government played little role in whatever success it enjoyed. Simply put, Westminster did not wish to intervene in "a matter of private enterprise."[64]

Perhaps such reluctance is unsurprising. As in France, private companies or development-minded individuals were doing an adequate job. During the interwar years, organizations such as the Butlin's Company continued to show private initiative, launching some of the first holiday camps—a cornerstone of postwar British tourism. Likewise, workers' organizations and trade unions provided "inexpensive excursions and holiday camps"—something in which they had long been involved.[65] Other non-profits such as "Youth Hostels, Cyclists Touring Club, Holiday Fellowship, Workers Travel Association, Co-operative Holidays Association and so-on" worked tirelessly to develop their own initiatives.[66]

Beyond Europe

For less developed countries outside of Europe, the preeminent reason for promoting tourism during the interwar years was economic growth. Although the number of people leaving Europe or the United States as tourists was still relatively small, there were those in many places who felt that the industry had promise. For some, it offered a means of rebuilding after bloody conflict. To others, tourism represented a chance to capitalize on colonial relationships. Yet even if profit was the greatest motive, tourism also suggested a way to make people proud of their own country and to alter international perceptions.

Mexico represents a case in point. The state faced a long climb back from violence and insurrection starting in the early 1920s. It had plunged into civil war in 1910 and continued to face outbreaks of conflict throughout much of the next twenty years. By 1928, the victorious political party was anxious to rebuild, constructing a capitalist economy while remaining true to its revolutionary ideals. Tourism seemed a panacea. It would raise money while at the same time replacing a postcolonial sense of inferiority with a self-confident sense of Mexico by showcasing its history and rich culture.

The new government officially undertook a tourism development policy in 1928 and promptly set about gathering as much information as it could regarding successful programs in other places.[67] Ministry of Foreign Affairs representatives abroad were responsible for gathering as much intelligence as they could, eventually generating reports about tourism in "Prague, Phoenix, St. Louis, Chicago, Galveston and Del Rio, Texas, Canada, and Cuba." Findings were tremendously promising, showing positive benefits both close to home in Canada and Cuba as well as further afield in Europe.[68] The range of products in these places varied considerably, but the overall message was encouraging. The country could make money by attracting visitors and encouraging travel while at the same time crafting a new and more positive image for outsiders.

American tourists represented the most auspicious market. The neighbors to the north already traveled to Canada and Cuba in large numbers and the easy automobile access to Mexico promised similar results.[69] Yet the road to getting Americans to cross the southern border was not without bumps. First, Mexico had a reputation for being unstable and dangerous.[70] Second, suitable tourist accommodations were lacking.[71] The new National Revolutionary Party (PNR) government was anxious to address these issues in order to improve relations with the United States, portray an image of Mexico that was modern while celebrating selected aspects of the country's ancient past, and "enter the race for the tourist dollar." The PNR adopted policies designed to make "travel to Mexico easy and safe." It built roadways, encouraged hotel development, and sought to create attractions that might be appealing to both European and American travelers, at the same time helping to enhance national feeling. Drawing visitors to "national treasures" such as ancient sites, gorgeous beaches, and colonial towns "inherently evoked pride in things uniquely Mexican."[72]

In the summer of 1936, the Nuevo Laredo-Mexico Highway opened, running from the US border to central Mexico. Various groups followed the debut by pushing for the development of visitor accommodations. Mexico City was "transformed by tourism development" during the late 1930s and early 1940s into a symbol of "a nation on the rise."[73]

Unfortunately the global economic crisis soon undermined top-down efforts. As in Britain and France, private initiative took over. Historian Dina Berger writes: "While economic depression crippled both government and even the emerging private tourist organizations, it made room for a growing number of supporters who rose to the occasion." Such boosters carried out lecture tours in the United States, published "laudatory articles about Mexico's tourism possibilities in US newspapers," and continued to instruct Mexicans that it was a good idea to create a vibrant tourism industry.[74] When the economic crisis started to wane, the groundwork was in place to launch much larger development efforts.

The challenges were different in Bali, but tourism still promised both economic growth and an opportunity to improve public perception of the country. The small island, east of Java in the Indonesian archipelago, was colonized in 1908. The conquest did not go smoothly. While en route to assume control of the royal residence, the Dutch army confronted utter horror. Rather than be defeated in battle, the local Rajah ordered his court to march from the palace and then to murder one another in full view of the advancing Europeans. Mortified, and facing fire from a furious crowd, the Dutch began shooting. It was a massacre.[75]

The European public was anything but pleased by the display. There was a growing anxiety about empire more generally as reports of colonial violence in places such as the Belgian Congo mortified those with a conscience. The slaughter at Bandung seemed more of the same and it was not the type of publicity that any government is keen to pursue. The Dutch had to reinvent perceptions of Bali and of their rule there. At the same time, the new governors needed to assure a revenue stream from a place largely void of resources. To be sure, the island was a fruitful source of opium, which the Dutch were happy to sell,[76] but drug sales did little to assuage the image of bloodshed. Tourism development and place marketing offered both money and positive public relations.

Europeans started to trickle into Bali very soon after the conquest, mostly artists and adventurers. They were thrilled by what they found: beautiful landscapes and attractive naked natives. It did not take long for an image of the island as a pre-modern paradise to gain currency. Here was a land of noble, as well as nubile, savages—a place where sensuality was everywhere and where every sexual taste was catered to.[77]

Exploitation efforts started quickly. The Association for Tourist Traffic in Netherlands India launched in 1908.[78] A regular steamship service started in 1924,[79] suddenly and dramatically raising the number of Europeans who made the trip. The first hotel opened in 1928.[80] Only 213 visitors traveled to Bali in 1924. By 1929 this increased to 1428. The global economic downturn kept numbers down over the next few years, but traffic rebounded in 1934. During that year, 250 people a month made the journey, enjoying ever-easier transportation and consistently improving accommodations.[81] The destination remained popular until the Japanese conquered the island in 1942.[82]

Conclusion

Regardless of the political regime, tourism and leisure were good politics during the interwar years. States could show concern about their citizens, draw contrasts with others, promote economic development, stress modernity, and build a stronger sense of nationalism. All of this campaigning served to make holiday travel that much more popular with the public. Groups—the French and German working classes, for example—who previously had little experience with taking time off from work had to learn how to do it. Once they mastered the lesson, paid holidays and the chance to get away from it all were difficult to shake.

World War II brought a temporary hiatus to the fun, but the conflict also generated new technologies, tastes, and tolerances that ushered in true mass tourism after the bloodshed. What is more, the efforts described above helped to assure that it would remain a political tool, both at state and international levels, during the postwar years.

9

Tourism in the postwar

World War II was both global and total. It was fought in the air, on land, and on the seas. The combatants leveled towns, destroyed factories, and decimated infrastructure. Once great cities such as Berlin, London, Dresden, Pisa, Coventry, Hiroshima, Nagasaki, and many others were rendered vast ruins, mountains of rubble. Millions died, both soldiers and, on a hitherto unheard of scale, civilians. There were refugees everywhere.[1]

Against this backdrop the story of tourism continued to unfold. Long-haul travel largely ceased for the duration of the conflict. Governments confiscated cruise ships and aircraft to aid the war effort, and it was too dangerous to move within or across many national borders. For those removed from ground combat, holidays were possible closer to home.[2] The British government "encouraged leisure activities and traditional travelling entertainments to help boost civilian morale."[3] As during the Great War, some places benefitted. Blackpool, for example, enjoyed a period of expansion and growth. It was removed from likely invasion points, was not bombed, and was used by the RAF to accommodate trainees. Many civil servants were even relocated there from London. Servicemen, especially Americans, were anxious to spend their wages on leisure pursuits.[4] More than ever, the war turned the British countryside into a haven, "a place of safety as well as leisure for the nation's urban population."[5] Other countries were less excited about travel; in Australia, for example, expensive fuel, an "austerity culture," and beaches strung with barbed wire assured that holidays were not foremost in people's minds.[6] To the extent that Americans traveled, they evidently opted to stay closer to home rather than explore the growing tourism facilities available even as close as in Mexico.[7] In a few countries such as Ireland—which was neutral—the war offered an opportunity to develop tourism infrastructure in anticipation of the conflict's end while officials tried to convince the populace, usually unsuccessfully, to visit national sites/sights.[8] With bombs falling and death tolls mounting, states seldom made creating leisure a top priority.

After the war the story was different. In only about forty years tourism became one of the world's leading industries. By the end of the 1950s, living standards reached previously unknown levels. The holidays with pay idea took deeper hold and many states extended paid vacation days well beyond what had been required before the outbreak of hostilities. People had time and money to travel, but there were other inducements. New technologies, often a product of the war effort, allowed individuals to move more cheaply than in the past. The industry was again the subject of political calculation, promoted by the United Nations as well as by most state governments. Resorts proliferated and private companies looked for ways to expand the range of attractions. Millions were anxious to take advantage of the new opportunities.

Pushing tourism

At the end of 1945 the United States was the only major power free of substantial damage. While many world cities, especially in Japan, Britain, Italy, and Germany, were hard hit by aerial bombing, the same was not true across the Atlantic. The American government was anxious to capitalize and the US almost effortlessly transitioned into a peacetime industrial stronghold, producing everything from heavy equipment to household luxuries. Consumer goods were everywhere, but consumers were harder to come by. In particular, Europeans wanted American goods and materials. They desperately needed food. American popular culture and products enjoyed a definite status. Yet money was scarce; a dollar shortage meant that neither governments nor the majority of European people could afford to buy the merchandise that their allies across the Atlantic hoped to sell.[9]

American and some European leaders had a second grave concern: the rise of what many politicians and intellectuals termed "totalitarianism." Former British Prime Minister Winston Churchill (1874–1965) was particularly outspoken. He worried that an "iron curtain" was dividing Europe and he insisted that the "safety of the world ... requires a unity" on the continent.[10] Russia was no longer willing to "co-operate"[11] and clouds of conflict brewed as a result. Fascism and communism were both examples of what philosopher Hannah Arendt (1906–75) called "totalitarian" government and they could not be separated.[12] During the war, Churchill and his colleagues in the West held their noses and allied with Joseph Stalin (1878–1953) for the sake of military expediency, but now they could not ignore what they viewed as a new Soviet threat.[13] It was important to avoid "disturbances arising as a result of the desperation of the people concerned" and to guard against "hunger, poverty, desperation and chaos"[14]—the things that traumatized Europe during the interwar years and that contributed to the rise of fascism.

American Secretary of State George C. Marshall (1880–1959) proposed a practical solution: provide millions of dollars in aid to European countries in order to promote rebuilding and economic growth. Stability would reign if Europe were back on its feet, unemployment reduced, and balances of trade and dollar earnings improved rapidly. Happy people do not resort to oppressive government. The European Recovery Program (ERP), or Marshall Plan, would rebuild Western Europe and would save the peace. Although many are aware that the program funneled money to agricultural and to industrial redevelopment, few realize that tourism was also a primary component of ERP efforts. Indeed,

> The industry was particularly intriguing because it offered twin benefits: "dollar-earning capacity of the tourist services proper" (including the purchase of European products while traveling) and the prospect of "stimulating the export of commodities to America" after the "American tourist traveling in Europe gets to know European goods, for which, on his return to America, he may help to create a demand." With so much to add to reconstruction, both Marshall Plan officials and the member countries of the Organisation for European Economic Co-operation (OEEC) saw tourism as a cornerstone of a sound economic future.[15]

Whereas agriculture assured that people were fed and industrial expansion promised ample job growth and a chance to close the dollar gap, tourism offered jobs, larger markets, improved infrastructure, an influx of currency, and even an opportunity for Americans to gain cultural capital by visiting the old country. As historian Christopher Endy puts it: "Saving Europe from Communism and poverty never seemed so easy." Certainly the notion of pushing tourism was popular across the political spectrum and commentators enthused that "[w]e might as well soak up a little old world culture for our dollars. It would be almost like eating our cake and having it too."[16]

As the ERP took shape, so too did a larger international tourism movement. It started with the formation of the First Constitutive Assembly of the International Union of Official Travel Organisations (IUOTO) at a meeting in London in 1946. The 41 countries that took part saw confusion in the tourism landscape. There was excessive red tape associated with crossing borders and too much decentralization. Consequently, the IUOTO established an international headquarters and started to work toward agreements on passport control and visa-related issues. It quickly gave birth to the European Travel Commission

(ETC), which concerned itself with publicity, travel conditions, and other issues on the continent. It did not take long before these organizations joined forces with the OEEC and ERP in common purpose.[17] Collectively they launched an international marketing campaign, sought to make crossing borders easier for travelers, worked to expand tourism infrastructure (hotels, roads, attractions), and strove to create opportunities for working-class tourists.[18]

The successful realization of the Marshall Planners' goals demanded two things. First, holidaymakers needed to find satisfactory accommodations in Europe. In particular, Americans were (and are) notoriously intolerant of poor hotels or unimproved facilities. While Europeans were long more accepting of shared bathrooms, small rooms, or less than stellar hygiene, Americans simply would not put up with such things. If efforts were to succeed, European standards had to match those found in the United States. In order to assure the necessary improvements, officials decided to send representatives from across Europe to the US on a fact-finding trip. These men, mostly from national tourist boards or major hotels, would "examine on the spot the arrangements and services which an American tourist expects when he travels in his own country."[19] In early 1950, experts from Austria, Belgium, Denmark, France, Germany, Greece, Ireland, Italy, Luxembourg, the Netherlands, Sweden, and Switzerland journeyed to the United States to "study hotel development and other tourism infrastructure questions."[20]

Significant changes resulted. The French, for example, altered their "customs to become more like Americans." They added shops to hotel lobbies, printed tourist maps, and highlighted important sites/sights. Gift shops sold specialty crafts. Menus drew attention to curious customs: wine pairings, then foreign to most Americans, for example. Tourism providers even altered the way that food was served and changed the design of the rooms in which this happened. Americans

> liked to be served ice water before a meal, and meals should be presented in a *prix fixe* scheme that offered multiple meal choices and included the cost of tea or coffee. Americans preferred to drink their tea or coffee ("served rather light") during their meal. Few Americans liked breakfast in their rooms. Instead, small tables should be provided in a room for this purpose, or failing that, in the regular dining room. Hotel rooms should be heated between twenty and twenty-two degrees Celsius. At the same time, the windows in a room should be easy to open because most Americans preferred to sleep with them open. Electric lights should be placed at the head of every bed and hot water should be available twenty-four hours a day. A small bar of soap should be placed on every sink and an English-language newspaper should be provided free every day.

It was not that European hotels should be completely like American ones, but they needed to have at least some of the trappings.[21]

Second, the United States was the only country in the world that could be expected to send legions of tourists abroad. Advertising was vital, but the challenges were real. The problem was that America is very large. As Irish tourism developers discovered when they attempted to breech the American market, advertising in New York or Chicago alone was roughly equivalent to operating in all of France or Germany.[22] Sizeable and comparatively wealthy countries such as the United Kingdom, France, or Italy might realistically expect to function in such a wide area, but smaller states simply could not. Joint advertising proved to be the solution and a sub-committee of the European Travel Commission successfully launched a program that united Austria, Belgium, Denmark, Great Britain, France, Italy, Luxembourg, Norway, Sweden, and Switzerland. Countries such as Great Britain, Italy, and France each paid $30,000 annually to the program, while others provided much less. Tiny Luxembourg, for example, contributed a mere $1000 but received substantial placement in the campaign. By the 1960s the reality that smaller countries got far more benefit for their investment than did bigger ones prompted the French and others to pull out of the scheme, but in the short term it proved remarkably successful.[23] By 1952, notes historian Brian A. McKenzie, "the only demographic group more numerous than Americans in Paris was Parisians."[24] The arrangement was so successful that other parts of the world adopted the joint advertising model. Within only a few years, similar initiatives were launched in Asia (Pacific Area Travel Association), South America (South American Travel Association), and Central America (Caribbean Tourist Association). Also following on the ETC's success, regional bodies under the auspices of the IUOTO were ultimately created in Africa (1949), the Middle East (1951), Central Asia (1956), and the Americas (1957).[25]

Marshall Planners were not above using financial coercion to assure that tourism development took place. Although it was neutral during World War II,[26] the European Recovery Program included Ireland. The country especially benefitted in terms of agricultural support.[27] While recognizing the long-term significance of farming in Irish life and certainly hoping to see further industrial development, Colonel Théo J. Pozzy (1901–95),[28] the Travel Development Section chief of the Economic Cooperative Administration (which oversaw the ERP), was utterly convinced that tourism signaled the road ahead. He noted Ireland's impressive historical sites and natural beauty. Tourism did not simply employ tour guides, travel agents, and guidebook writers; it expanded demand for food and other services, quickly reaching into every aspect of a national economy. Best of all, the initial financial investment, while significant, was less than was demanded by other types of development.

Pozzy and his group confronted significant problems in Ireland, however. At a time when the Emerald Isle faced a major housing crisis, widespread tuberculosis, and general poverty, tourism seemed a strange investment to many Irish voters. Why spend money on luxury hotels when thousands of Irish people lived in slums? Worse, the long time director of the Irish Tourist Board had few friends in government following a series of questionable decisions during the war years. Even when that director was removed, his successors proved largely unable to generate enthusiasm in the halls of the Irish parliament, Dáil Éireann. There was no real will among Irish officials to undertake tourism development.

Pozzy would have none of this. He made it known that if the Irish failed to pursue a significant reorganization of their tourism industry, including the installation of a new director, the ERP would cease to provide aid for agricultural or industrial expansion. Ireland would be out.[29] The strategy sparked results. Within months, the Irish government began a major review of its policies and administration. They took advantage of the Marshall-Plan-sponsored tourism fact-finding trips to the United States and solicited advice from a leading American hotelier. Within three years, the state had a new tourism development bill, *two* new statutory tourism bodies, and a major program of publicity and product creation that included a nationwide tourism festival, the revitalization of historic sites, and even a "tidy towns" scheme that ultimately prompted the almost total reinvention of Irish town and cityscapes. It is no exaggeration to say that the ERP played a major role in making tourism development a significant component of Irish political, economic, social, and cultural life.[30]

As the formation of the International Union of Official Travel Organisations makes clear, the Marshall Plan and the attendant desire to rebuild Europe was not the only tourism-related nexus for international politics. From at least the end of the Boer War (1899–1902), various voices looked to the British Empire as a model for successful international cooperation. The conflagration of World War I added to these calls and resulted in the creation of the impressive, if not entirely successful, League of Nations. That body was supposed to assure global peace, creating a format where conflicts might be resolved before bloodshed was necessary. It did not work for various reasons, the US Congress's failure to ratify the treaty among them.[31]

Following World War II, many were anxious to improve upon the league model (although they were careful not to play up any hint of continuity between the old organization and the new), learning from past mistakes to create a body that would cement the authority of the victorious powers by promoting world peace. This new organization, "basically a cooperative grouping of independent states ... rested on the doctrine of the sovereign equality of its members" and was called the United Nations.[32] It was far from perfect, but it did have four major objectives that are laudable: to avoid future wars, to reaffirm faith in human rights, to enforce justice through international law, and "to promote social progress and better standards of life."[33]

Although the relationship between travel, international politics, and the United Nations has yet to find its historian, it is fair to say that UN member states viewed tourism as one path toward improved living standards and a better life in many places around the world. Consequently, the IUOTO attained United Nations "consultative status" in 1948. During the 1950s, the international tourism body engaged in various activities, including working to ease travel across borders. In the 1960s, it further increased its efforts. In 1963, for example, the organization led the United Nations to hold a worldwide tourism conference, the United Nations Conference on Tourism and International Travel. Contemporary newspaper coverage of the initiative captures the growing political and economic reality:

> They made no bones about their commercial interest in the matter. All agreed that international tourism had cultural benefits and hopefully led to wider understanding and appreciation of foreign ways.
>
> But the emphasis clearly was on developing tourism because it is now recognized as an industry and as an important economic asset. Countries large and small remarked that tourism in a single year accounted for $5,000,000,000 in world foreign exchange, helping many a country to pay off its trade deficits.[34]

With cultural and financial benefits, leisure travel represented the best interest of the international community. Barriers had to be reduced and incentives increased. Cooperation was paramount. In 1967, the UN declared an "International Year of Tourism" under the lofty slogan: "Tourism, Passport to Peace." In 1970, they did away with the consultative status of the IUOTO and brought the body in-house under the heading World Tourism Organization (WTO).[35] The industry was simply too important not to be a formal part of the United Nations.

Getting there in the air

The postwar politics of internationalism played a major role in promoting the tourism industry and in encouraging people to travel. Changes in aviation played an equally (if not even more) critical role. Before World War II,

Figure 9.1 Passenger air travel expanded dramatically in the years after World War II. Aircraft could travel further, fly higher, and carry travelers in more comfort than ever before. At the same time, a new international political situation, greater affluence, and a growing interest in tourism helped to fuel expansion of the industry. Photo courtesy of John W. Hartman Center for Sales, Advertising & Marketing History, Duke University. Copyright permission courtesy of British Airways Heritage Collection.

most long-haul trips happened aboard ocean liners. These vast and ever-more speedy ships continued to have a place into the early 1950s, but ultimately they could not compete against improved aviation technologies, more efficient and expansive air routes, and dropping ticket prices.[36]

Aviation moved ahead by leaps and bounds during World War II. Long-distance bombing required planes that could fly both very far and very high. Thus, engineers devised more efficient engines that generated greater horsepower, perfected pressurized cabins, and created new materials that were lighter and stronger. Within a very short time, new aircraft such as the Lockheed Constellation, which could cover longer distances than any passenger plane before the war, joined the airlines' stables. There was an even more exciting development: the jet engine. Boeing introduced the first commercial jet aircraft, the 707, in October 1958. A year later, Douglas launched the DC-8. Such planes offered larger seating capacities and a longer flying range. Air India officials went so far as to project that just three 707s would service the same number of customers as ten Constellations.[37]

Soon, every country seemed to need an airline and an airport. Having one was a reflection of importance, an opportunity to increase both corporate and national earnings, and sometimes even a way to symbolize national identity—especially for newly independent states.[38] For example, Air India provided a chance to stress Indian identity after that country broke free from Britain in 1947. Stewardesses were "told that their task was to make every passenger feel like a Maharajah." Similarly, El Al, the Israeli airline, strictly observed Jewish dietary restrictions as a means of stressing identity.[39] Of course, having an airline was more than symbolic. Much of Brazil, for example, is remote. The national airline, VARIG, opened up the vast isolated spaces of the country and allowed for the construction of a new capital city called Brasília in the highland interior.[40]

The existence of many new carriers created logistical challenges and states needed to arrive at international rules concerning airspace and, in the process, overcome sometimes opposite ideas about national interest. For some countries, it seemed logical to open up the skies, to adopt a laissez-faire attitude to the stratosphere. Others believed that such an approach would only enhance American power and should therefore be resisted. It was an insoluble problem, resulting in a failure to reach a unified policy. Access to given countries and to particular routes was by individual agreement. Small countries suffered as a result, lacking the diplomatic muscle to negotiate the right to airspace wherever they might want it. Consequently, many states focused on short-haul routes, venturing little more than 500 or so miles in any direction. Meanwhile, major world powers found themselves in a global contest, their airlines seeking to provide the largest variety of long-haul routes possible. Perhaps ironically, this state of affairs assured that the United States was far in the lead.

Route-by-route, country-by-country negotiation assured that international politics and the Cold War were very much a part of air transport. Tourists could not simply go anywhere and whether one was in the American orbit or that of the Soviet Union mattered. US allies were not to fly within the Soviet sphere. In 1945, Pan Am dreamed of flights to the beautiful Central European city of Prague. By 1946, with tension growing between East and West, that fantasy evaporated. Similarly, the Soviet Union assured that its allies were limited to Eastern Bloc or Soviet destinations. For the Russians, "domestic services took center stage." Despite it all by the end of the 1940s

> something like a global air network emerged that extended beyond the prewar colonial context in Asia and Africa, which connected even South America ... now that aircraft had the range and payload to operate profitably across the South Atlantic. This fitted the high hopes of politicians and economists alike that air transport would not only contribute to the economic development of South America, but also that of the newly independent nations in Asia and Africa.[41]

None of this might have mattered had carriers not also tried to open air travel to those beyond the very rich. Prior to the war, airlines offered luxury. Stewards and stewardesses provided service befitting first-class passengers. The experience of flying was supposed to be relaxing and pleasant.[42] The noise and discomfort of pre-war planes assured that flight was never easy, but the idea of opulence informed how airlines imagined their offerings. After the war, these companies faced a dilemma: continue as before *or* look for ways to expand their customer base. The choice was fairly obvious.

The challenge was to fill enough seats so that financial targets were met. Doing so was not easy. Before 1958 companies such as Pan Am had to overcome the objections of the International Air Transport Association (IATA), a body formed after World War II to generate "inter-airline cooperation in promoting safe, reliable, secure and economical air services ... for the benefit of the world's consumers."[43] At first, the IATA objected to low-cost fares, only agreeing to change their policy after considerable lobbying and even then tickets remained too expensive for most middle-class travelers. A flight from Holland to North America, for example, cost "as much as $534 in Holland, which was quite a hefty amount for prospective passengers, about half the price of a small car in local currency."[44]

Prices only started to drop dramatically in the late 1970s. The Skytrain program, launched by Laker Airlines in 1977, precipitated much of the change by offering one-way trans-Atlantic flights for just £59. Despite some restrictions—one had to purchase tickets on the day of the flight and the trip itself was a rather spartan affair—people flocked to attain seats. In July, August, and September 1978 thousands took advantage of the fares, only to find themselves unable to get return flights to the States. One journalist described the result: hundreds of passengers camped out with barely the airfare in their pockets, hoping to get home. Although the scheme was a failure, Laker's policy had the effect of dismantling what was left of the "IATA-supported fare structure." The company demonstrated that there was a vast market for cheap tickets and competitors quickly offered lower prices.[45]

There was at least one noticeable result beyond an increase in passengers: a transformation in the way that airlines conceived of their routes. Instead of offering direct flights, carriers moved toward a "hubs-and-spokes" model whereby companies operated a handful of "hubs" that functioned as transfer points from which people could access smaller airports, or "spokes." To make it function properly, airlines had to schedule their flights in waves, assuring that planes arrived in close proximity to one another. The new approach worked. Economies of scale "became of overriding importance in air transport" wherever an airline was operating.[46]

Rising living standards and the expansion of time

The proliferation of airlines and decreases in ticket prices might have mattered little were they not accompanied by staggering economic change in both Europe and the United States. Many Americans enjoyed

> an historic reign of prosperity, longer lasting and more universally enjoyed than ever before in American history. National output of goods and services doubled between 1946 and 1956, and would double again by 1970, with private consumption expenditures holding steady at two-thirds of gross national product ... over the era. Certainly there were downturns ... [b]ut inevitably, recessions were followed by recoveries that each time lifted Americans' wage scales and living standards a little higher.[47]

Following a period of economic, social, and political turmoil after the war, Europeans also entered a boom period. The particulars varied. Germany, then Britain, then France and Italy experienced periods of economic expansion until

> every European country saw steadily growing rates of *per capita* GDP and GNP—Gross Domestic Product and Gross National Product—the newly sanctified measures of national strength and well-being. In the course of the 1950s, the average *annual* rate at which *per capita* national output grew in West Germany was 6.5 percent; in Italy 5.3 percent; in France 3.5 percent. The significance of such high and sustained growth rates is best appreciated when they are compared with the same countries' performance in earlier decades: in the years 1913-1950 the German growth rate *per annum* was just 0.4 percent, the Italian 0.6 percent, the French 0.7 percent. Even in the prosperous decades of the Wilhelminian Empire after 1870, the German economy had only managed an annual average of 1.8 percent.

Even when growth slowed in the 1960s, "economies still grew at historically unusual levels."[48]

Economic well-being meant that more individuals and families could buy consumer items, trips for example, than ever before. "People had money to spend and they were spending it."[49] Car ownership jumped,[50] paving the way for increases in car camping, motel availability, and other automobile-related travel opportunities.[51]

Many also had more time in which to spend their earnings. The holidays-with-pay movement of the 1930s did not disappear. Virtually everybody in continental Europe enjoyed two weeks of paid holiday. In Norway, Sweden, Denmark, and France workers had three weeks.[52] A number of countries added to what was promised previously. In Finland, for example, a succession of acts in 1946, 1959, 1960, 1965, and 1973 steadily increased the number of remunerated vacation days, topping out at a minimum of four weeks for all full-time employees.[53] By the turn of the century, only thirteen countries in the world, including the United States, did not mandate paid vacations.[54]

Tourism and national politics in the postwar world

Countries in virtually every part of the globe tried to benefit from this context, creating what Louis Turner and John Ash call the "pleasure periphery"—a belt of tourism-based economies surrounding "the great industrialized zones of the world," virtually all within only a few hours'flying distance.[55] Legions of leisure-seekers, whether from the United States, Europe, or Asia, took advantage.[56]

Mexico provides a fine example. Despite earlier sightseers and some development efforts, before the war relatively few tourists ventured, as singer Frank Sinatra (1915–98) crooned, "south of the border, down Mexico way."[57] Things changed afterward. By 1946 travel writers frequently wrote about the country and it even featured in a Hollywood movie entitled *Holiday in Mexico*.[58] In 1929 only 13,982 tourists, most of them Americans, crossed the Rio Grande; on the eve of World War II, the number was closer to 130,000. In 1946, 254,069 made the trip and 384,297 did so in 1950.[59]

While there were other groups working to expand tourism—including artists and boosters who created an artist colony and a partially invented past for visitors in the central Mexican town of San Miguel de Allende[60]—the real story is the role of the Mexican government. The ruling Institutional Revolutionary Party (PRI), which dominated Mexican politics for more than seventy years, decided to pursue a tourism policy based around the provision of resorts. Acapulco, an old port city that had seen better days, was the first to enjoy a makeover. Developers constructed luxury hotels, refurbished or rebuilt markets (and displaced longtime vendors), relocated the poor outside of tourist areas, and cleaned up beaches. By the late 1950s, going to Acapulco was little different from visiting any other modern resort.[61]

Tourists were pleased, but the PRI did not rest. It adopted a bolder plan: create tourism centers in underdeveloped parts of the country, especially on the Yucatán Peninsula at a place called Cancún. Officials wanted to "export paradise."[62] To provide visitors with the "'three esses'—sand, sun, and sex." The site would not only draw tourist dollars, it would help unify Mexico through the creation of infrastructure, the promotion of migration, and the provision of employment. The government first proposed the idea of building a new resort to the Inter-American Development Bank in 1964. There would be two zones: one for tourists, the other for service workers. The tourist sector would face the sea; the urban district would be set some distance away, removed from where outsiders might see it. Visitors were supposed to arrive by air, spend their days on the beach, take advantage of hotels and restaurants, and then go home.[63] Construction began in 1971 and the resort opened for business in 1976.[64]

The provision of the "three esses" was central to postwar development in other places as well. Fewer than 50,000 tourists visited Australia per year before the advent of speedy aircraft during the 1950s. With faster planes came more people and soon Australian tourism developers promised travelers sunshine and plenty of sand. At the same time, various airlines sought to complement their routes by offering hotels that would grant "improvement of the standard of accommodation" over what was present previously. These facilities offered the "ready availability of women, men, fun," and classiness. There were exotic island locations, organized tours of places such as North Queensland and Tasmania, and the promise of easy access to the beach.[65] For Australians themselves, the seaside holiday represented an "egalitarian Australia." Swimming costumes might leave little to the imagination, but they certainly hid class distinctions.[66] For those from the northern hemisphere, going "down under" offered a respite from the dreariness of winter just when it was most needed.

The Bahamas and their immediate neighbors also capitalized on the popularity of the sunny seaside. As with Jamaica, other islands in the Caribbean Sea underwent a process of evolution during the nineteenth century whereby they transformed from white men's graveyards into potentially desirable destinations. During the interwar period, a variety of wealthy tourists such as writer Ian Fleming (1908–64), playwright Noel Coward (1899–1973), and actor Errol Flynn (1909–59) spent time on the islands, often throwing lavish parties for guests.[67] Hollywood offered moviegoers an image of exotic beauty that was encapsulated in the picture of "a banana-bedecked Carmen Miranda" (1909–55) who sang and danced to the infectious tune of calypso music.[68] As the war drew to a close, American President Franklin D. Roosevelt (1882–1945) and Prime Minister Churchill discussed the economic future of America's southern neighbors, many of which were still British colonies. These talks spawned the creation of a body concerned with tourism development, the Anglo–American Commission, which was soon joined by the French and Dutch, who also had Caribbean holdings. In 1950, the organization changed its name to be more inclusive: Caribbean Tourist Association.

Cuba quickly capitalized. Fulgencio Batista (1901–73), the country's dictator, was anxious to promote economic growth and was easily persuaded by Meyer Lansky (1902–83), an American mobster, to introduce gambling tourism. A wave of hotel building followed and soon performers such as Eartha Kitt (1927–2008), Maurice Chevalier (1888–1972), Lena Horne (1917–2010), and Nat King Cole (1919–65) were regulars at popular nightspots. For visitors, the island provided a heady combination of strong drinks, high stakes gambling, and attractive beaches. The party might have gone on indefinitely had Batista not been overthrown by a young anti-imperialist named Fidel Castro (1926–) during the Cuban Revolution of 1953–8.[69]

The 1960s represented a period of still more change in the Caribbean. European empires crumbled and newly independent states sought ways to generate revenue. Tourism represented an easy answer, even if governments seldom took time to fully recognize the role that the growing industry might play in their economic forecasting. It was not always a happy story. Where once Caribbean islands looked to foreign states as their political leaders, now they became dependent on multinational companies and foreign visitors, most from the United States.[70]

The pleasure periphery was not limited to Mexico, Australia, or the Caribbean. In Europe, Mediterranean states from Portugal to Greece created resorts, attempted to capitalize on historic sites, and built hotels to accommodate a growing tide of middle and working-class tourists.[71] No place was more successful than Spain, where Francisco Franco's (1892–1975) right-wing government gradually realized and then capitalized on the potential of mass tourism. Officials hoped that the industry would generate revenue, while demonstrating to outsiders that the country was modern, forward-looking, and worthy of closer ties to the developing common market in Europe.

Tourism was not new in Spain. Formal initiatives dated back at least as far as the National Commission to Promote Artistic and Recreational Excursions of the Foreign Public which a "cadre of dynastic politicians" launched in 1905. Their research showed that other countries, notably Switzerland and Italy, already turned a significant profit from tourism and they were convinced that Spain could follow suit.[72] Later, during the Spanish Civil War (1936–9), Franco used tourism as a propaganda tool, a way to demonstrate "the tranquility and order which reign in the regions recently conquered by our arms."[73]

After the civil war, the Spanish government worried that tourism was out of keeping with a conservative Catholic vision of the country. Despite this initial anxiety, the industry grew proportionately faster than it did elsewhere in Europe. While somewhat tepid in their efforts, advancing tourism signaled that Spain was in line with UN, OEEC, and Marshall Plan efforts.[74] Tourism mattered. Despite currency challenges, inferior infrastructure, and other issues, tourist numbers climbed steadily during the 1950s.

Between 1957 and 1962, the regime grew more committed. Some officials believed that the industry should be a "singular objective," a source for foreign currency and national propaganda.[75] At the same time, liberalization of charter flight restrictions opened the way for airlines to provide low-cost flights to the Iberian Peninsula. Customers could fly direct from a number of European cities to the Spanish seaside where new hotels emerged at a quickening pace.[76] The outlays were still too much for industrial workers, but "those slightly higher on the pay scale found Spain well within reach."[77]

In 1962, the rise of a new minister for information and tourism, Manuel Fraga (1922–2012), ushered in an even greater period of growth.[78] The number of tourists to Spain soared. In 1954, there were 993,100 visitors. By 1962 it was 6,390,369. Only a few years later, in 1969, they exceeded 18 million. In 1973, 31,335,806 travelers made their way to Spain.[79] Within only a short period, the old English seaside holiday, a defining feature of working-class life from the late nineteenth century through the 1930s, declined dramatically in popularity while workers flooded into Spain, now the leading seaside destination in Western Europe.[80]

Further east, Soviet leaders also developed tourism in the years after World War II. Authorities believed it important to restore paid vacations quickly and even to add new opportunities for useful leisure. Unfortunately the majority of tourist facilities, mostly spas, were in ruins.[81] Initially, officials could only reward a few citizens with holidays[82] and what would-be holidaymakers found was "often memorable for its lack of comfort, service, medical attention, and recreation."[83] Still, the Soviets made progress. The state built new facilities. Spas in the mountains and along the Black Sea in Crimea arose from the ashes.[84]

As before the war, the Soviets emphasized "a distinctive combination of purpose and pleasure" while stressing the vacation as medicine.[85] Despite official effort this brand of tourism started to fray by the 1960s. An expanding number of tourists did not want a spa holiday and they did not want treatment. They dreamed about having fun and this meant different things to different people.[86] As a consequence, a new tourism marketplace started to appear, its proponents catering to the "tastes and demands of the growing consumer public."[87]

Conclusion

The transition was not unique to the Soviet Union. While tourism developers in Europe and the United States anxiously built resorts in the years after World War II, and tourists flocked to them, there were other trends afoot. Not everybody was anxious to spend time with thousands of their closest friends. The freedom of car-based tourism and the simple reality that not everybody was excited about sun, sand, and sea assured that there were alternatives to the beach.

Yet there was something else, perhaps born of affluence, or of consumer culture, maybe of other factors altogether that also mediated against a uniform tourist experience. From the 1960s, more and more people wanted to show, as the English rock band The Kinks put it, "I'm not like everybody else." Consumers wished to demonstrate that they were "cool," moving from group or family-related activities toward pursuits that were often more individual, more expressive, more apt to reflect self-defined difference. The implications were massive.

10

Mass tourism

Disneyland, the "happiest place on earth," opened on July 17, 1955. Fifteen thousand invited guests and a sizable television audience anxious to catch a first glimpse of the park joined company founder Walt Disney (1901–66) and hosts Art Linkletter (1912–2010), Ronald Reagan (1911–2004), and Bob Cummings (1910–90) for the event. The program spoke volumes about tourism as it then looked. In particular, family and young people were everywhere. Cummings and Linkletter both brought their wives and children and the little ones were more than passive participants. Linkletter asked his kids which area of the park they were most anxious to see. Diane, his six-year-old, was itching for Fantasyland, "where Sleeping Beauty is." Sharon, aged eight, hoped to see Frontierland, "when [*sic*] Davy Crockett fights the Indians." The youngest, Robert, was set on a boat trip down "the Congo." The eldest daughter, Dawn, dreamed of "a cruise to the moon in the rocket ship."[1] All of these things were possible.

Walt Disney amassed his fortune making animated films: especially movies based upon fairy tales and following the antics of characters such as Mickey and Minnie Mouse, Goofy, Clarabelle Cow, and Donald and Daisy Duck. Mickey launched the empire, but the cheery mouse was certainly not his creator's only secret for success. Disney owed much to context, and particularly to Americans' need for escape, even if only for a few minutes, from the dismal horror of the Great Depression.[2] The people of the United States were attracted to the fact that the cartoons were "completely removed from the workaday reality of contemporary life" while promising viewers affirmation of "the power of happy endings and virtuous actions."[3] It was an appealing mixture, rooted in Disney's "instinctive empathy and respect for his audience."[4]

After World War II, Walt Disney continued to rely on context. The Cold War offered an opportunity to celebrate a sort of "libertarian populism" that "stressed the autonomy of ordinary citizens in the face of overweening authority." Americans were good, "community-building" people, a profound contrast with those subject to "Communist collectivism and authoritarianism."[5] The community-heavy message fit neatly with Disney's nostalgia for the small town of his youth, something he believed was commonplace among his countrymen. "Many of us fondly remember our 'small home town' and its friendly way of life at the turn of the century," he wrote in a guidebook. "To me, this era represents an important part of our heritage," what he called "the crossroads of an era."[6]

The new theme park made the movies "real," rendering the company's famous characters in three dimensions and providing a fruitful venue for selling related products. Yet Disneyland was not simply a sales gimmick. As historian Steven Watts summarizes: "Disneyland was a unique embodiment of prosperous, middle-class, postwar America. As nothing else quite did, it stood, literally, as a monument to the American way of life. Millions of citizens journeyed there to pay homage to the idealized image of themselves created by a master cultural mediator."[7]

Walt Disney claimed that he had the idea for the park while on a walk with his young daughters. He found more traditional amusement parks, Coney Island in New York,[8] for example, to be abhorrent: "dirty, sleazy, money-grubbing places." Disneyland would be different. Although "a park for kids, a place scaled down to kids' size," it would nevertheless appeal to every generation.[9] To this end, it was divided into four parts. In Frontierland, tourists learned about the American past through a romanticized lens, a place where Davy Crockett and his trusty gun "Betsy" ruled the roost. Visitors to Adventureland experienced a sanitized version of the primitive "other," filled with exotic plants and stylized wild tribesmen. And in Tomorrowland, customers lived "predictions of things to come" and encountered what the world would be like in the distant future of 1986: there were rocket ships, an educational exhibit about atoms, and a superhighway, called Autopia, where children and adults could drive petrol-fueled mini-cars at eleven miles per hour.[10] At the heart of the park was a 5/8 scale Main Street, USA where the "clock has turned back half a century and you're on the main street of a small American town. The year is 1900." Disney filled the area with parades, band concerts, an 1898 car, and old-fashioned candies: things that "grandma" would both recognize and love.[11]

Together this represented a distinctly *American* narrative and the television broadcast left no doubt about the nationalist message. Disney himself informed viewers: "Disneyland is dedicated to the ideals, the dreams, and the hard facts that have created America." Moments later, Goodwin Knight (1896–1970), then governor of California, celebrated the park for showcasing "all the charm of the old world with all the progress and ingenuity of the new world." More, it was "all built by American labor and American capital under the belief that this is a God-fearing and a God-loving country ... we are the fortunate ones to be Americans."[12]

What the "fortunate ones" found was a paradox: a place that celebrated innovation while peering backward. Nostalgia was "jammed up against the needle-pointed promises of the future."[13] Disneyland welcomed the respectable regardless of race, while celebrating an age of small towns largely populated by whites. As suburbs overran the American landscape, Disney worked to keep them at bay. He built a massive dirt wall around his first facility, then started making plans to build an even larger theme park, far removed from urban life, in then undeveloped central Florida.[14] Main Street, USA was the antidote to urban sprawl, an escape into an idealized past where everybody knew one another and where life was simple and slow paced.

Disneyland stands as a powerful metaphor for the mass tourism of which it was a part. Attractions celebrated the past or the future, but it was all very much a product of the present.[15] The division of the site into multiple parts represented an effort to cater to the proliferation of tastes that define mass tourism, but these divisions were not enough. The park would need to change to keep up with evolving palates. Tourists imagine their experiences as "authentic" and that they are improved by travel. Yet while "even some of the most mindless and commodified forms of touristic behaviour" may be inspired by "the search for knowledge and an 'authentic' identity beyond the marketplace,"[16] there is often very little "authentic" on offer.[17] Tourists may seek to escape into the past through "heritage tourism," but that legacy is often invented or imagined. Leisure travel is associated with health, yet the multitude of tourists who leave home each year are inadvertently contributing to environmental destruction that could destroy the very pursuits they engage in. In short, the rise of mass tourism is a story of paradox.

Families and young people

In the years right after World War II, tourism was an expression of growing affluence and expanding family, but it also hinted at anxiety and unsettling change. In Britain, postwar suburbanization represented a response to the widespread devastation of wartime bombing and resultant housing shortages. Planners enjoyed the opportunity to move working-class slums, as existed in London's East End, to the fringes of the city in order to relieve congestion and to make room for the development of business and retail space. Creating "new towns" also allowed for a paternalistic restructuring of society at the expense of the social bonds that once defined working-class urban life.[18] Not everybody was pleased. Detractors saw in growing suburbs "a disorder and vagueness, a violent individualism, that is a direct negation of all that the civic spirit has implied for hundreds of years."[19] The task for critics was to create ways to reverse such trends by forming opportunities for young people and their families to rediscover community bonds.

The story in the United States was slightly different. As early as the mid-nineteenth century Americans saw the single-family, middle-class suburban home as a symbol of having attained success and status. Comfort came from a narrow focus on family. The mass production by the "millions of copies" of "verse and prose, pictures and prints with domestic themes" further stressed and promoted this prioritization.[20]

After the war, couples everywhere married younger than in the past and children were born (and survived) in greater numbers than was true previously. The 1950s family was thus something quite new and it did not embody the romanticized version depicted on television in programs such as *Leave It To Beaver* and *Father Knows Best*. There were substantial new pressures. Women, long the center of the idealized family, were compelled to create work for themselves in the home and "felt guilty when they did not do everything for themselves." Advertisers, anxious to capitalize, reported that women found housework "a medium of expression for ... [their] femininity and individuality." Both men and women learned that their very identities were supposed to be rooted in "familial and parental roles" and media representations were ever-present to remind them of the fact.[21]

Important elements of postwar tourism capitalized on and further enhanced the push toward a family and community ideal. As already noted, Walt Disney was anxious to offer his parks on a scale that appealed to young people, but he also stressed the idea that his attraction would be enjoyable for the whole family, from the littlest child to parents and grandparents. There was an emphasis on unity, on togetherness, and on a sense of community. Whether any of these things had ever really existed in the way depicted on Main Street, USA is open for debate, but the focus placed on them by tourism advocates and developers was not unique to Disney.

In the United Kingdom, holiday camps were one of the most popular vacation-time options for working-class families adapting to postwar life. Nobody is more closely associated with this development than Sir Billy Butlin (1899–1980). He was born in South Africa at the end of the nineteenth century and then spent time in both England and Canada while growing up.[22] In Canada, Butlin famously attended a "holiday camp" that featured games, canoes, and other "organized fun."[23] He recalled "the happy camaraderie of that far-off Canadian summer camp" and noted that the encounter led him to believe that the secret to creating a similar experience for visitors to his own facilities would demand finding "some way of getting the campers to mix." He decided to task special employees, dressed in easy to spot red coats, with offering entertainment and he scheduled organized leisure that would engage visitors and promote interaction between campers.[24]

Butlin entered the leisure business by first managing and later running amusement parks. In 1936 he secured a loan to open his first "luxury holiday camp" in Skegness, on the coast about forty-three miles east of Lincoln.[25] When the camp opened, most visitors came from the Midlands, but there were inquiries from across the rest of England, as well as from Scotland and Wales: a tribute to the man's marketing and promotional savvy.[26] Butlin opened his second camp in 1938, just as preparation for war was underway. Recognizing an opportunity to capitalize financially while also demonstrating a certain degree of patriotism, Butlin negotiated a deal whereby he would set up camps for military personnel while reserving the right to purchase them after the war at a price that was significantly lower than the cost of construction. He built the foundation of his leisure empire for pennies on the pound. Butlin modeled each camp on the one at Skegness, with dining hall, dormitories featuring hot/cold water and electricity, and various recreation facilities.[27] When the war ended, it was a relatively easy task to turn the wartime barracks into family-friendly fun.[28]

The goal of the Butlin's camps was to offer families "a week's holiday for a week's pay"—making the experience widely affordable. Customers came by the millions.[29] Each morning, a loudspeaker awakened people with the cry: "hi-di-hi!" Campers would reply: "hi-di-ho!"[30] During the days and evenings, tourists enjoyed a wealth of entertainment: dances, theatrical performances, opera, and both classical and popular music concerts (often offered by young men and women who went on to become some of Britain's most famous entertainers including musicians Dusty Springfield [1939–99], Cliff Richard [1940–], and Ringo Starr [1940–], among many others).[31] There were also amusement rides, beauty and "knobbly knees" competitions, and athletic activities.[32]

The focus on family was a way to combat what many believed to be the fragmentation of society. It was not simply the redesign of urban areas and the formation of suburbs. Critics claimed that "modern production techniques isolated workers" and that the cinema, for example, was a further sign of fracture. A constant threat of worker unrest and protest resulted. Holiday camps represented an antidote by promising "social harmony and togetherness through fun and games."[33] Advertisements celebrated the promise of family unity, often appealing to mothers with slogans such as "Butlin's, the perfect holiday for mother and, of course, the rest of the family too!"[34] Here was a place with plenty to do, and childcare too.

In the United States, family road trips were the holiday of choice. According to historian Susan Sessions Rugh, middle-class Americans clogged the roads starting just after World War II and they continued to explore their country by car "until the 1970s when family road trips declined in popularity."[35] Widespread automobile ownership, creation of campgrounds and other accommodations, and construction of roadways made it possible.[36] Postwar affluence made it reality. Middle-class families packed up their station wagons—the car of choice[37]—, tossed the kids into the back seat, consulted worn copies of gas station maps and Rand McNally camping guides (which were ubiquitous), and hit the road. Such a trip represented an affordable holiday. Campground fees ranged from $0.25 to $1.75 per night for a family; a two-week trip cost as little as $200 during the early 1950s.[38] While there were certainly plenty of squabbles, such vacations were a break from the day-to-day. Everybody chipped in:

> "Junior keeps the camp clean, gets the firewood, and perhaps proves to be a whiz as a packer and unpacker. Daughter sees to it that all the clothes are properly cared for and sleeping gear stays in top condition." Dad may have cooked, but women were in charge of cleaning up. Outdoors made it more pleasurable: "For Mom, dishwashing will be anything but drudgery with a mountain to look at and chipmunks for company." While camping, the rest of the family was more likely to help Mom with the housekeeping while performing their usual roles.[39]

These trips were not just about the camping. There were roadside attractions to see, beautiful and unique scenery, and wildlife to admire. What was more, these journeys were patriotic, a pilgrimage to "historic points of interest and national shrines in America."[40] Washington DC, the American capital, was a must-see location. "Every American," said a 1964 guidebook, "is imaginatively and emotionally attracted to see his nation's capital." Civil War battlefields were equally appealing and millions trekked to Gettysburg each year.[41]

The family vacation was a middle-class activity, but the middle class was not a uniform group. Despite the idealized view projected at Disneyland, racial and ethnic divisions were stark. Tourist activities reflected the fissures. Jews, for example, developed a holiday culture all their own in the Catskills, an area of New York state located only about ninety minutes from New York City. Facilities ranged from individual "bungalows" to luxury hotels such as Gossinger's, the "Waldorf in the Catskills."[42] Families often stayed for much of the summer, women and children remaining throughout the week, men commuting to the hills for weekends. There was much to occupy visitors: card games, stand-up comics, music, sports, swimming, and more. Entertainers were often very famous, or soon would be, and included comedian Joan Rivers (1933–2014) and singer Tony Bennett (1926–) among others.[43]

Middle-class African-Americans faced far greater challenges than Jews and were often humiliated by whites while trying to visit national "pilgrimage sites," especially in the South. During the 1950s and early 1960s, black families were frequently denied hotel and motel rooms, turned away from restaurants, and limited to beaches and pools unadorned by "Whites Only" signs. According to President Lyndon B. Johnson (1908–73), it was upon learning of the difficulties experienced by traveling African-Americans that he recognized the evils of segregation and so dedicated himself to what would become the 1964 Civil Rights Act. Johnson was told:

> We drive for hours and hours. We get hungry. But there's no place on the road we can stop and go in and eat. We drive some more. It gets pretty hot. We want to wash up. But the only bathroom we're allowed in is usually miles off the main highway. We keep goin' 'til night comes—'til we get so tired we can't stay awake anymore. We're ready to pull in. But it takes another hour or so to find a place to sleep.[44]

The will to travel was the same as for white families, but the lived experience was vastly different.

Family holidays of one sort or another were not limited to Britain and the United States. In Scandinavia, families took to the roads to engage in camping trips, to stay in holiday cottages, and to visit American-style motels that briefly attracted imitators in Europe.[45] In France, vacations represented "an ever-increasing focus of consumer spending" and families allocated between 6 and 8 percent of their budget toward getting away. An organization called Tourism and Labor worked "to offer healthy and enriching vacations" by administering day trips, trips abroad, and "running campgrounds and family vacation villages," often near the seaside. The first of these sites opened in 1959. It featured two restaurants, childcare, recreation and meeting rooms, a bar, as well as two and three bedroom bungalows. They were popular and such facilities expanded during the 1960s to include swimming pools, golf courses, and tennis courts—everything a family needed to enjoy time away from the daily grind.[46]

If family was important to tourism promoters, so too were young people. To some boosters, teenagers promised a chance to prevent future conflict and to promote world peace by creating global awareness and friendship. The youth hostel movement was the personification of this idea. The notion of creating low-cost accommodation for traveling youth was first suggested by Richard Schirrmann (1874–1961), a Prussian-born schoolteacher, a few years before World War I.[47] The number of hostels expanded dramatically in the 1920s, especially in Germany.[48] During the interwar years, hostels sprung up in Switzerland, Poland, the Netherlands, Norway, Denmark, Britain and Ireland, France, Belgium, Finland, Luxembourg, Czechoslovakia, Iceland, and even the United States.[49] The war did not end youth hosteling, but it certainly resulted in the closure of many hostels and slowed growth.

After the war, the movement enjoyed a new energy. The formation of an international youth hosteling federation prompted a statement of aims and goals, celebrating the notion that

> we live in a beautiful world, containing an infinite variety of natural beauty that is not confined to a few favoured countries but is shared by all... We strive to bring together the peoples of the world, so that around a common-room fire, or sharing a common meal, or wandering along the trail, they may learn to appreciate each other's viewpoint and outlook, and realize that we are a world brother-hood.

Youth hosteling could "become a rallying point of grace and friendship and reassurance in a world of frightened and discomfited peoples."[50] Soon hostels sprung up virtually everywhere across the globe and expanded in parallel.[51] By 1950, the movement was "firmly re-established, both nationally and internationally" and the number of "overnights" spent in hostels was up 60 percent.[52] Expansion continued thereafter, with locations started in India, Asia, Israel, North Africa, Latin America, the Arab world, and beyond. Use of Western European hostels grew by 88 percent. Internationally, the growth rate was even more impressive: 237 percent.[53]

Birth of the cool

The family holiday and the notion that young people might bring about social change through travel did not disappear in the 1970s and 1980s, but they were surpassed in popularity by a range of tourism products aimed at increasingly diverse market segments. Tastes had changed. Displaying one's individuality and success required more than a camping trip. The American family holiday declined in popularity starting around 1970. "It's not that the family vacation went away," writes Rugh:

> but it did cease to be recognized as a mass phenomenon. The family vacation declined in importance in the 1970s as the travel advertising focused on niche marketing... The family ideal of the 1950s was eclipsed by the culture of cool, where Peter Fonda's *Easy Rider* (1969) ... was hip, and the family road trip was definitely not.[54]

Similarly, leisure providers such as Billy Butlin faced the reality that family togetherness had its limits. Parents needed time alone. Young people now imagined themselves to be distinct from adults and wanted freedom and independence. It is true that by the late 1960s British holiday camps had a reputation for providing sexual adventure, but even that tantalizing prospect could not overcome the tide of developing youth culture. In 1975, The Who, a popular rock band, released their rock opera *Tommy*. It was scathing in its treatment of camp culture. According to historian Sandra Trudgen Dawson, the band

> ... satirized the mass appeal of the postwar holiday camps. Set in the immediate postwar years *Tommy* presented the holiday camp as a symbol of mass culture and one that stood in opposition to a more authentic culture and working-class experience. As war widow Mrs. Walker and her son arrive at 'Bernie's Holiday Camp' they are met by rows of orderly wooden huts and groups of happy campers engaged in energetic and regimented 'keep fit' activities and non-stop entertainment. The critique centres on the seemingly mechanical and mindless actions of the campers, as well as the broader suppression of working-class culture in postwar Britain. The Who sought to expose the emptiness of the mass culture in which individuality was subsumed in endless group activities.[55]

Such criticisms undermined holiday camp popularity and many, though not all, closed. In 2011 there were three Butlin's camps in operation with 1.3 million guests visiting each year, perhaps fueled by a nostalgic desire for the simpler days of the 1950s.[56]

The story was similar in the Soviet Bloc. State officials long wanted to establish a uniquely proletarian tourism, something different from the capitalist West. Toward this end, the USSR constructed a tourist infrastructure that offered healthful and productive leisure opportunities. Millions availed themselves. Yet by the late 1960s and after, a growing number wanted more. They sought something unique and hoped to escape the beaten track and to find individualized holidays. They took to the highways, deserted the old resorts, and made their own way. They were what officials deemed "wild tourists" and their approach to leisure "emerged as a viable alternative to the state-sponsored social tourism."[57]

Even Disneyland and Disney World (which opened in 1971) confronted change. At its start, Walt Disney emphasized "'cute' culture," rejecting "thrill rides" in favor of nostalgic, escapist, or futuristic attractions. By the 1970s the company had to change tack. There was more competition and "tweens" were anxious to go fast, be scared, and confront what was once called the sublime. In 1977, the company introduced its first thrill ride—Space Mountain—and others followed. Disney attempted a "careful compromise of the cute with the cool." There were other changes as well. Tomorrowland ceased to explore the future of technological development, instead drawing attention to the "place of the imagination and beyond." Once the park tried to cater to respectable middle-class people, insisting that visitors be clean-cut and employees adopt a particular look and behavior. "'Trouble making' youth" were even ejected from the parks for having "spiky black or teased hair" or for swearing. By the 1990s it was necessary to rely on "local crowds" and to accept all comers, foulmouthed or no.

Disney introduced cruises and wedding packages, added exclusively adult attractions where alcohol was served, and focused on providing "entertainment for every stage across the life course."[58] Being cool meant recognizing the reality that grown-ups increasingly wanted to be children. Youth culture submerged other forms of expression. As A. O. Scott, a cultural commentator and movie critic for the *New York Times,* argues: "Maybe nobody grows up anymore, but everyone gets older… The world is our playground, without a dad or a mom in sight."[59] The transformation worked. In 1989, Disney World attracted 30 million visitors[60] and the Florida park is just one of Disney's many global concerns.

Cool variety?

The decline of adulthood did not happen overnight and the process was arguably just beginning in 1970. Still, the tourism industry was quick to respond to changing tastes by generating a global playground of "cool" attractions. The catch is that what is cool one minute is passé the next. Just as youth movements have a limited lifecycle in which they appeal at first to a small "subculture," catch popular attention, draw in larger and larger numbers anxious to be part of something exciting and cutting edge, and then arrive as mainstream and thus cease to be cool,[61] so, too, the latest tourist attraction cannot remain trendy forever.

Tourism scholars often refer to a model developed by geographer R. W. Butler in which there are identifiable stages through which tourism sites progress. At first, there is an "exploration stage" in which small numbers of tourists explore a site. Next, during the "involvement stage," visitors become more regular and local residents start to provide services for these guests. During the "development stage," marketing efforts increase, facilities are improved, and attendance grows. The "consolidation stage" represents a turning point. The rate at which visitor numbers climbed starts to tail off. Tourists still come in droves, but growth is not what it once was. Numbers ultimately peak during the "stagnation phase" and then drop off during the "decline stage." Holidaymakers might visit on a day-trip, but the number traveling further to see the attraction is underwhelming.[62] Acquiring cultural capital through tourism demands going further afield than others, escaping from the maddening crowd.[63] This goal is impossible to achieve when everybody is touring the same places and seeing the same sites. Mass tourism demands the inclusion of everybody by creating targeted products, while keeping costs low requires that everything be standardized.[64] Marketers and developers must do their best to establish difference, to show holidaymakers that the place on offer is actually unique from every place else.

The result can be paradoxical. "Heritage tourism" is a case in point. It is rooted in a widespread desire to travel into a simpler past and it accounts for as much as $192 billion in the United States alone.[65] In Great Britain, "heritage" was worth £26.4 billion in 2013.[66] In developing countries, this branch of travel is arguably worth even more.[67] Not everybody is happy about the results. Neil Cossons (1939–), director of the Science Museum (London), once observed that "You can't project that sort of rate of growth much further before the whole country becomes one big open air museum, and you just join it as you get off at Heathrow [airport]"[68]—but there is too much money at stake to let such things slow development. Around the world, gas lamps, cobblestones, red brick, and iron railings became universal symbols of age and of a simplified past. Cities in virtually every part of the world launched redevelopment programs during the 1970s, 1980s, and 1990s to make their tourist districts look old and to stress local histories. Sometimes these places were legitimately long-standing and unique—there is only one Great Wall of China, Taj Mahal, Machu Picchu, or Stonehenge—but in other instances they reflect a more cynical desire to attract tourists by giving them what they want, something that seems genuinely old but that is in fact standardized and cookie-cutter.[69]

For some travelers, the pursuit of a unique place or experience demands greater effort. The only way to find this is to venture far off the beaten track. Antarctica, for example, is growing rapidly as a desirable tourist destination. During the 1980s, there were less than 2000 visitors a year who took cruises in the area and went ashore once or twice. Today the number is more than 35,000 and they are "much more action oriented. Now people want to go paragliding, waterskiing, diving or a variety of other things."[70] Tribes hidden away in isolated rainforests offer a comparable level of appeal, a type of tourism called "human safaris" in which travelers seek "voyeuristic sightings of members" of "uncontacted tribes."[71]

The summit of Mount Everest, the highest mountain on earth, offers yet another difficult-to-reach, high-prestige destination. While there is debate about the first successful ascent,[72] Edmund Hillary (1919–2008) and Tenzing Norgay (1914–86) became the first to reach the summit and to return alive in 1953.[73] After that, a few teams of superb climbers arrived at the top using various routes, but numbers were small. In the 1980s, traffic to the Himalayas increased. By the 1990s, author Jon Krakauer lamented that the mountain was "'debased and profaned' by the sheer number of amateurs flocking there." Anybody who was interested could pay to be led to the mountaintop. The peak was "commercialized" and "over-crowded."[74]

Similar things happen even when the destination is not as remote as the top or bottom of the world. "Voluntourism," spending one's holiday helping others, often in underdeveloped areas, started as a niche activity practiced by church groups and political organizations. It then became more commercialized and is now widespread with for-profit companies in place to help prospective voluntourists for a price.[75] Eating unique food was always a part of travel, but the advent of "foodie culture," as embodied by the Food Network and the rise of celebrity chefs, is now a booming industry in Italy and other places.[76] Visiting Holocaust sites had little appeal for all but a few people in the years after the Shoah.[77] Now Auschwitz alone attracts more than a million people every year, many of them Jews who see their attendance as a kind of pilgrimage,[78] and other camps such as Dachau draw hundreds of thousands more.[79] Similar points might be made about "hidden gems" of any number of types that are "discovered" by a few and become an attraction for the many. What starts as a minority practice or attraction soon develops the ruts characteristic of a heavily traveled path.

Impact of tourism

Those well-traveled tracks come at a cost. By the 1980s the implications of mass tourism for fragile ecosystems and cultures were increasingly obvious. According to Elisabeth Rosenthal of the *New York Times*, "One round-trip flight from New York to Europe or to San Francisco creates a warming effect equivalent to 2 or 3 tons of carbon dioxide per person. The average American generates about 19 tons of carbon dioxide a year; the average European, 10." Collectively, aircraft generate "about 5 percent of [global] warming" and that percentage is climbing"[80]—with significant implications for weather patterns, plant and animal life, and more. The ski resort at Kitzbühel in the Austrian Alps illustrates the problem. It depends on snow in order to attract ski tourists, creating a "vast economic engine for the surrounding region." Global warming is reducing the amount of snow and predictions by the Organization for Economic Co-operation and Development (OECD) hold that "Within two decades, there won't be enough snow to support skiing on the legendary slopes." The resort is not alone. Tourism is among the "most vulnerable sectors to the impacts of climate change."[81]

The arrival of huge numbers of tourists in often sensitive areas can cause soil erosion, deterioration of water resources and quality, deforestation, damage to plant life and altered animal behavior, and "pollution from litter, oil residues, and vehicle exhaust."[82] While not limited to tropical islands, these risks are particularly visible because "island ecosystems are fragile, vulnerable and under increasing stress as a consequence of forces stemming from coastal development, use of coastal resources and global environmental change. Yet island economies are generally in great need of foreign exchange earnings and they are often highly dependent on tourism as a source of income." As a consequence, coastal wetlands, mangroves, coral reefs, and even the beaches themselves face serious threats from anxious developers.[83]

Tourism has potentially negative cultural implications. It need not harm host cultures,[84] but it can easily lead to exploitation, to natives being made to dance for handouts or the subject of "human safaris" operated by tourism promoters promising "the wildest, rudest and possibly the most interesting" groups around.[85] When Cancún opened in 1976, it was designed to provide clear "segregation" between workers and tourists.[86] The effect was to create "a de jure social and economic apartheid," what amounts to "Cancún's Soweto."[87] For locals, the resort brought intense migration, demise of corn as a centerpiece of social life, overcrowding and slum conditions, a dearth of social services, and intense social and cultural change.[88]

Tourists can also be a danger to themselves. When Mount Everest emerged as a popular destination for people anxious to stand on the top of the world in the late 1980s and 1990s, they turned the base camp into a disgusting trash heap.[89] Beyond the rubbish, the ascent can be deadly. For experienced climbers, the South Col is considered to be "easy," featuring just one short section of technical climbing: the "Hillary Step," which is located at nearly 29,000 feet. Alpinists face a tight timeframe when climbing high mountains and must turn around with plenty of daylight left to descend to the safety of camp. With hundreds trying to reach the top, the Hillary Step forms a bottleneck. In 1996, a sudden storm combined with this traffic jam to cause the death of two top guides and six clients.[90] Paying customers were not put off. Between 2000 and 2005 "more people climbed to the top of the world than had summited during the previous fifty years."[91] In 2014, of the 800 people who attempted the summit, 90 percent had "no actual climbing skills, having paid between $30,000 and $120,000 for a guided trip up."[92] It is a recipe for disaster, but this hardly matters to would-be climbers. As journalist and mountaineer Nick Heil finds: "Too much has been written, said, filmed, and photographed for anyone going to Mount Everest not to be fully aware of the risks of climbing to 29,035 feet. Only a fool would put complete faith in someone else to guarantee their safety, or bail them out of trouble if a problem arises, though certainly the mountain continues to attract its share of fools."[93]

By 1987, authorities chimed in about the many threats posed by mass leisure and the World Commission on Environment and Development issued a report. *Our Common Future* argues for the adoption of "sustainable" tourism practices. Five years later, in 1992, the environmental impact of the industry was a significant topic of discussion at the Rio Earth Summit. A year later the scholarly journal *Sustainable Tourism* launched and a vast academic literature quickly emerged. Today, there is widespread recognition of the need to balance tourist demand, the wants of various interest groups, and social and environmental impact when developing and managing tourist sites.[94] With traveler numbers steadily climbing, many anxious to experience something new and different, it is an uphill fight.

Conclusion

Tourism is not always harmful, of course. It can be beneficial. If Cancún reflects the potential negatives for native populations, then Ireland—where Irish-run agencies, local developers, and even community groups largely directed tourist development efforts in the decades after that country's civil war—offers a counterpoint.[95] The rise of sustainable tourism and the effort of various governments and pressure groups to fight against "human safaris" is an indication that there are responsible people anxious to balance interests and impacts, however challenging that may be.[96]

In the end, mass tourism is quite simply complicated. One can celebrate inclusiveness, noting that leisure is no longer the purview of a tiny elite, however there is a price to be paid in terms of environmental impact. With legions of travelers visiting major tourist attractions, there is a loss of privacy. It can be hard to appreciate a sublime landscape with countless others doing the same. What constitutes an authentic experience? Many vacationers express a desire to get off the beaten track, to experience something new, to see cultural traditions or pasts different from their own, to see things that are *real*. It follows that Disneyland must be inauthentic, home to "little hyper-real celluloid animal deities, not dead, and not alive either."[97] Walt Disney did not see it this way. He imagined that his park might be educational. Tomorrowland, for example, featured attractions that were designed to teach. Even Autopia, with its eleven miles-per-hour go-carts, was supposed to teach children to "learn respect for one another and for the rules of the road."[98] Leisure travel generates many such questions and is probably part of the reason that tourism represents one of the faster growing areas of scholarly enquiry, with numerous new books and articles appearing every year.

Tomorrowland looked toward an imagined future that was premised on the best guesses available in 1957 about what would happen over the ensuing thirty years. The dramatic arrival of mass tourism invites similar flights of fancy. The industry is growing rapidly, but will it continue? Tourism did not always exist; it was a product of the particular contexts described in these pages and it changed with time. Will the future bring further changes or even the dissolution of tourism?

Conclusion: "Never ask an historian about the future"

In the second decade of the twenty-first century tourism looks different than when elite males (and a few well-off women) embarked on trips around Europe more than two hundred and fifty years ago. There are similarities, an accretion of the past. Politics remain an important element of the story, even if in an altered way from when Queen Elizabeth I paid the best and brightest Britons to go abroad to learn about the neighbors. The notion that travel is good for you, that it will make you a better, more rounded person, is very much in play. As was true for spa- and beach-goers almost three hundred years ago, today people link health with leisure. Modern tourists maintain a desire to find the sublime and beautiful, even if they do not use those terms. Despite living in an age of Instagram, Twitter, and Facebook, postcards and other souvenirs still fill shops at major attractions and sightseers race to buy. But the overall scale is now larger. Once, tourists journeyed almost exclusively in Western Europe. Today they go nearly everywhere. Once critics remarked on the presence of a few hundred British visitors in Rome, today the figure stands in the millions. Once tourism was the purview of elites, today it occupies the minds of virtually everybody, at least in the developed world. Most striking, while in the past elites used tourism as a means of identifying themselves as part of a social group who all did roughly the same thing, today far more niche travel options help people express their claim to the "cool," a state that is inherently about being above the crowd.

The statistics do not lie. Tourism is expanding at an astonishing pace. In 1950 there were 25 million international arrivals. Totals shot up dramatically after that: 278 million in 1980, 528 million in 1995, and an amazing 1087 million in 2013. None of these tallies include domestic tourists—roughly 5 or 6 billion people in that same year. Altogether the tourism industry represented 9 percent of the global GDP, accounted for one in eleven jobs, and earned US$1.4 trillion in exports (equal to 6 percent of the world total).[1] What is more, in 2013, in the United States the industry "created jobs at a 40 percent faster pace than the rest of the economy."[2] Figures increase year to year at a rate of roughly 5 percent, with some place-to-place, continent-to-continent variation. In fact, in the most recent figures available at the time of writing, only the Middle East saw no growth, and it was host to two wars, frequent bombings, and considerable political tension.

As far as the World Tourism Organization is concerned, there is no reason to believe that this state of affairs will change. In fact, it projects 1.8 billion international tourist arrivals in 2030, increasing by an average of roughly 3.3 percent a year. The trend toward "emerging economies" is also slated to continue and these locations "are expected to exceed those in advanced economies by 2020." 57 percent of international arrivals, the organization predicts for 2030, will be in emerging economy destinations (versus 30 percent in 1980) and 43 percent in advanced economy destinations (versus 70 percent in 1980).[3]

The history of tourism since World War II may seem to support such bullish projections, but nothing is certain. The famous historian A.J.P. Taylor (1906–90) is often said to have quipped to a reporter: "Dear boy, you should never ask an historian to predict the future—frankly we have a hard enough time predicting the past."[4] Whether Taylor actually said this is debatable, but it is certainly correct. The past is terribly complicated. As Taylor once wrote, "Only death is inevitable. Short of that, nothing is inevitable until it happens and everything is inevitable once it has happened. The historian deals with past events and therefore to him all history is inevitable."[5] That a few hundred aristocrats traveled around Europe many years ago did not need to lead to billions of tourists today. This only took place because of numerous combinations of happenings, developments, needs and solutions, inventions, desires, and conscious actions—some of which are discussed in this book. The future is even more daunting because we cannot know what the context will be.

Even if the past is unable to tell us the future, it remains worthy of intensive study and tourism history is particularly intriguing because it so clearly coincides with so many aspects of life. This book shows that tourism overlaps with aesthetics, science and medicine, economics, politics, geography and environment, technological innovation, and more besides. Each is interesting in its own right. At the same time, tourism history demands that we think very broadly as well. For example, it is worth considering the past in a way that is not bounded by national borders. Much of the existing literature about tourism focuses on Great Britain. There are good reasons for this; as the first country to industrialize, British people enjoyed higher standards of living earlier and could therefore afford to travel before many of those from other places. And yet what took place in the United Kingdom happened within a larger international context. The Grand Tour was born of an age of expanding trade and global politics. It was partly a response to the rising employment of diplomats pioneered in Italy. Touristic aesthetics were the result of work by artists and scientists, authors and engineers drawn from many different countries. England hosted the first world's fair, but these events quickly became a nearly global phenomenon, fueling interest in travel. Politics played a role in tourism history from the start, but it was the global competition between political ideologies, each competing for mass support, that truly politicized tourism. Thinking about tourism history in a transnational way opens up the possibility of seeing connections and complexities that might otherwise be missed.

To know the history of tourism is to realize that few things are as simple as they might initially seem. At first blush, leisure travel may appear very uncomplicated. It is what we do when we are not being productive workers. It is mindless pastime. Yet as this book makes clear, such a view misses the reality. Tourism is a reflection of how we see the world around us. We can use it to help define ourselves by social class, education, gender, or nationality. It follows that tourism can also be used as a pedagogical tool. Leisure has ideological content and it can be, as in the case of Kraft durch Freude, disturbing. Far from an innocent diversion, tourism deserves the same careful thought and reflection that we give other aspects of life.

Finally, studying what came before should show us that we live in specific contexts. The lenses through which we see our age are as much a product of our time as our ancestors' experiences were a result of theirs. Looking at the story of tourism as it played out over hundreds of years illustrates this point very nicely. It makes it possible to see that things we take for granted—that beaches and mountains are beautiful, for example—are the outcome of many factors that are chronologically contingent. This is not simply a question of what tourists do or what they see. It defines who they *are*. Once they hoped to establish themselves as part of particular social groups, now leisure travel is very much about distinguishing oneself as an individual. The long-term narrative of tourism may offer significant clues about why this happened: a fascinating convergence of aesthetics, politics, industrialization and consumerism, economics, and health among other factors. Studying the past obviously teaches us about the past, but it can also tell us a tremendous amount about ourselves—*if* we learn the lessons of context.

Despite the optimistic forecasts discussed above, there are good reasons to wonder what will come next for tourism. The industry faces many challenges, beginning with the anxiety about international terrorism that started on September 11, 2001 when hijackers associated with a global Islamist terror network known as Al-Qaeda flew passenger jets into the World Trade Center in New York City, the Pentagon in Washington, DC, and a field in Stoystown, Pennsylvania after passengers thwarted a plan to strike a more high-profile target.[6] The United States government immediately grounded commercial air travel in its airspace for the four days after the attacks.[7] Months later, many still felt nervous boarding aircraft.[8] Partly to assuage this anxiety, airport security increased. Authorities demanded that shoes be removed, added more random identity checks, beefed up technology, and eventually required passengers to dramatically reduce the amount of fluids they carried onto aircraft.[9] Sometimes passengers chafed at the requirements, but officials such as Janet Napolitano, head of the Department of Homeland Security, a new agency created by the George W. Bush administration in the wake of the attacks, insisted that "It's all about security. It's all about everybody recognizing their role."[10] Grumbling gave way to acceptance.

Even as officials endeavored to make people feel secure, it was clear that total safety is a mirage and there were countless risks involved in going from one place to another. Shortly after the destruction of the Twin Towers, on November 12, 2001, American Airlines Flight 587 crashed in Queens, New York killing all 260 people on board.[11] It was not terrorism; rather, the plane was caught in turbulence generated by another aircraft. Yet the tragedy raised questions about the design of the airplane and about the skill of the pilots.[12]

There *were* more terror attacks in the following months and years; fear was present far from the "friendly skies." For example, in March 2004, 192 people died as a result of a train bombing in Madrid, Spain that was carried out by men affiliated with Al-Qaeda.[13] In 2005, three bombs exploded in London almost simultaneously on the London Underground and a forth destroyed a bus at Tavistock Square about an hour later.[14] And, as this book was being completed, Paris was gripped by shootings at the *Charlie Hebdo* satirical newspaper.[15] No place is entirely safe from those anxious to do harm; violence might erupt anywhere.

Risks extended beyond terrorism or crashing aircraft to a much older threat: disease. In 2003 an illness called Severe Acute Respiratory Syndrome (SARS) appeared in Asia and started to spread to other areas. Many world governments responded with programs intended to prevent a catastrophic global pandemic.[16] Carriers of the mysterious disease were deemed to be "more dangerous than bombers."[17] In 2009, anxiety again spiked when a flu strain referred to as H1N1, or "Swine Flu," appeared in a number of countries. Measures were once again taken to prevent the worst.[18] Even more recently, the dramatic spread of Ebola in West Africa and a handful of subsequent cases of the disease elsewhere, primarily among aid workers returning from the "hot zone," caused near panic across the United States. Politicians quickly politicized the situation, perhaps anxious to gain electoral support.[19]

For many, fiscal issues represented an even bigger worry. In the fall of 2008, the global economy collapsed: stocks plummeted, the American property market spiraled downward, a debt crisis rocked Europe, and unemployment climbed.[20] Almost no place was safe. As families tried to keep themselves afloat, annual holidays seemed one logical place to save and many popular destinations showed marked declines in traffic. Prague, capital of the Czech Republic, reported an 11 percent drop in visitor numbers during the first half of 2009 relative to the previous year.[21] Spain suffered an 8.7 percent decrease.[22]

In response, a growing number of people embraced a new form of vacation: the "staycation." The *Washington Times* interviewed one staycationer who commented simply: "Traveling is just so exhausting. The lines are long at the airport; the security takes forever; and I'm sick of schlepping and rushing, all for the chance to relax. I'd rather spend my money doing something quiet and low-key."[23] It was not a phenomenon limited to the United States. It exists in the United Kingdom as well. In July 2013, the *Manchester Evening News* reported: "A record two thirds of us are planning a break at home this summer."[24]

In Fall 2014, news outlets relayed that "U.S. workers forfeited $52.4 billion in time-off benefits in 2013 and took less vacation time than at any point in the past four decades. American workers turned their backs on a total of 169 million days of paid time off, in effect 'providing free labor for their employers, at an average of $504 per employee.'"[25] They have taken "almost a full work-week less compared to pre-2000." [26] The reasons for this are as yet unclear, but the trend is certainly in striking contrast to the rise in vacation travel between the 1930s and the turn of the century.

What does all of this mean? How will the context of today shape the tourism industry of tomorrow? Are there changes underway that will fundamentally transform the way that we look at the world, developments that will only become clear with the benefit of hindsight? The past cannot tell us, but if carefully considered it certainly gives us a lot of possibilities to consider.

Notes

Introduction

1 See: United Nations World Tourism Organization, *Tourism Highlights*, 2014 ed. (Madrid: UNWTO, 2014), 2 and United Nations World Tourism Organization, *UNWTO Annual Report 2013* (Madrid: UNWTO, 2013), 2, 11.
2 While I use the term "mobility" to describe the movement of people from place to place, scholars increasingly have a more complicated view. It may not be immediately obvious to the casual observer. Mobility might involve ideas as much as the people who have them. Rootedness can be as important as movement. For an example of current discussion, see: Stephen Greenblatt, ed., *A Mobility Studies Manifesto* (Cambridge: Cambridge University Press, 2009).
3 This point is not universally agreed upon. Some claim that once they evolved in southern Africa, humans soon spread outward, populating the rest of the globe. Other academics argue that the emergence of our distant ancestors occurred through a process of hybridization whereby migrating populations met, mated, and changed. Still others posit that humans are a result of "gene flow," of some populations surviving while others died out. Yet another group of anthropologists believes that humans appeared almost independently in Europe, Africa, and Asia from populations that had left Africa much earlier. See: Chris Stringer, "Modern Human Origins: Progress and Prospects," *Philosophical Transactions: Biological Sciences* 357, no. 1420 (29 April 2002): 563–79.
4 "New Evidence Puts Man in North America 50,000 Years Ago," *Science Daily*, 18 November 2004, accessed 6 February 2011, http://www.sciencedaily.com/releases/2004/11/041118104010.htm.
5 Israel Finkelstein and Neil Asher Silberman, *The Bible Unearthed: Archaeology's New Vision of Ancient Israel and the Origin of Its Sacred Texts* (New York: Free Press, 2001), 63.
6 Timothy Taylor, *The Buried Soul: How Humans Invented Death* (Boston, MA: Beacon Press, 2005), 31.
7 Michael Cook, *A Brief History of the Human Race* (New York: W.W. Norton, 2003), 21–2.

8 S.H. Katz and M. Voight, "Bread and Beer: The Early Use of Cereals in the Human Diet," *Expedition* 28, no. 2 (1987): 23–34.
9 Monica L. Smith, "The Substance and Symbolism of Long-distance Exchange: Textiles and Desired Trade Goods in the Bronze Age Middle Asian Interaction Sphere," in *Connections and Complexity: New Approaches to the Archaeology of South Asia*, eds, Dhinu Anna Abraham, Praveena Gullapalli, Teresa P. Raczek, and Uzma Z. Rizvi (Walnut Creek, CA: Left Coast Press, 2013), 143–60. See especially page 143. See also: Guillermo Algaze, *Ancient Mesopotamia at the Dawn of Civilization: The Evolution of an Urban Landscape* (Chicago, IL: University of Chicago Press, 2008), 93–9.
10 John R. McNeill and William H. McNeill, *The Human Web: A Bird's Eye View of World History* (New York: W.W. Norton, 2003), 3.
11 Patrick E. McGovern, *Uncorking the Past: The Quest for Wine, Beer, and other Alcoholic Beverages* (Berkeley, CA: University of California Press, 2009), 180–2. Also see Tom Standage, *A History of the World in Six Glasses* (New York: Walker and Co., 2005).
12 Avraham Faust and Ehud Weiss, "Judah, Philistia, and the Mediterranean World: Reconstructing the Economic System of the Seventh Century, B.C.E.," *Bulletin of the American Schools of Oriental Research* 338 (May 2005): 71–92. See page 85.
13 David Sacks and Oswyn Murray, *Encyclopedia of the Ancient Greek World*, rev. ed. (New York: Facts on File, 2005), 265.
14 For more on Roman trade in the East, see: Raoul McLaughlin, *Rome and the Distant East: Trade Routes to the Ancient Lands of Arabia, India and China* (London: Continuum, 2010).
15 For example, see: Else Roesdahl, *The Vikings*, trans. Susan M. Margeson and Kirsten Williams (London: Penguin, 1998).
16 Eric J. Leed, *Mind of the Traveler: From Gilgamesh to Global Tourism* (New York: Basic Books, 1991), 27.
17 Andrew George, trans. *The Epic of Gilgamesh* (New York: Penguin, 2003).
18 For a discussion of Alexander the Great, see: Norman F. Cantor, *Alexander the Great: Journey to the End of the Earth* (New York: Harper Perennial, 2005). For more on the Mongols, see: David Morgan, *The Mongols*, 2nd ed. (Malden, MA: Blackwell, 2007).
19 For more on the life of Henry the Navigator, see: Peter Russell, *Prince Henry "the Navigator": A Life* (New Haven, CT: Yale University Press, 2000).
20 More on the age of exploration can be found in: J.H. Parry, *The Age of Reconnaissance: Discovery, Exploration, and Settlement, 1450-1650* (London: Phoenix Press, 1962) and Glenn J. Ames, *The Globe Encompassed: The Age of European Discovery (1500-1700)* (New York: Pearson, 2007).

For a more expansive history of exploration itself, see: Felipe Fernández-Armesto, *Pathfinders: A Global History of Exploration* (New York: W.W. Norton, 2006).

21 Lionel Casson, *Travel in the Ancient World* (1974, repr., Baltimore, MD: Johns Hopkins University Press, 1994), 32.

22 Ibid., 35.

23 See: O. Kimball Armayor, "Did Herodotus Ever Go To Egypt?," *Journal of the American Research Center in Egypt* 15 (1978): 59–73 and O. Kimball Armayor, "Did Herodotus Ever Go To the Black Sea?" *Harvard Studies in Classical Philology* 82 (1978): 45–62. For an interesting account of Herodotus's writing about travel: James Redfield, "Herodotus the Tourist," *Classical Philology* 80, no. 2 (April 1985): 97–118.

24 Casson, *Travel*, 85.

25 Loykie Lomine, "Tourism in Augustan Society (44BC-AD69)," in *Histories of Tourism: Representation, Identity and Conflict*, ed. John K. Walton (Clevedon: Channel View Publications, 2005), 69.

26 Ibid., 73–4.

27 Ibid., 83. Kevin D. O'Gorman explores the history of hospitality in his textbook, *The Origins of Hospitality and Tourism* (Woodeaton, UK: Goodfellow Publishers, 2010). He finds that hospitality is a factor in much (if not all) of human history, but focuses his attentions on antiquity through to the Renaissance. O'Gorman offers a useful discussion of Greek and Roman hospitality in Chapters 4 and 5 of his book.

28 Lomine, "Tourism in Augustan Society," 86.

29 For a selection of essays concerning the spread of Buddhism out of India, see: Ann Heirman and Stephen Peter Bumbacher, eds, *The Spread of Buddhism* (Leiden: Brill, 2007).

30 For a history of Islam and its geographic reach, see: Adam J. Silverstein, *Islamic History: A Very Short Introduction* (Oxford: Oxford University Press, 2010). It is also worth stressing that every Muslim who is financially and physically capable is required to take part in the Hajj, a religious pilgrimage to Mecca, "at least once in a lifetime." For a detailed history, see: F.E. Peters, *The Hajj: The Muslim Pilgrimage to Mecca and the Holy Places* (Princeton, NJ: Princeton University Press, 1994). Quote appears on page xxi.

31 Robert L. Montgomery offers a sociological study designed to explain why Christianity successfully spread north and west from the Holy Land, but had a more difficult road moving eastward. See Robert L. Montgomery, *Lopsided Spread of Christianity: Toward an Understanding of the Diffusion of Religions* (Westport, CT: Praeger, 2001). During the early Middle Ages a significant number of Muslim "men of letters" traveled in pursuit of knowledge, to carry out survey work, and for other purposes.

Many wrote of their experiences. For a thorough account, see: Houari Touati, *Islam and Travel in the Middle Ages* (Chicago, IL: University of Chicago Press, 2010).

32 J. Stopford, *Pilgrimage Explored* (York, UK: York Medieval Press, 1999), ix.

33 Nelson H.H. Graburn, "Secular Ritual: A General Theory of Tourism," in *Hosts and Guests Revisited: Tourism Issues of the 21st Century*, eds, Valene L. Smith and Maryann Brent (Elmsford, NY: Cognizant Communications, 2001), 42–50. See pages 42–3.

34 For an interesting discussion of the tourist/pilgrim distinction, see: Valene L. Smith, "The Nature of Tourism," in *Hosts and Guests Revisited: Tourism Issues of the 21st Century*, eds, Valene L. Smith and Maryann Brent (Elmsford, NY: Cognizant Communications, 2001), 53–68. See pages 66–7.

35 Jacques Le Goff, *The Birth of Europe* (Oxford: Blackwell, 2007), 65.

36 For an excellent introduction to medieval pilgrimage, see: Diana Webb, *Medieval European Pilgrimage, c. 700-c.1500* (Basingstoke: Palgrave, 2002).

37 Sidney Heath, *Pilgrim Life in the Middle Ages* (Boston, MA and New York: Houghton Mifflin, 1912), 36.

38 Sarah Hopper, *To Be a Pilgrim: The Medieval Pilgrimage Experience* (Stroud: Sutton, 2002), 132–3.

39 For further discussion of the "interface" between tourism and religion, see: Erik Cohen, *Contemporary Tourism: Diversity and Change* (New York: Elsevier, 2004), 147–58.

40 Rudy Koshar, *German Travel Cultures* (Oxford: Berg, 2000), 8. There are other definitions of tourism, of course. Ascem Anand, for example, describes it as "a composite phenomenon which embraces the incidence of [a] mobile population of travellers who are strangers to the places they visit. It is essentially a pleasure activity in which money earned in one's normal domicile is spent in the place visited." Ascem Anand, *Advance Dictionary of Tourism* (New Delhi: Sarup & Sons, 1997), 41. While Anand suggests that tourism is not tied to making money, historian Cindy Aron describes a conflicted relationship in which workers justify leisure by suggesting that it will help them work more efficiently—thus giving tourism an important role in productive labor. See: Cindy S. Aron, *Working At Play: A History of Vacations in the United States* (Oxford: Oxford University Press, 1999), 5–6. For still more discussion of definitions and distinctions, see: Cohen, *Contemporary Tourism*, 17–36.

41 Even within Europe, the division between "early modern" and "modern" history varies from place to place. In Britain, for example, modern history often starts with the Glorious Revolution in 1688, while in France the transition is often seen with the French Revolution in 1789.

42 Cited in Dipesh Chakrabarty, "The Muddle of Modernity," *American Historical Review* 116, no. 3 (June 2011): 663–75. See page 671.

43 Carol Gluck, "The End of Elsewhere: Writing Modernity Now," *American Historical Review* 116, no. 3 (June 2011): 676–87. See page 676.
44 Gurminder K. Bhambra, "Historical Sociology, Modernity, and Postcolonial Critique," *American Historical Review* 116, no. 3 (June 2011): 653–62. See page 655.
45 Stuart B. Schwartz, ed., *Implicit Understandings: Observing, Reporting, and Reflecting on the Encounters Between Europeans and Other Peoples in the Early Modern Era* (Cambridge: Cambridge University Press, 1994), 3.

Chapter 1

1 Edward Gibbon, *Memoirs of My Life and Writings of Edward Gibbon* (Boston, MA and London: Ginn & Company, 1898), 48.
2 Ibid., 47.
3 Ibid., 82.
4 Ibid., 142.
5 Jeremy Black, *The British Abroad: The Grand Tour in the Eighteenth Century* (New York: St. Martin's Press, 1992), 7–12.
6 Orvar Löfgren, *On Holiday: A History of Vacationing* (Berkeley, CA: University of California Press, 1999), 19.
7 Chloe Chard writes that Grand Tour travel accounts reflected and encouraged a growing sense of "personal adventure." For more, see: *Pleasure and Guilt on the Grand Tour: Travel Writing and Imaginative Geography, 1600–1830* (Manchester, UK: Manchester University Press, 1999), 11.
8 Bruce Redford, *Venice and The Grand Tour* (New Haven, CT: Yale University Press, 1996), 14.
9 Louise McReynolds, "The Prerevolutionary Russian Tourist: Commercialization in the Nineteenth Century," in *Turizm: The Russian and East European Tourist Under Capitalism and Socialism*, eds, Anne E. Gorsuch and Diane P. Koenker (Ithaca, NY: Cornell University Press, 2006), 17.
10 Johann Wolfgang von Goethe, *Goethe's Letters from Switzerland and Travels in Italy* (New York: Worthington, 1885).
11 Cesare De Seta, "Grand Tour: The Lure of Italy in the Eighteenth Century," in *Grand Tour: The Lure of Italy in the Eighteenth Century*, eds, Andrew Wilton and Ilaria Bignamini (London: Tate Gallery Publishing, 1996), 14.
12 Chard, *Pleasure and Guilt*, 15.
13 Brian Dolan, *Ladies of the Grand Tour: British Women in Pursuit of Enlightenment and Adventure in Eighteenth-Century Europe* (New York: HarperCollins, 2001).
14 Tobias Smollett, *Travels through France and Italy*, ed. Frank Felsenstein (Buffalo, NY: Broadview, 2011; first published 1766).

15 Hugh Brigstocke, "The 5th Earl of Exeter as Grand Tourist and Collector," *Papers of the British School at Rome* 72 (2004): 331–56.
16 De Seta, "Grand Tour," 14.
17 For a short discussion of the plague and some of its implications, see: Norman F. Cantor, *In the Wake of the Plague: The Black Death and the World It Made* (New York: Perennial, 2001).
18 S.J. Payling, "Social Mobility, Demographic Change, and Landed Society in Late Medieval England," *Economic History Review*, New Series, 45, no. 1 (February 1992): 51–73.
19 Paul Johnson, *The Renaissance: A Short History* (New York: The Modern Library, 2002), 14–15.
20 Cited in Jacques Le Goff, *The Birth of Europe* (Oxford: Blackwell, 2007), 178.
21 Le Goff, *Birth of Europe*, 178–81. See also: Johnson, *Renaissance*, 15–16.
22 Michael A. Di Giovine, "Review Article: Identities and Nation-Building in Early Modern Travel Accounts," *Journeys: International Journal of Travel and Travel Writing* 12, no. 1 (September 2011): 93–105.
23 Italy did not become a unified state until the *Risorgimento* during the second half of the nineteenth century.
24 Garrett Mattingly, *Renaissance Diplomacy* (Baltimore, MD: Penguin Books, 1964), 10 and 55.
25 Colin Martin and Geoffrey Parker, *The Spanish Armada* (Manchester, UK: Mandolin, 1988), 57–70.
26 Edward Chaney, *The Evolution of the Grand Tour: Anglo-Italian Cultural Relations since the Renaissance* (London: Frank Cass, 1998), xiii.
27 Felipe Fernández-Armesto, *The Spanish Armada: The Experience of War in 1588* (Oxford: Oxford University Press, 1989), 112.
28 Charles Beem and Carole Levin, "Why Elizabeth Never Left England," in *The Foreign Relations of Elizabeth I*, ed. Charles Beem (New York: Palgrave Macmillan, 2011), 4.
29 Susan Doran, *Elizabeth I and Foreign Policy, 1558–1603* (London: Routledge, 2000), 48–9 and 67.
30 Paul Grendler, "The Universities of the Renaissance and Reformation," *Renaissance Quarterly* 57, no. 1 (Spring 2004): 1–42.
31 For a scathing indictment of the nature of the education provided during the seventeenth, eighteenth, and nineteenth centuries at Oxford and Cambridge, see Andrew Lockhart Walker, *The Revival of the Democratic Intellect* (Edinburgh: Polygon, 1994), 38–57.
32 Geoffrey Trease, *The Grand Tour* (New York: Holt, Rinehart and Winston, 1967), 16–17; and, Christopher Hibbert, *The Grand Tour* (New York: G.P. Putnam's Sons, 1969), 10–11.
33 Francis Bacon, *Bacon's Essay with Annotations by Richard Whately*, 2nd ed., rev. and enl. (Freeport, NY: Books for Libraries, 1973), 194–6.

34 Hibbert, *Grand Tour*, 11–15.
35 Jeremy Black, *The Grand Tour in the Eighteenth Century* (Stroud, UK: Alan Sutton, 1992), 10. See also: De Seta, "Grand Tour," 14.
36 It should be noted that historians debate this chronology. Some argue that the "aristocratic Grand Tour" peaked in roughly 1760, transforming into something else thereafter. After 1760, according to this view, the efficacy of the tour was evermore challenged, the objectives changed, the type of people traveling expanded, and even the destinations evolved to include more rural locations than were attractive before. See: Rosemary Sweet, *Cities and the Grand Tour: The British in Italy, c. 1690–1820* (Cambridge: Cambridge University Press, 2012), 7.
37 Jeremy Black offers an extended discussion of tourist numbers and of popular destinations. See: *Grand Tour*, 7–12 and 14–80. See also: Roger Hudson, ed., *The Grand Tour: 1592–1796* (London: Folio Society, 1993), 21.
38 Bruce Redford, *Venice and the Grand Tour* (New Haven, CT: Yale University Press, 1996), 15–16.
39 Hibbert, *Grand Tour*, 24.
40 Thomas William Heyck, *The Peoples of the British Isles: A New History, Vol. II: From 1688 to 1870* (Chicago, IL: Lyceum Books, 2008), 48–9.
41 The rise of radical politics, the gradual erosion of aristocratic power, and the attitudes held by the elites themselves is the subject of extensive historical discussion. H.T. Dickinson offers a good introduction to the structure of eighteenth-century British politics as well as to the growth of radical politics in *The Politics of the People in Eighteenth Century Britain* (New York: St. Martin's Press, 1994). Eric J. Evans introduces both the unreformed political system and the story of the 1832 Reform Act in his very concise *The Great Reform Act of 1832*, 2nd ed. (London: Routledge, 1994). While their argument is the subject of considerable debate, Lawrence and Jeanne Stone's *An Open Elite? England, 1540–1880* (Oxford: Oxford University Press, 1984) provides a useful look at the challenges facing Britain's upper-crust during the sixteenth, seventeenth, eighteenth, and nineteenth centuries.
42 Redford, *Venice and the Grand Tour*, 16.
43 Black, *Grand Tour*, 86–107. To put these costs into perspective, according to the British National Archives' currency calculator, £1 in 1750 was equivalent to £85.16 in 2005. This means that an average annual expenditure of £300 in 1750 would equal £25,548 today. "Currency Converter." Available from the (British) National Archives at: http://www.nationalarchives.gov.uk/currency/. Accessed 4 February 2012.
44 Hibbert, *Grand Tour*, 19.
45 For example, see W. Hamish Fraser, *The Coming of the Mass Market, 1850–1914* (Hamden, CT: Archon Books, 1981) and Rosalind H. Williams,

Dream Worlds: Mass Consumption in Late Nineteenth-Century France (Berkeley, CA: University of California Press, 1982).

46 Christopher Dyer is especially aggressive in this regard. See: "The Consumer and the Market in the Later Middle Ages," *Economic History Review*, 2nd ser. 41, no. 3 (1989): 305–27.

47 Miles Hadfield, *A History of British Gardening* (London: Penguin, 1985), 452.

48 Ian Ousby, *The Englishman's England: Taste, Travel and the Rise of Tourism* (Cambridge: Cambridge University Press, 1990), 58–91.

49 Brigstocke, "The 5th Earl of Exeter," 331–56.

50 Numerous paintings from both Britain and Continental Europe reflect this trend. Thomas Gainsborough's "Mr. and Mrs. Andrews" (1750), in which a young married couple stands with their lands extending into the background (taking up nearly the entire left of the portrait), is among the most famous.

51 Lorna Weatherill, "A Possession of One's Own: Women and Consumer Behavior in England, 1660–1740," *Journal of British Studies* 25 (April 1986): 131–56.

52 Colin Campbell, *The Romantic Ethic and the Spirit of Modern Consumerism* (Oxford: Basil Blackwell, 1987), 202–27.

53 Orvar Löfgren provides a very useful discussion of picture postcards, photographs, and souvenirs in *On Holiday*, 72–88.

54 For a discussion of major routes, see: Black, *British Abroad*, 14–80. See also: Hibbert, *Grand Tour*. It is worth stressing that the Grand Tour, at least before 1750 when changing tastes (see Chapter 2) inspired trips to mountains and beaches, was overwhelmingly *urban* in focus. See: Sweet, *Cities and the Grand Tour*, 2–3.

55 Hibbert, *Grand Tour*, 224–7.

56 Black, *British Abroad*, 196.

57 Lawrence Stone, *The Family, Sex and Marriage in England, 1500–1800*, Abr. ed. (New York: Harper and Row, 1979), 334–5.

58 Black, *British Abroad*, 195.

59 Ibid., 191.

60 Jessica Warner, *Craze: Gin and Debauchery in an Age of Reason* (New York: Random House, 2003), 3.

61 Paul Jennings, *The Local: A History of the English Pub* (Stroud, UK: Tempus, 2007), 51.

62 Black, *British Abroad*, 206.

63 Ibid., 207.

64 Wollstonecraft, at least, was differentiated from many male travelers by her choice of destination as well. While most went to France, Italy, Switzerland, and the Netherlands, the proto-feminist author journeyed to Scandinavia in June 1795. See: Mary Wollstonecraft, *Letters Written*

in Sweden, Norway, and Denmark, ed. Tone Brekke and Jon Mee (1796; Oxford: Oxford University Press, 2009), ix.

65 Patricia Jean Behenna Meyer, "No Land Too Remote: Women Travellers in the Georgian Age, 1750–1830" (Ph.D. diss., University of Massachusetts-Amherst, 1978), 275.

66 Brian Dolan, *Ladies of the Grand Tour* (New York: HarperCollins, 2001), 7.

67 Ibid., 5–8.

68 James Boswell, *The Life of Samuel Johnson, Vol. 2* (1791; London: J.M. Dent & Sons, 1911), 251.

69 Gibbon, *Memoirs*, 72–3.

70 Bacon, *Bacon's Essays*, 196.

71 Hibbert, *Grand Tour*, 230.

72 Sweet, *Cities and the Grand Tour*, 11–13. Richard Mullen and James Munson pick up the story of British travelers in *"The Smell of the Continent": The British Discover Europe, 1814–1914* (London: Macmillan, 2009).

73 Sweet, *Cities and the Grand Tour*, 11–13.

Chapter 2

1 Coleridge suffered from "Atonic Gout," but it appears that he often used this complaint "to mask a deeper psychological need for sedation." See: Dorothy Wordsworth, *Recollections of a Tour Made in Scotland* (New Haven, CT: Yale University Press, 1997; first published 1874), 14–15.

2 Coleridge to Sara Hutchinson, "Eskdale, 6 August 1802," in *Collected Letters of Samuel Taylor Coleridge, Vol. II, 1801-1806*, ed. Earl Leslie Griggs (Oxford: Clarendon Press, 1966), 841.

3 Robert Macfarlane, *Mountains of the Mind: How Desolate and Forbidding Heights Were Transformed into Experiences of Indomitable Spirit* (New York: Pantheon Books, 2003), 82.

4 Coleridge to Hutchinson, "Eskdale, 6 August 1802," 841–3.

5 Margaret B. Fergusson, "The Ascent of Olympus," *Greece and Rome* 12, no. 21 (May 1938): 129–36. See pages 129–30.

6 Exodus, 19:2, 19:12-14.

7 Constanza Ceruti, "Human Bodies as Objects of Dedication in Inca Mountain Shrines (North-Western Argentina)," *World Archaeology* 36, no. 1 (March 2004): 103–22.

8 Christopher Hibbert, *The Grand Tour* (New York: Putnam's Sons, 1969), 88.

9 Lyell Asher, "Petrarch at the Peak of Fame," *PMLA* 108, no. 5 (October 1993): 1050–63. See pages 1050–1.

10 Alain Corbin, *The Lure of the Sea: The Discovery of the Seaside in the Western World, 1750-1840* (Berkeley, CA: University of California Press, 1994), 1.
11 Ibid., 1–18. Especially page 9. See also Chet Van Duzer, *Sea Monsters on Medieval and Renaissance Maps* (London: The British Library, 2013).
12 Huston Smith, *The World's Religions*, 50th anniversary ed. (New York: HarperCollins, 2009), 365–83.
13 Corbin, *Lure of the Sea*, 102 and Macfarlane, *Mountains of the Mind*, 24.
14 Macfarlane, *Mountains of the Mind*, 22–31.
15 Corbin, *Lure of the Sea*, 3, 102.
16 Macfarlane, *Mountains of the Mind*, 31–3.
17 Ibid., 33–4.
18 Ibid., 36–44.
19 Adam Smith, *The Wealth of Nations* (New York: P.F. Collier & Son, 1902; first published 1776), 155.
20 Corbin, *Lure of the Sea*, 33.
21 William H. TeBrake, "Taming the Waterwolf: Hydraulic Engineering and Water Management in the Netherlands during the Middle Ages," Special issue: Water Technology in the Netherlands, *Technology and Culture* 43, no. 3 (July 2002): 475–99. See pages 476–7.
22 S.J. Fockema Andreae, "Embanking and Drainage Authorities in the Netherlands during the Middle Ages," *Speculum* 27, no. 2 (April 1952): 158–67. The evolutionary process did not end with the Middle Ages. For more, see: Harry Lintsen, "Two Centuries of Central Water Management in the Netherlands," Special issue: Water Technology in the Netherlands, *Technology and Culture* 43, no. 3 (July 2002): 549–68.
23 Corbin, *Lure of the Sea*, 33.
24 Ibid., 33–4.
25 Macfarlane, *Mountains of the Mind*, 76; and, Casper C. de Jonge, "Dionysius and Longinus on the Sublime: Rhetoric and Religious Language," *American Journal of Philology* 133, no. 2 (Summer 2012): 271–300.
26 Dennis O'Keeffe, *Edmund Burke* (New York: Continuum, 2010), xv, 1–4.
27 Edmund Burke, *A Philosophical Enquiry into the Origin of Our Ideas of the Sublime and Beautiful*, ed. Adam Philips (Oxford: Oxford University Press, 2008; first published 1757), 113.
28 Ibid., 31–3.
29 Ibid., 36–7.
30 Macfarlane, *Mountains of the Mind*, 77.
31 Edward Gibbon, *Memoirs of My Life and Writings of Edward Gibbon* (Boston, MA and London: Ginn & Co., 1898), 82.
32 Samuel Johnson and James Boswell, *A Journey to the Western Islands of Scotland and A Journal of a Tour to the Hebrides* (New York: Penguin, 1984; first published 1775 and 1786), 46–7.

33 Ibid., 211–12.
34 Ibid., 46–7.
35 Macfarlane, *Mountains of the Mind*, 151–2.
36 Orvar Löfgren, *On Holiday: A History of Vacationing* (Berkeley, CA: University of California Press, 1999), 22–5.
37 For an interesting discussion of this painting and its relationship to the cult of climbing, see Macfarlane, *Mountains of the Mind*, 157–8.
38 Peter H. Hansen, *The Summits of Modern Man: Mountaineering after the Enlightenment* (Cambridge, MA: Harvard University Press, 2013), 32.
39 Peter H. Hansen, "Albert Smith, the Alpine Club, and the Invention of Mountaineering in Mid-Victorian Britain," *Journal of British Studies* 34, no. 3 (July 1995): 300–24.
40 Macfarlane, *Mountains of the Mind*, 157. For an extended discussion of Victorians and their obsession with the mountains (especially with the colonization of the Alps by climbers anxious to find the sublime), see: Ann C. Colley, *Victorians and the Mountains: Sinking the Sublime* (Farnham, UK: Ashgate, 2010). Readers may also wish to explore how at least some thinkers responded to the rapid growth of such forms of tourism and by so responding helped to further shape a sense of aesthetics and desirable practice. For example, see: Keith Hanley and John K. Walton, *Constructing Cultural Tourism: John Ruskin and the Tourist Gaze* (Bristol, UK: Channel View, 2010).
41 Hansen, "Albert Smith," 305.
42 Macfarlane, *Mountains of the Mind*, 89.
43 Hansen, "Albert Smith," 309–10.
44 Corbin, *Lure of the Sea*, 38.
45 Ibid., 37–40.
46 E.A. Wrigley and R.S. Schofield, *The Population History of England, 1541-1871* (Cambridge, MA: Harvard University Press, 1981), 175, 588.
47 Asa Briggs, *Victorian Cities* (New York: Harper & Row, 1970), 56.
48 Thomas William Heyck, *A History of the Peoples of the British Isles, Vol. II: From 1688-1914* (Chicago, IL: Lyceum, 2002), 180.
49 Paul Bairoch and Gary Goertz, "Factors of Urbanization in the Nineteenth Century Developed Countries: A Descriptive and Econometric Analysis," *Urban Studies* 23 (1986): 285, 288.
50 David F. Crew, *Town on the Ruhr* (New York: Columbia University Press, 1979). See pages 8–9 for a brief summation of the speed of change.
51 Friedrich Engels provides a sobering description of working-class living conditions in *The Condition of the Working Class in England*, ed. Victor Kiernan (London: Penguin, 2005; first published 1845), especially in his chapter addressing "The Great Towns," 68–110.

52 John Kelly, *The Great Mortality: An Intimate History of the Black Death, the Most Devastating Plague of All Time* (New York: HarperCollins, 2005), 169–71.
53 Readers interested in changing ideas about smell, as well as about the relationship between health and scent in European thought, should consult Alain Corbin, *The Foul and the Fragrant: Odor and the French Social Imagination* (Cambridge, MA: Harvard University Press, 1988).
54 Roy Porter, *London: A Social History* (Cambridge, MA: Harvard University Press, 1994), 259–66.
55 For an overview, see: Norman Longmate, *King Cholera: The Biography of a Disease* (London: Hamish Hamilton, 1966).

Chapter 3

1 Harold Perkin, *The Age of the Railway* (New York: Drake, 1973), 15–44.
2 Perkin, *Age of the Railway*, 61–70. For a more continental perspective on the importance of new roadway technologies, see: Bruno Blondé, "At the Cradle of the Transport Revolution?: Paved Roads, Traffic Flows, and Economic Development in Eighteenth-Century Britain," *Journal of Transport History* 31, no. 1 (June 2010): 89–111.
3 For a wide-ranging discussion of what life was like during the age of sail, see: Dorothy Denneen Volo and James M. Volo, *Daily Life in the Age of Sail* (Westport, CT: Greenwood Press, 2002).
4 John Malcolm Brinnin, *The Sway of the Grand Saloon: A Social History of the North Atlantic* (New York: Delacorte Press, 1971), 6–8.
5 James S. Donnelly, Jr., *The Great Irish Potato Famine* (Stroud: Sutton, 2002), 33.
6 David Fitzpatrick, "Flight from Famine," in *The Great Irish Famine*, ed. Cathal Póirtéir (Dublin: Mercier Press, 1995), 179.
7 Brinn, *Sway of the Grand Saloon*, 16.
8 Volo and Volo, *Daily Life*, 160–1.
9 Ibid., 121–3, 168–9.
10 Brinnin, *Sway of the Grand Saloon*, 17–19.
11 Stuart Hylton, *The Grand Experiment: The Birth of the Railway Age: 1820-45* (Hersham: Ian Allan, 2007), 18.
12 Christian Wolmar, *Fire and Steam: A New History of the Railways in Britain* (London: Atlantic Books, 2007), 1–4.
13 Ibid., 14. See also: Perkin, *Age of the Railway*, 71–2.
14 Wolmar, *Fire and Steam*, 16.
15 Perkin, *Age of the Railway*, 87–8.

16 Michael Freeman, *Railways and the Victorian Imagination* (New Haven, CT: Yale University Press, 1999), 51.
17 Wolmar, *Fire and Steam*, 9–10.
18 Asa Briggs, *Victorian Cities* (New York: Harper & Row, 1970), 56.
19 "The Railway Centenary," *Manchester Guardian*, 12 August 1930. See also: "Opening of the *Manchester and Liverpool Railway*," *Manchester Guardian*, 20 September 1830.
20 Hylton, *Grand Experiment*, 45.
21 "The Locomotive Engine Trial," *Manchester Guardian*, 17 October 1829.
22 Perkin, *Age of the Railway*, 79.
23 "Dreadful Accident to Mr. Huskisson," *Observer*, 20 September 1830.
24 "Death of the Right Hon. W. Huskisson, MP," *Observer*, 19 September 1830. For more on changing attitudes toward death, see: Philippe Ariès, *Western Attitudes Toward Death: From the Middle Ages to the Present* (Baltimore, MD: Johns Hopkins University Press, 1975).
25 Perkin, *Age of the Railway*, 180–1.
26 P.J.G. Ransom, *The Victorian Railway and How It Evolved* (London: Heinemann, 1990), 79, 110.
27 T.G. Otte and Keith Neilson, "'*Railpolitik*': An Introduction," in *Railways and International Politics: Paths of Empire, 1848-1945*, eds, T.G. Otte and Keith Neilson (London: Routledge, 2012), 3.
28 John F. Stover, *American Railroads* (Chicago, IL: University of Chicago Press, 1961), 19–29.
29 Marquerite S. Shaffer, *See America First: Tourism and National Identity, 1880-1940* (Washington, DC: Smithsonian Institution Press, 2001), 7–8.
30 Stover, *American Railroads*, 74–5.
31 Ibid., 83.
32 Otte and Neilson, "'*Railpolitik*,'" 7.
33 Richard Mowbray Haywood, *Russia Enters the Railway Age, 1842-1855* (New York: Columbia University Press, 1998).
34 Nigel Brailey, "The Railway-Oceanic Era, the India-China and India-Singapore Railway Schemes, and Siam," in *Railways and International Politics: Paths of Empire, 1848-1945*, eds, T.G. Otte and Keith Neilson (London and New York: Routledge, 2006), 95.
35 Roopa Srinivasan, Manish Tiwari, and Sandeep Silas, eds, *Our Indian Railways: Themes in India's Railway History* (Delhi: Foundation Books, 2006), xiv–xv.
36 For more on the Chinese case, see: Brailey, "Railway-Oceanic Era." Christian Wolmar provides a narrative history of global railway construction in *Blood, Iron and Gold: How the Railways Transformed the World* (London: Atlantic Books, 2009).
37 Hylton, *Grand Experiment*, 84–100.

38 Joe Welsh and Bill Howes, *Travel By Pullman: A Century of Service* (St. Paul, MN: Andover Junction Publications, 2004), 18.
39 Wolmar, *Blood, Iron and Gold*, 246–62.
40 Jeffrey Richards and John M. MacKenzie, *The Railway Station: A Social History* (Oxford: Oxford University Press, 1986), 3.
41 Ibid., 25.
42 Ibid., 37.
43 Ibid., 59.
44 Ibid., 67.
45 Asta von Buch, "In the Image of the Grand Tour: Railway Station Embellishment and the Origins of Mass Tourism," *Journal of Transport History* 28, no. 2 (September 2007): 252–71.
46 Freeman, *Railways and the Victorian Imagination*, 27–9.
47 Otte and Neilson "'*Railpolitik*,'" 3.
48 Quoted in Wolmer, *Blood, Iron and Gold*, 29.
49 Hylton, *Grand Experiment*, 101–4; see also: Richards and MacKenzie, *Railway Station*, 96–8.
50 Hylton, *Grand Experiment*, 103–4.
51 Richards and MacKenzie, *Railway Station*, 94. It should be noted that additional developments also contributed to the adoption of "clock time" and of GMT. For a discussion of clock time, see: E.P. Thompson, "Time, Work-Discipline, and Industrial Capitalism," *Past and Present* 38 (December 1967); 56–97. For more on how technological innovations such as the wireless telegraph, telephone, and bicycle shaped notions of "time and space," see: Stephen Kern, *The Culture of Time and Space, 1880-1918* (Cambridge, MA: Harvard University Press, 2003).
52 Melvin Maddocks, *The Great Liners* (Alexandria, VA: Time-Life Books), 17.
53 Perkin, *Age of the Railway*, 66–7.
54 Alastair J. Durie, *Scotland for the Holidays: Tourism in Scotland, c.1780-1939* (East Linton: Tuckwell, 2003), 47–55.
55 Jack Simmons, *The Victorian Railway* (New York: Thames and Hudson, 1991), 271–2.
56 Maddocks, *Great Liners*, 17. For more on the profound impact that the development of these early steam routes had for the growth of early resorts and excursions, see John Armstrong and David M. Williams, "The Steamboat and Popular Tourism," *Journal of Transport History* 26, no. 1 (March 2005): 61–77.
57 Brinnin, *Sway of the Grand Saloon*, 26, 36.
58 Maddocks, *Great Liners*, 18.
59 Brinnin, *Sway of the Grand Saloon*, 93–103 and Maddocks, *Great Liners*, 22–6.
60 Maddocks, *Great Liners*, 28–32.
61 Philip Dawson, *The Liner: Retrospective and Renaissance* (New York: W.W. Norton, 2005), 31, 39, 42.

62 For a contemporary discussion of some of the changes (originally published in 1872) that were introduced, see: Francis Trevithick, *Life of Richard Trevithick: With an Account of His Inventions* (Cambridge: Cambridge University Press, 2011), 384–6.
63 Dawson, *Liner*, 58–9.
64 Alexis Gregory, *The Golden Age of Travel, 1880-1939* (London: Cassell, 1991), 195.
65 For more on the history of grand hotels, see: Elaine Denby, *Grand Hotels: Reality and Illusion* (Chicago, IL: University of Chicago Press, 1998).
66 Dawson, *Liner*, 47–53. On public spaces aboard the great ocean liners, see: Douglas Hart, "Sociability and 'Separate Spheres' on the North Atlantic: The Interior Architecture of British Atlantic Liners, 1840-1930," *Journal of Social History* 44, no. 1 (Fall 2010): 189–212.
67 William H. Miller, *Floating Palaces: The Great Atlantic Liners* (Stroud: Amberley, 2012), 11. See also: Gregory, *Golden Age*, 190–2.
68 Dawson, *Liner*, 54. See also Gregory, *Golden Age*, 192.
69 Miller, *Floating Palaces*, 11. Many liners had a fourth smoke stack entirely because steerage passengers equated the stack with power and speed. The association was so strong that many companies even insisted on the addition of a fourth "dummy" stack that was in no way attached to the engines.
70 Dawson, *Liner*, 57.
71 Mark Rennella and Whitney Walton, "Planned Serendipity: American Travelers and the Transatlantic Voyage in the Nineteenth and Twentieth Centuries," *Journal of Social History* 38, no. 2 (Winter 2004): 365–83. See especially pages 367–72.
72 For a detailed account, see: Lorraine Coons and Alexander Varias, *Tourist Third Cabin: Steamship Travel in the Interwar Years* (New York: Palgrave Macmillan, 2003). It is worth adding that the motivation for creating tourist and cabin classes was not a sudden up-tick in demand for trans-Atlantic tourism, though that demand grew with faster boats and new classes of travel. Instead, these new categories were added after the United States instituted a new immigration quota system that quickly undermined the market for steerage.

Chapter 4

1 Jack Simmons, *The Victorian Railway* (New York: Thames and Hudson, 1991), 270–1.
2 David Norman Smith, *The Railways and Its Passengers: A Social History* (Newton Abbot: David & Charles, 1988), 115. British historians have long debated the impact of industrialization on the standard of living

among the working class during the first stage of industrialization, dividing roughly into "optimist" and "pessimist" camps. Virtually all agree, however, that things got better after roughly 1840. For a short introduction to the debate, see: Eric J. Hobsbawm, "The British Standard of Living, 1750-1850," *Economic History Review*, New Series 10, no. 1 (1957): 46–61.

3 For more on the unique nature of British excursions, see Simmons, *Victorian Railway*, 290–2.

4 Susan Barton, *Working-Class Organisations and Popular Tourism, 1840-1970* (Manchester: Manchester University Press, 2005), 29–35.

5 Smith, *Railways and Its Passengers*, 116–7.

6 Ibid., 118.

7 Ibid., 121; and, Simmons, *Victorian Railway*, 272.

8 Simmons, *Victorian Railway*, 273–4.

9 John K. Walton, "Thomas Cook: Image and Reality," in *Giants of Tourism*, eds, Richard W. Butler and Roslyn A. Russell (Wallingford: CABI International, 2010), 81–92.

10 Piers Brendon, *Thomas Cook: 150 Years of Popular Tourism* (London: Secker and Warburg, 1991), chapter 2. For another book-length treatment of Cook's life, readers may also consult Jill Hamilton, *Thomas Cook: The Holiday-Maker* (Stroud: Sutton, 2005).

11 Paul Jennings, *The Local: A History of the English Pub* (Stroud: Tempus, 2007), 57–63. The quotation appears on page 63.

12 Walton, "Thomas Cook," 84.

13 Jack Simmons, "Thomas Cook of Leicester," *Leicestershire Archaeological and Historical Society* 49 (1973–4): 20.

14 Brendon, *Thomas Cook*, 36–7. See also Simmons, "Thomas Cook," 25.

15 Much has been written about the history of the relationship between "Highland" and "Lowland" cultures in Scotland. For example, see: Peter Womack, *Improvement and Romance: Constructing the Myth of the Highlands* (London: Macmillan, 1989) and Hugh Trevor-Roper, "The Invention of Tradition: The Highland Tradition in Scotland," in *The Invention of Tradition*, eds, Eric Hobsbawm and Terence Ranger (Cambridge: Cambridge University Press, 1983), 15–41.

16 For an exceptional account of the relationship between England and Scotland as played out through tourism, see Katherine Haldane Grenier, *Tourism and Identity in Scotland, 1770-1914: Creating Caledonia* (Aldershot: Ashgate, 2005). Grenier explores the attraction of Scottish Sabbatarianism to English visitors in "'The Traditional Peculiarities of Scottish Worship': Nineteenth-Century Tourism and Religion in Scotland," in *Tourism Histories in Ulster and Scotland: Connections and Comparisons, 1800-1939*, eds, Kevin J. James and Eric G.E. Zuelow (Belfast: Ulster Historical Society, 2013), 112–30.

17 See: Erica Lee German, "'Royal Deeside' and the Public/Private Divide: Nineteenth-Century Tourism Promotion and the Royal Residence of Balmoral," in *Tourism Histories in Ulster and Scotland: Connections and Comparisons, 1800-1939*, eds, Kevin J. James and Eric G.E. Zuelow (Belfast: Ulster Historical Society, 2013), 54–72, and Eric G.E. Zuelow, "'Kilts versus Breeches': The Royal Visit, Tourism, and Scottish National Memory," *Journeys: The International Journal of Travel and Travel Writing* 7, no. 2 (2006): 33–53. See especially page 47.
18 Brendon, *Thomas Cook*, 38–40, 42–3.
19 Jeffrey A. Auerbach, *The Great Exhibition of 1851: A Nation on Display* (New Haven, CT: Yale University Press, 1999), 23.
20 Smith, *Railway and Its Passengers*, 119.
21 Auerbach, *Great Exhibition*, 138.
22 Ibid., 137.
23 Walton, "Thomas Cook," 86.
24 Smith, *Railway and Its Passengers*, 119.
25 Brendon, *Thomas Cook*, 54.
26 Ibid., 52. Cook believed deeply in the educational value of his trips. See: Trent S. Newmeyer, "'Moral Renovation and Intellectual Exaltation': Thomas Cook's Tourism as Practical Education," *Journal of Tourism and Cultural Change* 6, no. 1 (December 2008): 1–16.
27 Brendon, *Thomas Cook*, 55. Incomes were higher because Britain industrialized before other countries. Although the first wave of industrialization brought considerable hardship, it eventually assured higher wages and an improved standard of living for many Britons.
28 Ian Bradley, *Water: A Spiritual History* (London: Bloomsbury, 2012), 1–10.
29 Ibid., 13, 23.
30 Phyllis Hembry, *The English Spa: 1560-1815* (London: Athlone Press, 1990), 1.
31 Karl E. Wood, *Health and Hazard: Spa Culture and the Social History of Medicine in the Nineteenth Century* (Newcastle upon Tyne: Cambridge Scholars Publishing, 2012), 14–16.
32 Hembry, *English Spa*, 2, 9–20.
33 Douglas Peter Mackaman, *Leisure Settings: Bourgeois Culture, Medicine, and the Spa in Modern France* (Chicago, IL: University of Chicago Press, 1998), 16–22; Hembry, *English Spa*, 10–20; Bradley, *Water*, 105–13.
34 Quoted in Mackaman, *Leisure Settings*, 19. During the nineteenth century yet another type of water therapy, hydropathy, attained popularity and the trajectory of such spas closely reflects that of the spas described in this section. Initially the trip was about health, growing more about leisure as time passed and it was necessary to compete for patrons. Hydropathy cures were more varied than simply immersing

oneself in a pool or drinking foul smelling mineral water by the glass. Physicians offered a host of options after careful consultation, of course. One might be wrapped in a wet sheet for an hour, consume cod liver oil, get sprayed by a powerful hose, or be bled and encased in wet bandages. See Alastair J. Durie, *Water is Best: The Hydros and Health Tourism in Scotland, 1840-1940* (Edinburgh: John Donald, 2006).

35 Mackaman, *Leisure Settings*, 16, 30.

36 See Hembry, *English Spa*, 39–52 and Bradley, *Water*, 112, for example.

37 Mackaman, *Leisure Settings*, 16.

38 Ibid., 35.

39 Wood, *Health and Hazard*, 19; and, Mackaman, *Leisure Settings*, 34–5.

40 Mackaman, *Leisure Settings*, 51.

41 John K. Walton, *The English Seaside Resort: A Social History, 1750-1914* (New York: St. Martin's Press, 1983), 10–11.

42 See: Kathryn Ferry, *The British Seaside Holiday* (Oxford: Shire Books, 2009), 68.

43 Alain Corbin, *The Lure of the Sea: The Discovery of the Seaside in the Western World, 1750-1840* (Berkeley, CA: University of California Press, 1994), 65–71. For a description of the bathing process itself, see especially pages 68–9.

44 For more on the disease, its prevalence among European royals, and the George III case, see: Ida Macalpine and Richard Hunter, *George III and the Mad Business* (1969; London: Pimlico, 1991).

45 Kathryn Ferry, *Beach Huts and Bathing Machines* (Oxford: Shire Books, 2009), 9–10. See also: Walton, *English Seaside Resort*, 12.

46 Walton, *English Seaside Resort*, 14.

47 Ibid., 13.

48 John K. Walton, *Blackpool* (Edinburgh: Edinburgh University Press, 1998), 14. See also, John K. Walton, *The Blackpool Landlady* (Manchester: Manchester University Press, 1978), 14–15.

49 Barton, *Working-Class Organisations*, 33–4. Historians use the term "labor aristocracy" to refer to skilled laborers whose incomes placed them at the top of the working-class pay scale.

50 For more on the Bank Holiday Act, see: Ibid., 88–91.

51 Walton, *English Seaside Resort*, 31.

52 Ferry, *Beach Huts*, 5–24.

53 Walton, *English Seaside Resort*, 16–17.

54 Barton, *Working-Class Organisations*, 34.

55 See: Walton, *English Seaside Resort*, chapter 7.

56 Walton, *Blackpool*, 50–1.

57 Walton, *English Seaside Resort*, 38.

58 Ferry, *British Seaside Holiday*, 7.

59 John Hannavy, *The English Seaside in Victorian and Edwardian Times* (Risborough: Shire, 2003), 9–10. See also: Walton, *English Seaside Resort*, 163–7.
60 For a thorough discussion of English piers and various seaside entertainments, see Walton, *English Seaside Resort*, chapter 7.
61 Ibid., 188–91. Quote on pages 190–1.
62 Peter J. Hugill, "Social Conduct on the Golden Mile," *Annals of the Association of American Geographers* 65, no. 2 (June 1975): 214–28. See especially pages 219–21.
63 Walton, *English Seaside Resorts*, 192.
64 Corbin, *Lure of the Sea*, 262.
65 Ibid., 273.
66 Ibid., 276.
67 Ibid., 267.
68 Ibid., 278. Diverging ideas about seaside sex continue to be a source of conflict in many places. See, for example: Stephen L. Harp, "The 'Naked City' of Cap d'Agde: European Nudism and Tourism in Postwar France," in *Touring Beyond the Nation: A Transnational Approach to European Tourism History*, ed. Eric G.E. Zuelow (Farnham: Ashgate, 2011), 37–58.
69 Lena Lenček and Gideon Bosker, *The Beach: The History of Paradise on Earth* (New York: Viking, 1998), 140–9.
70 Ferry, *British Seaside Holiday*, 68–9. For more on this revised view of the sun, see: George L. Mosse, *Nationalism and Sexuality: Middle-Class Morality and Sexual Norms in Modern Europe* (Madison, WI: University of Wisconsin Press, 1985), 50–3.

Chapter 5

1 E.M. Forster, *A Room with A View* (New York: Vintage Books, 1989; first published 1908), 14–22.
2 Rudy Koshar, "'What Ought to Be Seen': Tourists' Guidebooks and National Identities in Modern Germany and Europe," *Journal of Contemporary History* 33, no. 3 (July 1998): 323–40.
3 Forster, *Room with A View*, 25.
4 John Urry, *The Tourist Gaze: Leisure and Travel in Contemporary Societies* (Newbury Park, CA: Sage Publications, 1990).
5 David M. Bruce, "Baedeker: The Perceived 'Inventor' of the Formal Guidebook—A Bible for Travellers in the 19th Century," in *Giants of Tourism*, eds, Richard W. Butler and Roslyn A. Russell (Wallingford: CABI, 2010), 95–6.

6 Katherine Haldane Grenier, *Tourism and Identity in Scotland, 1770-1914: Creating Caledonia* (Aldershot: Ashgate, 2005), 66.
7 Jan Palmowski, "Travels with Baedeker—The Guidebook and the Middle Classes in Victorian and Edwardian Britain," in *Histories of Leisure*, ed. Rudy Koshar (Oxford: Berg, 2002), 105.
8 The obsession with self-improvement was largely tied to the popularity of Samuel Smiles' *Self-Help; with Illustrations of Character and Conduct*, New ed. (London: John Murray, 1876; first published 1859).
9 Bruce, "Baedeker," 97.
10 Bruce, "Baedeker," 94; Palmowski, "Travels with Baedeker," 105, 108.
11 Palmowski's chapter "Travels with Baedeker" offers a useful description of some of these guides.
12 G.H. Martin, "Sir George Samuel Measom (1818-1901), and His Railway Guides," in *The Impact of the Railway on Society in Britain: Essays in Honour of Jack Simmons*, eds, A.K.B. Evans and J.V. Gough (Aldershot: Ashgate, 2003), 225–40.
13 Palmowski, "Travels with Baedeker," 109.
14 Robert Burns-related tourism was among the first literary tourism practiced in Europe. Guidebooks and travel writing encouraging people to visit Ayrshire in Scotland started as early as 1822 and proliferated after 1840. See: Karyn Wilson-Costa, "The Land of Burns: Between Myth and Heritage," in *Literary Tourism and Nineteenth-Century Culture*, ed. Nicola J. Watson (New York: Palgrave Macmillan, 2009), 37–48.
15 Alan Sillitoe, *Leading the Blind: A Century of Guidebook Travel, 1815-1914* (London: Macmillan, 1995).
16 Palmowski, "Travels with Baedeker," 118–19.
17 Ibid., 116–17.
18 Quoted in Rudy Koshar, *German Travel Cultures* (Oxford: Berg, 2000), 1.
19 James Buzard, *The Beaten Track: European Tourism, Literature, and the Ways of Culture, 1800-1918* (Oxford: Oxford University Press, 1993).
20 Hans Magnus Enzensberger, "A Theory of Tourism," Special issue on literature, *New German Critique* 68 (Spring-Summer 1996): 124.
21 Rudy Koshar offers a useful discussion of the commoditization of travel through guidebooks in *German Travel Cultures*, 2–3.
22 Koshar, "'What Ought to Be Seen,'" 325–6, 339.
23 Palmowski, "Travels with Baedeker," 122.
24 Bruce, "Baedeker," 98–9.
25 John M. Mackenzie, "Empires of Travel: British Guide Books and Cultural Imperialism in the 19th and 20th Centuries," in *Histories of Tourism: Representation, Identity and Conflict*, ed. John K. Walton (Clevedon: Channel View, 2005), 19–38.

26 *Black's Picturesque Tourist of Scotland,* 19th ed. (Edinburgh: Adam and Charles Black, 1872), 281–4.
27 Karl Baedeker, *A Handbook for Travellers on the Rhine, from Switzerland to Holland* (London and Coblenz: Karl Baedeker, 1861), 83–4.
28 For more on the role of mediators such as tourist guidebooks and postcards and the production of place, see: Erica Lea German, "'Royal Deeside' and the Public/Private Divide: Nineteenth-Century Tourism Promotion and the Royal Residence of Balmoral," in *Tourism Histories in Ulster and Scotland: Connections and Comparisons, 1800-1939,* eds, Kevin J. James and Eric G.E. Zuelow (Belfast: Ulster Historical Foundation, 2013), 54–72.
29 Ousby, *Englishman's England,* 162–3.
30 Eric G.E. Zuelow, *Making Ireland Irish: Tourism and National Identity since the Irish Civil War* (Syracuse, NY: Syracuse University Press, 2009), 139–40.
31 For a fascinating analysis of the arguments (such as they were) against preservation during the nineteenth century, see: Peter Mandler, "Rethinking the 'Powers of Darkness': An Anti-History of the Preservation Movement in Britain," in *Towards World Heritage: International Origins of the Preservation Movement, 1870-1930,* ed. Melanie Hall (Farnham: Ashgate, 2011), 221–39.
32 John Gaze, *Figures in a Landscape: A History of the National Trust* (London: Barrie & Jenkins, 1988), 12, 32.
33 Gaze, *Figures,* 34, 35–9. For more on the development of the National Trust, see: Robin Fedden, *The Continuing Purpose: A History of the National Trust, Its Aims and Work* (London: Longmans, 1968) and Jennifer Jenkins and Patrick James, *From Acorn to Oak Tree: The Growth of the National Trust, 1895-1994* (London: Macmillan, 1994). It is worth mentioning that American author Paula Weideger criticizes the Trust for being less than forthcoming about its activities, wondering "Why was there no book about the Trust?... By a person who was not of it, that is." See *Gilding the Acorn: Behind the Façade of the National Trust* (London: Simon and Schuster, 1994), 2.
34 Zuelow, *Making Ireland Irish,* 205.
35 Andrea Witcomb and Kate Gregory, *From the Barracks to the Burrup: The National Trust in Western Australia* (Sydney, NSW: University of New South Wales), 23.
36 "A Brief History of the National Trust," National Trust for Historical Preservation, accessed 25 October 2014, http://www.preservationnation.org/who-we-are/history.html#.U8aSUGk-s2E.
37 Ousby, *Englishman's England,* 118–20.
38 Ibid., 101.

39 For example, see: Ernest Gellner, *Nations and Nationalism* (Ithaca, NY: Cornell University Press, 1983); Conor Cruise O'Brien, "Nationalism and the French Revolution," in *The Permanent Revolution: The French Revolution and its Legacy, 1789-1989*, ed. Geoffrey Best (Chicago, IL: University of Chicago Press, 1988); Eric Hobsbawm, *Nations and Nationalism since 1780: Programme, Myth, Reality* (Cambridge: Cambridge University Press, 1990).

40 See Peter Lambert, "Paving the 'Peculiar Path': German Nationalism and Historiography since Ranke," in *Imagining Nations*, ed. Geoffrey Cubitt (Manchester: Manchester University Press, 1998), 92–109. Quotation appears on page 92. Virtually every discussion of nations and nationalism addresses the importance of history to a group's self-understanding. Anthony D. Smith's notion of "ethno-symbolism" is especially concerned with the role of history because it is one of the ingredients from which "modern national identities are reconstituted in each generation." See Montserrat Guibernau and John Hutchinson, "History and National Identity," *Nations and Nationalism* 10, no. 1–2 (January 2004): 1.

41 See James Boswell, *Boswell on the Grand Tour: Germany and Switzerland*, ed. Frederick Pottle (New York: McGraw-Hill, 1953; first published 1764).

42 Nicola J. Watson, *The Literary Tourist: Readers and Places in Romantic & Victorian Britain* (Basingstoke: Palgrave, 2006), 2–3.

43 Ibid., 60–1.

44 Paul Hubbard and Keith Lilley, "Selling the Past: Heritage Tourism and Place Identity in Stratford-upon-Avon," *Geography* 85, no. 3 (July 2000): 223–4, 226. For more on the establishment of Stratford as a tourist destination, see: Julia Thomas, "Bringing Down the House: Restoring the Birthplace," in *Literary Tourism and Nineteenth-Century Culture*, ed. Nicola J. Watson (New York: Palgrave, 2009), 73–83.

45 Karl Baedeker, *Great Britain: England, Wales, and Scotland As Far As Loch Maree and the Cromarty Firth: Handbook for Travellers* (London: Karl Baedeker Publisher, 1887), 245–9.

46 Ibid., 246.

47 Karyn Wilson-Costa, "The Land of Burns: Between Myth and Heritage," in *Literary Tourism and Nineteenth-Century Culture*, ed. Nicola J. Watson (New York: Palgrave, 2009), 38.

48 Richard Gall, *Poems and Songs, with a Memoir of the Author* (Oxford: Oxford University Press, 1819), 58–60.

49 Erin Hazard, "The Author's House: Abbotsford and Wayside," in *Literary Tourism and Nineteenth-Century Culture*, ed. Nicola J. Watson (New York: Palgrave, 2009), 68–9, 73; Wilson-Costa, "The Land of Burns," 39–40.

50 *Oliver and Boyd's Scottish Tourist: with Seventy-One Engravings on Steel, and Seventeen Travelling Maps and Charts* (Edinburgh: Oliver and Boyd, 1852), 361, 363–4, 365–6, 369, 370, 373–4, 377–8, 381, 386–7.
51 John Glendening, "Keats's Tour of Scotland: Burns and the Anxiety of Hero Worship," *Keats-Shelley Journal* 41 (1992): 92.
52 Polly Atkin, "Ghosting Grasmere: the Musealisation of Dove Cottage," in *Literary Tourism and Nineteenth-Century Culture*, ed. Nicola J. Watson (New York: Palgrave, 2009), 88.
53 Atkin, "Ghosting Grasmere," 84–94.
54 For more on Abbotsford, see: Alastair J. Durie, "Tourism in Victorian Scotland: The Case of Abbotsford," *Journal of Scottish Economic and Social History* 12, no. 1 (1992): 42–5. See also: Hazard, "The Author's House," 63–72.
55 Pamela Corpron Parker, "Elizabeth Gaskell and Literary Tourism," in *Literary Tourism and Nineteenth-Century Culture*, ed. Nicola J. Watson (New York: Palgrave, 2009), 128–38.
56 See: Alison Booth, "Time-Travel in Dickens' World," in *Literary Tourism and Nineteenth Century Culture*, ed. Nicola J. Watson (New York: Palgrave, 2009), 150–63.
57 Diane Roberts, "Harriet Beecher Stowe and Florida Tourism," in *Literary Tourism and Nineteenth-Century Culture*, ed. Nicola J. Watson (New York: Palgrave, 2009), 196–209. See also: Paul Westover, "How America 'Inherited' Literary Tourism," in *Literary Tourism and Nineteenth-Century Culture*, ed. Nicola J. Watson (New York: Palgrave, 2009), 184–95.
58 Lindy Stiebel, "On the Trail of Rider Haggard in South Africa," in *Literary Tourism and Nineteenth-Century Culture*, ed. Nicola J. Watson (New York: Palgrave, 2009), 210–19.
59 Monica MacDonald, "Railway Tourism in the 'Land of Evangeline,'" *Acadiensis* 35, no. 1 (Autumn 2005): 158–80.
60 Orvar Löfgren, *On Holiday: A History of Vacationing* (Berkeley, CA: University of California Press, 1999), 77.
61 See: Jessica Warner, *Craze: Gin and Debauchery in an Age of Reason* (New York: Random House, 2003), 194–9.
62 Martin Willoughby, *A History of Postcards* (Secaucus, NJ: Wellfleet Press, 1992), 22–32, 46, 56.
63 Willoughby, *History of Postcards*, 67–8.
64 Ibid., 10.
65 Ibid., 120.
66 Tom Kelly, "Just Too Saucy! The Bawdy Seaside Postcards the Censors Banned 50 Years Ago," *Daily Mail Online*, 6 August 2010, http://www.dailymail.co.uk/news/article-1300763/Just-saucy-The-bawdy-seaside-postcards-censors-banned-50-years-ago.html.
67 Löfgren, *On Holiday*, 81–2.

68 Irish Museum of Modern Art, *Hindesight* (Dublin: Irish Museum of Modern Art, 1993), 18–9.
69 Jan De Fouw, interview by the author, Dublin, 14 October 2002.
70 Irish Museum of Modern Art, *Hindesight*, 18–19, 36.
71 Ibid., 38.
72 Buzard, *Beaten Track*.

Chapter 6

1 This phrase is drawn from Eric Hobsbawm, *The Age of Empire: 1875-1914* (New York: Random House, 1989). In addition, there are many excellent surveys of British and European imperialism. Piers Brendon's, *The Decline and Fall of the British Empire, 1781-1997* (New York: Vintage, 2010) is particularly readable. Bernard Porter emphasizes the degree of difference between colonies, stressing how their acquisition varied considerably from one to the other, in his very accessible *The Lion's Share: A Short History of British Imperialism, 1850-2004* (New York: Pearson, 2004). Interested readers will find a brief discussion of German colonial expansion in Hans-Ulrich Wehler's *The German Empire, 1871-1918* (Oxford: Berg, 1985), Chapters 6 and 7. French imperialism during the fin de siècle is covered in James J. Cooke's *New French Imperialism, 1880-1910: The Third Republic and Colonial Expansion* (New Haven, CT: Archon Books, 1973).
2 For examples and discussion, see: Edward Said, *Orientalism*, 25th anniversary ed. (New York: Vintage, 1994); John E. Crowley, *Imperial Landscapes: Britain's Global Visual Culture, 1745-1820* (New Haven, CT: Yale University Press, 2011); Chandrika Kaul, ed., *Media and the British Empire* (Basingstoke: Palgrave, 2006); Graham Dawson, *Soldier Heroes: British Adventure, Empire, and the Imagining of Masculinities* (New York: Routledge, 1994); Zohreh T. Sullivan, *Narratives of Empire: The Fictions of Rudyard Kipling* (Cambridge: Cambridge University Press, 1993).
3 Henry Morton Stanley's account is well worth reading. It is an exciting (if disturbing) narrative and a valuable document of European attitudes toward Africa during the last half of the nineteenth century: *How I Found Livingston: Travels, Adventures, and Discoveries in Central Africa including Four Months' Residence with Dr. Livingston* (Montreal, QC: Dawson, 1872).
4 Perhaps the most famous explanation of the initial development of nations and nationalism relative to industrialization is to be found in Ernest Gellner, *Nations and Nationalism* (Ithaca, NY: Cornell, 1983). Quote appears on page 25.

5 Benedict Anderson, *Imagined Communities: Reflections on the Origin and Spread of Nationalism* (London: Verso, 1991), 5–7.
6 Eric Hobsbawm, *Nations and Nationalism since 1789: Programme, Myth, Reality* (Cambridge: Cambridge University Press, 1990), 101–30; Michel Winock, *Nationalism, Antisemitism, and Fascism in France* (Palo Alto, CA: Stanford University Press, 2000), 5–26.
7 For a history of modern racial thought and of racism, see: George L. Mosse, *Toward the Final Solution: A History of European Racism* (Madison, WI: University of Wisconsin Press, 1985).
8 For an interesting primary source about this new racial science, especially as it stratified whites, see: Robert Knox, M.D., *The Races of Men: A Fragment* (Philadelphia, PA: Lea & Blanchard, 1850). For scholarly discussion, see: Peter Mandler, *The English National Character: The History of an Idea from Edmund Burke to Tony Blair* (New Haven, CT: Yale University Press, 2006), 59–99.
9 Brendon, *Decline and Fall*, 71. See also pages 150–3. For an excellent discussion of British efforts to create a narrative justifying their empire in India, see: Thomas R. Metcalf, *Ideologies of the Raj* (Cambridge: Cambridge University Press, 1995), especially pages 66–159.
10 Peter Whitfield, *Travel: A Literary History* (Oxford: Bodleian Library, 2011), 181.
11 Patricia Jean Behenna Meyer offers a window onto the extent of female travel during the height of the Grand Tour and early years of the nineteenth century through a survey of a number of travel narratives by lesser-known authors. See: "No Land Too Remote: Women Travellers in the Georgian Age, 1750-1830" (Ph.D. diss., University of Massachusetts-Amherst, 1978).
12 Jeffrey A. Auerbach, *The Great Exhibition of 1851: A Nation on Display* (New Haven, CT: Yale University Press, 1999), 15, 23.
13 Richard D. Mandell, *Paris 1900: The Great World's Fair* (Toronto, ON: University of Toronto Press, 1967), 8.
14 Auerbach, *Great Exhibition*, 148, 185.
15 C.B. Norton, *World's Fairs from London 1851 to Chicago 1893: Illustrated with Views and Portraits* (Chicago, IL: Milton Weston Co., 1893).
16 Angela Schwarz, "'Come to the Fair': Transgressing Boundaries in World's Fairs Tourism," in *Touring Beyond the Nation: A Transnational Approach to European Tourism History*, ed. Eric G.E. Zuelow (Farnham: Ashgate, 2011), 81–2.
17 Schwarz, "'Come to the Fair,'" 99.
18 T.J. Boisseau and Abigail M. Markwyn, "World's Fairs in Feminist Historical Perspective," in *Gendering the Fair: Histories of Women and Gender at World's Fairs*, eds, T.J. Boisseau and Abigail M. Markwyn (Urbana, IL: University of Illinois Press, 2010), 2.

19 Oswald M. Mohl, *Die Wunder der Weltausstellung zu Paris: Schilderungen der Erlebnisse in einer Weltstadt im Jahre 1867* (Leipzig: Otto Spamer, 1868), 70, quoted in Angela Schwarz, "'Come to the Fair,'" 96–7.
20 Schwarz, "'Come to the Fair,'" 80, 89–90, 98.
21 Christopher Quinn, "The Irish Villages at the 1893 World's Columbian Exposition: Constructing, Consuming, and Contesting Ireland at Chicago" (M.A. thesis, University of Guelph, 2011), 50, 90.
22 Schwarz, "'Come to the Fair,'" 91.
23 Mandell, *Paris 1900*, 12.
24 Ibid., 65–8.
25 Ibid., x.
26 Schwarz, "'Come to the Fair,'" 91.
27 Ibid., 99.
28 Quinn, "The Irish Villages," 25, 28, 53. Irish political, social, and cultural life has long been divided between "nationalists," anxious for separation from Britain, and "unionists" who wish to remain part of the union.
29 Eric Hobsbawm and Terence Ranger coined the phrase "invention of tradition" in their edited collection *The Invention of Tradition* (Cambridge: Cambridge University Press, 1992; originally published 1983).
30 Cristina Della Coletta, *World's Fairs Italian Style: The Great Expositions in Turin and their Narratives, 1860-1915* (Toronto, ON: University of Toronto Press, 2006), 4, 33–5.
31 Interested readers may wish to explore connections between the Ottomans, the Hajj, and the evolution of travel facilities and documentation by consulting F.E. Peters, *The Hajj: The Muslim Pilgrimage to Mecca and the Holy Places* (Princeton, NJ: Princeton University Press, 1994). This book does a fine job of using travel writing to paint a vivid picture of the experience of travel as it evolved over hundreds of years.
32 Susan Nance, "A Facilitated Access Model and Ottoman Empire Tourism," *Annals of Tourism Research* 34, no. 4 (2007): 1056–77. See especially pages 1056–7.
33 Martin Anderson, "The Development of British Tourism in Egypt, 1815-1850," *Journal of Tourism History* 4, no. 3 (November 2012): 259–79. Especially pages 260–2.
34 F. Robert Hunter, "Tourism and Empire: The Thomas Cook & Son Enterprise on the Nile, 1868-1914," *Middle Eastern Studies* 40, no. 5 (September 2004): 28–54. Quotation appears on page 28.
35 While there is little scholarship about the relationship between imperialism and tourism development during the nineteenth and early twentieth centuries, much more is available about how Europeans interpreted the "other" and how they expressed these impressions through travel writing. For more, see Mary Louise Pratt, *Imperial Eyes: Travel*

Writing and Transculturation, 2nd ed. (London: Routledge, 2008); Sara Mills, *Discourses of Difference: An Analysis of Women's Travel Writing and Colonialism* (London: Routledge, 1991); and Monica Anderson, *Women and the Politics of Travel, 1870-1914* (Madison, NJ: Fairleigh Dickinson University Press, 2006). Edward Said's *Orientalism*, 25th anniversary ed. (1978; New York: Vintage, 1994) remains a classic text, informing much of the contemporary scholarship. Postmodernists such as Homi Bhabha have also added quite a lot to knowledge of this subject. Further work explores how people from the white dominions reacted upon traveling to Europe. On this front, readers should consult Cecilia Morgan, *"A Happy Holiday": English Canadians and Transatlantic Tourism, 1870-1930* (Toronto, ON: University of Toronto Press, 2008).

36 See especially: Eric T. Jennings, *Curing the Colonizers: Hydrotherapy, Climatology, and French Colonial Spas* (Durham, NC: Duke University Press, 2006).

37 For example, Dane Kennedy, *The Magic Mountains: Hills Stations and the British Raj* (Berkeley, CA: University of California Press, 1996).

38 Greg Gillespie, *Hunting for Empire: Narratives of Sport in Rupert's Land, 1840-70* (Vancouver, BC and Toronto, ON: University of British Columbia Press, 2007), 35–7.

39 E.P. Thompson, *Whigs and Hunters: The Origins of the Black Act* (New York: Pantheon Books, 1975).

40 M.S.S. Pandian, "Gendered Negotiations: Hunting and Colonialism in Late Nineteenth Century Nilgiris," *Contributions to Indian Sociology* 20, no. 1–2 (1995): 239–64.

41 Gillespie, *Hunting for Empire*, 41.

42 Ibid., 48.

43 John R. Gold and Margaret M. Gold, *Imagining Scotland: Tradition, Representation, and Promotion in Scottish Tourism since 1750* (Aldershot: Ashgate, 1995), 80, 109–13. See also: Alastair J. Durie, *Scotland for the Holidays: Tourism in Scotland, c.1780-1939* (East Linton: Tuckwell, 2003), Chapter 5.

44 Gillespie, *Hunting for Empire*, 49, 110–11.

45 Patricia Jane Jasen, *Wild Things: Nature, Culture, and Tourism in Ontario, 1790-1914* (Toronto, ON: University of Toronto Press, 1995), 16–17, 80–1.

46 Ibid., 87.

47 Brendon, *Decline and Fall*, 75–86, 281–93; Wallace Clement, *Understanding Canada: Building on the New Canadian Political Economy* (Montreal, QC: McGill-Queen's University Press, 1997), 198–200.

48 Peter White, "Out of the Woods," in *Beyond Wilderness: The Group of Seven, Canadian Identity, and Contemporary Art*, eds, John O'Brian and Peter White (Montreal, QC: McGill-Queen's University Press, 2007), 14–15.

49 Zuelow, *Making Ireland Irish*, xxix–xxx.
50 Brendon, *Decline and Fall*, 20–4, 152–4; Bernard Porter, *The Lion's Share: A Short History of British Imperialism, 1850-1994*, 3rd ed. (London and New York: Longman, 1996), 53; and Philippa Levine, *The British Empire: Sunrise to Sunset* (London: Pearson-Longman, 2007), 18–19, 21.
51 Frank Fonda Taylor, *To Hell with Paradise: A History of the Jamaican Tourist Industry* (Pittsburgh, PA: University of Pittsburgh Press, 1993), 13–16.
52 For a superb discussion of malaria, resistance to the disease, and the development of various strategies and treatments for fighting it, see: James Webb, Jr., *Humanity's Burden: A Global History of Malaria* (Cambridge: Cambridge University Press, 2009).
53 Taylor, *To Hell with Paradise*, 17, 22–7.
54 Ibid., 37–51.
55 Ibid., 68–89.
56 Ibid., 113.
57 Ibid., 122–4.
58 Ibid., 111.
59 Ibid., 144.
60 Jim Davidson and Peter Spearritt, *Holiday Business: Tourism in Australia since 1870* (Carlton, VIC: The Miegunyah Press at Melbourne University Press, 2000), 1.
61 L.L. Wynn, *Pyramids and Nightclubs: A Travel Ethnography of Arab and Western Imaginations of Egypt, from King Tut and a Colony of Atlantis to Rumors of Sex Orgies, Urban Legends about a Marauding Prince, and Blonde Belly Dancers* (Austin, TX: University of Texas Press, 2007), 5–6.
62 Levine, *British Empire*, 89–91; Brendon, *Decline and Fall*, 178–80; and Porter, *Lion's Share*, 90–4.
63 Anderson, "British Tourism in Egypt," 260–2.
64 Ibid., 275. Europeans referred to themselves as "Franks" when touring Egypt.
65 Ibid., 278.
66 Although not developed here for lack of space, John Mason Cook played a remarkable role in the development of the Cook travel business and especially in the expansion of the company's offerings beyond Europe. He is notable for playing a key part in the creation of a voucher (or coupon) system whereby travelers anxious to journey on their own could buy tickets for rooms, meals, and other amenities at hotels and restaurants with whom the company had formed relationships. John Mason Cook also introduced "Circular Notes" in 1874. These "forerunners of traveller's cheques" made it possible for "tourists to obtain currency in exchange for a paper note." The program was so successful that Thomas Cook & Son opened a banking and exchange department in 1878—still

one of the most visible elements of the company's business. See: Jill Hamilton, *Thomas Cook: The Holiday-Maker* (Stroud: Sutton, 2005), quote appears on 190–1. Piers Brendon addresses these developments at length in *Thomas Cook: 150 Years of Popular Tourism* (London: Secker and Warburg, 1991).

67 Hunter, "Tourism and Empire," 28–54. Especially pages 31, 33, 34, and 37.

68 Ibid., 36.

69 Ibid., 42–3.

70 Brendon, *Thomas Cook*, 141–51.

71 Davidson and Spearritt, *Holiday Business*, 1–28.

72 Zuelow, *Making Ireland Irish*, xxiii–xxx.

73 For further discussion, see: William W. Stowe, *Going Abroad: European Travel in Nineteenth-Century American Culture* (Princeton, NJ: Princeton University Press, 1994); Harvey Levenstein, *Seductive Journey: American Tourists in France from Jefferson to the Jazz Age* (Chicago, IL: University of Chicago Press, 1998) and *Always Have Paris: American Tourists in France since 1930* (Chicago, IL: University of Chicago Press, 2004); Daniel Kilbride, *Being American in Europe: 1750-1860* (Baltimore, MD: Johns Hopkins University Press, 2013).

74 John F. Sears, *Sacred Places: American Tourist Attractions in the Nineteenth Century* (Amherst, MA: University of Massachusetts Press, 1989), 4; and Marguerite S. Shaffer, *See America First: Tourism and National Identity, 1880-1940* (Washington, DC: Smithsonian Institution Press, 2001), 12–16.

75 Sears, *Sacred Places*, 4–15.

76 Richard H. Gassan, *The Birth of American Tourism: New York, the Hudson Valley, and American Culture, 1790-1830* (Amherst, MA: University of Massachusetts Press), 28–31.

77 Dona Brown, *Inventing New England: Regional Tourism in the Nineteenth Century* (Washington, DC: Smithsonian Institution Press, 1995), 37, 62.

78 Jasen, *Wild Things*, 31, 36–7.

79 Karen Dubinsky, *The Second Greatest Disappointment: Honeymooning and Tourism at Niagara Falls* (New Brunswick, NJ: Rutgers University Press, 1999), 40. See also Jasen, *Wild Things*, 32–5.

80 Sears, *Sacred Places*, 14–6 and Jasen, *Wild Things*, 47–9.

81 Quote appears in Sears, *Sacred Places*, 16. See also: Dubinsky, *Disappointment*, 31–4 and Jasen, *Wild Things*, 43–7.

82 William E. Tunis, *Tunis's Topographical and Pictorial Guide to Niagara: Containing, also, A Description of the Route Through Canada, and the Great Northern Route, from Niagara Falls to Montreal, Boston, and Saratoga Springs. Also Full and Accurate Tables of Distances, on all Railroads Running to and From Niagara Falls* (Niagara Falls, NY: W.E. Tunis, Publisher, 1856), 22–3.

83 Sears, *Sacred Places*, 23–7.
84 Dubinsky, *Disappointment*, 47–8.
85 Ibid., 33–5.
86 Sears, *Sacred Places*, 184–9.
87 Ibid., 12–30, 87–121.
88 Brown, *Inventing New England*, 75–104; and Randall Balmer, "From Frontier Phenomenon to Victorian Institution: The Methodist Camp Meeting in Ocean Grove, New Jersey," *Methodist History* 25, no. 3 (1987): 194–200.
89 Sears, *Sacred Places*, 99–121. See also: Sarah Tarlow, "Landscapes of Memory: The Nineteenth-Century Garden Cemetery," *European Journal of Archaeology* 3, no. 2 (2000): 217–39; Peter Thorsheim, "The Corpse in the Garden: Burial, Health, and the Environment in Nineteenth-Century London," *Environmental History* 16 (January 2011): 38–68; and James Stevens Curl, *The Victorian Celebration of Death* (Newton Abbott: David & Charles, 1980).
90 Sears, *Sacred Places*, 124.
91 James Mason Hutchings, *In the Heart of the Sierras* (Oakland, CA: Pacific Press Publishing House, 1888; first published 1886).
92 Sears, *Sacred Places*, 125.
93 Ibid., 128, 130.
94 Ibid.
95 Shaffer, *See America First*, 8–11, 16.
96 Sears, *Sacred Places*, 156–7, 161–2.
97 Ibid., 163.
98 For a thorough discussion of the "See America First" idea see Shaffer, *See America First*.

Chapter 7

1 David V. Herlihy, *Bicycle: The History* (New Haven, CT: Yale University Press, 2006), 15, 21.
2 Ibid., 75.
3 Christopher S. Thompson, "Bicycling, Class, and the Politics of Leisure in Belle Epoque France," in *Histories of Leisure*, ed. Rudy Koshar (Oxford: Berg, 2002), 135.
4 Richard Harmond, "Progress and Flight: An Interpretation of the American Cycle Craze of the 1890s," *Journal of Social History* 5, no. 2 (Winter 1971–2): 235–57. See pages 236–7.
5 Thompson, "Bicycling," 135; Harmond, "Progress and Flight," 237–8.

6 Thompson, "Bicycling," 135; Christopher S. Thompson, *The Tour de France: A Cultural History* (Berkeley, CA: University of California Press, 2008); Eugene Weber, "Forward," in *Tour de France, 1903-2003: A Century of Sporting Structures, Meanings and Values*, eds, Hugh Dauncey and Geoff Hare (London: Frank Cass, 2003), xii–xvi and Philippe Gaboriau, "The Tour de France and Cycling's Belle Epoque," in *Tour de France, 1903-2003*, 54–75.

7 Andrew Richie, *Major Taylor: The Extraordinary Career for a Champion Bicycle Racer* (San Francisco, CA: Bicycle Books, 1988). Pages 9–10 briefly summarize the widespread popularity of bicycle racing in America at the end of the nineteenth century. Readers, however, will want to read the whole book, which tells the fascinating and surprisingly unknown story of one of the first professional African-American athletes in America while also painting a vivid picture of the "bicycle craze" in the United States. Also see: Todd Balf, *Major: A Black Athlete, A White Era, and the Fight to be the World's Fastest Human Being* (New York: Crown Publishing, 2008), 2, 57; Michael C. Gabriele, *The Golden Age of Bicycle Racing in New Jersey* (Charleston, SC: The History Press, 2011), 13, 17–58.

8 Peter Joffre Nye, *The Six-Day Bicycle Races* (San Francisco, CA: Cycle Publishing, 2006), 10.

9 Georges Vigarello, "The Tour de France," in *Realms of Memory: The Construction of the French Past, Vol. 2: Traditions*, ed. Pierre Nora (New York: Columbia University Press, 1997), 469–500. See also: Christophe Campos, "Beating the Bounds: The Tour de France and National Identity," in *Tour de France, 1903-2003: A Century of Sporting Structures, Meanings and Values*, eds, Hugh Dauncey and Geoff Hare (London: Frank Cass, 2003), 148–73.

10 Thompson, "Bicycling," especially pages 133–6; Harmond, "Progress and Flight."

11 David Rubinstein, "Cycling in the 1890s," *Victorian Studies* 21, no. 1 (Autumn 1977): 47–71. See page 47.

12 Rubinstein, "Cycling," 49.

13 Christopher Thompson and Fiona Ratkoff, "Un Troisieme Sexe? Les Bourgeoises et la Bicyclette dans la France Fin de Siecle," *Le Mouvement Social* 192 (July–September 2000): 9–39. See especially page 9.

14 Löfgren, *On Holiday*, 58–9.

15 Cotton Seiler, *Republic of Drivers: A Cultural History of Automobility in America* (Chicago, IL: University of Chicago Press, 2008), 41–2.

16 Engineers did eventually figure out how to use steam to power automobiles. The Stanley Motor Carriage Company (1902–24) is probably the most famous manufacturer of steam cars. The "Stanley Steamer" performed exceptionally well, capable of speeds over 100 miles per hour. See: Kit Foster, *The Stanley Steamer: America's Legendary Steam Car*

(Kingfield, ME: The Stanley Museum, 2004). For a fun video of one of these cars in action, see: "1906 Stanley Steamer Vanderbilt Cub Racer—Jay Leno's Garage," YouTube video, 28:55, posted by "Jay Leno's Garage," 26 April 2012, accessed 1 November 2014, http://www.youtube.com/watch?v=5Me8b0ed59s.

17 James J. Flink, *The Car Culture* (Cambridge, MA: MIT Press, 1975), 5–11.
18 Ibid., 7.
19 Sean O'Connell, *The Car in British Society: Class, Gender and Motoring, 1896-1939* (Manchester: Manchester University Press, 1998), 13.
20 Flink, *Car Culture*, 12.
21 Gordon Pirie, "Automobile Organizations Driving Tourism in Pre-Independence Africa," *Journal of Tourism History* 5, no. 1 (April 2013): 73–91. See pages 74–7. For more about the American Automobile Association, see: John A. Jakle and Keith A. Sculle, *Motoring: The Highway Experience in America* (Athens, GA: University of Georgia Press, 2008), 37.
22 Michael Frederik Wagner, "The Rise of Autotourism in Danish Leisure, 1910-1970," *Journal of Tourism History* 5, no. 3 (November 2013): 268.
23 Russell H. Anderson, "The First Automobile Race in America," *Journal of the Illinois State Historical Society* 47, no. 4 (Winter 1954): 343–59.
24 Flink, *Car Culture*, 14.
25 Jakle and Sculle, *Motoring*, 11.
26 Seiler, *Republic*, 46–7.
27 Rudy Koshar, "Driving Cultures and the Meanings of Roads," in *The World Beyond the Windshield: Roads and Landscapes in the United States and Europe*, eds, Christof Mauch and Thomas Zeller (Athens, OH: University of Ohio Press, 2008), 18.
28 "To Klondyke by Automobile," *Washington Post*, 12 March 1900.
29 "Automobile Topics of Interest," *New York Times*, 30 August 1903.
30 "Through the Mountains by Automobile," *New York Times*, 28 June 1903.
31 Koshar, "Driving Cultures," 19–21.
32 "Automobile Off for the West," *New York Times*, 14 July 1899.
33 For a highly engaging account of the journey: Dayton Duncan, *Horatio's Drive: America's First Road Trip* (New York: Alfred A. Knopf, 2003). See also Koshar, "Driving Cultures," 22–3.
34 Flink, *Car Culture*, 18–20.
35 Seiler, *Republic*, 51–5.
36 Quoted in Jakle and Sculle, *Motoring*, 21.
37 O'Connell, *Car in British Society*, 15, 18.
38 Koshar, "Driving Cultures," 24–8.
39 Seiler, *Republic*, 37.
40 Flink, *Car Culture*, 19.
41 Ibid., 53. See also: Jakle and Sculle, *Motoring*, 9–10, 14–17.

42 Flink, *Car Culture*, 67. The Ford Model T inspires a great deal of nostalgia among aficionados of vintage automobiles and is the subject of numerous books. Floyd Clymer's *Henry's Wonderful Model T: 1908-1927* (New York: Bonanza Books, 1955) is one particularly enjoyable example, filled with photographs, jokes, stories, and an account of the rise and fall of this important car.
43 O'Connell, *Car in British Society*, 19–22.
44 Automobiles inspire tremendous excitement and fascination. Consequently, there is no shortage of books addressing the story of automotive design and engineering among other myriad topics. Interested readers, in addition to other texts, may enjoy: Marco Matteucci, *History of the Motor Car* (New York: Crown Publishers, 1970) and Pierre Dumont, Ronald Barker, and Douglas B. Tubbs, *Automobiles and Automobiling* (New York: Viking, 1965). Both feature numerous vintage illustrations and photographs and cover the development of cars in the United States and Europe in an engaging way.
45 Jakle and Sculle, *Motoring*, 33.
46 Marguerite Shaffer, *See America First: Tourism and National Identity, 1880-1940* (Washington, DC: Smithsonian Institution Press, 2001), 138, 140.
47 W. Pierrepont White, "Good Roads for the People," in *Motoring in America: The Early Years*, ed. Frank Oppel (Secaucus, NJ: Castle Books, 1989), 109.
48 Jakle and Sculle, *Motoring*, 39–53.
49 David Louter, "Glaciers and Gasoline: The Making of a Windshield Wilderness, 1900-1915," in *Seeing and Being Seen: Tourism in the American West*, eds, David M. Wrobel and Patrick T. Long (Lawrence, KS: University of Kansas Press, 2001), 253–5.
50 Ibid., 260–1.
51 John A. Heitmann, *The Automobile and American Life* (Jefferson, NC: McFarland & Co., 2009), 75.
52 Drake Hokanson, *The Lincoln Highway: Main Street across America* (Iowa City, IA: University of Iowa Press, 1988), 7–15. Although the Lincoln Highway is no longer the major route across the United States, it continues to inspire considerable nostalgia and at least some people every year venture forth to drive some of or the entire route. There is also a small publishing industry devoted to popular books on the topic. It carefully informs readers that the highway is for travelers, not tourists. Michael Wallis and Michael S. Williamson's work is one such example. The Lincoln Highway is a route that takes one from the beaten track, leading to "a memorable place or a person they will never find again." Michael Wallis and Michael S. Williamson, *The Lincoln Highway: Coast to Coast from Times Square to the Golden Gate* (New York: W.W. Norton, 2007), 1.

53 Heitmann, *Automobile and American Life*, 74, 76–9. For an extensive and fascinating case study of the motivations for and conflicts often associated with constructing these scenic driving routes, see: Anne Mitchell Whisnant, *Super-Scenic Motorway: The Blue Ridge Parkway History* (Chapel Hill, NC: University of North Carolina Press, 2006).

54 Timothy Davis, "The Rise and Decline of the American Parkway," in *The World Beyond the Windshield: Roads and Landscapes in the United States and Europe*, eds, Christof Mauch and Thomas Zeller (Athens, OH: University of Ohio Press, 2008), 35–7. For an interesting discussion of the expansion of available roadways in Scotland, see: John R. Gold and Margaret M. Gold, *Imagining Scotland: Tradition, Representation and Promotion in Scottish Tourism since 1750* (Aldershot: Ashgate, 1995), 124–6.

55 Alastair J. Durie, *Scotland for the Holidays: Tourism in Scotland, c. 1780-1939* (East Linton: Tuckwell Press, 2003), 164–6.

56 Paul S. Sutter, *Driven Wild: How the Fight Against Automobiles Launched the Modern Wilderness Movement* (Seattle, WA: University of Washington Press, 2002), x–xi, 3–7. According to author Brian Ladd, the automobile inspired disgust on many fronts; see, *Autophobia: Love and Hate in the Automotive Age* (Chicago, IL: University of Chicago Press, 2008).

57 O'Connell, *Car in British Society*, 77.

58 Justine Greenwood, "Driving Through History: The Car, *The Open Road*, and the Making of History Tourism in Australia, 1920-1940," *Journal of Tourism History* 3, no. 1 (April 2011): 21–37. See page 25.

59 Wagner, "Rise of Autotourism," 272–3. I am very grateful to Michael Wagner for supplying me with information about Bagge.

60 Löfgren, *On Holiday*, 63.

61 Jakle and Sculle, *Motoring*, 107.

62 Greenwood, "Driving Through History."

63 Gold and Gold, *Imagining Scotland*, 128–31.

64 Stephen L. Harp, *Marketing Michelin: Advertising and Cultural Identity in Twentieth-Century France* (Baltimore, MD: Johns Hopkins University Press, 2001), especially pages 1–14, 54–88, 89–125, 225–68. See also: Herbert R. Lottman, *The Michelin Men: Driving An Empire* (New York: I.B. Tauris, 2003).

65 Dona Brown, *Inventing New England: Regional Tourism in the Nineteenth Century* (Washington, DC: Smithsonian Institution Press, 1995), 15–40. Especially pages 23–31.

66 See: John A. Jakle, Keith A. Sculle, and Jefferson S. Rogers, *The Motel in America* (Baltimore, MD: Johns Hopkins University Press, 1996); Per Lundin, "Confronting Class: The American Motel in Early Post-War Sweden," *Journal of Tourism History* 5, no. 3 (November 2013): 305–24.

67 Susan Barton, *Working-Class Organisations and Popular Tourism, 1840-1970* (Manchester: Manchester University Press, 2005), 169–72. Also see Gold and Gold, *Imagining Scotland*, 116–18. Scotland offered the possibility of getting away from it all, camping in more remote areas.
68 Sutter, *Driven Wild*, 28–33 and Löfgren, *On Holiday*, 61.
69 Sutter, *Driven Wild*, 35–9.
70 Tara Mitchell Mielnik, *New Deal, New Landscape: The Civilian Conservation Corps and South Carolina's State Parks* (Columbia, SC: University of South Carolina Press, 2011), 65–74. Especially pages 66–8.
71 Per Østby, "Car Mobility and Camping Tourism in Norway, 1950-1970," *Journal of Tourism History* 5, no. 3 (November 2013): 287–304. See pages 291–4.
72 Jakle and Sculle, *Motoring*, 109–10.
73 Jakle and Sculle, *Motoring*, 114.
74 For a discussion of roadside America and its memory, preservation, and legacy, see: John A. Jakle and Keith A. Sculle, *Remembering Roadside America: Preserving the Recent Past as Landscape and Place* (Knoxville, TN: University of Tennessee Press, 2011). There are many popular books on this topic, often featuring glossy photographs that depict the sort of attractions mentioned here. For two examples, see: Eric Peterson, *Roadside Americana* (Lincolnwood, IL: Publications International, 2004) and Brian Butko, *Roadside Attractions: Cool Cafes, Souvenir Stands, Route 66 Relics, & Other Road Trip Fun* (Mechanicsburg, PA: Stackpole Books, 2007).
75 Jakle and Sculle, *Motoring*, 116.
76 "Stock footage – WRIGHT BROTHERS FIRST FLIGHT," YouTube video, 1:29, film of Wilbur Wright near Le Mans, France, Fall 1908, posted by "MyFootage.com," 24 January 2007, accessed 9 February 2011, http://www.youtube.com/watch?v=A-CvkEUSAO4. See also: John W.R. Taylor and Kenneth Munson, *History of Aviation* (New York: Crown Publishers, 1976), 47.
77 Taylor and Munson, *History of Aviation*, 47.
78 Taylor and Munson, *History of Aviation*, 50. See also: Henry R. Palmer, Jr., *This Was Air Travel: A Pictorial History of Aeronauts and Aeroplanes from the Beginning to Now!* (New York: Bonanza Books, 1962), 28–9.
79 Palmer, Jr., *This Was Air Travel*, 34–5.
80 Palmer, Jr., *This Was Air Travel*, 73–4.
81 John Hamilton, *Aircraft of World War I* (Edina, MN: ABDO & Daughters, 2004), 7.
82 Kevin Hillstrom, *Defining Moments: World War I and the Age of Modern Warfare* (Detroit, MI: Omnigraphics, 2013), 25, 44, 46, 54.
83 James R. Mellow, *Charmed Circle: Gertrude Stein and Company* (New York: Henry Holt, 1974), 273–4.

84 Hillstrom, *Defining Moments*, 47–50.
85 Maryam Philpott, *Air and Sea Power in World War I: Combat and Experience in the Royal Flying Corps and the Royal Navy* (London: I.B. Tauris, 2013), 2–5, 101.
86 Taylor and Munson, *History of Aviation*, 118–19.
87 Robert Wohl, *A Passion for Wings: Aviation and the Western Imagination, 1908-1918* (New Haven, CT and London: Yale University Press, 1994), 207–8.
88 Taylor and Munson, *History of Aviation*, 120.
89 Wohl, *Passion for Wings*, 203, 232, and 235; Peter Fritzsche, *A Nation of Flyers: German Aviation and the Popular Imagination* (Cambridge, MA: Harvard University Press, 1992), 59–101; and George L. Mosse, *Fallen Soldiers: Reshaping the Memory of the World Wars* (Oxford: Oxford University Press, 1990), 119–25.
90 Virginia Woolf, *Mrs Dalloway* (New York: Harcourt Brace Jovanovich, 1981; first published 1925), 20–1. Italics mine.
91 Kenneth Hudson and Julian Pettifer, *Diamonds in the Sky: A Social History of Air Travel* (London: Bodley Head, 1979), 12.
92 A.S. Jackson, *Imperial Airways and the First British Airlines* (Levenham: Terence Dalton, Ltd.), 6.
93 Marc Dierikx, *Clipping the Clouds: How Air Travel Changed the World* (Westport, CT: Praeger, 2008), 10–12.
94 Jackson, *Imperial Airways*, 16–20. See also: Peter Fearon, "The Growth of Aviation in Britain," *Journal of Contemporary History* 20, no. 1 (January 1985): 21–40. Especially pages 27–8.
95 Jackson, *Imperial Airways*, 3–9.
96 Hudson and Pettifer, *Diamonds in the Sky*, 15–19.
97 Joseph J. Corn, "Making Flying 'Thinkable': Women Pilots and the Selling of Aviation, 1927-1940," *American Quarterly* 31, no. 4 (Autumn 1979): 556–71. Especially pages 558–61, 563, 567, 570.
98 Dierikx, *Clipping the Clouds*, 10–12; Jackson, *Imperial Airways*, 39–94; and Hudson and Pettifer, *Diamonds in the Sky*, 58–89.
99 Jackson, *Imperial Airways*, 44.
100 Hudson and Pettifer, *Diamonds in the Sky*, 54–5.
101 Dierikx, *Clipping the Clouds*, 26.
102 Jackson, *Imperial Airways*, 104–15.
103 Quoted in Hudson and Pettifer, *Diamonds in the Sky*, 62. See pages 61–3 for a more detailed discussion of Zeppelins.
104 "Hindenburg Disaster with Sound" (Stock Footage, 1937), video (Pathograms) and sound (WLS Radio), 1:20, from Internet Archive, accessed 3 November 2014, http://archive.org/details/SF145.
105 See Dierikx, *Clipping the Clouds*, 38–41 and 64–71. Also see: Hudson and Pettifer, *Diamonds in the Sky*, 121, 124–5, 130–52.

Chapter 8

1 Eric Hobsbawm, *The Age of Extremes: A History of the World, 1914-1991* (New York: Vintage Books, 1996), xiii, 6, 14. Scholarly discussion concerning the impact of World War I is vast. For a starting place, see: Modris Eksteins, *Rites of Spring: The Great War and the Birth of the Modern Age* (Boston, MA: Houghton Mifflin, 1989); Jay Winter, *Sites of Memory, Sites of Mourning: The Great War in European Cultural History* (Cambridge: Cambridge University Press, 1995); and, Wolfgang J. Mommsen, "Society and War: Two New Analyses of the First World War," *Journal of Modern History* 47, no. 33 (September 1975): 530–8.

2 Mark Mazower, *Dark Continent: Europe's Twentieth Century* (New York: Vintage, 1998), xi.

3 John K. Walton, *Blackpool* (Edinburgh: Edinburgh University Press, 1998), 108–9.

4 Alastair J. Durie, *Scotland for the Holidays: Tourism in Scotland, c.1780-1939* (East Linton: Tuckwell Press, 2003), 171–91.

5 Marguerite S. Shaffer, *See America First: Tourism and National Identity, 1880-1940* (Washington, DC: Smithsonian Institution Press, 2001), 100–1.

6 While not addressed here, tourism also played a role in the promotion of preservation and urban development efforts during the interwar years. For two American case studies, see: Stephanie E. Yuhl, *A Golden Haze of Memory: The Making of Historic Charleston* (Chapel Hill, NC: University of North Carolina Press, 2005) and Anthony J. Stanonis, *Creating the Big Easy: New Orleans and the Emergence of Modern Tourism, 1918-1945* (Athens, GA: University of Georgia Press, 2006).

7 For a discussion of this debate and examples of various definitions, see: Stanley Payne, *A History of Fascism, 1914-1945* (Madison, WI: University of Wisconsin Press, 1995), 3–22.

8 Jeffrey Herf, *Reactionary Modernism: Technology, Culture, and Politics in Weimar and the Third Reich* (Cambridge: Cambridge University Press, 1986).

9 It is worth adding that many states of all ideological stripes were concerned with the promotion of healthful activity during the interwar years. For more, see: Charlotte MacDonald, *Strong, Beautiful and Modern: National Fitness in Britain, New Zealand, Australia, and Canada* (Vancouver, BC: University of British Columbia Press, 2013). Fitness and sport were closely connected to ideas about national identity. See: Hans Bonde, *Gymnastics and Politics: Niels Bukh and Male Aesthetics*, trans. Simon Frost (Copenhagen: Museum Tusculanum Press, 2006) and Ana Carden-Coyne, *Reconstructing the Body: Classicism, Modernism, and the First World War* (Oxford: Oxford University Press, 2009).

10 Roger Eatwell, *Fascism: A History* (New York: Allen Lane, 1996), 43–88.
11 Victoria De Grazia, *The Culture of Consent: Mass Organisation of Leisure in Fascist Italy* (Cambridge: Cambridge University Press, 1981), 24–6. Quote on page 26.
12 Ibid., 33–4.
13 Ibid., 35.
14 Ibid., 179, 181–2.
15 See: Richard F. Hamilton, *Who Voted for Hitler?* (Princeton, NJ: Princeton University Press, 1982); and Thomas Childers, *Nazi Voter: The Social Foundations of Fascism in Germany, 1919-1933* (Chapel Hill, NC: University of North Carolina Press, 1983).
16 Detlev Peukert, *Inside Nazi Germany: Conformity, Opposition, and Racism in Everyday Life* (New Haven, CT: Yale University Press, 1987), 103.
17 Shelley Baranowski, *Strength Through Joy: Consumerism and Mass Tourism in the Third Reich* (Cambridge: Cambridge University Press, 2004), 40.
18 It should be noted that market-based leisure co-existed in Nazi Germany alongside the KdF model. See: Kristin Semmens, *Seeing Hitler's Germany: Tourism in the Third Reich* (Basingstoke: Palgrave Macmillan, 2005).
19 Baranowski, *Strength Through Joy*, 44–50 and Shelley Baranowski, "Strength Through Joy: Tourism and National Integration in the Third Reich," in *Being Elsewhere: Tourism, Consumer Culture, and Identity in Modern Europe and North America*, eds, Shelley Baranowski and Ellen Furlough (Ann Arbor, MI: University of Michigan Press, 2004), 213–36. See especially pages 215–16.
20 Baranowski, *Strength Through Joy*, 53–4.
21 Ibid., 67–70 and Baranowski, "Strength Through Joy," 220–1.
22 Baranowski, *Strength Through Joy*, 67–70 and Baranowski, "Strength Through Joy," 223–4.
23 Baranowski, *Strength Through Joy*, 71.
24 Baranowski, *Strength Through Joy*, 130–4 and Baranowski, "Strength Through Joy," 224.
25 Kenneth R. Olwig, "Landscape, Monuments, and National Identity," in *Nations and Nationalism: A Global Historical Overview*, eds, Guntram H. Herb and David H. Kaplan (Santa Barbara, CA: ABC-CLIO, 2008), 59–71. See page 70.
26 Baranowski, *Strength Through Joy*, 124, 127–9. For more about the ideological goals associated with hiking see: Scott Moranda, "Maps, Markers, and Bodies: Hikers Constructing the Nation in German Forests," *The Nationalism Project*, last modified 1 December 2000, http://www.nationalismproject.org/articles/Moranda/moranda.html.
27 Baranowski, *Strength Through Joy*, 162–3, 192–3, 197–8.
28 Ibid., 144.

29 Ibid., 148.
30 Ibid., 134–7.
31 Ibid., 58.
32 Shelley Baranowski, "A Family Vacation for Workers: The Strength through Joy Resort at Prora," *German History* 25, no. 4 (October 2007): 539–59. See page 542.
33 For a concise overview: David G. Williamson, *The Age of the Dictators: A Study of the European Dictators, 1918-53* (Harlow: Pearson, 2007), 29–85.
34 Louise McReynolds, "The Prerevolutionary Russian Tourist: Commercialization in the Nineteenth Century," in *Turizm: The Russian and East European Tourist under Capitalism and Socialism*, eds, Anne E. Gorsuch and Diane P. Koenker (Ithaca, NY: Cornell University Press, 2006), 17–42.
35 Diane P. Koenker, "The Proletarian Tourist in the 1930s: Between Mass Excursion and Mass Escape," in *Turizm: The Russian and East European Tourist under Capitalism and Socialism*, eds, Anne E. Gorsuch and Diane P. Koenker (Ithaca, NY: Cornell University Press, 2006), 119–40. See page 119.
36 Christian Noack, "Building Tourism in One Country? The Sovietization of Vacationing, 1917-41," in *Touring Beyond the Nation: A Transnational Approach to European Tourism History*, ed. Eric G.E. Zuelow (Farnham: Ashgate, 2011), 171–93.
37 Diane P. Koenker, *Club Red: Vacation, Travel and the Soviet Dream* (Ithaca, NY: Cornell University Press, 2013), 15.
38 The practice of splitting up couples on holiday often meant license to pursue casual affairs. Ironically, the pervasiveness of this type of behavior meant that single vacationers were often considered to be "too complicated" by others who feared the expectation of longer-term commitment. See Koenker, *Club Red*, 36–7.
39 Ibid., 49.
40 Ibid., 53–4.
41 Noack, "Building Tourism," 183.
42 Koenker, *Club Red*, 57.
43 Ibid., 59.
44 Noack, "Building Tourism," 185.
45 Ibid., 186.
46 Gary Cross, "Vacations for All: The Leisure Question in the Era of the Popular Front," *Journal of Contemporary History* 24, no. 4 (October 1989): 599–621. See page 599. Cross offers a more extensive discussion of the "leisure question," including exploration of the push for weekends and an eight-hour workday during the nineteenth century, in: *A Quest for Time: The Reduction of Work in Britain and France, 1840-1940* (Berkeley, CA: University of California Press, 1989).

47 Cross, "Vacations for All," 603.
48 Ibid., 605.
49 Ibid., 609.
50 Ibid., 609–10.
51 Ibid., 608. It is worth mentioning that this notion was prevalent beyond Europe as well. Australia also debated and ultimately implemented paid holidays in the late 1930s and early 1940s. See: Richard White, *On Holidays: A History of Getting Away in Australia* (North Melbourne, VIC: Pluto Press, 2005), 112–16.
52 Cross, "Vacations for All," 601–2.
53 Ibid., 599, 601.
54 Ellen Furlough, "Making Mass Vacations: Tourism and Consumer Culture in France, 1930s to 1970s," *Comparative Studies in Society and History* 40, no. 2 (April 1998): 247–86. See page 253.
55 Kristin Semmens, "'Tourism and Autarky are Conceptually Incompatible': International Tourism Conferences in the Third Reich," in *Touring Beyond the Nation: A Transnational Approach to European Tourism History*, ed. Eric G.E. Zuelow (Farnham: Ashgate, 2011), 195–214. See pages 195–6.
56 Eric G.E. Zuelow, *Making Ireland Irish: Tourism and National Identity since the Irish Civil* War (Syracuse, NY: Syracuse University Press, 2009), 52.
57 Cross, "Vacations for All," 612.
58 Furlough, "Making Mass Vacations," 252.
59 Cross, "Vacations for All," 608–9.
60 Furlough, "Making Mass Vacations," 255.
61 Ibid.
62 Cross, "Vacations for All," 611.
63 John Beckerson, "Marketing British Tourism: Government Approaches to the Stimulation of a Service Sector, 1880-1950," in *The Making of Modern Tourism: The Cultural History of the British Experience, 1600-2000*, eds, Hartmut Berghoff, Barbara Korte, Ralf Schneider, and Christopher Harvie (Basingstoke: Palgrave, 2002), 133–58. See page 138.
64 Beckerson, "Marketing," 141–3. See also: Victor T.C. Middleton and L.J. Lickoris, *British Tourism: The Remarkable Story of Growth* (Burlington, MA: Elsevier Butterworth-Heinemann, 2005).
65 Cross, "Vacations for All," 613.
66 Middleton and Lickoris, *British Tourism*, 4–5.
67 Dina Berger, *The Development of Mexico's Tourism Industry: Pyramids by Day, Martinis by Night* (New York: Palgrave Macmillan, 2006), 7.
68 Ibid., 16.
69 Ibid., 18.
70 Ibid., 15.
71 Ibid., 29.

72 Ibid., 11–13, 119. See also: Dina Berger, "Goodwill Ambassadors on Holiday," in *Holiday in Mexico: Critical Reflections on Tourism and Tourist Encounters*, eds, Dina Berger and Andrew Grant Wood (Durham, NC: Duke University Press, 2010), 107–29. Especially pages 114–19.
73 Berger, *Development*, 93–4. See also: Andrew Grant Wood, "On the Selling of Rey Momo: Early Tourism and the Marketing of Carnival in Veracruz," in *Holiday in Mexico: Critical Reflections on Tourism and Tourist Encounters*, eds, Dina Berger and Andrew Grant Wood (Durham, NC: Duke University Press, 2010), 77–106. Especially pages 86–90.
74 Berger, *Development*, 28.
75 David Shavit, *Bali and the Tourist Industry: A History, 1906-1942* (Jefferson, NC: McFarland & Co., 2003), 5.
76 Ibid., 11–12.
77 Ibid., 22, 56–7.
78 Ibid., 24.
79 Ibid., 27.
80 Ibid., 3, 50–1.
81 Ibid., 53.
82 Ibid., 3. For more information about the history of tourism in Bali, see: Adrian Vickers, *Bali: A Paradise Created*, 2nd ed. (Hong Kong: Periplus Editions, 1990) and Michel Picard, *Bali: Cultural Tourism and Touristic Culture*, trans. Diana Darling (Singapore: Archipelago Press, 1996).

Chapter 9

1 Tony Judt offers an extended discussion of the causalities, both human and material, in *Postwar: A History of Europe Since 1945* (New York: Penguin Books, 2006), 14–27.
2 Chris Sladen, "Holidays at Home in the Second World War," *Journal of Contemporary History* 37, no. 1 (January 2002): 67–89.
3 Sandra Trudgen Dawson, *Holiday Camps in Twentieth-Century Britain: Packaging Pleasure* (New York: Manchester University Press, 2011), 123; Sladen, "Holidays at Home," 68–70.
4 John K. Walton, *Blackpool* (Edinburgh: Edinburgh University Press, 1998), 137.
5 Dawson, *Holiday Camps*, 122.
6 Richard White, *On Holiday: A History of Getting Away in Australia* (North Melbourne, VIC: Pluto Press, 2005), 116–17.
7 Dennis Merrill, *Negotiating Paradise: U.S. Tourism and Empire in Twentieth-Century Latin America* (Chapel Hill, NC: University of North Carolina Press, 2009), 100–1.

8 Eric G.E. Zuelow, *Making Ireland Irish: Tourism and National Identity since the Irish Civil War* (Syracuse, NY: Syracuse University Press, 2009), 35–44.

9 Consumerism, the economic situation in Europe, and the formation of the Marshall Plan are widely addressed by historians. For example: Richard F. Kuisel, "Coca-Cola and the Cold War: The French Face of Americanization, 1948-1953," *French Historical Studies* 17, no. 1 (Spring 1991): 96–116; Greg Castillo, "Domesticating the Cold War: Household Consumption as Propaganda in Marshall Plan Germany," *Journal of Contemporary History* 40, no. 2 (April 2005): 261–88; C.C.S. Newton, "The Sterling Crisis of 1947 and the British Response to the Marshall Plan," *Economic History Review* New Series 37, no. 3 (August 1984): 391–408; Manfred Knapp, Wolfgang F. Stolper, and Michael Hudson, "Reconstruction and West-Integration: The Impact of the Marshall Plan on Germany," *Journal of Institutional and Theoretical Economics* 137 (September 1981): 415–33; Arthur Schlesinger, Jr., "Origins of the Cold War," *Foreign Affairs* 46 (1967): 22–52; and Reinhold Wagnleitner, *Coca-Colonization and the Cold War: The Cultural Mission of the United States in Austria after the Second World War* (Chapel Hill, NC: University of North Carolina Press, 1994). Tony Judt's well-received *Postwar* addresses many of the calculations and concerns in a remarkably gripping and accessible fashion. See especially pages 82–8.

10 Winston S. Churchill, "Iron Curtain Speech," 5 March 1946, *The Modern History Sourcebook*, Fordham University, accessed 8 February 2009, http://www.fordham.edu/halsall/mod/churchill-iron.html.

11 Mary Saran, "Europe and the Marshall Plan," *The Antioch Review* 8, no. 1 (Spring 1948): 26–32.

12 Hannah Arendt, *The Origins of Totalitarianism*, rev. ed. (New York: Schocken, 2004).

13 For an extended history of the developing idea of totalitarianism, see: Benjamin L. Alpers, *Dictators, Democracy, and American Public Culture: Envisioning the Totalitarian Enemy, 1920s-1950s* (Chapel Hill, NC: University of North Carolina Press, 2003). Tony Judt describes the settlement that ended World War II as "impossible." Trust was in scarce supply during the war and afterward and, with Europe divided, that mistrust only grew as each "now had responsibility for large tracts of the European continent." See Judt, *Postwar*, 88–90, 100–64.

14 George C. Marshall, "The Marshall Plan Speech," *The George C. Marshall Foundation*, accessed 11 August 2014, http://marshallfoundation.org/marshall/the-marshall-plan/marshall-plan-speech/.

15 Eric G.E. Zuelow, "The Necessity of Touring Beyond the Nation: An Introduction," in *Touring Beyond the Nation: A Transnational Approach to European Tourism History*. ed. Eric G.E. Zuelow (Farnham: Ashgate, 2011), 5.

16 Christopher Endy, *Cold War Holidays: American Tourism in France* (Chapel Hill, NC: University of North Carolina Press, 2004), 33–4, 43.
17 Kenneth Campbell, "'U.N.' for Traveler: International Body is Formed to Deal with Simplification of Passports," *New York Times*, 19 October 1947; "History," United Nations World Tourism Organization (UNWTO), accessed 26 July 2013, http://www2.unwto.org/en/content/history-0; also see, Endy, *Cold War Holidays*, 49.
18 Zuelow, "Necessity," 5.
19 "Tourist Traffic with USA: Development," 1949, National Archives Ireland (hereafter NAI), Department of the Taoiseach (hereafter DT), Ms. S5472B. Quoted in Zuelow, "Necessity," 6.
20 "Dispatch of Teams of Experts to Study Tourist Equipment in the United States, December 16, 1949, folder 305/57/128, pt. 1, Economic Cooperation Administration, NAI, Department of Foreign Affairs. Quoted in Zuelow, "Necessity," 6.
21 Brian A. McKenzie, "Creating a Tourist's Paradise: The Marshall Plan and France, 1948-1952," *French Politics, Culture and Society* 21, no. 1 (Spring 2003): 40. For more, see: Endy, *Cold War Holidays*, 81–99.
22 Michael Gorman (Bord Fáilte, retired), interview conducted by the author, Dublin, 11 October 2002.
23 Zuelow, "Necessity," 6.
24 McKenzie, "Creating a Tourist's Paradise," 48.
25 Zuelow, "Necessity," 7; and, "History," UNWTO.
26 See Tony Gray, *The Lost Years: The Emergency in Ireland, 1939-45* (London: Little, Brown, and Company, 1997); Geoffrey Roberts and Brian Garvan, eds, *Ireland and the Second World War: Politics, Society, and Remembrance* (Dublin: Four Courts Press, 2000).
27 See Bernadette Whelan, *Ireland and the Marshall Plan, 1947-57* (Dublin: Four Courts Press, 2000).
28 For more on Pozzy, see: Endy, *Cold War Holidays*, 45.
29 Zuelow, *Making Ireland Irish*, 44–56.
30 Ibid., 58–71.
31 Mark Mazower, *No Enchanted Place: The End of Empire and the Ideological Origins of the United Nations* (Princeton, NJ: Princeton University Press, 2009), 14–15, 31–45, 193.
32 Ibid., 149.
33 "Charter of the United Nations: Preamble," *United Nations*, accessed 29 July 2013, http://www.un.org/en/documents/charter/preamble.shtml.
34 Kathleen Teltsch, "U.N. in Accord on Tourism," *New York Times*, 7 May 1961.
35 "History," UNWTO.

36 For a discussion of the decline of shipping (and the rise of cruise ships) see: Gaetano Cerchiello, "Cruise Market: A Real Opportunity for Transatlantic Shipping Lines in the 1960s – The Case of the Spanish Company Ybarra," *Journal of Tourism History* 6, no. 1 (April 2014): 16–37.
37 Marc Dierikx, *Clipping the Clouds: How Air Travel Changed the World* (Westport, CT: Praeger, 2008), 38–41; Kenneth Hudson and Julian Pettifer, *Diamonds in the Sky: A Social History of Air Travel* (London: Bodley Head, 1979), 121–4, 143–4.
38 Following World War II, Great Britain rapidly divested itself of overseas colonies—partly due to pressure from the United States, but largely because the onetime economic powerhouse could no longer afford to administer distant holdings. The decolonization story is varied and complicated, but interested readers will find a useful overview in Piers Brendon, *The Decline and Fall of the British Empire, 1781-1997* (New York: Vintage Books, 2010).
39 Hudson and Pettifer, *Diamonds in the Sky*, 164–6.
40 Ibid., 172–8.
41 Dierikx, *Clipping the Clouds*, 42–6.
42 Hudson and Pettifer, *Diamonds in the Sky*, 112.
43 "The Founding of the IATA," *IATA*, accessed 31 July 2013, http://www.iata.org/about/Pages/history.aspx.
44 Dierikx, *Clipping the Clouds*, 59–60. See also Hudson and Pettifer, *Diamonds in the Sky*, 130–52.
45 Hudson and Pettifer, *Diamonds in the Sky*, 196–8.
46 Dierikx, *Clipping the Clouds*, 126–7. For still more on the relationship between aviation and tourism, see: Roger Bray and Vladimir Raitz, *Flight to the Sun: The Story of the Holiday Revolution* (London: Continuum, 2001).
47 Lizabeth Cohen, *A Consumers' Republic: The Politics of Mass Consumption in Postwar America* (New York: Vintage Books, 2004), 121.
48 Judt, *Postwar*, 325.
49 Ibid., 338.
50 Ibid., 339–41.
51 For several case studies illustrating this point, see Eric G.E. Zuelow, ed., "Nordic Tourism," Special section, *Journal of Tourism History* 5, no. 3 (November 2013); also, see: Judt, *Postwar*, 342–3.
52 Judt, *Postwar*, 342.
53 Anu-Hanna Anttila, "Leisure as a Matter of Politics: The Construction of the Finnish Democratic Model of Tourism from the 1940s to the 1970s," *Journal of Tourism History* 5, no. 3 (November 2013): 330–2.
54 Katie Johnston, "Nearly 1 in 4 US Workers Go Without Paid Time Off," *Boston Globe*, 4 August 2014.
55 Louis Turner and John Ash, *The Golden Hordes: International Tourism and the Pleasure Periphery* (New York: St. Martin's Press, 1976), 11–12.

56 Ibid., 93–112.

57 For discussion of sightseeing in Mexico among nineteenth-century soldiers, see: Andrea Boardman, "The U.S.-Mexican War and the Beginnings of American Tourism in Mexico," in *Holiday in Mexico: Critical Reflections on Tourism and Tourist Encounters*, eds, Dina Berger and Andrew Grant Wood (Durham, NC: Duke University Press, 2010), 21–53.

58 Dina Berger, *The Development of Mexico's Tourism Industry: Pyramids by Day, Martinis by Night* (New York: Palgrave Macmillan, 2006), 113–4.

59 Ibid., 121. It is worth adding that prohibition in the United States, as well as a taste for gambling, inspired somewhat less reputable development along the US-Mexico border. See: Paul J. Vanderwood, *Satan's Playground: Mobsters and Movie Stars at America's Greatest Gaming Resort* (Durham, NC: Duke University Press, 2010).

60 Lisa Pinley Covert, "Colonial Outpost to Artists' Mecca: Conflict and Collaboration in the Development of San Miguel de Allende's Tourist Industry," in *Holiday in Mexico: Critical Reflections on Tourism and Tourist Encounters*, eds, Dina Berger and Andrew Grant Wood (Durham, NC: Duke University Press, 2010), 183–220.

61 Andrew Sackett, "Fun in Acapulco? The Politics of Development on the Mexican Riviera," in *Holiday in Mexico: Critical Reflections on Tourism and Tourist Encounters*, eds, Dina Berger and Andrew Grant Wood (Durham, NC: Duke University Press, 2010), 161–82. See especially pages 168–9, 170–1, 172–5, 178.

62 Michael Clancy, *Exporting Paradise: Tourism and Development in Mexico* (London: Pergamon, 2001).

63 Daniel Hiernaux-Nicolas, "Cancún Bliss," in *The Tourist City*, eds, Dennis R. Judd and Susan S. Fainstein (New Haven, CT: Yale University Press, 1999), 124–39. See pages 128–31.

64 M. Bianet Castellanos, "Cancún and the Campo: Indigenous Migration and Tourism Development in the Yucatán Peinsula," in *Holiday in Mexico: Critical Reflections on Tourism and Tourist Encounters*, eds, Dina Berger and Andrew Grant Wood (Durham, NC: Duke University Press, 2010), 244; and Hiernaux-Nicolas, "Cancún Bliss," 131. The "three esses" are also frequently listed as "sun, sand, and sea."

65 Jim Davidson and Peter Spearritt, *Holiday Business: Tourism in Australia since 1870* (Carlton, VIC: The Miegunya Press at Melbourne University Press, 2000), 290–1, 301–2, 304–5.

66 White, *On Holidays*, 132.

67 Polly Pattullo, *Last Resorts: The Cost of Tourism in the Caribbean* (London: Cassell, 1996), 8–9.

68 Mimi Sheller, *Consuming the Caribbean: From Arawaks to Zombies* (London: Routledge, 2003), 100.

69 Turner and Ash, *Golden Hordes*, 102–3.
70 Pattullo, *Last Resorts*, 4–6.
71 See: Luciano Segreto, Carles Manera, and Manfred Pohl, eds, *Europe at the Seaside: The Economic History of Mass Tourism in the Mediterranean* (New York: Berghahn Books, 2009).
72 Sasha Pack, *Tourism and Dictatorship: Europe's Peaceful Invasion of Franco's Spain* (New York: Palgrave Macmillan, 2006), 25.
73 Ibid., 33.
74 Ibid., 39–40.
75 Ibid., 84.
76 Ibid., 98–102.
77 Ibid., 97.
78 Ibid., 105–6.
79 Ibid., 108.
80 Susan Barton, *Working-Class Organisations and Popular Culture, 1840-1970* (Manchester: Manchester University Press, 2005), 198–213. For more on the tendency of British tourists to visit sunny Mediterranean destinations (and especially Spain), see: Peter Lyth, "Flying Visits: The Growth of British Air Package Tours, 1945-1975," in *Europe at the Seaside: The Economic History of Mass Tourism in the Mediterranean*, eds, Luciano Segreto, Carles Manera, and Manfred Pohl (New York: Berghahn Books, 2009), 11–30.
81 Diane P. Koenker, *Club Red: Vacation Travel and the Soviet Dream* (Ithaca, NY: Cornell University Press, 2013), 128–31.
82 Ibid., 131.
83 Ibid., 135.
84 Ibid., 150.
85 Ibid., 163.
86 Ibid., 179.
87 Ibid., 191.

Chapter 10

1 "1955 Disneyland Opening Day [Complete ABC Broadcast]," YouTube video, 1:13:01, televised as "Dateline Disneyland" on ABC on 17 July 1955, posted by "Marcio Disney," 26 July 2011, accessed 13 September 2014, https://www.youtube.com/watch?v=JuzrZET-3Ew.
2 Steven Watts, *The Magic Kingdom: Walt Disney and the American Way of Life* (Boston, MA: Houghton Mifflin, 1997), 63–100.
3 Ibid., 110.

4 Ibid., 160.

5 Ibid., 288.

6 Ibid., 22. Historian Lisa McGirr finds that Orange County, California was an especially suitable setting for Disneyland. Anaheim's nice weather was certainly a factor in Walt Disney's decision to locate the park there, but Disneyland also mirrored the values of its neighboring population. Not only were residents of Orange County strident anticommunists, they were also newly arrived to the region from the Midwest. They happily embraced Disney's "Main Street" out of nostalgia for their lost pasts and a desire for community and old-fashioned values that they struggled to maintain in suburbia. Their high salaries and professional jobs also allowed them the time and money to visit the park. See: Lisa McGirr, *Suburban Warriors: The Origins of the New American Right* (Princeton, NJ: Princeton University Press, 2001), 20–1, 28.

7 Watts, *Magic Kingdom*, 384.

8 Those interested in the history of Coney Island should consult: Woody Register's *The Kid of Coney Island: Fred Thompson and the Rise of American Amusements* (Oxford: Oxford University Press, 2001).

9 Watts, *Magic Kingdom*, 384.

10 "1955 Disneyland Opening Day."

11 Ibid.

12 Ibid.

13 The park was often celebrated as "a particularly impressive display of American technical achievement and free enterprise" as well "a marvel of city planning, municipal construction, landscaping, architectural design, interior and exterior lighting, air compression, hydraulic mechanics, and the innovative use of materials such as plastics." See Watts, *Magic Kingdom*, 393, 395.

14 Gary S. Cross and John K. Walton, *The Playful Crowd: Pleasure Places in the Twentieth Century* (New York: Columbia University Press, 2005), 181.

15 Lawrence Culver, *The Frontier of Leisure: Southern California and the Shaping of Modern America* (Oxford: Oxford University Press, 2010). See pages 1–2 for a short summary of Culver's argument.

16 Rudy Koshar, "'What Ought to Be Seen': Tourists' Guidebooks and National Identities in Modern Germany and Europe," *Journal of Contemporary History* 33, no. 3 (July 1998): 325.

17 The role of authenticity in tourism is widely discussed by scholars. For more, see: Dean MacCannell, *The Tourist: A New Theory of the Leisure Class* (Berkeley, CA: University of California Press, 1999; first published 1976) and Dean MacCannell, *Empty Meeting Grounds: The Tourist Papers* (London: Routledge, 1992). Erik Cohen takes things a little further, noting that the importance of authenticity may be waning as tourists grow

increasingly content with "contrived" sites: see, *Contemporary Tourism: Diversity and Change* (New York: Elsevier, 2004), 3–6, 87–100, 131–43.

18 Rodney Lowe, *The Welfare State in Britain since 1945* (Basingstoke: Palgrave Macmillan, 2005), 253–4; Roy Porter, *London: A Social History* (Cambridge, MA: Harvard University Press, 1994), 349–53. See also: Charles More, *Britain in the Twentieth Century* (Harlow: Pearson-Longman, 2007), 154–5.

19 David Matless, *Landscape and Englishness* (London: Reaktion Books, 1998), 35.

20 Kenneth T. Jackson, *Crabgrass Frontier: The Suburbanization of the United States* (Oxford: Oxford University Press, 1985), 48–9.

21 Stephanie Coontz, *The Way We Never Were: American Families and the Nostalgia Trap* (New York: Basic Books, 1993), 27–8.

22 Sir Billy Butlin, *The Billy Butlin Story: A Showman to the End* (London: Robson Books, 1993), 33–40.

23 Sandra Trudgen Dawson, *Holiday Camps in Twentieth-Century Britain: Packaging Pleasure* (Manchester: Manchester University Press, 2011), 54.

24 Butlin, *Billy Butlin Story*, 114.

25 Dawson, *Holiday Camps*, 54–5.

26 Ibid., 58–9.

27 Ibid.; Butlin, *Billy Butlin Story*, 130–9.

28 Dawson, *Holiday Camps*, 147–8, 159–63.

29 Over two million stayed at Butlin's and Pontin's (a less famous competitor) holiday camps in 1960 alone. Ibid., 212.

30 Butlin, *Billy Butlin Story*, 118.

31 Dawson, *Holiday Camps*, 220.

32 For a sample itinerary, see: Ibid., 165.

33 Ibid., 110.

34 Ibid., 169.

35 Susan Sessions Rugh, *Are We There Yet? The Golden Age of Family Vacations* (Lawrence, KS: University of Kansas Press, 2008), 2.

36 See Warren James Belasco, *Americans on the Road: From Autocamps to the Motel, 1910-1945* (Cambridge, MA: MIT Press, 1979) for a more detailed account of both camping and motels.

37 Rugh, *Are We There Yet*, 20–3.

38 Ibid., 122–3.

39 Ibid., 126.

40 Ibid., 51.

41 Ibid., 59.

42 Ibid., 169–71.

43 Ibid., 173.

44 Quoted in Ibid., 89.

45 See: Per Østby, "Car Mobility and Camping Tourism in Norway, 1950-1970," *Journal of Tourism History* 5, no. 3 (August 2014): 287–304 and Per Lundin, "Confronting Class: The American Motel in Early Post-War Sweden," *Journal of Tourism History* 5, no. 3 (August 2014): 305–24.

46 Ellen Furlough, "Making Mass Vacations: Tourism and Consumer Culture in France, 1930s to 1970s," *Comparative Studies in Society and History* 40, no. 2 (April 1998): 247–86. Especially pages 262, 266, 271, and 276.

47 Anton Grassl and Graham Heath, *The Magic Triangle: A Short History of the World Youth Hostel Movement* (Antwerp: International Youth Hostel Federation, 1982), 13–14. There are a number of short histories of youth hosteling, most published by the hosteling organizations themselves. For another example, see: Youth Hostels Association, *A Short History of the YHA* (St. Albans: Youth Hostels Association [of England and Wales], 1969).

48 Grassl and Heath, *Magic Triangle*, 17.

49 Ibid., 30–49, 60–3.

50 Ibid., 91–2.

51 Ibid., 93, 96–107.

52 Ibid., 113–4.

53 Ibid., 117–33.

54 Rugh, *Are We There Yet*, 180–1.

55 Dawson, *Holiday Camps*, 221.

56 Ibid., 225.

57 Christian Noack, "Coping with the Tourist: Planned and 'Wild' Tourism on the Soviet Black Sea Coast," in *Turizm: The Russian and East European Tourist Under Capitalism and Socialism*, eds, Anne E. Gorsuch and Diane P. Koenker (Ithaca, NY: Cornell University Press, 2006), 281–305. See page 304.

58 Cross and Walton, *Playful Crowd*, 194–202.

59 A.O. Scott, "The Death of Adulthood in American Culture," *New York Times*, 11 September 2014.

60 As a partial measure of the numbers in question, in 1989 alone, Disney's Orlando-area park, Disney World, drew 30 million people. See Richard E. Foglesong, *Married to the Mouse: Walt Disney World and Orlando* (New Haven, CT: Yale University Press, 2001), 3.

61 Dick Hebdige, *Subculture: The Meaning of Style* (London: Routledge, 1979).

62 R.W. Butler, "The Concept of a Tourist Area Cycle of Evolution: Implications for Management of Resources," *Canadian Geographer* 24, no. 1 (1980): 5–12.

63 Michel Peillon, "Tourism—The Quest for Otherness," *Crane Bag* 8, no. 2 (1984): 165–8.

64 Louis Turner and John Ash, *The Golden Hordes: International Tourism and the Pleasure Periphery* (New York: St. Martin's Press, 1976), 111.

65 Cathleen R. Litvack, "Heritage Tourism in New Jersey," *State of New Jersey Historic Trust*, accessed 11 November 2014, http://www.njht.org/dca/njht/touring/plan/.

66 "Heritage Tourism Boosts UK Economy by £26.4bn per year," Shakespeare Birthplace Trust, published on 13 July 2013, accessed 11 November 2014, http://www.shakespeare.org.uk/visit-the-houses/latest-news/heritage-tourism-boosts-uk-economy-by-atilde.html.

67 Kathleen Newland and Carylanna Taylor, "Heritage Tourism and Nostalgia Trade: A Diaspora Niche in the Development Landscape" (Washington, DC: Migration Policy Institute, September 2010). This widespread importance is clear when exploring the vast scholarly literature dealing with "heritage." Several examples (among countless others) include: Carol E. Henderson and Maxine Weisgrau, eds, *Raj Rhapsodies: Tourism, Heritage, and the Seduction of History* (Aldershot: Ashgate, 2007); Joseph L. Scarpaci, *Plazas and Barrios: Heritage Tourism and Globalization in the Latin American Centro Histórico* (Tucson, AZ: University of Arizona Press, 2005); Emma Waterton and Steve Watson, eds, *Culture, Heritage and Representation: Perspectives on Visuality and the Past* (Aldershot: Ashgate, 2010); Dallen J. Timothy and Gyan P. Nyaupane, eds, *Cultural Heritage and Tourism in the Developing World: A Regional Perspective* (London: Routledge, 2009); and Michael Hitchcock, Victor T. King, and Michael Parnwell, eds, *Heritage Tourism in Southeast Asia* (Honolulu: University of Hawai'i Press, 2010).

68 Robert Hewison, *The Heritage Industry: Britain in a Climate of Decline* (London: Methuen, 1987), 24.

69 G.J. Ashworth, "Is Heritage a Globalisation of the Local or a Localisation of the Global?," paper presented at the conference Ireland's Heritages: Critical Perspectives on Consumption, Method and Memory, Galway-Mayo Institute of Technology, Castlebar, Ireland, 19 October 2002.

70 "Antarctica Concerns Grow as Tourism Numbers Rise," *USA Today*, 16 March 2013, http://www.usatoday.com/story/travel/destinations/2013/03/16/antarctica-tourism-rise/1993181/.

71 Adam Bridge, "Manu, Peru: Is Tourism Harming Remote Tribes?" *Telegraph*, 11 September 2014.

72 Jochen Hemmleb, Larry A. Johnson, and Eric R. Simonson, *Ghosts of Everest: The Search for Mallory and Irvine* (Seattle, WA: Mountaineers Books, 1999).

73 Gordon T. Stewart, "Tenzing's Two Wrist-Watches: The Conquest of Everest and Late Imperial Culture in Britain 1921-1953," *Past and Present* 149 (November 1995): 170–97. See also: Peter H. Hansen, "Debate: Tenzing's Two Wrist-Watches: The Conquest of Everest and Late Imperial Culture in Britain, 1921-1953," *Past and Present* 153 (November 1997): 159–77.

74 Nick Heil, *Dark Summit: The True Story of Everest's Most Controversial Season* (New York: Holt & Co., 2008). Ann C. Colley describes how areas in the Alps became similarly overrun during the nineteenth century as large numbers of sportsmen and women sought to experience the sublime and to conquer the mountains. See *Victorians in the Mountains: Sinking the Sublime* (Farnham: Ashgate, 2010), especially Chapter 2.

75 Timothy G. Fogarty, "Searching for Solidarity in Nicaragua: Faith-Based NGOs as Agents of Trans-cultural Voluntourism," in *Bridging the Gaps: Faith-Based Organizations, Neoliberalism, and Development in Latin America and the Caribbean*, eds, Tara Hefferan, Julie Adkins, and Laura Occhipinti (Lanham, MD: Lexington Books, 2009), 83–102. See pages 84–5. To explore some of the various commercial firms, see: VolunTourism, accessed 17 September 2014, http://www.voluntourism.org/.

76 For scholarly exploration of culinary tourism see: Lucy M. Long, ed., *Culinary Tourism* (Lexington, KY: University of Kentucky Press, 2004).

77 Harold Marcuse, "Reshaping Dachau for Visitors, 1933-2000," in *Horror and Human Tragedy Revisited: The Management of Sites of Atrocities for Tourism*, eds, Greg Ashworth and Rudi Hartmann (New York: Cognizant Communications, 2005), 118–48.

78 Jack Kugelmass, "Rites of the Tribe: The Meaning of Poland for American Jewish Visitors," in *Tourists and Tourism: A Reader*, ed. Sharon Bohm Gmelch (Long Grove, IL: Waveland Press, 2010), 369–96.

79 "Auschwitz Memorial visited by 1.33 million people in 2013," *Auschwitz-Birkenau Memorial and Museum*, published 3 January 2014, accessed 7 November 2014, http://en.auschwitz.org/m/index.php?option=com_content&task=view&id=1153&Itemid=7; Tony Paterson, "Dachau Makes a Fresh Start: Young Families Moving in from Munich are Helping the Town to Move on From Its Nazi Shame," *The Independent*, 28 August 2013.

80 Elisabeth Rosenthal, "Your Biggest Carbon Sin May Be Air Travel," *New York Times*, 27 January 2013.

81 Joe Kelly, "Tourism Relies on Jet-Setters, but Travel is Destroying Attractions," *Vancouver Sun*, 14 January 2012.

82 Jaime A. Seba, *Ecotourism and Sustainable Tourism: New Perspectives and Studies* (Toronto, ON: Apple Academic Press, 2012), 46.

83 Stefan Gössling, "Tourism and Development in Tropical Islands: Political Ecology Perspectives," in *Tourism Development in Tropical Islands: Political Ecology Perspectives*, ed. Stefan Gössling (Cheltenham: Edward Elgar, 2003), 1–13. See pages 1, 7.

84 Simone Abram, "Performing for Tourists in Rural France," in *Tourists and Tourism: Identifying People and Places*, eds, Simone Abram, Jacqueline Waldren, and Donald V.L. Macleod (Oxford: Berg, 1997), 29–49. See especially page 45.

85 Gethin Chamberlain, "Tourists in India Told to Avoid 'Human Safaris' as Row Widens," *The Observer*, 22 January 2012. See also: Cohen, *Contemporary Tourism*, 275–316.
86 Daniel Hiernaux-Nicolas, "Cancún Bliss," in *The Tourist City*, eds, Denis R. Judd and Susan S. Fainstein (New Haven, CT: Yale University Press, 1999), 124–42. See page 129.
87 Tamar Diana Wilson, "Economic and Social Impacts of Tourism in Mexico," Special issue: The Impact of Tourism in Latin America, *Latin American Perspectives* 35, no. 3 (May 2008): 37–52. See page 47. Soweto is a famous South African apartheid-era slum outside of Johannesburg.
88 Alicia Re Cruz, "A Thousand and One Faces of Cancun," Special issue: Circum-Caribbean Tourism, *Urban Anthropology and Studies of Cultural Systems and World Economic Development* 25, no. 3 (Fall 1996): 283–310. See especially pages 304–8. Readers interested in tourism in Latin America should also consult Anthropologist Florence E. Babb's study of tourism in "post-conflict" states including Cuba, Mexico, Nicaragua, and Peru; see, *The Tourism Encounter: Fashioning Latin American Nations and Histories* (Stanford, CA: Stanford University Press, 2011).
89 Lindsay Abrams, "Mount Everest's Massive Trash Problem: Nepal Cracks Down on Littering Tourists," *Salon*, 4 March 2014, http://www.salon.com/2014/03/04/mount_everests_massive_trash_problem_nepal_cracks_down_on_littering_tourists/.
90 See Jon Krakauer, *Into Thin Air: A Personal Account of the Mt. Everest Disaster* (New York: First Anchor Books, 1997) for a firsthand account of the incident. It is both a gripping and horrifying read.
91 Heil, *Dark Summit*, 6.
92 Abrams, "Mount Everest's Massive Trash Problem."
93 Heil, *Dark Summit*, 250.
94 Colin Hunter, "Aspects of the Sustainable Tourism Debate from a Natural Resources Perspective," in *Sustainable Tourism: A Global Perspective*, eds, Rob Harris, Peter Williams, and Tony Griffin (Oxford: Butterworth Heinemann, 2002), 3-23. See page 3; and, Sonya Graci and Rachel Dodds, *Sustainable Tourism in Island Destinations* (London: Earthscan, 2010), 10–11.
95 Eric G.E. Zuelow, *Making Ireland Irish: Tourism and National Identity Since the Irish Civil War* (Syracuse, NY: Syracuse University Press, 2009).
96 For example: Gethin Chamberlain, "Tourists in India Told to Avoid 'Human Safaris,'" *Telegraph*, 11 September 2015; and Megan Alpert, "'They Come, They Photograph, But They Don't Help': How Ecotourism in the Amazon Shortchanges the Locals," *Guardian*, 11 March 2015.
97 MacCannell, *Empty Meeting Grounds*, 75–5.

98 This idea failed miserably because "the children loved the ride mainly for the excitement and hilarity of smashing into one another," assuring that only six of the original thirty-six cars survived the first two weeks. Watts, *Magic Kingdom*, 388.

Conclusion

1 United Nations World Tourism Organization, *UNWTO Tourism Highlights*, 2014 ed. (Madrid: UNWTO, 2014).
2 US Travel Association, "Press Release: Travel Industry Employment Reaches an All-Time High, November 7, 2014," accessed 10 November 2014, https://www.ustravel.org/news/press-releases/travel-industry-employment-reaches-all-time-high.
3 United Nations World Tourism Organization, *UNWTO Tourism Highlights*.
4 *Wikipedia*, s.v. "A.J.P. Taylor," last modified 14 February 2015, http://en.wikipedia.org/wiki/A._J._P._Taylor.
5 Quoted in Louis Decimus Rubin, *The Summer the Archduke Died: Essays on Wars and Warriors* (Columbia, MO: University of Missouri Press, 2008), 18–19.
6 For an account of these events, see: Kevin Hillstrom, *Defining Moments: September 11 Terrorist Attacks* (Detroit, MI: Omnigraphics, 2012), 57–82.
7 Robin Pomeroy, "Limit Aid for Airlines, EU Transport Boss Says: Compensation Only for U.S. Airspace was Closed," *Financial Times*, 17 October 2001.
8 "Expert Says You Should Not Be Afraid to Fly, Really," *San Mateo County Times*, 3 December 2001.
9 For more about airport security, see: Amelia K. Voegele, ed., *Airport and Aviation Security* (New York: Nova Science Publishers, 2010).
10 "U.S. Officials Defend Stepped-Up Airport Security," *NBCNEWS.com*, published 15 November 2010, accessed 17 July 2013, http://www.nbcnews.com/id/40194439/ns/travel-news/t/us-officials-defend-stepped-up-airport-security/#.UebQvmk-s_s.
11 "Search for Clues as New York Faces Grief Again," *New Zealand Herald*, 14 November 2001.
12 Sara Kehaulani, "Airbus, American and Pilots Blame Each Other for Crash," *Washington Post*, 4 March 2004.
13 Bill Hutchinson, "Madrid Train Bombs Kill 192: Eye on Al Qaeda & Basque Groups in Train Blasts," *New York Daily News*, 12 March 2004.
14 Annabel Crabb, "One Minute of Mayhem: Underground Bombs Went Off Together," *Sunday Age* (Melbourne, Australia), 10 July 2005.
15 "11 Dead, 10 Wounded in Paris Shooting," *China Daily*, 7 January 2015.

16 Moch N. Kurniawan, "Flu-Like Illness has Potential to Spread to Indonesia," *Jakarta Post*, 19 March 2003; Lawrence K. Altman and Keith Bradsher, "Officials War on Spread of SARS; Disease May be Airborne or Contracted Through Close Contact," *International Herald Tribune*, 1 April 2003.
17 Neal H. Cruz, "SARS Carriers More Dangerous Than Bombers," *Korea Herald*, 3 April 2003.
18 Sean Lengell, "U.S. Warns of Swine Flu Spread; CDC Declares Emergency to Clear Red Tape for Federal Funds," *Washington Times*, 27 April 2009.
19 DeWayne Wickham, "Politics Keeps Coming Before Science in Threat of Ebola," *The Daily Advertiser* (Lafayette, LA), 12 November 2014.
20 "Crash Course: The Origins of the Financial Crisis," *The Economist*, 7 September 2013.
21 "Tourist Numbers to Prague Show Sharp Decline," *Deutsche Press-Agentur*, 6 October 2009.
22 "Tourist Arrivals in Spain Dropped 8.7 Percent in 2009," *Indo-Asian News Service*, 23 January 2010.
23 Andrea Billups, "'Staycation' Trend Has Travelers Going Nowhere Fast," *Washington Times*, 23 March 2008.
24 "Staycations on the Rise," *Manchester Evening Post*, 1 July 2013.
25 Chuck Thompson, "Americans Taking Fewest Vacation Days in Four Decades," *CNN.com*, 23 October 2014, http://www.cnn.com/2014/10/22/travel/u-s-workers-vacation-time/.
26 "Executive Summary. All Work, No Pay: The Impact of Forfeited Time Off," *Travel Effect*, 21 October 2014, http://traveleffect.com/resources/fact-sheets/all-work-no-pay-impact-forfeited-time-executive-summary.

Bibliography

Primary Sources

Archives

National Archives, Ireland
Department of the Taoiseach
Department of Foreign Affairs

Interviews

Jan de Fouw, graphic designer, *Ireland of the Welcomes*. Dublin, 15 October 2002.

Michael Gorman, Bord Fáilte, retired. Dublin, 6 August 2002 and 11 October 2002.

Michael Kevin O'Doherty, Bord Fáilte, retired. Dublin, 29 April 2002 and 30 July 2002.

Newspapers, Magazines, and News Websites

Boston Globe (United States)
China Daily (China)
CNN.com (United States)
The Daily Advertiser (Lafayette, Louisiana)
Daily Mail Online (United Kingdom)
Deutsche Press-Agentur (Germany)
Economist (United Kingdom)
Financial Times (United Kingdom)
Independent (United Kingdom)
Indo-Asian News Service (India)
International Herald Tribune (France)
Jakarta Post (Indonesia)
Korea Herald (South Korea)
Manchester Evening Post (United Kingdom)

Manchester Guardian (United Kingdom)
NBCNEWS.com (United States)
New York Daily News (United States)
New York Times (United States)
New Zealand Herald (New Zealand)
Observer (United Kingdom)
Salon.com (United States)
San Mateo County Times (United States)
ScienceDaily.com (United States)
Sunday Age (Melbourne, Australia)
Telegraph (United Kingdom)
Travel Effect (United States)
USA Today (United States)
Vancouver Sun (Canada)
Washington Post (United States)
Washington Times (United States)

Published Primary Sources

Arendt, Hannah. *The Origins of Totalitarianism*. Rev. ed. New York: Schocken, 2004.

Bacon, Francis. *Bacon's Essays with Annotations by Richard Whately*. 5th ed., rev. and enl. Freeport, NY: Books for Libraries, 1973. First published 1860.

Baedeker, Karl. *Great Britain: England, Wales, and Scotland as Far as Loch Maree and the Cromarty Firth: Handbook for Travelers*. London: Karl Baedeker Publisher, 1887.

———. *A Handbook for Travellers on the Rhine, from Switzerland to Holland*. London and Coblenz: Karl Baedeker, 1861.

Black, Adam and Charles Black. *Black's Picturesque Tourist of Scotland*. 19th ed. Edinburgh: Adam and Charles Black, 1872.

Boswell, James. *The Life of Samuel Johnson, Vol. 2*. London: J.M. Dent & Sons, 1911. First published 1791.

———. *Boswell on the Grand Tour: Germany and Switzerland*, edited by Frederick Pottle. New York: McGraw-Hill, 1953. First published 1764.

Burke, Edmund. *A Philosophical Enquiry into the Origin of Our Ideas of the Sublime and Beautiful*, edited by Adam Phillips. Oxford: Oxford University Press, 2008. First published 1757.

Butlin, Sir Billy. *The Billy Butlin Story: A Showman to the End*. London: Robson Books, 1993.

Coleridge, Samuel Taylor. Samuel Taylor Coleridge to Sara Hutchinson, 6 August 1802. In *Collected Letters of Samuel Taylor Coleridge*, Vol. II, 1801-1806, edited by Earl Leslie Griggs. Oxford: Clarendon Press, 1966.

Engels, Friedrich. *The Condition of the Working Class in England*, edited by Victor Kiernan. London: Penguin, 2005. First published 1845 (in German) by Otto Wigand.

Forster, E.M. *A Room with a View*. New York: Vintage, 1989. First published 1908 by Edward Arnold.

Gall, Richard. *Poems and Songs, with a Memoir of the Author*. Oxford: Oxford University Press, 1819.

George, Andrew, trans. *The Epic of Gilgamesh*. New York: Penguin, 2003.

Gibbon, Edward. *Memoirs of My Life and Writings*. Boston, MA and London: Ginn & Co., 1898.

Herodotus. *The Histories*. Translated by David Grene. Chicago, IL: University of Chicago Press, 1987.

Hutchings, James Mason. *In the Heart of the Sierras*. Oakland, CA: Pacific Press Publishing House, 1888. First published 1886 by Pacific Press Publishing House.

Johnson, Samuel and James Boswell. *A Journey to the Western Islands of Scotland and A Journal of a Tour to the Hebrides*, edited by Peter Levi. New York: Penguin, 1984. First published 1775 and 1786.

Knox, M.D. Robert. *The Races of Men: A Fragment*. Philadelphia, PA: Lea & Blanchard, 1850.

Kraukauer, Jon. *Into Thin Air: A Personal Account of the Mt. Everest Disaster*. New York: First Anchor Books, 1997.

Mohl, Oswald M. *Die Wunder der Weltausstellung zu Paris: Schilderungen der Erlebnisse in einer Weltstadt im Jahre 1867*. Leipzig: Otto Spamer, 1868.

Norton, C.B. *World's Fairs from London 1851 to Chicago 1893: Illustrated with Views and Portraits*. Chicago, IL: Milton Western Co., 1893.

Oliver and Boyd's Scottish Tourist: with Seventy-One Engravings on Steel and Seventeen Travelling Maps and Charts. Edinburgh: Oliver and Boyd, 1852.

Smiles, Samuel. *Self-Help; with Illustrations of Character and Conduct*. New ed. London: John Murray, 1876. First published 1859 by John Murray.

Smith, Adam. *The Wealth of Nations*. New York: P.F. Collier & Son, 1902. First published 1776 by W. Strahan and T. Cadell.

Smollett, Tobias. *Travels through France and Italy*, edited by Frank Felsenstein. Buffalo, NY: Broadview, 2011. First published 1766.

Stanley, Henry Morton. *How I Found Livingston: Travels, Adventures, and Discoveries in Central Africa including Four Months' Residence with Dr. Livingston*. Montreal, QC: Dawson, 1872.

Trevithick, Francis. *Life of Richard Trevithick: With an Account of His Inventions*. Cambridge: Cambridge University Press, 2011. First published 1872 by E. & F.N. Spon.

Tunis, William E. *Tunis's Topographical and Pictorial Guide to Niagara: Containing, also, A Description of the Route Through Canada, and the Great Northern Route, from Niagara Falls to Montreal, Boston, and Saratoga Springs.*

Also Full and Accurate Tables of Distances, on all Railroads Running to and From Niagara Falls. Niagara Falls, NY: W.E. Tunis, 1856.

von Goethe, Johann Wolfgang. *Goethe's Letters from Switzerland and Travels in Italy*. New York: Worthington, 1885.

White, W. Pierrepont. "Good Roads for the People." In *Motoring in America: The Early Years*, edited by Frank Oppel. Secaucus, NJ: Castle Books, 1989, 221–8. First published 1907 in *The Outing Magazine*.

Wollstonecraft, Mary. *Letters Written in Sweden, Norway, and Denmark*, edited by Tone Brekke and Jon Mee. Oxford: Oxford University Press, 2009. First published 1796 in London by J. Johnson.

Woolf, Virginia. *Mrs. Dalloway*. New York: Harcourt Brace Jovanovich, 1981. First published 1925 by Hogarth Press.

Wordsworth, Dorothy. *Recollections of a Tour Made in Scotland*. New Haven, CT: Yale University Press, 1997. First published 1874 by G.P. Putnam's Sons.

Industry Reports

Newland, Kathleen and Carylanna Taylor. *Heritage Tourism and Nostalgia Trade: A Diaspora Niche in the Development Landscape*. Washington, DC: Migration Policy Institute, September 2010.

United Nations World Tourism Organization. *Tourism Highlights*. 2014 ed. Madrid: UNWTO, 2014.

———. *UNWTO Annual Report 2013*. Madrid: UNWTO, 2013.

Websites

"Auschwitz Memorial visited by 1.33 million people in 2013." Auschwitz-Birkenau Memorial and Museum. Published 3 January 2014. Accessed 7 November 2014. http://en.auschwitz.org/m/index.php?option=com_content&task=view&id=1153&Itemid=7.

Churchill, Winston S. "Iron Curtain Speech," 5 March 1946. Modern History Sourcebook. Fordham University. Accessed 8 February 2009. http://www.fordham.edu/halsall/mod/churchill-iron.html.

"Hindenburg Disaster with Sound" (Stock Footage, 1937). From Internet Archive. Video (Pathograms) and sound (WLS Radio), 1:20. Accessed 3 November 2014. http://archive.org/details/SF145.

IATA. "The Founding of the IATA." Accessed 31 July 2013. http://www.iata.org/about/Pages/history.aspx.

Litvack, Cathleen R. "Heritage Tourism in New Jersey." State of New Jersey Historic Trust. Accessed 11 November 2014. http://www.njht.org/dca/njht/touring/plan/.

Marshall, George C. "The Marshall Plan Speech." The George C. Marshall Foundation. Accessed 11 August 2014. http://marshallfoundation.org/marshall/the-marshall-plan/marshall-plan-speech/.

National Trust for Historical Preservation. "A Brief History of the National Trust." Accessed 25 October 2014. http://www.preservationnation.org/who-we-are/history.html#.U8aSUGk-s2E.

"1955 Disneyland Opening Day [Complete ABC Broadcast]." YouTube video, 1:13:01. Posted by "Marcio Disney," 16 July 2011. Televised as "Dateline Disneyland" on ABC on 17 July 1955. Accessed 13 September 2014. https://www.youtube.com/watch?v=JuzrZET-3Ew.

"1906 Stanley Steamer Vanderbilt Cub Racer—Jay Leno's Garage." YouTube video, 28:55. Posted by "Jay Leno's Garage," 26 April 2012. Accessed 1 November 2014. http://www.youtube.com/watch?v=5Me8b0ed59s.

Shakespeare Birthplace Trust. "Heritage Tourism Boosts UK Economy by £26.4bn Per Year." Published 13 July 2013. Accessed 11 November 2014. http://www.shakespeare.org.uk/visit-the-houses/latest-news/heritage-tourism-boosts-uk-economy-by-atildc.html.

"Stock footage – WRIGHT BROTHERS FIRST FLIGHT." YouTube video, 1:29. Posted by "MyFootage.com," 24 January 2007. Film of Wilbur Wright near Le Mans, France, Fall 1908. Accessed 9 February 2011. http://www.youtube.com/watch?v=A-CvkEUSAO4.

United Nations. "Charter of the United Nations: Preamble." Accessed 29 July 2013. http://www.un.org/en/documents/charter/preamble.shtml.

United Nations World Tourism Organization. "History." Accessed 26 July 2013. http://www2.unwto.org/en/content/history-0.

US Travel Association. "Press Release: Travel Industry Employment Reaches All-Time High, November 7, 2014." Accessed 10 November 2014. https://www.ustravel.org/news/press-releases/travel-industry-employment-reaches-all-time-high.

VolunTourism. Accessed 17 September 2014. http://www.voluntourism.org/.

Unpublished Secondary Sources

Conference Paper

Ashworth, G.J. "Is Heritage a Globalisation of the Local or a Localisation of the Global?" Paper presented at the conference Ireland's Heritages: Critical Perspectives on Consumption, Method and Memory, Galway-Mayo Institute of Technology, Castlebar, Ireland, 19 October 2002.

Theses

Meyer, Patricia Jean Behenna. "No Land Too Remote: Women Travellers in the Georgian Age, 1750-1830." Ph.D. diss., University of Massachusetts-Amherst, 1978.

Quinn, Christopher. "The Irish Villages at the 1893 World's Columbian Exposition: Constructing, Consuming and Contesting Ireland at Chicago." M.A. thesis, University of Guelph, 2011.

Published Secondary Sources on Tourism

Author's Note: *As the tourism industry expands, so, too, does the literature. This bibliography is designed both to draw attention to secondary sources cited in this book and to point readers toward additional scholarly books and articles. It is not comprehensive, but it should, nevertheless, provide a useful starting point, especially for students working on papers about tourism or related themes.*

Selected Scholarly Tourism Journals

Anatolia: An International Journal of Tourism and Hospitality Research
Annals of Leisure Research
Annals of Tourism Research
ASEAN Journal on Hospitality and Tourism
Asia Pacific Journal of Tourism Research
Cornell Hospitality Quarterly
Current Issues in Tourism
e-Review of Tourism Research
European Journal of Tourism Research
Hospitality Review Journal
Information Technology of Tourism
International Journal of Contemporary Hospitality Management
International Journal of Culture, Tourism and Hospitality Research
International Journal of Event and Festival Management
International Journal of Knowledge Management in Tourism and Hospitality
International Journal of Mobility Studies
International Journal of Sport Policy
International Journal of Tourism Policy
International Journal of Tourism Research
Journal of China Tourism Research
Journal of Convention and Event Tourism

Journal of Convention and Exhibition Management
Journal of Ecotourism
Journal of Heritage Tourism
Journal of Hospitality, Leisure, Sport & Tourism Education
Journal of Hospitality Marketing & Management
Journal of Hospitality and Tourism Education
Journal of Hospitality and Tourism Management
Journal of Hospitality and Tourism Research
Journal of Human Resources in Hospitality and Tourism
Journal of Leisurability
Journal of Leisure Research
Journal of Park and Recreation Administration
Journal of Policy Research in Tourism, Leisure and Events
Journal of Quality Assurance in Hospitality & Tourism
Journal of Retail and Leisure Property
Journal of Service Management
Journal of Sport & Tourism
Journal of Sustainable Tourism
Journal of Teaching in Travel & Tourism
Journal of Tourism Consumption and Practice
Journal of Tourism and Cultural Change
Journal of Tourism History
Journal of Travel & Tourism Marketing
Journal of Travel and Tourism Research
Journal of Travel Research
Journal of Vacation Marketing
Journeys: International Journal of Travel and Travel Writing
Leisure/Loisir: Journal of the Canadian Association of Leisure Studies
Leisure Sciences: An Interdisciplinary Journal
Leisure Studies
Managing Leisure
Mobilities
Pacific Tourism Review
PASOS: Journal of Tourism and Cultural Heritage
Progress in Tourism and Hospitality Research
Research in Transportation Business and Management
Scandinavian Journal of Hospitality and Tourism
Sport Management Review
Studies in Travel Writing
Tourism Analysis
Tourism, Culture & Communication
Tourism Economics

Tourism Geographies: An International Journal of Tourism Space, Place and Environment
Tourism and Hospitality Planning and Development
Tourism & Hospitality Research: The Surrey Quarterly Review
Tourism: An International Interdisciplinary Journal
Tourism Management
Tourism Management Perspectives
Tourism in Marine Environments
Tourism Planning and Development
Tourism Recreation Research
Tourism Review (The Tourist Review)
Tourism Review International
Tourismos: An International Multidisciplinary Journal of Tourism
Tourist Studies
Transfers: Interdisciplinary Journal of Mobility Studies
UNLV Journal of Hospitality, Tourism and Leisure Science
Visitor Studies
World Leisure Journal

Tourism-Related Books and Articles

Abraham, Shinu Anna, Praveena Gullapalli, Teresa P. Raczek, and Uzma Z. Rizvi, eds. *Connections and Complexity: New Approaches to the Archaeology of South Asia*. Walnut Creek, CA: Left Coast Press, 2013.

Abram, Simone. "Performing for Tourists in Rural France." In *Tourists and Tourism: Identifying People and Places*, edited by Simone Abram, Jacqueline Waldren, and Donald V.L. Macleod, 29–49. Oxford: Berg, 1997.

Abram, Simone, Jacqueline Waldren, and Donald V.L. Macleod, eds. *Tourists and Tourism: Identifying People and Places*. Oxford: Berg, 1997.

Anand, Ascem. *Advance Dictionary of Tourism*. New Delhi: Sarup & Sons, 1997.

Anderson, Martin. "The Development of British Tourism in Egypt, 1815-1850." *Journal of Tourism History* 4, no. 3 (November 2012): 259–79.

Anderson, Monica. *Women and the Politics of Travel, 1870-1914*. Madison, NJ: Fairleigh Dickinson University Press, 2006.

Anderson, Russell H. "The First Automobile Race in America." *Journal of the Illinois State Historical Society* 47, no. 4 (Winter 1954): 343–59.

Anttila, Anu-Hanna. "Leisure as a Matter of Politics: The Construction of the Finnish Democratic Model of Tourism from the 1940s to the 1970s." *Journal of Tourism History* 5, no. 3 (November 2013): 325–45.

Armayor, O. Kimball. "Did Herodotus Ever Go To Egypt?" *Journal of the American Research Center in Egypt* 15 (1978): 59–73.

———. "Did Herodotus Ever Go To the Black Sea?" *Harvard Studies in Classical Philology* 82 (1978): 45–62.

Armstrong, John and David M. Williams. "The Steamboat and Popular Tourism." *Journal of Transport History* 26, no. 1 (March 2005): 61–77.

Aron, Cindy S. *Working at Play: A History of Vacations in the United States*. Oxford: Oxford University Press, 1999.

Atkin, Polly. "Ghosting Grasmere: the Musealisation of Dove Cottage." In *Literary Tourism and Nineteenth-Century Culture*, edited by Nicola J. Watson, 84–94. New York: Palgrave Macmillan, 2009.

Auerbach, Jeffrey A. *The Great Exhibition of 1851: A Nation on Display*. New Haven, CT: Yale University Press, 1999.

Babb, Florence E. *The Tourism Encounter: Fashioning Latin American Nations and Histories*. Stanford, CA: Stanford University Press, 2011.

Balmer, Randall. "From Frontier Phenomenon to Victorian Institution: The Methodist Camp Meeting in Ocean Grove, New Jersey." *Methodist History* 25, no. 3 (1987): 194–200.

Baranowski, Shelley. "A Family Vacation for Workers: The Strength through Joy Resort at Prora." *German History* 25, no. 4 (October 2007): 539–59.

———. *Strength Through Joy: Consumerism and Mass Tourism in the Third Reich*. Cambridge: Cambridge University Press, 2004.

———. "Strength Through Joy: Tourism and National Integration in the Third Reich." In *Being Elsewhere: Tourism, Consumer Culture, and Identity in Modern Europe and North America*, edited by Shelley Baranowski and Ellen Furlough, 213–36. Ann Arbor, MI: University of Michigan Press, 2004.

Baranowski, Shelley and Ellen Furlough, eds. *Being Elsewhere: Tourism, Consumer Culture, and Identity in Modern Europe and North America*. Ann Arbor, MI: University of Michigan Press, 2004.

Barton, Susan. *Working-Class Organisations and Popular Tourism, 1840-1970*. Manchester: Manchester University Press, 2005.

Beattie, Andrew. *The Alps: A Cultural History*. Oxford: Oxford University Press, 2006.

Beckerson, John. "Marketing British Tourism: Government Approaches to the Stimulation of a Service Sector, 1880-1950." In *The Making of Modern Tourism: The Cultural History of the British Experience, 1600-2000*, edited by Hartmut Berghoff, Barbara Korte, Ralf Schneider, and Christopher Harvie, 133–58. Basingstoke: Palgrave Macmillan, 2002.

Belasco, Warren James. *Americans on the Road: From Autocamps to the Motel, 1910-1945*. Cambridge, MA: MIT Press, 1979.

Berger, Dina. *The Development of Mexico's Tourism Industry: Pyramids by Day, Martinis by Night*. New York: Palgrave Macmillan 2006.

———. "Goodwill Ambassadors on Holiday." In *Holiday in Mexico: Critical Reflections on Tourism and Tourist Encounters*, edited by Dina Berger and Andrew Grant Wood, 107–29. Durham, NC: Duke University Press, 2010.

Berger, Dina and Andrew Grant Wood, eds. *Holiday in Mexico: Critical Reflections on Tourism and Tourist Encounters*. Durham, NC: Duke University Press, 2010.

Berghoff, Hartmut, Barbara Korte, Ralf Schneider, and Christopher Harvie, eds. *The Making of Modern Tourism: The Cultural History of the British Experience, 1600-2000*. Basingstoke: Palgrave Macmillan, 2002.

Black, Jeremy. *The British Abroad: The Grand Tour in the Eighteenth Century*. New York: St. Martin's Press, 1992.

———. *The British and the Grand Tour*. Dover, NH: Croom Helm, 1985.

———. *France and the Grand Tour*. Basingstoke: Palgrave Macmillan, 2003.

———. *The Grand Tour in the Eighteenth Century*. Stroud: Alan Sutton, 1992.

———. *Italy and the Grand Tour*. New Haven, CT: Yale University Press, 2003.

Blondé, Bruno. "At the Cradle of the Transport Revolution? Paved Roads, Traffic Flows and Economic Development in Eighteenth-Century Brabant." *Journal of Transport History* 31, no. 1 (June 2010): 89–111.

Boardman, Andrea. "The U.S.-Mexican War and the Beginnings of American Tourism in Mexico." In *Holiday in Mexico: Critical Reflections on Tourism and Tourist Encounters*, edited by Dina Berger and Andrew Grant Wood, 21–53. Durham, NC: Duke University Press, 2010.

Boisseau, T.J. and Abigail M. Markwyn. "World's Fairs in Feminist Historical Perspective." In *Gendering the Fair: Histories of Women and Gender at World's Fairs*, edited by T.J. Boisseau and Abigail M. Markwyn, 1–16. Urbana, IL: University of Illinois Press, 2010.

———, eds. *Gendering the Fair: Histories of Women and Gender at World's Fairs*. Urbana, IL: University of Illinois Press, 2010.

Bonde, Hans. *Gymnastics and Politics: Niels Bukh and Male Aesthetics*. Translated by Simon Frost. Copenhagen: Museum Tusculanum Press, 2006.

Bonington, Chris. *The Climbers: A History of Mountaineering*. London: BBC Books, 1992.

Booth, Alison. "Time-Travel in Dickens' World." In *Literary Tourism and Nineteenth-Century Culture*, edited by Nicola J. Watson, 150–63. New York: Palgrave Macmillan, 2009.

Bradley, Ian. *Water: A Spiritual History*. London: Bloomsbury, 2012.

Brailey, Nigel. "The Railway-Oceanic Era, the India-China and India-Singapore Railway Schemes, and Siam." In *Railways and International Politics: Paths of Empire, 1848-1945*, edited by T.G. Otte and Keith Neilson, 94–111. London and New York: Routledge, 2006.

Brendon, Piers. *Thomas Cook: 150 Years of Popular Tourism*. London: Secker and Warburg, 1991.

Brigstocke, Hugh. "The 5th Earl of Exeter as Grand Tourist and Collector." *Papers of the British School at Rome* 72 (2004): 331–56.

Brinnin, John Malcolm. *The Sway of the Grand Saloon: A Social History of the North Atlantic*. New York: Delacorte Press, 1971.

Brown, Dona. *Inventing New England: Regional Tourism in the Nineteenth Century*. Washington, DC: Smithsonian Institution Press, 1995.

Brown, Ian, ed. *Literary Tourism, the Trossachs, and Walter Scott*, Occasional Papers: No. 16. Glasgow, UK: Scottish Literature International, 2012.

Bruce, David M. "Baedeker: The Perceived 'Inventor' of the Formal Guidebook – A Bible for Travellers in the 19th Century." In *Giants of Tourism*, edited by Richard W. Butler and Roslyn A. Russell, 93–110. Wallingford: CABI International, 2010.

Butko, Brian. *Roadside Attractions: Cool Cafes, Souvenir Stands, Route 66 Relics, and Other Road Trip Fun*. Mechanicsburg, PA: Stackpole Books, 2007.

Butler, R.W. "The Concept of a Tourist Area Cycle of Evolution: Implications for Management of Resources." *Canadian Geographer* 24, no. 1 (1980): 5–12.

Butler, Richard W. and Roslyn Russell, eds. *Giants of Tourism*. Wallingford: CABI International, 2010.

Buzard, James. *The Beaten Track: European Tourism, Literature, and the Ways of Culture, 1800-1918*. Oxford: Oxford University Press, 1993.

Campos, Christophe. "Beating the Bounds: The Tour de France and National Identity." In *Tour de France, 1903-2003: A Century of Sporting Structures, Meanings and Values*, edited by Hugh Dauncey and Geoff Hare, 148–73. London: Frank Cass, 2003.

Carden-Coyne, Ana. *Reconstructing the Body: Classicism, Modernism, and the First World War*. Oxford: Oxford University Press, 2009.

Casson, Lionel. *Travel in the Ancient World*. Baltimore, MD: Johns Hopkins University Press, 1994. First published 1974 by George Allen & Unwin Ltd.

Castellanos, M. Bianet. "Cancún and the Campo: Indigenous Migration and Tourism Development in the Yucatán Peinsula." In *Holiday in Mexico: Critical Reflections on Tourism and Tourist Encounters*, edited by Dina Berger and Andrew Grant Wood, 241–64. Durham, NC: Duke University Press, 2010.

Cerchiello, Gaetano. "Cruise Market: A Real Opportunity for Transatlantic Shipping Lines in the 1960s – The Case of the Spanish Company Ybarra." *Journal of Tourism History* 6, no. 1 (April 2014): 16–37.

Chaney, Edward. *The Evolution of the Grand Tour: Anglo-Italian Cultural Relations since the Renaissance*. London: Frank Cass, 1998.

Chard, Chloe. *Pleasure and Guilt on the Grand Tour: Travel Writing and Imaginative Geography, 1600-1830*. Manchester: Manchester University Press, 1999.

Clancy, Michael. *Exporting Paradise: Tourism and Development in Mexico*. London: Pergamon, 2001.

Clifford, James. *Routes: Travel and Translation in the Late Twentieth Century.* Cambridge, MA: Harvard University Press, 1997.

Cocco, Sean. *Watching Vesuvius: A History of Science and Culture in Early Modern Italy.* Chicago, IL: University of Chicago Press, 2013.

Cohen, Erik. *Contemporary Tourism: Diversity and Change.* New York: Elsevier, 2004.

Cohen, Erik H. *Youth Tourism to Israel: Educational Experiences of the Diaspora.* Clevedon: Channel View, 2008.

Colbert, Benjamin. *Travel Writing and Tourism in Britain and Ireland.* Basingstoke: Palgrave Macmillan, 2012.

Colley, Ann C. *Victorians in the Mountains: Sinking the Sublime.* Farnham: Ashgate, 2010.

Coons, Lorraine and Alexander Varias. *Tourist Third Cabin: Steamship Travel in the Interwar Years.* New York: Palgrave Macmillan, 2003.

Corbin, Alain. *The Lure of the Sea: The Discovery of the Seaside in the Western World, 1750-1840.* Berkeley, CA: University of California Press, 1994.

Corn, Joseph J. "Making Flying 'Thinkable': Women Pilots and the Selling of Aviation, 1927-1940." *American Quarterly* 31, no. 4 (Autumn 1979): 556–71.

Covert, Lisa Pinley. "Colonial Outpost to Artists' Mecca: Conflict and Collaboration in the Development of San Miguel de Allende's Tourist Industry." In *Holiday in Mexico: Critical Reflections on Tourism and Tourist Encounters,* edited by Dina Berger and Andrew Grant Wood, 183–220. Durham, NC: Duke University Press, 2010.

Cronin, Michael and Barbara O'Connor, eds. *Irish Tourism: Image, Culture and Identity.* Clevedon: Channel View, 2003.

Cross, Gary. *A Quest for Time: The Reduction of Work in Britain and France, 1840-1940.* Berkeley, CA: University of California Press, 1989.

Cross, Gary S. "Vacations for All: The Leisure Question in the Era of the Popular Front." *Journal of Contemporary History* 24, no. 4 (October 1989): 599–621.

Cross, Gary S. and John K. Walton. *The Playful Crowd: Pleasure Places in the Twentieth Century.* New York: Columbia University Press, 2005.

Crouch, David and Nina Lübbren, eds. *Visual Culture and Tourism.* Oxford: Berg, 2003.

Culver, Lawrence. *The Frontier of Leisure: Southern California and the Shaping of Modern America.* Oxford: Oxford University Press, 2010.

Davidson, Jim and Peter Spearritt. *Holiday Business: Tourism in Australia since 1870.* Carlton, VIC: The Miegunya Press at Melbourne University Press, 2000.

Davis, Timothy. "The Rise and Decline of the American Parkway." In *The World Beyond the Windshield: Roads and Landscapes in the United States and*

Europe, edited by Christof Mauch and Thomas Zeller, 35–58. Athens, OH: University of Ohio Press, 2008.

Dawson, Philip. *The Liner: Retrospective and Renaissance*. New York: W.W. Norton, 2005.

Dawson, Sandra Trudgen. *Holiday Camps in Twentieth-Century Britain: Packaging Pleasure*. New York: Manchester University Press, 2011.

De Grazia, Victoria. *The Culture of Consent: Mass Organisation of Leisure in Fascist Italy*. Cambridge: Cambridge University Press, 1981.

Della Coletta, Cristina. *World's Fairs Italian Style: The Great Expositions in Turin and their Narratives, 1860-1915*. Toronto, ON: University of Toronto Press, 2006.

DeLuca, Richard. *Post Roads and Iron Horses: Transportation in Connecticut from Colonial Times to the Age of Steam*. Middletown, CT: Wesleyan University Press, 2011.

Denby, Elaine. *Grand Hotels: Reality and Illusion*. Chicago, IL: University of Chicago Press, 1998.

Denning, Andrew. *Skiing into Modernity: A Cultural and Environmental History*. Berkeley, CA: University of California Press, 2015.

De Seta, Cesare. "Grand Tour: The Lure of Italy in the Eighteenth Century." In *Grand Tour: The Lure of Italy in the Eighteenth Century*, edited by Andrew Wilton and Ilaria Bignamini, 13–19. London: Tate Gallery Publishing, 1996.

Dierikx, Marc. *Clipping the Clouds: How Air Travel Changed the World*. Westport, CT: Praeger, 2008.

Di Giovine, Michael A. "Review Article: Identities and Nation-Building in Early Modern Travel Accounts." *Journeys: International Journal of Travel and Travel Writing* 12, no. 1 (September 2011): 93–105.

Dolan, Brian. *Ladies of the Grand Tour: British Women in Pursuit of Enlightenment and Adventure in Eighteenth-Century Europe*. New York: HarperCollins, 2001.

Dubinsky, Karen. *The Second Greatest Disappointment: Honeymooning and Tourism at Niagara Falls*. New Brunswick, NJ: Rutgers University Press, 1999.

Duncan, Dayton. *Horatio's Drive: America's First Road Trip*. New York: Alfred A. Knopf, 2003.

Durie, Alastair J. *Scotland for the Holidays: Tourism in Scotland, c.1780-1939*. East Linton: Tuckwell, 2003.

———. "Tourism in Victorian Scotland: The Case of Abbotsford." *Journal of Scottish Economic and Social History* 12, no. 1 (1992): 42–54.

———. *Water Is Best: The Hydros and Health Tourism in Scotland, 1840-1940*. Edinburgh: John Donald, 2006.

Endy, Christopher. *Cold War Holidays: American Tourism in France*. Chapel Hill, NC: University of North Carolina Press, 2004.

Enzensberger, Hans Magnus. "A Theory of Tourism." Special issue on literature, *New German Critique* 68 (Spring–Summer 1996): 117–35.

Evans, A.K.B. and J.V. Gough, eds. *The Impact of the Railway on Society in Britain: Essays in Honour of Jack Simmons*. Aldershot: Ashgate, 2003.

Fearon, Peter. "The Growth of Aviation in Britain." *Journal of Contemporary History* 20, no. 1 (January 1985): 21–40.

Fedden, Robin. *The Continuing Purpose: A History of the National Trust, Its Aims and Work*. London: Longmans, 1968.

Feifer, Maxine. *Tourism in History: From Imperial Rome to the Present*. Briarcliff Manor, NY: Stein and Day, 1985.

Fergusson, Margaret B. "The Ascent of Olympus." *Greece and Rome* 12, no. 21 (May 1938): 129–36.

Fernández-Armesto, Felipe. *Pathfinders: A Global History of Exploration*. New York: W.W. Norton, 2006.

Ferry, Kathryn. *Beach Huts and Bathing Machines*. Oxford: Shire, 2009.

———. *The British Seaside Holiday*. Oxford: Shire, 2009.

Flink, James J. *The Car Culture*. Cambridge, MA: MIT Press, 1975.

Fogarty, Timothy G. "Searching for Solidarity in Nicaragua: Faith-Based NGOs as Agents of Trans-cultural Voluntourism." In *Bridging the Gaps: Faith-Based Organizations, Neoliberalism, and Development in Latin America and the Caribbean*, edited by Tara Hefferan, Julie Adkins, and Laura Occhipinti, 83–102. Lanham, MD: Lexington Books, 2009.

Foglesong, Richard E. *Married to the Mouse: Walt Disney World and Orlando*. New Haven, CT: Yale University Press, 2001.

Foley, Malcolm and John Lennon. *Dark Tourism: The Attraction of Death and Disaster*. London: Continuum, 2000.

Freeman, Michael. *Railways and the Victorian Imagination*. New Haven, CT: Yale University Press, 1999.

Fritzsche, Peter. *A Nation of Flyers: German Aviation and the Popular Imagination*. Cambridge, MA: Harvard University Press, 1992.

Furlong, Irene. *Irish Tourism: 1880-1980*. Portland, OR: Irish Academic Press, 2009.

Furlough, Ellen. "Making Mass Vacations: Tourism and Consumer Culture in France, 1930s to 1970s." *Comparative Studies in Society and History* 40, no. 2 (April 1998): 247–86.

Fussell, Paul. *Abroad: British Literary Traveling Between the Wars*. Oxford: Oxford University Press, 1980.

———, ed. *The Norton Book of Travel*. New York: W.W. Norton, 1987.

Gaboriau, Philippe. "The Tour de France and Cycling's Belle Epoque." In *Tour de France, 1903-2003: A Century of Sporting Structures, Meanings and Values*, edited by Hugh Dauncey and Geoff Hare, 54–75. London: Frank Cass, 2003.

Gassan, Richard H. *The Birth of American Tourism: New York, the Hudson Valley, and American Culture, 1790-1830.* Amherst, MA: University of Massachusetts Press, 2008.

Gaze, John. *Figures in a Landscape: A History of the National Trust.* London: Barrie & Jenkins, 1988.

German, Erica Lee. "'Royal Deeside' and the Public/Private Divide: Nineteenth-Century Tourism Promotion and the Royal Residence of Balmoral." In *Tourism Histories in Ulster and Scotland: Connections and Comparisons, 1800-1939,* edited by Kevin J. James and Eric G.E. Zuelow, 54–72. Belfast: Ulster Historical Foundation, 2013.

Gillespie, Greg. *Hunting for Empire: Narratives of Sport in Rupert's Land, 1840-70.* Vancouver, BC and Toronto, ON: University of British Columbia Press, 2007.

Glendening, John. "Keats's Tour of Scotland: Burns and the Anxiety of Hero Worship." *Keats-Shelley Journal* 41 (1992): 76–99.

Gmelch, Sharon Bohm, ed. *Tourists and Tourism: A Reader.* Long Grove, IL: Waveland Press, 2010.

Gold, John R. and Margaret M. Gold. *Imagining Scotland: Tradition, Representation, and Promotion in Scottish Tourism since 1750.* Aldershot: Ashgate, 1995.

Goldstone, Patricia. *Making the World Safe for Tourism.* New Haven, CT: Yale University Press, 2001.

Goodale, Thomas and Geoffrey Godbey. *The Evolution of Leisure.* State College, PA: Venture Publishing, 1988.

Gorsuch, Anne E. and Diane P. Koenker, eds. *Turizm: The Russian and East European Tourist under Capitalism and Socialism.* Ithaca, NY: Cornell University Press, 2006.

Gössling, Stefan. "Tourism and Development in Tropical Islands: Political Ecology Perspectives." In *Tourism Development in Tropical Islands: Political Ecology Perspectives,* edited by Stefan Gössling, 1–13. Cheltenham: Edward Elgar, 2003.

Graburn, Nelson H.H. "Secular Ritual: A General Theory of Tourism." In *Hosts and Guests Revisited: Tourism Issues of the 21st Century,* edited by Valene L. Smith and Maryann Brent, 42–50. Elmsford, NY: Cognizant Communications, 2001.

Graci, Sonya and Rachel Dodds. *Sustainable Tourism in Island Destinations.* London: Earthscan, 2010.

Grassl, Anton and Graham Heath. *The Magic Triangle: A Short History of the World Youth Hostel Movement.* Antwerp: International Youth Hostel Federation, 1982.

Greenwood, Justine. "Driving Through History: The Car, *The Open Road,* and the Making of History Tourism in Australia, 1920-1940." *Journal of Tourism History* 3, no. 1 (April 2011): 21–37.

Gregory, Alexis. *The Golden Age of Travel, 1880-1939*. London: Cassell, 1991.

Grenier, Katherine Haldane. *Tourism and Identity in Scotland, 1770-1914: Creating Caledonia*. Aldershot: Ashgate, 2005.

———. "'The Traditional Peculiarities of Scottish Worship': Nineteenth-Century Tourism and Religion in Scotland." In *Tourism Histories in Ulster and Scotland: Connections and Comparisons, 1800-1939*, edited by Kevin J. James and Eric G.E. Zuelow, 112–30. Belfast: Ulster Historical Foundation, 2013.

Hall, C.S. and S.J. Page. *The Geography of Tourism and Recreation: Environment, Place and Space*. London: Routledge, 1999.

Hall, Melanie, ed. *Towards World Heritage: International Origins of the Preservation Movement, 1870-1930*. Farnham: Ashgate, 2011.

Hamilton, Jill. *Thomas Cook: The Holiday-Maker*. Stroud: Sutton, 2005.

Hamilton, John. *Aircraft of World War I*. Edina, MN: ABDO & Daughters, 2004.

Hanley, Keith and John K. Walton. *Constructing Cultural Tourism: John Ruskin and the Tourist Gaze*. Bristol: Channel View, 2010.

Hanna, Stephen P. and Vincent J. Del Casino, Jr., eds. *Mapping Tourism*. Minneapolis, MN: University of Minnesota Press, 2003.

Hannavy, John. *The English Seaside Resort in Victorian and Edwardian Times*. Princes Risborough: Shire, 2003.

Hansen, Peter H. "Albert Smith, the Alpine Club, and the Invention of Mountaineering in Mid-Victorian Britain." *Journal of British Studies* 34, no. 3 (July 1995): 300–24.

———. "Debate: Tenzing's Two Wrist-Watches: The Conquest of Everest and Late Imperial Culture in Britain, 1921-1953." *Past and Present* 153 (November 1997): 159–77.

———. *The Summits of Modern Man: Mountaineering after the Enlightenment*. Cambridge, MA: Harvard University Press, 2013.

Harmond, Richard. "Progress and Flight: An Interpretation of the American Cycle Craze of the 1890s." *Journal of Social History* 5, no. 2 (Winter 1971–2): 235–57.

Harp, Stephen L. *Marketing Michelin: Advertising and Cultural Identity in Twentieth-Century France*. Baltimore, MD: Johns Hopkins University Press, 2001.

———. "The 'Naked City' of Cap d'Agde: European Nudism and Tourism in Postwar France." In *Touring Beyond the Nation: A Transnational Approach to European Tourism History*, edited by Eric G.E. Zuelow, 37–58. Farnham: Ashgate, 2011.

Harris, Rob, Peter Williams, and Tony Griffin, eds. *Sustainable Tourism: A Global Perspective*. Oxford: Butterworth Heinemann, 2002.

Hart, Douglas. "Sociability and 'Separate Spheres' on the North Atlantic: The Interior Architecture of British Atlantic Liners, 1840-1930." *Journal of Social History* 44, no. 1 (Fall 2010): 189–212.

Haywood, Richard Mowbray. *Russia Enters the Railway Age, 1842-1855*. New York: Columbia University Press, 1998.

Hazard, Erin. "The Author's House: Abbotsford and Wayside." In *Literary Tourism and Nineteenth-Century Culture*, edited by Nicola J. Watson, 63–72. New York: Palgrave Macmillan, 2009.

Heath, Sidney. *Pilgrim Life in the Middle Ages*. Boston, MA and New York: Houghton Mifflin, 1912.

Hefferan, Tara, Julie Adkins, and Laurie Occhipinti, eds. *Bridging the Gaps: Faith-Based Organizations, Neoliberalism, and Development in Latin America and the Caribbean*. Lanham, MD: Lexington Books, 2009.

Heil, Nick. *Dark Summit: The True Story of Everest's Most Controversial Season*. New York: Holt & Co., 2008.

Heitmann, John A. *The Automobile and American Life*. Jefferson, NC: McFarland & Co., 2009.

Hembry, Phyllis. *The English Spa: 1560-1815*. London: Athlone Press, 1990.

Hemmleb, Jochen, Larry A. Johnson, and Eric R. Simonson. *Ghosts of Everest: The Search for Mallory and Irvine*. Seattle, WA: Mountaineers Books, 1999.

Henderson, Carol E. and Maxine Weisgrau, eds. *Raj Rhapsodies: Tourism, Heritage, and the Seduction of History*. Aldershot: Ashgate, 2007.

Herlihy, David V. *Bicycle: The History*. New Haven, CT: Yale University Press, 2006.

Hewison, Robert. *The Heritage Industry: Britain in a Climate of Decline*. London: Methuen, 1987.

Hibbert, Christopher. *The Grand Tour*. New York: G.P. Putnam's Sons, 1969.

Hiernaux-Nicolas, Daniel. "Cancún Bliss." In *The Tourist City*, edited by Dennis R. Judd and Susan S. Fainstein, 124–39. New Haven, CT: Yale University Press, 1999.

Hitchcock, Michael, Victor T. King, and Michael Parnwell, eds. *Heritage Tourism in Southeast Asia*. Honolulu: University of Hawai'i Press, 2010.

Hokanson, Drake. *The Lincoln Highway: Main Street across America*. Iowa City, IA: University of Iowa Press, 1988.

Hopper, Sarah. *To Be a Pilgrim: The Medieval Pilgrimage Experience*. Stroud: Sutton, 2002.

Horgan, Donal. *The Victorian Visitor in Ireland: Irish Tourism, 1840-1910*. Cork: Imagimedia, 2002.

Hubbard, Paul and Keith Lilley. "Selling the Past: Heritage Tourism and Place Identity in Stratford-upon-Avon." *Geography* 85, no. 3 (July 2000): 221–32.

Hudson, Kenneth and Julian Pettifer. *Diamonds in the Sky: A Social History of Air Travel*. London: Bodley Head, 1979.

Hudson, Roger, ed. *The Grand Tour: 1592-1796*. London: Folio Society, 1993.

Hugill, Peter J. "Social Conduct on the Golden Mile." *Annals of the Association of American Geographers* 65, no. 2 (June 1975): 214–28.

Hunter, Colin. "Aspects of the Sustainable Tourism Debate from a Natural Resources Perspective." In *Sustainable Tourism: A Global Perspective*, edited by Rob Harris, Tony Griffin, and Peter Williams, 3–23. Oxford: Butterworth Heinemann, 2002.

Hunter, F. Robert. "Tourism and Empire: The Thomas Cook & Son Enterprise on the Nile, 1868-1914." *Middle Eastern Studies* 40, no. 5 (September 2004): 28–54.

Hylton, Stuart. *The Grand Experiment: The Birth of the Railway Age: 1820-45*. Hersham: Ian Allan, 2007.

Irish Museum of Modern Art. *Hindesight*. Dublin: Irish Museum of Modern Art, 1993.

Jackson, A.S. *Imperial Airways and the First British Airlines*. Levenham: Terence Dalton, Ltd., 1995.

Jacobs, Martin. *Reorienting the East: Jewish Travelers to the Medieval Muslim World*. Philadelphia, PA: University of Pennsylvania Press, 2014.

Jacobson, Miriam. *Barbarous Antiquity: Reorienting the Past in the Poetry of Early Modern England*. Philadelphia, PA: University of Pennsylvania Press, 2014.

Jakle, John A. *The Tourist: Travel in Twentieth-Century North America*. Lincoln, NE: University of Nebraska Press, 1985.

Jakle, John A. and Keith A. Sculle. *Motoring: The Highway Experience in America*. Athens, GA: University of Georgia Press, 2008.

———. *Remembering Roadside America: Preserving the Recent Past as Landscape and Place*. Knoxville, TN: University of Tennessee Press, 2011.

Jakle, John A., Keith A. Sculle, and Jefferson S. Rogers. *The Motel in America*. Baltimore, MD: Johns Hopkins University Press, 1996.

James, Kevin J. and Eric G.E. Zuelow, eds. *Tourism Histories in Ulster and Scotland: Connections and Comparisons, 1800-1939*. Belfast: Ulster Historical Foundation, 2013.

Jasen, Patricia Jane. *Wild Things: Nature, Culture, and Tourism in Ontario, 1790-1914*. Toronto, ON: University of Toronto Press, 1995.

Jenkins, Jennifer and Patrick James. *From Acorn to Oak Tree: The Growth of the National Trust, 1895-1994*. London: Macmillan, 1994.

Jennings, Eric T. *Curing the Colonizers: Hydrotherapy, Climatology, and French Colonial Spas*. Durham, NC: Duke University Press, 2006.

———. *Imperial Heights: Dalat and the Making and Undoing of French Indochina*. Berkeley, CA: University of California Press, 2011.

———. *Vichy in the Tropics: Pétain's National Revolution in Madagascar, Guadeloupe, and Indochina, 1940-1944*. Stanford, CA: Stanford University Press, 2001.

Jewett, Sarah. "'We're Sort of Imposters': Negotiating Identity at Home and Abroad." *Critical Inquiry* 40, no. 5 (2010): 635–56.

Jolliffe, Lee. *Tea and Tourism: Tourists, Traditions and Transformations*. Clevedon: Channel View, 2007.

———, ed. *Coffee Culture, Destinations and Tourism*. Clevedon: Channel View, 2010.

Judd, Dennis R. and Susan S. Fainstein. *The Tourist City*. New Haven, CT: Yale University Press, 1999.

Karp, Ivan and Steven D. Lavine, eds. *Exhibiting Cultures: The Poetics and Politics of Museum Display*. Washington, DC: Smithsonian Institution Press, 1991.

Kennedy, Dane. *The Magic Mountains: Hills Stations and the British Raj*. Berkeley, CA: University of California Press, 1996.

Kilbride, Daniel. *Being American in Europe: 1750-1860*. Baltimore, MD: Johns Hopkins University Press, 2013.

Kirshenblatt-Gimblett, Barbara. *Destination Culture: Tourism, Museums, and Heritage*. Berkeley, CA: University of California Press, 1998.

Kockel, Ullrich, ed. *Culture, Tourism and Development: The Case of Ireland*. Liverpool: Liverpool University Press, 1994.

Koenker, Diane P. *Club Red: Vacation Travel and the Soviet Dream*. Ithaca, NY: Cornell University Press, 2013.

———. "The Proletarian Tourist in the 1930s: Between Mass Excursion and Mass Escape." In *Turizm: The Russian and East European Tourist under Capitalism and Socialism*, edited by Anne E. Gorsuch and Diane P. Koenker, 119–40. Ithaca, NY: Cornell University Press, 2006.

Koshar, Rudy. "Driving Cultures and the Meanings of Roads." In *The World Beyond the Windshield: Roads and Landscapes in the United States and Europe*, edited by Christof Mauch and Thomas Zeller, 14–34. Athens, OH: University of Ohio Press, 2008.

———. *German Travel Cultures*. Oxford: Berg, 2000.

———, ed. *Histories of Leisure*. Oxford: Berg, 2002.

———. "'What Ought to Be Seen': Tourists' Guidebooks and National Identities in Modern Germany and Europe." *Journal of Contemporary History* 33, no. 3 (July 1998): 323–40.

Kugelmass, Jack. "Rites of the Tribe: The Meaning of Poland for American Jewish Visitors." In *Tourists and Tourism: A Reader*, edited by Sharon Bohm Gmelch, 369–96. Long Grove, IL: Waveland Press, 2010.

Ladd, Brian. *Autophobia: Love and Hate in the Automotive Age*. Chicago, IL: University of Chicago Press, 2008.

Larrabee, Eric and Rolf Meyersohn, eds. *Mass Leisure*. Glencoe, IL: Free Press, 1958.

Leed, Eric J. *Mind of the Traveler: From Gilgamesh to Global Tourism*. New York: Basic Books, 1991.

Lenček, Lena and Gideon Bosker. *The Beach: The History of Paradise on Earth*. New York: Viking, 1998.

Levenstein, Harvey. *Seductive Journey: American Tourists in France from Jefferson to the Jazz Age*. Chicago, IL: University of Chicago Press, 1998.

———. *We'll Always Have Paris: American Tourists in France since 1930.* Chicago, IL: University of Chicago Press, 2004.

Lindgren, Eva, Urban Lindgren, and Thomas Pettersson. "Driving from the Centre to the Periphery?" *Journal of Transport History* 31, no. 2 (December 2010): 164–81.

Lippard, Lucy R. *On the Beaten Track: Tourism, Art, and Place.* New York: New Press, 1999.

Littlewood, Ian. *Sultry Climates: Travel and Sex.* Cambridge, MA: Da Capo Press, 2001.

Lloyd, David W. *Battlefield Tourism: Pilgrimage and the Commemoration of the Great War in Britain, Australia, and Canada, 1919-1939.* New York: Berg, 1998.

Löfgren, Orvar. *On Holiday: A History of Vacationing.* Berkeley, CA: University of California Press, 1999.

Lomine, Loykie. "Tourism in Augustan Society (44BC-AD69)." In *Histories of Tourism: Representation, Identity and Conflict*, edited by John K. Walton, 69–87. Clevedon: Channel View, 2005.

Long, Lucy M., ed. *Culinary Tourism.* Lexington, KY: University of Kentucky Press, 2004.

Long, Philip and Nicola J. Palmer, eds. *Royal Tourism: Excursions around Monarchy.* Clevedon: Channel View, 2008.

Lottman, Herbert R. *The Michelin Men: Driving an Empire.* New York: I.B. Tauris, 2003.

Louter, David. "Glaciers and Gasoline: The Making of a Windshield Wilderness, 1900-1915." In *Seeing and Being Seen: Tourism in the American West*, edited by David M. Wrobel and Patrick T. Long, 248–70. Lawrence, KS: University of Kansas Press, 2001.

Lowenthal, David. *The Past is a Foreign Country.* Cambridge: Cambridge University Press, 1985.

Luciano Segreto, Carles Manera, and Manfred Pohl, eds. *Europe at the Seaside: The Economic History of Mass Tourism in the Mediterranean.* New York: Berghahn Books, 2009.

Lundin, Per. "Confronting Class: The American Motel in Early Post-War Sweden." *Journal of Tourism History* 5, no. 3 (November 2013): 305–24.

Lyth, Peter. "Flying Visits: The Growth of British Air Package Tours, 1945-1975." In *Europe at the Seaside: The Economic History of Mass Tourism in the Mediterranean*, edited by Luciano Segreto, Carles Manera, and Manfred Pohl, 11–30. New York: Berghahn Books, 2009.

MacCannell, Dean. *Empty Meeting Grounds: The Tourist Papers.* London: Routledge, 1992.

———. *The Tourist: A New Theory of the Leisure Class.* 3rd ed. Berkeley, CA: University of California Press, 1999.

MacDonald, Charlotte. *Strong, Beautiful and Modern: National Fitness in Britain, New Zealand, Australia, and Canada*. Vancouver, BC: University of British Columbia Press, 2013.

MacDonald, Monica. "Railway Tourism in the 'Land of Evangeline.'" *Acadiensis* 35, no. 1 (Autumn 2005): 158–80.

Macfarlane, Robert. *Mountains of the Mind: How Desolate and Forbidding Heights Were Transformed Into Experiences of Indomitable Spirit*. New York: Pantheon Books, 2003.

Mack, John. *The Sea: A Cultural History*. Oxford: Oxford University Press, 2011.

Mackaman, Douglas Peter. *Leisure Settings: Bourgeois Culture, Medicine, and the Spa in Modern France*. Chicago, IL: University of Chicago Press.

Maddocks, Melvin. *The Great Liners*. Alexandria, VA: Time-Life Books, 1978.

Mandell, Richard D. *Paris 1900: The Great World's Fair*. Toronto, ON: University of Toronto Press, 1967.

Mandler, Peter. "Rethinking the 'Powers of Darkness': An Anti-History of the Preservation Movement in Britain." In *Towards World Heritage: International Origins of the Preservation Movement, 1870-1930*, edited by Melanie Hall, 221–39. Farnham: Ashgate, 2011.

Marcuse, Harold. "Reshaping Dachau for Visitors, 1933-2000." In *Horror and Human Tragedy Revisited: The Management of Sites of Atrocities for Tourism*, edited by Gregory John Ashworth and Rudi Hartmann, 118–48. Elmsford, NY: Cognizant Communications, 2005.

Markwyn, Abigail M. *Empress San Francisco: The Pacific Rim, the Great West, and California at the Panama-Pacific International Exposition*. Lincoln: University of Nebraska Press, 2014.

Martin, G.H. "Sir George Samuel Measom (1818-1901), and his Railway Guides." In *The Impact of the Railway on Society in Britain: Essays in Honour of Jack Simmons*, edited by A.K.B. Evans and J.V. Gough, 225–40. Aldershot: Ashgate, 2003.

Martin, Scott C. *Killing Time: Leisure and Culture in Southwestern Pennsylvania, 1800-1850*. Pittsburgh, PA: University of Pittsburgh Press, 1995.

Mason, Courtney W. *Spirits of the Rockies: Reasserting an Indigenous Presence in Banff National Park*. Toronto, ON: University of Toronto Press, 2014.

Matless, David. *Landscape and Englishness*. London: Reaktion Books, 1998.

Mauch, Christof and Thomas Zeller, eds. *The World Beyond the Windshield: Roads and Landscapes in the United States and Europe*. Athens, OH: University of Ohio Press, 2008.

McKenzie, Brian A. "Creating a Tourist's Paradise: The Marshall Plan and France, 1948-1952." *French Politics, Culture and Society* 21, no. 1 (Spring 2003): 35–54.

McReynolds, Louise. "The Prerevolutionary Russian Tourist: Commercialization in the Nineteenth Century." In *Turizm: The Russian and East European*

Tourist Under Capitalism and Socialism, edited by Anne E. Gorsuch and Diane P. Koenker, 17–42. Ithaca, NY: Cornell University Press, 2006.

Merrill, Dennis. *Negotiating Paradise: U.S. Tourism and Empire in Twentieth-Century Latin America*. Chapel Hill, NC: University of North Carolina Press, 2009.

Middleton, Victor T.C. and L.J. Lickoris. *British Tourism: The Remarkable Story of Growth*. Burlington, MA: Elsevier Butterworth-Heinemann, 2005.

Mielnik, Tara Mitchell. *New Deal, New Landscape: The Civilian Conservation Corps and South Carolina's State Parks*. Columbia, SC: University of South Carolina Press, 2011.

Miller, William H. *Floating Palaces: The Great Atlantic Liners*. Stroud: Amberley, 2012.

Mills, Sara. *Discourses of Difference: An Analysis of Women's Travel Writing and Colonialism*. London: Routledge, 1991.

Moranda, Scott. "Maps, Markers, and Bodies: Hikers Constructing the Nation in German Forests." *The Nationalism Project*. Last modified 1 December 2000. http://www.nationalismproject.org/nationalism.htm.

———. *The People's Own Landscape: Nature, Tourism, and Dictatorship in East Germany*. Ann Arbor, MI: University of Michigan Press, 2014.

Morgan, Cecilia. *"A Happy Holiday": English Canadians and Transatlantic Tourism, 1870-1930*. Toronto, ON: University of Toronto Press, 2008.

Mullen, Richard and James Munson. *"The Smell of the Continent": The British Discover Europe, 1814-1914*. London: Macmillan, 2009.

Murphy, Graham. *Founders of the National Trust*. London: Christopher Helm, 1987.

Nance, Susan. "A Facilitated Access Model and Ottoman Empire Tourism." *Annals of Tourism Research* 34, no. 4 (2007): 1056–77.

Newmeyer, Trent S. "'Moral Renovation and Intellectual Exaltation': Thomas Cook's Tourism as Practical Education." *Journal of Tourism and Cultural Change* 6, no. 1 (December 2008): 1–16.

Noack, Christian. "Building Tourism in One Country? The Sovietization of Vacationing, 1917-41." In *Touring Beyond the Nation: A Transnational Approach to European Tourism History*, edited by Eric G.E. Zuelow, 171–93. Farnham: Ashgate, 2011.

———. "Coping with the Tourist: Planned and 'Wild' Tourism on the Soviet Black Sea Coast." In *Turizm: The Russian and East European Tourist Under Capitalism and Socialism*, edited by Anne E. Gorsuch and Diane P. Koenker, 281–305. Ithaca, NY: Cornell University Press, 2006.

O'Connell, Sean. *The Car in British Society: Class, Gender and Motoring, 1896-1939*. Manchester: Manchester University Press, 1998.

O'Connor, Barbara and Michael Cronin, eds. *Tourism in Ireland: A Critical Analysis*. Cork: Cork University Press, 1993.

O'Gorman, Kevin D. *The Origins of Hospitality and Tourism*. Woodeaton: Goodfellow Publishers, 2010.

Østby, Per. "Car Mobility and Camping Tourism in Norway, 1950-1970." *Journal of Tourism History* 5, no. 3 (November 2013): 287–304.

Otte, T.G. and Keith Neilson. "'*Railpolitik*: An Introduction." In *Railways and International Politics: Paths of Empire, 1848-1945*, edited by T.G. Otte and Keith Neilson, 1–20. London: Routledge, 2012.

———, eds. *Railways and International Politics: Paths of Empire, 1848-1945*. London: Routledge, 2012.

Ousby, Ian. *The Englishman's England: Taste, Travel and the Rise of Tourism*. Cambridge: Cambridge University Press, 1990.

Pack, Sasha. *Tourism and Dictatorship: Europe's Peaceful Invasion of Franco's Spain*. New York: Palgrave Macmillan, 2006.

Palmer, Jr., Henry R. *This Was Air Travel: A Pictorial History of Aeronauts and Aeroplanes from the Beginning to Now!* New York: Bonanza Books, 1962.

Palmowski, Jan. "Travels with Baedeker—The Guidebook and the Middle Classes in Victorian and Edwardian Britain." In *Histories of Leisure*, edited by Rudy Koshar, 105–30. Oxford: Berg, 2002.

Parker, Pamela Corpron. "Elizabeth Gaskell and Literary Tourism." In *Literary Tourism and Nineteenth-Century Culture*, edited by Nicola J. Watson, 128–38. New York: Palgrave Macmillan, 2009.

Parry, J.H. *The Age of Reconnaissance: Discovery, Exploration, and Settlement, 1450-1650*. London: Phoenix Press, 1962.

Pattullo, Polly. *Last Resorts: The Cost of Tourism in the Caribbean*. London: Cassell, 1996.

Peillon, Michel. "Tourism—The Quest for Otherness." *Crane Bag* 8, no. 2 (1984): 165–8.

Peiss, Kathy. *Cheap Amusements: Working Women and Leisure in Turn-of-the-Century New York*. Philadelphia, PA: Temple University Press, 1986.

Perkin, Harold. *The Age of the Railway*. New York: Drake, 1973.

Peters, F.E. *The Muslim Pilgrimage to Mecca and the Holy Places*. Princeton, NJ: Princeton University Press, 1994.

———. *The Hajj: The Muslim Pilgrimage to Mecca and the Holy Places*. Princeton, NJ: Princeton University Press, 1994.

Peterson, Eric. *Roadside Americana*. Lincolnwood, IL: Publications International, 2004.

Philpott, William. *Vacationland: Tourism and the Environment in the Colorado High Country*. Seattle, WA: University of Washington Press, 2014.

Picard, Michel. *Bali: Cultural Tourism and Touristic Culture*. Translated by Diana Darling. Singapore: Archipelago Press, 1996.

Pirie, Gordon. "Automobile Organizations Driving Tourism in Pre-Independence Africa." *Journal of Tourism History* 5, no. 1 (April 2013): 73–91.

Pratt, Mary Louise. *Imperial Eyes: Travel Writing and Transculturation*. 2nd ed. London: Routledge, 2008.

Ransom, P.J.G. *The Victorian Railway and How It Evolved*. London: Heinemann, 1990.

Re Cruz, Alicia. "A Thousand and One Faces of Cancun." Special issue: Circum-Caribbean Tourism, *Urban Anthropology and Studies of Cultural Systems and World Economic Development* 25, no. 3 (Fall 1996): 283–310.

Redfield, James. "Herodotus the Tourist." *Classical Philology* 80, no. 2 (April 1985): 97–118.

Redford, Bruce. *Venice and The Grand Tour*. New Haven, CT: Yale University Press, 1996.

Register, Woody. *The Kid of Coney Island: Fred Thompson and the Rise of American Amusements*. Oxford: Oxford University Press, 2001.

Rennella, Mark and Whitney Walton. "Planned Serendipity: American Travelers and the Transatlantic Voyage in the Nineteenth and Twentieth Centuries." *Journal of Social History* 38, no. 2 (Winter 2004): 365–83.

Richards, Jeffrey and John M. MacKenzie. *The Railway Station: A Social History*. Oxford: Oxford University Press, 1986.

Roger, Bray and Vladimir Raitz. *Flight to the Sun: The Story of the Holiday Revolution*. London: Continuum, 2001.

Rojek, Chris and John Urry, eds. *Touring Cultures: Transformations of Travel and Theory*. London: Routledge, 1997.

Rollins, William H. "Whose Landscape? Technology, Fascism, and Environmentalism on the National Socialist Autobahn." *Annals of the Association of American Geographers* 85, no. 3 (September 1995): 494–520.

Rosenthal, Michael. *The Character Factory: Baden-Powell's Boy Scouts and the Imperatives of Empire*. New York: Pantheon Books, 1986.

Rubinstein, David. "Cycling in the 1890s." *Victorian Studies* 21, no. 1 (Autumn 1977): 47–71.

Rugh, Susan Sessions. *Are We There Yet? The Golden Age of Family Vacations*. Lawrence, KS: University of Kansas Press, 2008.

Russell, Peter. *Prince Henry "the Navigator": A Life*. New Haven, CT: Yale University Press, 2000.

Sackett, Andrew. "Fun in Acapulco? The Politics of Development on the Mexican Riviera." In *Holiday in Mexico: Critical Reflections on Tourism and Tourist Encounters*, edited by Dina Berger and Andrew Grant Wood, 161–82. Durham, NC: Duke University Press, 2010.

Scarpaci, Joseph L. *Plazas and Barrios: Heritage Tourism and Globalization in the Latin American Centro Histórico*. Tucson, AZ: University of Arizona Press, 2005.

Schwarz, Angela. "'Come to the Fair': Transgressing Boundaries in World's Fairs Tourism." In *Touring Beyond the Nation: A Transnational Approach to European Tourism History*, edited by Eric G.E. Zuelow, 79–100. Farnham: Ashgate: 2011.

Schwartz, Stuart B., ed. *Implicit Understandings: Observing, Reporting, and Reflecting on the Encounters Between Europeans and Other Peoples in the Early Modern Era*. Cambridge: Cambridge University Press, 1994.

Sears, John F. *Sacred Places: American Tourist Attractions in the Nineteenth Century*. Amherst, MA: University of Massachusetts Press, 1989.

Seba, Jaime A. *Ecotourism and Sustainable Tourism: New Perspectives and Studies*. Toronto, ON: Apple Academic Press, 2012.

Segreto, Luciano, Carles Manera, and Manfred Pohl, eds. *Europe at the Seaside: The Economic History of Mass Tourism in the Mediterranean*. New York: Berghahn Books, 2009.

Seiler, Cotton. *Republic of Drivers: A Cultural History of Automobility in America*. Chicago, IL: University of Chicago Press, 2008.

Semmens, Kristin. *Seeing Hitler's Germany: Tourism in the Third Reich*. Basingstoke: Palgrave Macmillan, 2005.

———. "'Tourism and Autarky are Conceptually Incompatible': International Tourism Conferences in the Third Reich." In *Touring Beyond the Nation: A Transnational Approach to European Tourism History*, edited by Eric G.E. Zuelow, 195–213. Farnham: Ashgate, 2011.

Shaffer, Marquerite S. *See America First: Tourism and National Identity, 1880-1940*. Washington, DC: Smithsonian Institution Press, 2001.

Sharpley, Richard and Philip R. Stone, eds. *The Darker Side of Travel: The Theory and Practice of Dark Tourism*. Clevedon: Channel View, 2009.

Shavit, David. *Bali and the Tourist Industry: A History, 1906-1942*. Jefferson, NC: McFarland & Co., 2003.

Sheller, Mimi. *Consuming the Caribbean: From Arawaks to Zombies*. London: Routledge, 2003.

Sheehan, James J. *Museums in the German Art World: From the End of the Old Regime to the Rise of Modernism*. Oxford: Oxford University Press, 2000.

Sillitoe, Alan. *Leading the Blind: A Century of Guidebook Travel, 1815-1914*. London: Macmillan, 1995.

Simmons, Jack. *The Victorian Railway*. New York: Thames and Hudson, 1991.

———. "Thomas Cook of Leicester." *Leicestershire Archaeological and Historical Society* 49 (1973–4): 18–32.

Sion, Brigitte, ed. *Death Tourism: Disaster Sites as Recreational Landscape*. Salt Lake City, UT: Seagull Books, 2014.

Sladen, Chris. "Holidays at Home in the Second World War." *Journal of Contemporary History* 37, no. 1 (January 2002): 67–89.

Smith, David Norman. *The Railways and Its Passengers: A Social History*. Newton Abbot: David & Charles, 1988.

Smith, Valene L. "The Nature of Tourism." In *Hosts and Guests Revisited: Tourism Issues of the 21st Century*, edited by Valene L. Smith and Maryann Brent, 53–68. Elmsford, NY: Cognizant Communications, 2001.

Smith, Valene L. and Maryann Brent, eds. *Hosts and Guests Revisited: Tourism Issues of the 21st Century*. Elmsford, NY: Cognizant Communications, 2001.

Srinivasan, Roopa, Manish Tiwari, and Sandeep Silas, eds. *Our Indian Railways: Themes in India's Railway History*. Delhi: Foundation Books, 2006.

Stanonis, Anthony J. *Creating the Big Easy: New Orleans and the Emergence of Modern Tourism, 1918-1945*. Athens, GA: University of Georgia Press, 2006.

Stewart, Gordon T. "Tenzing's Two Wrist-Watches: The Conquest of Everest and Late Imperial Culture in Britain 1921-1953." *Past and Present* 149 (November 1995): 170–97.

Stiebel, Lindy. "On the Trail of Rider Haggard in South Africa." In *Literary Tourism and Nineteenth-Century Culture*, edited by Nicola J. Watson, 210–19. New York: Palgrave Macmillan, 2009.

Stopford, J. *Pilgrimage Explored*. York: York Medieval Press, 1999.

Stover, John F. *American Railroads*. Chicago, IL: University of Chicago Press, 1961.

Stowe, William W. *Going Abroad: European Travel in Nineteenth-Century American Culture*. Princeton, NJ: Princeton University Press, 1994.

Sutter, Paul S. *Driven Wild: How the Fight Against Automobiles Launched the Modern Wilderness Movement*. Seattle, WA: University of Washington Press, 2002.

Sweet, Rosemary. *Cities and the Grand Tour: The British in Italy, c. 1690-1820*. Cambridge: Cambridge University Press, 2012.

Swift, Earl. *The Big Roads: The Untold Story of the Engineers, Visionaries, and Trailblazers Who Created the American Superhighways*. Boston, MA: Houghton Mifflin Harcourt, 2011.

Taylor, Frank Fonda. *To Hell with Paradise: A History of the Jamaican Tourist Industry*. Pittsburgh, PA: University of Pittsburgh Press, 1993.

Taylor, John W.R. and Kenneth Munson. *History of Aviation*. New York: Crown Publishers, 1976.

Thomas, Julia. "Bringing Down the House: Restoring the Birthplace." In *Literary Tourism and Nineteenth-Century Culture*, edited by Nicola J. Watson, 73–83. New York: Palgrave, 2009.

Thompson, Christopher S. "Bicycling, Class, and the Politics of Leisure in Belle Epoque France." In *Histories of Leisure*, edited by Rudy Koshar, 131–46. Oxford: Berg, 2002.

Thompson, Christopher S. and Fiona Ratkoff. "Un Troisieme Sexe? Les Bourgeoises et la Bicyclette dans la France Fin de Siecle." *Le Mouvement Social* 192 (July–September 2000): 9–39.

Timothy, Dallen J. and Gyan P. Nyaupane, eds. *Cultural Heritage and Tourism in the Developing World: A Regional Perspective*. London: Routledge, 2009.
Touati, Houari. *Islam and Travel in the Middle Ages*. Chicago, IL: University of Chicago Press, 2010.
Trease, Geoffrey. *The Grand Tour*. New York: Holt, Rinehart and Winston, 1967.
Turner, Louis and John Ash. *The Golden Hordes: International Tourism and the Pleasure Periphery*. New York: St. Martin's Press, 1976.
Urry, John. *The Tourist Gaze: Leisure and Travel in Contemporary Societies*. Newbury Park, CA: Sage Publications, 1990.
Urry, John and Jonas Larsen. *The Tourist Gaze: 3.0*. Los Angeles, CA: Sage Publications, 2011.
Vanderwood, Paul J. *Satan's Playground: Mobsters and Movie Stars at America's Greatest Gaming Resort*. Durham, NC: Duke University Press, 2010.
Vickers, Adrian. *Bali: A Paradise Created*. Hong Kong: Periplus Editions, 1990.
Voegele, Amelia K., ed. *Airport and Aviation Security*. New York: Nova Science Publishers, 2010.
Volo, Dorthy Denneen and James M. Volo. *Daily Life in the Age of Sail*. Westport, CT: Greenwood Press, 2002.
von Buch, Asta. "In the Image of the Grand Tour: Railway Station Embellishment and the Origins of Mass Tourism." *Journal of Transport History* 28, no. 2 (September 2007): 252–71.
Wagner, Michael Frederik. "The Rise of Autotourism in Danish Leisure, 1910-1970." *Journal of Tourism History* 5, no. 3 (November 2013): 265–86.
Wallis, Michael and Michael S. Williamson. *The Lincoln Highway: Coast to Coast from Times Square to the Golden Gate*. New York: W.W. Norton, 2007.
Walton, John K. *Blackpool*. Edinburgh: Edinburgh University Press, 1998.
———. *The Blackpool Landlady*. Manchester: Manchester University Press, 1978.
———. *The English Seaside Resort: A Social History, 1750-1914*. New York: St. Martin's Press, 1983.
———, ed. *Histories of Tourism: Representation, Identity and Conflict*. Clevedon: Channel View, 2005.
———. "Thomas Cook: Image and Reality." In *Giants of Tourism*, edited by Richard W. Butler and Roslyn A. Russell, 81–92. Wallingford: CABI International, 2010.
Walton, John K. and James Walvin, eds. *Leisure in Britain: 1780-1939*. Manchester: Manchester University Press, 1983.
Waterson, Merlin. *The National Trust: The First Hundred Years*. London: BBC Books, 1994.
Waterton, Emma and Steve Watson, eds. *Culture, Heritage and Representation: Perspectives on Visuality and the Past*. Aldershot: Ashgate, 2010.
Watson, Nicola J., ed. *Literary Tourism and Nineteenth-Century Culture*. New York: Palgrave Macmillan, 2009.

———. *The Literary Tourist: Readers and Places in Romantic & Victorian Britain*. Basingstoke: Palgrave Macmillan, 2006.

Watts, Steven. *The Magic Kingdom: Walt Disney and the American Way of Life*. Boston, MA: Houghton Mifflin, 1997.

Webb, Diana. *Medieval European Pilgrimage, c.700-c.1500*. Basingstoke: Palgrave, 2002.

Weber, Eugene. "Forward." In *Tour de France, 1903-2003: A Century of Sporting Structures, Meanings and Values*, edited by Hugh Dauncey and Geoff Hare, xi–xvi. London: Frank Cass, 2003.

Weideger, Paula. *Gilding the Acorn: Behind the Façade of the National Trust*. London: Simon and Schuster, 1994.

Welsh, Joe and Bill Howes. *Travel By Pullman: A Century of Service*. St. Paul, MN: Andover Junction Publications, 2004.

Westover, Paul. "How America 'Inherited' Literary Tourism." In *Literary Tourism and Nineteenth-Century Culture*, edited by Nicola J. Watson, 184–95. New York: Palgrave Macmillan, 2009.

Whisnant, Anne Mitchell. *Super-Scenic Motorway: A Blue Ridge Parkway History*. Chapel Hill, NC: University of North Carolina Press, 2006.

White, Leanne and Elspeth Frew, eds. *Dark Tourism and Place Identity: Managing and Interpreting Dark Places*. London: Routledge, 2013.

White, Richard. *On Holidays: A History of Getting Away in Australia*. North Melbourne, VIC: Pluto Press, 2005.

Whitfield, Peter. *Travel: A Literary History*. Oxford: Bodleian Library, 2011.

Williams, Paul. *Memorial Museums: The Global Rush to Commemorate Atrocities*. Oxford: Berg, 2007.

Williams, William H.A. *Creating Irish Tourism: The First Century, 1750-1850*. London: Anthem Press, 2010.

———. *Tourism, Landscape, and the Irish Character: British Travel Writers in Pre-Famine Ireland*. Madison, WI: University of Wisconsin Press, 2008.

Willoughby, Martin. *A History of Postcards*. Secaucus, NJ: Wellfleet Press, 1992.

Wilson, Tamar Diana. "Economic and Social Impacts of Tourism in Mexico." Special issue: The Impact of Tourism in Latin America, *Latin American Perspectives* 35, no. 3 (May 2008): 37–52.

Wilson-Costa, Karyn. "The Land of Burns: Between Myth and Heritage." In *Literary Tourism and Nineteenth-Century Culture*, edited by Nicola J. Watson, 37–48. New York: Palgrave Macmillan, 2009.

Wilton, Andrew and Ilaria Bignamini, eds. *Grand Tour: The Lure of Italy in the Eighteenth Century*. London: Tate Gallery Publishing, 1996.

Witcomb, Andrea and Kate Gregory. *From the Barracks to the Burrup: The National Trust in Western Australia*. Sydney, NSW: University of New South Wales, 2009.

Withey, Lynne. *Grant Tours and Cooks Tours: A History of Leisure Travel, 1750-1915.* New York: William Morrow and Co., 1997.

Wohl, Robert. *A Passion for Wings: Aviation and the Western Imagination, 1908-1918.* New Haven, CT: Yale University Press, 1994.

Wolmar, Christian. *Blood, Iron and Gold: How the Railways Transformed the World.* London: Atlantic Books, 2009.

———. *Fire and Steam: A New History of the Railways in Britain.* London: Atlantic Books, 2007.

Wood, Andrew Grant. "On the Selling of Rey Momo: Early Tourism and the Marketing of Carnival in Veracruz." In *Holiday in Mexico: Critical Reflections on Tourism and Tourist Encounters*, edited by Dina Berger and Andrew Grant Wood, 77–106. Durham, NC: Duke University Press, 2010.

Wood, Karl E. *Health and Hazard: Spa Culture and the Social History of Medicine in the Nineteenth Century.* Newcastle upon Tyne: Cambridge Scholars Publishing, 2012.

Wrobel, David M. and Patrick T. Long, eds. *Seeing and Being Seen: Tourism in the American West.* Lawrence, KS: University Press of Kansas, 2001.

Wynn, L.L. *Pyramids and Nightclubs: A Travel Ethnography of Arab and Western Imaginations of Egypt, from King Tut and a Colony of Atlantis to Rumors of Sex Orgies, Urban Legends about a Marauding Prince, and Blonde Belly Dancers.* Austin, TX: University of Texas Press, 2007.

Young, Patrick. *Enacting Brittany: Tourism and Culture in Provincial France.* London: Ashgate, 2012.

Youth Hostels Association. *A Short History of the YHA.* St. Albans: Youth Hostels Association [of England and Wales], 1969.

Yuhl, Stephanie E. *A Golden Haze of Memory: The Making of Historic Charleston.* Chapel Hill, NC: University of North Carolina Press, 2005.

Zeller, Thomas. *Driving Germany: The Landscape of the German Autobahn, 1930-1970.* New York: Berghahn Books, 2006.

Zuelow, Eric G.E. "'Kilts versus Breeches': The Royal Visit, Tourism, and Scottish National Memory." *Journeys: The International Journal of Travel and Travel Writing* 7, no. 2 (2006): 33–53.

———. *Making Ireland Irish: Tourism and National Identity since the Irish Civil War.* Syracuse, NY: Syracuse University Press, 2009.

———, ed. "Nordic Tourism." Special section, *Journal of Tourism History* 5, no. 3 (November 2013).

———. "The Necessity of Touring Beyond the Nation: An Introduction." In *Touring Beyond the Nation: A Transnational Approach to European Tourism History*, edited by Eric G.E. Zuelow, 1–16. Farnham: Ashgate, 2011.

———, ed. *Touring Beyond the Nation: A Transnational Approach to European Tourism History.* Farnham: Ashgate, 2011.

Contextual Secondary Reading (Non-Tourism)

Algaze, Guillermo. *Ancient Mesopotamia at the Dawn of Civilization: The Evolution of an Urban Landscape.* Chicago, IL: University of Chicago Press, 2008.

Alpers, Benjamin L. *Dictators, Democracy, and American Public Culture: Envisioning the Totalitarian Enemy, 1920s-1950s.* Chapel Hill, NC: University of North Carolina Press, 2003.

Ames, Glenn J. *The Globe Encompassed: The Age of European Discovery. 1500-1700.* New York: Pearson, 2007.

Anderson, Benedict. *Imagined Communities: Reflections on the Origin and Spread of Nationalism.* London: Verso, 1991.

Andreae, S.J. Fockema. "Embanking and Draining Authorities in the Netherlands during the Middle Ages." *Speculum* 27, no. 2 (April 1952): 158–67.

Ariès, Philippe. *Western Attitudes Toward Death: From the Middle Ages to the Present.* Baltimore, MD: Johns Hopkins University Press, 1975.

Asher, Lyell. "Petrarch at the Peak of Fame." *PMLA* 108, no. 5 (October 1993): 1050–63.

Bairoch, Paul and Gary Goertz. "Factors of Urbanization in the Nineteenth Century Developed Countries: A Descriptive and Econometric Analysis." *Urban Studies* 23 (1986): 285–305.

Balf, Todd. *Major: A Black Athlete, A White Era, and the Fight to be the World's Fastest Human Being.* New York: Crown Publishing, 2008.

Beem, Charles, ed. *The Foreign Relations of Elizabeth I.* New York: Palgrave Macmillan, 2011.

Beem, Charles and Carole Levin. "Why Elizabeth Never Left England." In *The Foreign Relations of Elizabeth I,* edited by Charles Beem, 3–26. New York: Palgrave Macmillan, 2011.

Bhambra, Gurminder K. "Historical Sociology, Modernity, and Postcolonial Critique." *American Historical Review* 116, no. 3 (June 2011): 653–62.

Brendon, Piers. *The Decline and Fall of the British Empire, 1781-1997.* New York: Vintage, 2010.

Briggs, Asa. *Victorian Cities.* New York: Harper & Row, 1970.

Campbell, Colin. *The Romantic Ethic and the Spirit of Modern Consumerism.* Oxford: Basil Blackwell, 1987.

Cantor, Norman F. *Alexander the Great: Journey to the End of the Earth.* New York: Harper Perennial, 2005.

———. *In the Wake of the Plague: The Black Death and the World It Made.* New York: Perennial, 2001.

Castillo, Greg. "Domesticating the Cold War: Household Consumption as Propaganda in Marshall Plan Germany." *Journal of Contemporary History* 40, no. 2 (April 2005): 261–88.

Ceruti, Constanza. "Human Bodies as Objects of Dedication in Inca Mountain Shrines (North-Western Argentina)." *World Archaeology* 36, no. 1 (March 2004): 103–22.

Chakrabarty, Dipesh. "The Muddle of Modernity." *American Historical Review* 116, no. 3 (June 2011): 663–75.

Childers, Thomas. *Nazi Voter: The Social Foundations of Fascism in Germany, 1919-1933.* Chapel Hill, NC: University of North Carolina Press, 1983.

Clement, Wallace. *Understanding Canada: Building on the New Canadian Political Economy.* Montreal, QC: McGill-Queen's University Press, 1997.

Clymer, Floyd. *Henry's Wonderful Model T: 1908-1927.* New York: Bonanza Books, 1955.

Cohen, Lizabeth. *A Consumer's Republic: The Politics of Mass Consumption in Postwar America.* New York: Vintage Books, 2004.

Cook, Michael. *A Brief History of the Human Race.* New York: W.W. Norton, 2003.

Cooke, James J. *New French Imperialism, 1880-1910: The Third Republic and Colonial Expansion.* New Haven, CT: Archon Books, 1973.

Coontz, Stephanie. *The Way We Never Were: American Families and the Nostalgia Trip.* New York: Basic Books, 1993.

Corbin, Alain. *The Foul and the Fragrant: Odor and the French Social Imagination.* Cambridge, MA: Harvard University Press, 1988.

Crew, David F. *Town on the Ruhr.* New York: Columbia University Press, 1979.

Crowley, John E. *Imperial Landscapes: Britain's Global Visual Culture, 1745-1820.* New Haven, CT: Yale University Press, 2011.

Curl, James Stevens. *The Victorian Celebration of Death.* Newton Abbot: David & Charles, 1980.

Dauncey, Hugh and Geoff Hare, eds. *Tour de France, 1903-2003: A Century of Sporting Structures, Meanings and Values.* London: Frank Cass, 2003.

Dawson, Graham. *Soldier Heroes: British Adventure, Empire, and the Imagining of Masculinities.* New York: Routledge, 1994.

de Jonge, Casper C. "Dionysius and Longinus on the Sublime: Rhetoric and Religious Language." *American Journal of Philology* 133, no. 2 (Summer 2012): 271–300.

Dickinson, H.T. *The Politics of the People in Eighteenth-Century Britain.* New York: St. Martin's Press, 1994.

Donnelly, Jr., James S. *The Great Irish Potato Famine.* Stroud: Sutton, 2002.

Doran, Susan. *Elizabeth I and Foreign Policy, 1558-1603.* London: Routledge, 2000.

Dumont, Pierre, Ronald Barker, and Douglas B. Tubbs. *Automobiles and Automobiling.* New York: Viking, 1965.

Dyer, Christopher. "The Consumer and the Market in the Later Middle Ages." *Economic History Review*, 2nd ser. 41, no. 3 (1989): 305–27.

Eatwell, Roger. *Fascism: A History*. New York: Allen Lane, 1996.
Eksteins, Modris. *Rites of Spring: The Great War and the Birth of the Modern*. Boston, MA: Houghton Mifflin, 1989.
Evans, Eric J. *The Great Reform Act of 1832*. 2nd ed. London: Routledge, 1994.
Faust, Avraham and Ehud Weiss. "Judah, Philistia, and the Mediterranean World: Reconstructing the Economic System of the Seventh Century, B.C.E." *Bulletin of the American Schools of Oriental Research* 338 (May 2005): 71–92.
Fernández-Armesto, Felipe. *The Spanish Armada: The Experience of War in 1588*. Oxford: Oxford University Press, 1989.
Finkelstein, Israel and Neil Asher Silberman. *The Bible Unearthed: Archaeology's New Vision of Ancient Israel and the Origin of Its Sacred Texts*. New York: Free Press, 2001.
Fitzpatrick, David. "Flight from Famine." In *The Great Irish Famine*, edited by Cathal Póirtéir, 174–84. Dublin: Mercier Press, 1995.
Foster, Kit. *The Stanley Steamer: America's Legendary Steam Car*. Kingfield, ME: The Stanley Museum, 2004.
Fraser, W. Hamish. *The Coming of the Mass Market, 1850-1914*. Hamden, CT: Archon Books, 1981.
Gabriele, Michael C. *The Golden Age of Bicycle Racing in New Jersey*. Charleston, SC: The History Press, 2011.
Gellner, Ernest. *Nations and Nationalism*. Ithaca, NY: Cornell University Press, 1983.
Glandering, John. "Keat's Tour of Scotland: Burns and the Anxiety of Hero Worship." *Keats-Shelley Journal* 41 (1992): 76–99.
Gluck, Carol. "The End of Elsewhere: Writing Modernity Now." *American Historical Review* 116, no. 3 (June 2011): 676–87.
Gray, Tony. *The Lost Years: The Emergency in Ireland, 1939-45*. London: Little, Brown, and Company, 1997.
Greenblatt, Stephen, ed. *A Mobility Studies Manifesto*. Cambridge: Cambridge University Press, 2009.
Grendler, Paul. "Universities of the Renaissance and Reformation." *Renaissance Quarterly* 57, no. 1 (Spring 2004): 1–42.
Guibernau, Montserrat and John Hutchinson. "History and National Destiny." *Nations and Nationalism* 10, no. 1–2 (January 2004): 1–8.
Hadfield, Miles. *A History of British Gardening*. London: Penguin, 1985.
Hamilton, Richard F. *Who Voted for Hitler?* Princeton, NJ: Princeton University Press, 1982.
Hebdige, Dick. *Subculture: The Meaning of Style*. London: Routledge, 1979.
Heirman, Ann and Stephen Peter Bumbacher, eds. *The Spread of Buddhism*. Leiden: Brill, 2007.
Herb, Guntram H. and David H. Kaplank, eds. *Nations and Nationalism: A Global Historical Overview*. Santa Barbara, CA: ABC-CLIO, 2008.

Herf, Jeffrey. *Reactionary Modernism: Technology, Culture, and Politics in Weimar and the Third Reich*. Cambridge: Cambridge University Press, 1986.

Heyck, Thomas William. *The Peoples of the British Isles: A New History, From 1688 to 1914*. Chicago, IL: Lyceum Books, 2014.

———. *The Peoples of the British Isles: A New History, Vol. II: From 1688 to 1870*. Chicago, IL: Lyceum Books, 2008.

Hillstrom, Kevin. *Defining Moments: September 11 Terrorist Attacks*. Detroit, MI: Omnigraphics, 2012.

———. *Defining Moments: World War I and the Age of Modern Warfare*. Detroit, MI: Omnigraphics, 2013.

Hobsbawm, Eric. *The Age of Empire: 1875-1914*. New York: Random House, 1989.

———. *Age of Extremes: 1914-1991*. New York: Vintage Books, 1996.

———. "The British Standard of Living, 1750-1850." *Economic History Review*, New Series 10, no. 1 (1957): 46–61.

———. *Nations and Nationalism since 1780: Programme, Myth, Reality*. Cambridge: Cambridge University Press, 1990.

Hobsbawm, Eric and Terence Ranger, eds. *The Invention of Tradition*. 2nd ed. Cambridge: Cambridge University Press, 1992. First published 1983 by Cambridge University Press.

Jackson, Kenneth T. *Crabgrass Frontier: The Suburbanization of the United States*. Oxford: Oxford University Press, 1985.

Jennings, Paul. *The Local: A History of the English Pub*. Stroud: Tempus, 2007.

Johnson, Paul. *The Renaissance: A Short History*. New York: The Modern Library, 2002.

Judt, Tony. *Postwar: A History of Europe since 1945*. New York: Penguin, 2006.

Katz, S.H. and M. Voight. "Bread and Beer: The Early Use of Cereals in the Human Diet." *Expedition* 28, no. 2 (1987): 23–34.

Kaul, Chandrika, ed. *Media and the British Empire*. Basingstoke: Palgrave, 2006.

Kelly, John. *The Great Mortality: An Intimate History of the Black Death, the Most Devastating Plague of All Time*. New York: HarperCollins, 2005.

Kern, Stephen. *The Culture of Time and Space, 1880-1918*. Cambridge, MA: Harvard University Press, 1983.

Knapp, Manfred, Wolfgang F. Stolper, and Michael Hudson. "Reconstruction and West-Integration: The Impact of the Marshall Plan on Germany." *Journal of Institutional and Theoretical Economics* 137 (September 1981): 415–33.

Kuisel, Richard F. "Coca-Cola and the Cold War: The French Face of Americanization, 1948-1953." *French Historical Studies* 17, no. 1 (Spring 1991): 96–116.

Lambert, Peter. "Paving the 'Peculiar Path': German Nationalism and Historiography since Ranke." In *Imagining Nations*, edited by Geoffrey Cubitt, 92–109. Manchester: Manchester University Press, 1998.

Le Goff, Jacques. *The Birth of Europe*. Oxford: Blackwell, 2007.
Levine, Philippa. *The British Empire: Sunrise to Sunset*. London: Pearson-Longman, 2007.
Lintsen, Harry. "Two Centuries of Central Water Management in the Netherlands." Special issue: Water Technology in the Netherlands, *Technology and Culture* 43, no. 3 (July 2002): 549–68.
Longmate, Norman. *King Cholera: The Biography of a Disease*. London: Hamish Hamilton, 1966.
Lowe, Rodney. *The Welfare State in Britain since 1945*. Basingstoke: Palgrave Macmillan, 2005.
Macalpine, Ida and Richard Hunter. *George III and the Mad Business*. London: Pimlico, 1991. First published 1969 by Allen Lane.
Mandler, Peter. *The English National Character: The History of an Idea from Edmund Burke to Tony Blair*. New Haven, CT: Yale University Press, 2006.
Martin, Colin and Geoffrey Parker. *The Spanish Armada*. Manchester: Mandolin, 1988.
Matteucci, Marco. *History of the Motor Car*. New York: Crown Publishing, 1970.
Mattingly, Garrett. *Renaissance Diplomacy*. Baltimore, MD: Penguin Books, 1964.
Mazower, Mark. *Dark Continent: Europe's Twentieth Century*. New York: Vintage, 1998.
———. *No Enchanted Place: The End of Empire and the Ideological Origins of the United Nations*. Princeton, NJ: Princeton University Press, 2009.
McGirr, Lisa. *Suburban Warriors: The Origins of the New American Right*. Princeton, NJ: Princeton University Press, 2001.
McGovern, Patrick E. *Uncorking the Past: The Quest for Wine, Beer, and other Alcoholic Beverages*. Berkeley, CA: University of California Press, 2009.
McLaughlin, Raoul. *Rome and the Distant East: Trade Routes to the Ancient Lands of Arabia, India and China*. London: Continuum, 2010.
McNeill, John R. and William H. McNeill. *The Human Web: A Bird's Eye View of World History*. New York: W.W. Norton, 2003.
Mellow, James R. *Charmed Circle: Gertrude Stein and Company*. New York: Henry Holt, 1974.
Metcalf, Thomas R. *Ideologies of the Raj*. Cambridge: Cambridge University Press, 1995.
Mommsen, Wolfgang J. "Society and War: Two New Analyses of the First World War." *Journal of Modern History* 47, no. 3 (September 1975): 530–8.
Montgomery, Robert L. *Lopsided Spread of Christianity: Toward an Understanding of the Diffusion of Religions*. Westport, CT: Praeger, 2001.
More, Charles. *Britain in the Twentieth Century*. Harlow: Pearson-Longman, 2007.
Morgan, David. *The Mongols*. 2nd ed. Malden, MA: Blackwell, 2007.

Mosse, George L. *Fallen Soldiers: Reshaping Memory of the World Wars.* Oxford: Oxford University Press, 1990.

———. *Nationalism and Sexuality: Middle-Class Morality and Sexual Norms in Modern Europe.* Madison, WI: University of Wisconsin Press, 1985.

———. *Toward the Final Solution: A History of European Racism.* Madison, WI: University of Wisconsin Press, 1985.

Newton, C.C.S. "The Sterling Crisis of 1947 and the British Response to the Marshall Plan." *Economic History Review,* New Series 37, no. 3 (August 1984): 391–408.

Nye, Peter Joffre. *The Six-Day Bicycle Races.* San Francisco, CA: Cycle Publishing, 2006.

O'Brian, John and Peter White, eds. *Beyond Wilderness: The Group of Seven, Canadian Identity, and Contemporary Art.* Montreal, QC: McGill-Queen's University Press, 2007.

O'Brien, Conor Cruise. "Nationalism and the French Revolution." In *The Permanent Revolution: The French Revolution and its Legacy, 1789-1989,* edited by Geoffrey Best, 17–48. Chicago, IL: University of Chicago Press, 1988.

O'Keeffe, Dennis. *Edmund Burke.* New York: Continuum, 2010.

Olwig, Kenneth R. "Landscape, Monuments, and National Identity." In *Nations and Nationalism: A Global Historical Overview,* edited by Guntram H. Herb and David H. Kaplan, 59–71. Santa Barbara, CA: ABC-CLIO, 2008.

Pandian, M.S.S. "Gendered Negotiations: Hunting and Colonialism in Late Nineteenth Century Nilgiris." *Contributions to Indian Sociology* 29, no. 1–2 (1995): 239–64.

Parry, J.H. *The Age of Reconnaissance: Discovery, Exploration, and Settlement, 1450-1650.* London: Phoenix Press, 1962.

Payling, S.J. "Social Mobility, Demographic Change, and Landed Society in Late Medieval England." *Economic History Review,* New Series 45, no. 1 (February 1992): 51–73.

Payne, Stanley. *A History of Fascism, 1914-1945.* Madison, WI: University of Wisconsin Press, 1995.

Peukert, Detlev. *Inside Nazi Germany: Conformity, Opposition, and Racism in Everyday Life.* New Haven, CT: Yale University Press, 1987.

Philpott, Maryam. *Air and Sea Power in World War I: Combat Experience in the Royal Flying Corps and the Royal Navy.* London: I.B. Tauris, 2013.

Porter, Bernard. *The Lion's Share: A Short History of British Imperialism.* 3rd ed. New York: Longman, 1996.

Porter, Roy. *London: A Social History.* Cambridge, MA: Harvard University Press, 1994.

Richie, Andrew. *Major Taylor: The Extraordinary Career of a Champion Bicycle Racer.* San Francisco, CA: Bicycle Books, 1988.

Roberts, Geoffrey and Brian Garvan, eds. *Ireland and the Second World War: Politics, Society, and Remembrance*. Dublin: Four Courts Press, 2000.

Roesdahl, Else. *The Vikings*. Translated by Susan M. Margeson and Kirsten Williams. London: Penguin, 1998.

Rubin, Louis Decimus. *The Summer the Archduke Died: Essays on Wars and Warriors*. Columbia, MO: University of Missouri Press, 2008.

Sacks, David and Oswyn Murray. *Encyclopedia of the Ancient Greek World*. New York: Facts on File, 2005.

Said, Edward. *Orientalism*. 25th anniversary ed. New York: Vintage, 1994.

Saran, Mary. "Europe and the Marshall Plan." *The Antioch Review* 8, no. 1 (Spring 1948): 26–32.

Schlesinger, Jr., Arthur. "Origins of the Cold War." *Foreign Affairs* 46 (1967): 22–52.

Silverstein, Adam J. *Islamic History: A Very Short Introduction*. Oxford: Oxford University Press, 2010.

Smith, Huston. *The World's Religions*. 50th anniversary ed. New York: HarperCollins, 2009.

Standage, Tom. *A History of the World in Six Glasses*. New York: Walker and Co., 2005.

Stone, Lawrence. *The Family, Sex and Marriage in England, 1500-1800*. Abr. ed. New York: Harper and Row, 1979.

Stone, Lawrence and Jeanne Stone. *An Open Elite? England, 1540-1880*. Oxford: Oxford University Press, 1984.

Stringer, Chris. "Modern Human Origins: Progress and Prospects." *Philosophical Transactions: Biological Sciences* 357, no. 1420 (29 April 2002): 563–79.

Sullivan, Zohreh T. *Narratives of Empire: The Fictions of Rudyard Kipling*. Cambridge: Cambridge University Press, 1993.

Tarlow, Sarah. "Landscapes of Memory: The Nineteenth-Century Garden Cemetery." *European Journal of Archaeology* 3, no. 2 (2000): 217–39.

Taylor, Timothy. *The Buried Soul: How Humans Invented Death*. Boston, MA: Beacon Press, 2005.

TeBrake, William H. "Taming the Waterwolf: Hydraulic Engineering and Water Management in the Netherlands during the Middle Ages." Special issue: Water Technology in the Netherlands, *Technology and Culture* 43, no. 3 (July 2002): 475–99.

Thompson, Christopher S. *The Tour de France: A Cultural History*. Berkeley, CA: University of California Press, 2008.

Thompson, E.P. "Time, Work-Discipline, and Industrial Capitalism." *Past and Present* 38 (December 1967): 56–97.

———. *Whigs and Hunters: The Origins of the Black Act*. New York: Pantheon Books, 1975.

Thorsheim, Peter. "The Corpse in the Garden: Burial, Health, and the Environment in Nineteenth-Century London." *Environmental History* 16 (January 2011): 38–68.

Trevor-Roper, Hugh. "The Invention of Tradition: The Highland Tradition in Scotland." In *The Invention of Tradition,* edited by Eric Hobsbawm and Terence Ranger, 15–41. Cambridge: Cambridge University Press, 1983.

Van Duzer, Chet. *Sea Monsters on Medieval and Renaissance Maps*. London: The British Library, 2013.

Vigarello, Georges. "The Tour de France." In *Realms of Memory: The Construction of the French Past, Vol. 2: Traditions,* edited by Pierre Nora, 469–500. New York: Columbia University Press, 1997.

Wagnleitner, Reinhold. *Coca-Colonization and the Cold War: The Cultural Mission of the United States in Austria after the Second World War.* Chapel Hill, NC: University of North Carolina Press, 1994.

Walker, Andrew Lockhart. *The Revival of the Democratic Intellect.* Edinburgh: Polygon, 1994.

Warner, Jessica. *Craze: Gin and Debauchery in an Age of Reason.* New York: Random House, 2003.

Weatherill, Lorna. "A Possession of One's Own: Women and Consumer Behavior in England, 1660-1740." *Journal of British Studies* 25 (April 1986): 131–56.

Webb, Jr., James. *Humanity's Burden: A Global History of Malaria.* Cambridge: Cambridge University Press, 2009.

Wehler, Hans-Ulrich. *The German Empire, 1871-1918.* Oxford: Berg, 1985.

Whelan, Bernadette. *Ireland and the Marshall Plan, 1947-57.* Dublin: Four Courts Press, 2000.

White, Peter. "Out of the Woods." In *Beyond Wilderness: The Group of Seven, Canadian Identity, and Contemporary Art,* edited by John O'Brian and Peter White, 11–20. Montreal, QC: McGill-Queen's University Press, 2007.

Williams, Rosalind H. *Dream Worlds: Mass Consumption in Late Nineteenth-Century France.* Berkeley, CA: University of California Press, 1982.

Williamson, David G. *The Age of Dictators: A Study of the European Dictators, 1918-53.* Harlow: Pearson, 2007.

Winock, Michel. *Nationalism, Antisemitism, and Fascism in France.* Palo Alto, CA: Stanford University Press, 2000.

Winter, Jay. *Sites of Memory, Sites of Mourning: The Great War in European Cultural History.* Cambridge: Cambridge University Press, 1995.

Womack, Peter. *Improvement and Romance: Constructing the Myth of the Highlands*. London: Macmillan, 1989.

Wrigley, E.A. and R.S. Schofield. *The Population History of England, 1541-1871.* Cambridge, MA: Harvard University Press, 1981.

Index